HOW THE STOCK MARKET WORKS

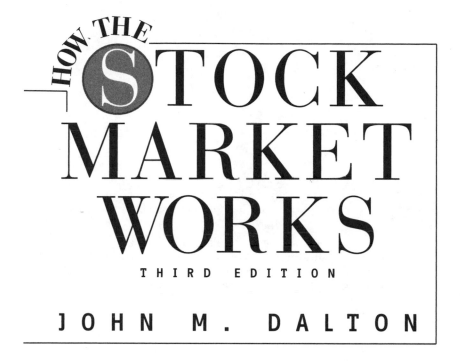

HOW THE STOCK MARKET WORKS

THIRD EDITION

JOHN M. DALTON

NEW YORK INSTITUTE OF FINANCE

NEW YORK • TORONTO • SYDNEY • TOKYO • SINGAPORE

NEW YORK INSTITUTE OF FINANCE
NYIF and NEW YORK INSTITUTE OF FINANCE are trademarks of
Executive Tax Reports, Inc., used under license by Penguin Putnam Inc.

This publication is designed to provide accurate and authoritative information in regard to the subject matter covered. It is sold with the understanding that the publisher is not engaged in rendering legal, accounting, or other professional service. If legal advice or other expert assistance is required, the services of a competent professional person should be sought.
—*From the Declaration of Principles jointly adopted by a Committee of the American Bar Association and a Committee of Publishers and Associations*

Library of Congress Cataloging-in-Publication Data

How the stock market works / [edited by] John M. Dalton.—3rd ed.
     p. cm.
    Includes index.
    ISBN 0-7352-0183-8
    1. Stock exchanges. 2. Stocks. I. Dalton John

  HG4515.D29 2001
  332.64'273—dc21   00-050090

Printed in the United States of America

10 9 8 7 6 5

DEDICATION

This book is dedicated to my wife, Rosemary; my children, John, Danielle, and Steven; my parents; and Ruby (they are truly my blue chips); and to my emerging "growth stock," my three grandchildren, Lauren, Karen, and Andrew.

OTHER BOOKS IN THIS SERIES

How the Bond Market Works, Second Edition

How the Economy Works, Second Edition

How the Foreign Exchange Market Works

How the Futures Markets Work, Second Edition

How Municipal Bonds Work

How Mutual Funds Work, Second Edition

How the Option Markets Work

ACKNOWLEDGMENTS

The story of the stock market has a long ancestry. So has this book. Many people and experiences have influenced me throughout my career and this book began a long time ago as I worked with many traders, specialists, Exchange floor members and staff, Nasdaq staff, educators and authors. No man is an island and no one takes on a project such as this alone. In this context it is an honor to mention and to thank some individuals whose help to me has been invaluable. Professionals such as Ralph Acampora, recognized as an industry leader, author and educator in the field of technical analysis, William Rini, educator and author, who has spent his entire professional life in the financial services industry; Allan Pessin, noted author, lecturer, member firm executive and regulatory expert, but above all, a teacher, and each of them an instructor without equal at the New York Institute of Finance; Greg Galinskie, professional trader who, although he will never teach me to golf, has taught me a great deal about trading, and reaction to market psychology; Ron Armitage, Compliance Consultant; Paul Fitzgerald, floor broker and member of the New York Stock Exchange, whose market understanding has always been clear and pivotal to me; James J. Maguire, Specialist, New York Stock Exchange, who taught me the true principles of maintaining a fair and orderly market; Arne Michelson, Senior Vice President, American Stock Exchange, whose guidance in analyzing and communicating the principles of specialist market making is without equal; Mark Gundersen, Nasdaq Media; and Tim McCormick, NASD Academic Liaison, whose help and guidance in presenting the Nasdaq chapter was instrumental; and to William Fredreck, Esq., attorney extraordinaire, whose stock market, legal and New York Mets conversations I will miss forever; James Britton, former American Stock Exchange Member who taught me the methods of floor order execution; and to the staff members of my office: Margaret T. Contino, Katherine J. Johnson, Heather Hanley-Lombardi, Suzanne Ascher, Esq., Rosemary Grillo and Amy Gunning, who did above and beyond what was necessary, and some of whom literally burned the midnight oil, to get the job done; and finally, to Gloria Fuzia, my Editor, for her help, guidance and patience: THANK YOU ONE AND ALL.

CONTENTS

Introduction   xv

■ Chapter 1
The Stock Market: What the Stock Market
Has to Offer   1
Why Stocks Are Offered   1
The Size of the Stock Market   2
A Word About Bonds   3
Why Individuals and Institutions Buy Stocks   3
Dividends   4
Capital Gains, or Growth   5
Short Selling   6
Risks and Rewards of Investing   8
Common Stocks   10
Preferred Stocks   12
Stock Rights   17
Stock Warrants   18
Summary   18

■ Chapter 2
Reading the Financial Press: Determining Share
Value, Determining Your Investment Return   20
Cash Accounts   20
Margin Accounts   21
Security Positions: Long, Short, Flat   23
Pricing Stocks: Points and Fractions   25

The Figuration of Current Yield   27
Newspaper Listings   28

■ **Chapter 3**
The Initial Public Offering: Getting the Stocks to the Marketplace   **32**
    The Primary Market—How Busineses
      Are Capitalized   34
    Incorporating the Business   35
    The Initial Public Offering (IPO)   40
    After the Offering Is Completed   54

■ **Chapter 4**
Inside the Brokerage Firm: Who Does What?   **55**
    Full Service Versus Discount   57
    Selecting a Brokerage Firm and an Account Executive   62
    The Sales Assistant   66

■ **Chapter 5**
The Secondary Market: Executing Orders on the Exchange Floor   **68**
    The New York Stock Exchange   68
    Listing Requirements and Criteria of the NYSE   69
    NYSE Maintenance Listing Requirements/Delisting
      from NYSE   71
    The NYSE Floor   72
    The Delivery of Orders to the NYSE: Superdot
      and the Broker Booth Support System   78
    NYSE's Online Comparison System   80
    The Auction System   80
    How Orders Are Executed in the Crowd   83
    Crossing Stock   88
    After (Off) Hours Trading—A/K/A
      Crossing Sessions   89
    The Short Sale   91
    Institutional Trades   93
    Decimalization   95

Other Important Features of the NYSE 95
AMEX—The American Stock Exchange 101

■ **Chapter 6**
The Specialist: Riding the Bulls and Bears **105**
The Specialist's Role: As Dealer, as Broker 106
The Role of Automation and Telecommunication 110
Other Duties of the Specialist 112
Odd-Lot Trading 116
Assigning Securities to the Specialist 120
Conclusion 121

■ **Chapter 7**
The Secondary Market:
Over-the-Counter Trading **122**
Following an Order Being Executed OTC 126
The Over-the-Counter Bulletin Board: OTCBB 130
Types of Orders 133
Compliance Regulations of the NASD 135
NASD Rules of Fair Practice 137

■ **Chapter 8**
The Nasdaq: Ongoing Changes **140**
NASD: National Association of Securities
Dealers, Inc. 140
Requirements for Securities to Become Listed
on Nasdaq 142
November 1998 Merger with the American
Stock Exchange 146
Nasdaq-100 Index Tracking Stock (AMEX
Symbol QQQ) 147
The Major Nasdaq Stock Market Indexes 147
Expansion of Nasdaq Worldwide: Globalization
of Stock Trading 149
Monitoring the Markets 150
Other Major Developments with the Nasdaq 151
Conclusion 158

■ **Chapter 9**
Investment Companies: Closed-End and Open-End
Funds—The "Package Plan" Approach   **159**
    Investment Companies   160
    Management Companies: Closed-End
       and Open-End Funds   162
    Pricing a Closed-End Fund   163
    Pricing an Open-End Fund   163
    Variety of Types of Open-End (Mutual) Funds
       for Bonds   168
    Conclusion   169

■ **Chapter 10**
Stock Options: Multipurpose Instruments   **170**
    The OCC and the Exchanges That Offer
       Option Trading   171
    Options: A Definition and Explanation of How
       Stock Option Contracts Generally Function   172
    Types of Option Contracts: Puts and Calls   176
    Option Premium: The Price of the Option Contract   182
    Options as a Hedging Tool   190
    Miscellaneous Option Topics   192
    Conclusion   193

■ **Chapter 11**
The Back Offices: Following the Long
Paper Trail   **194**
    The Depository and Clearing House   196
    The Order Department   198
    P&S Department   199
    Margin Department   206
    Stock Record Department   210
    Accounting Department   212
    Dividend Department   214
    Proxy Department   218

■ Chapter 12
**Stock Market Theories: Can Prices Really
Be Predicted?** **220**
The First American Analyst 222
The Analysts 231
The Technical Approach 241

■ Chapter 13
Analyzing Stocks: The Corporation's "Report Card" **260**
Current Assets and Current Liabilities 261
Can the Corporation Pay Its Way? 262
Using Debt and Capital Structure of a Corporation
as Sources of Long-Term Funds 263
The Income Statement 264

■ Chapter 14
**Online Trading in the Stock Market: How
Technology Has Changed the Financial Landscape** **269**
Brokerage Firms in the World of Online Trading 270
How an Investor Establishes Online Trading 273
Wireless and Touch Tone Trading 274
The Risks of Online Trading 275
Protection for Online Investors 279
Conclusion 281

■ Chapter 15
**Globalization of the Stock Market: Expanding
Opportunities for Investors** **282**
Stock Markets Around the World 283
Global Investing 286
Effect of Extended/After-Hours Trading
on Globalization 287
Globalization: The Stock Exchanges 288
Brokerage Firms and Online Access 292
Conclusion 293

■ **Chapter 16**
Taxation: How Dividends and Capital Gains
Are Taxed   **294**
    The Taxation of Interest   295
    The Taxation of Dividends   295
    The Taxation of Capital Gains   296
    Multiple Positions   297
    Stock Gifts to Minors   298
    Stocks Received as Gifts and Inheritances:
        Taxable Amounts and Basis   298

■ **Chapter 17**
In the Tank or, Even Worse, Crash, but Then
a Reversal: How the Stock Market Works
Under Pressure   **303**
    The Fair and Orderly Market   306
    Program Trading Myths   313
    The Global Crash   314
    The Stock Market and the Economy   317
    Conclusion   319

Glossary   **320**

Index   **399**

About the Author   **423**

INTRODUCTION

Inevitably, almost everyone becomes involved with the stock market although it is not necessary to purchase stocks directly to do so. The insurance companies that accept our premiums in exchange for protecting our lives and assets—the banks with which we are involved as borrower or saver—our pension funds and profit-sharing arrangements—are all intimately concerned with the stock market.

The "market" is an important part of all our lives. It is the principal means through which companies raise capital to expand their operations—and the medium used by millions of investors to trade for capital gain or invest for dividend income. The stock market reflects a country's prosperity and prospects. Every nation gives top priority to the development or enhancement of a stock exchange and think of it as a symbol of capital growth and maturity. The stock exchanges of the world will ultimately be linked together, providing the means for both individuals and institutions to purchase and sell securities, at fair prices, almost instantaneously.

The mechanism for trading stock is truly remarkable. Investments in any dollar amount can be made from a "menu" of over 10,000 different stocks. This text describes this mechanism and the products that are traded. Three new chapters have been added to this edition. The new material includes information on the Nasdaq, online trading, globalization, reading the financial press, technical analysis, stock charts, and other topics of interest to those interested in an overview of the investment world.

The possibilities afforded by the stock market are endless. This is true whether the individual is an investor, hedger, or trader, or merely interested in the fascinating world of bulls, bears, and Dow Jones averages. Regardless, this book will provide you with the essentials.

THE STOCK MARKET
What the Stock Market Has to Offer

"Businesses" usually evolve, over time, from one-man operations (sole proprietorships) to partnerships and ultimately to full-fledged corporations. Corporations traditionally meet their short-term cash requirements, for carrying inventory or for similar reasons, by borrowing from banks. When corporations need long-term financing, they may sell ownership interests in the company (common stocks and/or preferred stocks) to the public—or borrow from the public by selling bonds.

There are two major subdivisions of the stock market: the primary market and the secondary market. The *primary market* involves only new issues, while the *secondary market* handles retail sales of securities from an original owner to a new purchaser. Chapter 3 explains the primary market; Chapters 5 and 7 describe the secondary market. In this text we refer to this entire market, both primary and secondary, as the well-functioning "stock market."

■ WHY STOCKS ARE OFFERED

Stocks exist to enable companies in need of long-term financing to "sell" interests in the business—stocks (equity securities)—in exchange for cash. This is the principal method of raising business capital other than by issuing bonds. When the stocks of these corporations, which all corporations *must* issue, are owned by the public at large—including both private investors and institutions—they are said to be *publicly held*. These publicly held shares can be easily traded (sold) to other investors in the stock market, and are thus said to be *liquid*, or readily converted to cash.

The primary stock market, described in Chapter 3, is for newly issued shares, both common stock and preferred stock, which are sold by the issuer (the corporation in need of capital) to the investing public. Stock brokerage firms usually serve as intermediaries in these transactions, acquiring the new securities at "wholesale" prices from the issuer and then reselling them to the investing public at "retail prices." This is, effectively, what happens when you buy a new car. General Motors produces the car, a "new issue," and then sells it to you through a dealer. You exchange cash for the car. General Motors gets the bulk of the cash, and the dealer earns a commission because of efforts in arranging the transaction.

■ THE SIZE OF THE STOCK MARKET

Approximately 5,000 different stock issues are currently traded on stock exchanges throughout the United States (so-called *listed* securities) and about 5,000 other issues are traded over the counter. Generally speaking, commonly known value asset companies opt for listing on one or more exchanges, while the over-the-counter (OTC) market is where newer and, in most cases, smaller companies are traded. There are some notable exceptions to this, and quite a few companies that are able to meet the most exacting exchange listing requirements prefer to stay OTC, due to the growth and technological expansion of Nasdaq.

The stock market also includes thousands of different mutual funds and thousands of different options to purchase stocks. All mutual funds and some stock options trade OTC. The New York Stock Exchange—the nation's largest exchange—handles an average daily trading volume of one billion shares. It is an extremely efficient marketplace where accurate quotations and prices are instantly available, and buy and sell orders can be effected in a matter of moments.

■ A WORD ABOUT BONDS

This text covers the stock market. There are several other securities markets including the money market (debt instruments with less than one year to maturity) and the bond market. The bond market, where debt instruments of longer maturities are traded, is even bigger than the stock market. Unlike stocks, which represent ownership—a piece of the action—bonds represent a loan by the purchasing bondholder of the issuing company. The bondholder usually receives interest payments rather than dividends, does not have the right to vote, and is promised that, at maturity, the loan value called the principal or face value will be repaid. A bond is a fixed-income security, a "senior" security, and its interest payments must be paid in full before shareholders in that same company can receive any dividends.

Investors generally purchase bonds for the stream of relatively safe, stable income. Bonds are priced differently from stocks, and the vast majority are traded OTC. Common stocks are equity (ownership) securities; bonds are debt securities. Most investment portfolios contain both stocks and bonds. Determining the proper "mix" of these investment instruments, for various investment purposes and degrees of risk, is known as *asset allocation*. (For further information on debt securities refer to the *How the Bond Market Works* in this same series.)

■ WHY INDIVIDUALS AND INSTITUTIONS BUY STOCKS

Stocks are purchased as investments, to make additional money on the money invested. There are many other investment vehicles including real estate, precious metals, and rare paintings, etc., but investing in stocks offers a great number of advantages. Among these advantages are the relatively low commission costs, the ease with which purchased securities can be safeguarded (brokerage firms will hold them for clients upon request), the speed at which they can be bought and sold, the ability to determine your investments' exact market value in a matter of minutes, and, most importantly, their "track record." Over the long term, investments in stocks have proven to be an excellent way to exceed keeping pace with the erosive effects of inflation.

■ DIVIDENDS

Many common stocks and all preferred stocks pay dividends. Most dividend-paying stocks declare the dividend to be paid annually, but make their distributions on a quarterly basis (four times a year). That schedule is not a legal requirement, but most companies stick to it. The amount and timing of dividend payments are at the discretion of the corporation's board of directors. Most profitable corporations share their profits with their investors by paying them a cash dividend. A very general rule is that one-half the profit gets paid to the shareholders, and the remaining half gets reinvested in the company. Companies in an aggressive growth period might elect to reinvest most, or even all, of their profits to fuel expansion, paying only token cash dividends or even none at all.

There is no law that states that a company *must* pay a dividend on its common shares, even if the company is profitable. The board of directors, which is the elected governing body of the corporation (elected, of course, by majority vote of the common stockholders), can raise, reduce, or eliminate a company's dividend rate. Dividends on common stock are flexible, therefore, but companies try to maintain a fairly even flow of them, increasing the dividend when the company enjoys a growth in net earnings. A company with an annual dividend rate of $1.20 would be paid at $0.30 per quarter. (Dividends may also be paid in additional shares of stock (*stock dividends*) in lieu of, or in addition to, cash.)

The expected receipt of dividend income called "yield" is sometimes justification enough for investing in a given stock, particularly if the yield on the investment exceeds the return afforded by savings accounts or CDs. Stocks that pay out a fairly generous dividend are known as *income stocks*. These are generally popular with individuals or institutions that are satisfied with the rate of return in and of itself. Such dependable income producers are usually in stable industries such as utilities and food stocks. While the receipt of income is important to many investors and, as stated previously, sometimes the *only* reason for purchasing a stock, most investors hope to gain an additional return in the form of *capital gains*.

■ CAPITAL GAINS, OR GROWTH

When a stock is purchased at a given price, then subsequently sold at a higher price, the resultant profit is known as a *capital gain*. Trying for such "buy-low, sell-high" profits over a short time span is an activity known as *short-term trading*. Often the securities are held only for a single day, sometimes for as little as several hours or even minutes, and is referred to as Day Trading. Many individual and institutional investors, however, have a much longer time horizon and will hold stocks for many years.

Companies that are expected to grow over time are known as *growth stocks*. Investors buy such stocks in anticipation that their per-share value will increase over time as the company prospers, and as its per-share earnings and dividends increase. When stocks that have been held for more than a year are sold at a profit, the profit is *long-term*. *Short-term* profits are the result of profitable trades on securities that have been held for one year or less. Chapter 16 deals with this subject in greater detail. A capital gain will also result from a *short sale* that occurs when a security is first sold and then subsequently purchased (covered) at a lower price.

Investors sometimes purchase securities only for their capital gains potential. Many growth stocks pay out very little in dividends, sometimes not at all. It is probably fair to say that relatively conservative investors are attracted to income stocks, while those who are more adventurous, and more willing to take risks, gravitate toward Day Trading and/or growth stocks. While certain stocks are dividend payers with little chance for speculator growth in price (cash cows), and others offer small dividend potential but a chance for capital gains (*venture capital, special situations*), many stocks—probably *most* stocks—offer possible rewards both through a combination of dividends *and* capital gains.

Ultimately, that is why stocks are purchased: for dividends and/or capital gains—for *investment*. Most well-rounded portfolios have a balance between income situations and stocks with capital gains potential. Some investors achieve this aim by buying a package of securities with such a mix, typically exemplified by growth-income mutual funds. (Investments such as these are described at length in Chapter 9.)

■ SHORT SELLING

Most of us think of making a "killing" by buying something at a low price and subsequently selling it at a much higher price. With most investment vehicles (undeveloped real estate, rare paintings and coins, art treasures), this is the only way to profit. Such investments rarely produce income while they are held, unlike stocks, and one's only hope for gain is to be astute enough to buy at the right time—at a low price—and to sell later at a higher price. The "buy-low, sell-high" principle is, after all, the essence of making capital gains. The stock market affords another method for striving for capital gains, and that is through the medium of the *short sale*.

Investors (and speculators) who believe a stock is selling at a bargain price will purchase it in anticipation of later selling the security at a higher price. They are *bullish* on the stock and expect it to increase in price. But what about investors who believe the price of a security will drop because it is *overpriced*? Such situations also offer the opportunity for capital gains through the medium of the short sale. Someone who thinks that a stock is selling at too high a price, and that it will decline, is said to be *bearish* on the stock. As unlikely as it sounds, it is possible (at least in the stock market) to sell this supposedly overpriced item first, and to buy it later! That's right; first sell at the high price and then buy at the lower price. The difference between the sale price and the purchase price represents the investor's profit or loss. Naturally the short-seller wishes the stock to *decline* in value after the sale, so that the purchase (the *covering* transaction) will be at a lower price.

Let's look at an example. John Bear believes that XYZ stock overpriced at $89 per share and that it is due for a fall. He *shorts* (sells short) 100 shares at $89 and then keeps his fingers crossed. XYZ does decline in price, and Mr. Bear covers the short position by buying 100 shares of XYZ at $76 per share. He first *sold* for $8,900 and then *purchased* for $7,600, making a profit of $1,300. Instead of buying at a low price and then selling at a high price, Mr. Bear first sold at a high price and then bought at a low price. It's backwards, but it works!

The mechanics of selling something you don't own are quite interesting. When you sell the stock short, where does the stock come from? Since you don't own the stock being sold, it must come from someone who owns it and who lends it to you. This borrowed stock is then used to complete delivery of the sale transaction. Since you have sold borrowed stock, you are obligated to return that borrowed stock eventually. "He who sells what isn't his'n, must buy it back or go to prison."

Short selling is very different from "investing." Individual and institutional investors purchase stocks for their investment potential. They hope to make money on their invested capital through the receipt of dividends and/or capital gains. But capital gains profits may result from both long sales and short sales. As will be demonstrated, short selling is a very risky undertaking and is normally not practiced by the average individual investor. Short selling is usually best left to traders, institutional traders and arbitragers.

■ RISKS AND REWARDS OF INVESTING

When we buy a lottery ticket, we know that our maximum loss will be the price of the ticket. The same thing is true when we buy a stock; the most we can lose is what we paid for the stock. While the lottery offers a grand prize, there is no definitive "prize" when you purchase a stock for investment. But how high can a stock price go? Some have been going up for years—and are still going up! Stocks, therefore (at least in theory), have unlimited profit potential. Investing in the stock market has proven to be extremely rewarding over time. Although stocks go up and down, sometimes rather dramatically, they generally have been in an uptrend for more than 60 years. Historically stocks have "returned" (dividends and capital gains) more than 10 percent annually, more than keeping pace with inflation. That's probably their greatest attraction; they are a proven investment medium that outpaces inflation.

There is no magic formula for making money in the stock market, but *patience* probably comes closest. Historically, five years generally "bridges" most market declines, and, for those prepared to wait out a bear market, the market is *comparatively* safe. There have been only six losing five-year periods in the last 60 such periods. Patient investors who hold a well diversified portfolio of stocks have been rewarded handsomely. Most financial advisors consider stocks a *must* investment for virtually all investors.

Brokerage accounts are insured, by SIPC, for $500,000. This is *not* insurance against bad judgment in the selection and/or timing of stock purchases, but purely protection against the failure (bankruptcy) of brokerage firms. It is always a possibility that you will lose everything you have invested in an individual stock. Even if you don't lose everything, substantial losses can—and too often do—occur. The market does *fluctuate*, and that is both the good news and the bad news. One can profit from an upward move (selling long) and from a downward move (selling short). Guess incorrectly and you can certainly lose with either approach.

For investors who own securities, their potential loss is their entire investment, while there is no limit (theoretically) to the amount they can make. Short sellers have very different risks and rewards. Since the short seller makes his maximum profit from a downward movement in a stock's price, he is hoping that the stock falls in price as far as possible. In effect, he is hoping that the stock goes bankrupt so that he can "cover" for zero and thus make a profit equal to the proceeds of the original short sale. That's as far down as a stock can go—to zero—so that's the short seller's maximum profit potential.

The short seller is a bear who wants the stock's price to decline. What the short seller *doesn't* want is for the stock to go up! Remember, he has sold the stock at what he believes is too high a price and hopes to buy it back more cheaply. He doesn't want to have to buy it back at a higher price since this will result in a loss. There is no limit to the amount the short seller can lose. That's the inherent danger in short selling—the specter of unlimited losses.

While the short seller's profit is limited, the buyer has an unlimited profit potential—but can lose his entire investment. A further consideration for the short seller is that the stock he sold was borrowed from someone else and that it must ultimately be returned. If he shorts a dividend-paying stock, he will not receive the dividends but he himself will have to pay them out! Since he has borrowed the stock, he must make good the dividends to the one he borrowed the stock from. This results in a negative cash flow for the short seller.

In a broad sense, bonds and money market funds are safest, since their prices generally do not change erratically (referred to as volatility) while preferred stocks have slightly more risk and common stocks are the riskiest of all. The offset is that the high-risk situations offer the most potential reward. In general, the higher the potential risk is, the higher the potential reward. While stocks are generally risky, they have outperformed all other financial instruments over the long term. For all but the most ultraconservative investors, one of the greatest risks might be to *not* invest in stocks!

■ COMMON STOCKS

All corporations *must* issue common stock. These shares of common stock represent ownership in the corporation. The total number of shares that investors (both individuals and institutions) own at any one time is known as the *outstanding shares*.

An owner of common stock has, in effect, a "piece of the action." Called ownership or equity, common stocks are a type of *equity* (ownership) security. If a company has 1,000,000 shares of common stock outstanding, and you own 100,000 of those shares, then you are a 10 percent *owner* of the corporation (100,000 ÷ 1,000,000 = 10 percent).

The rights of the common stockholder vary from company to company, but normally they include the following:

1. The right to vote.
2. The receipt of dividends.
3. The right to sell or liquidity.
4. Residual rights.

THE RIGHT TO VOTE

Almost all common stocks carry the right to vote. Occasionally a company will issue several different classes of common stock, only some of which may be voting stock. This is comparatively rare. Shareholders vote for, among other things, the selection of directors who are elected to manage the corporation, determine policy, appoint officers, including the Chief Executive Officer or CEO, and see that the company is operated in accordance with the terms of the corporate charter. The directors attend to day-to-day operations, sometimes directly and sometimes with or through a slate of officers. Shareholders are also asked to vote on extraordinary events such as mergers and acquisitions, changes in the company's capitalization, stock splits, and other unusual actions.

Voting is usually conducted either on a statutory basis or a cumulative basis. Under *statutory voting* (the most common method), if four different directorships are up for election and you own 100 voting common shares, then you can cast up to 100 votes for your favorite for each of the four open Director seats, on a one share, one vote basis. If you favor Mary, John, Lucy, and Pete, then you may give each of those candidates a maximum of 100 votes. Under this method, holders of more than half the voting shares have absolute control over the directorships since they will always outvote everyone else. Fifty-one-percent ownership thus assures 100 percent control. Under *cumulative voting*, you may "allocate" your votes and split them up any way you wish. Given the same four directorships, you might opt to vote none of your 100 shares for Mary, John, or Lucy, but instead vote 400 shares for Pete. Cumulative voting thus gives minority shareholders their best chance at gaining representation on the board of directors, however it is rare and must be specifically authorized by the Corporation's charter which is the license under which a corporation does business.

THE RECEIPT OF DIVIDENDS

Common stockholders have the privilege to receive dividends *when, as, and if* declared by the board of directors. The dividend is under their absolute control and is not vested in the corporation's officers. Generally, while bonds pay a fixed amount of interest and preferred stocks pay a fixed amount of dividend, the dividend on common stock varies, usually in direct proportion to the company's earnings. Growth stocks usually exhibit a long-term pattern of increasing dividends through the years.

RESIDUAL RIGHTS

When a company is dissolved, either voluntarily or involuntarily, many claims must be satisfied before the common stockholders can claim any "salvage" rights. Even though they are the owners of the company, their claims come dead last. All salaries and taxes must first be satisfied, then general creditors and unsecured bondholders are paid, then preferred shareholders. And *then* common shareholders get to share whatever may be left. Usually there is nothing left for the common stockholder since even the bondholders and holders of the preferred issues rarely get paid in full. Some rare exceptions to this occur when a company is overly rich in assets. In such cases the company may be "worth more dead than alive," and the common shareholders benefit when the company is dissolved.

The *par value* of a common stock is *not* an important consideration. Par value bears no direct relationship to a common stock's initial price, its dividend rate, or what it is worth in the current marketplace or in dissolution (book value). A company's par value is of minimum use only to provide a control stated bookeeping value. For most U.S. corporations, a par value of between $0.01 and $1.00 is usually assigned, and sometimes a common stock is listed as having *no* par value!

■ PREFERRED STOCKS

Many corporations issue preferred stock, although they are under no legal obligation to do so. Preferred shares generally pay a fixed dividend which is announced when the shares are first offered in the marketplace. Most corporations have only one class of common stock outstanding, but, for corporations that do elect to issue preferred stock, they usually issue several different such issues over time. When we say that someone owns "XYZ" stock it is understood that we are referring to common stock. Just "XYZ" is description enough; we don't have to say "XYZ common stock." When referring to preferred stocks, however, we must add something to the description of the preferred stock to distinguish it from the *other* issues of preferred stock that that same company probably issued. To avoid confusion, companies elect to name their different preferred issues in several ways. Here are some:

Method 1	Method 2	Method 3
ABC $8.00 preferred	CYA 7 percent preferred	RFQ A preferred
ABC $10.00 preferred	CYA 11 percent preferred	RFQ B preferred
ABC $12.60 preferred	CYA 13.2 percent preferred	RFQ C preferred

Method 1. ABC company preferred issues are distinguished, one from the other, by the dollar amount of the *annual* dividend. Note that preferred stocks, like most dividend-paying common stocks, pay their dividends every three months (quarterly), or four times each year. ABC $8.00 preferred has a fixed dividend rate of $8.00 per year ($2.00 per quarter). The ABC $10.00 preferred pays an annual dividend of $10.00 ($2.50 quarterly). The $12.60 preferred pays that amount annually ($3.15 quarterly).

Method 2. The different CYA company preferred issues show a percent (%) rather than a dollar amount. This is the percent of each preferred stock's par value that the company has agreed to pay annually as the dividend on that particular issue. While many preferred stocks have a $100 par value, others are generally pared at $50 or $25.

Preferred issue par values, unlike common stock par values, are important to know. Most preferred issues are originally offered or sold at their par values. [When a preferred issue is callable (more on this later), the shareowner is entitled to par, and sometimes a small premium over par.]

In this method, then, when the preferred dividend is expressed as a percent, the par value must be known so that you can figure out exactly how much of a dividend will be paid. If the issuer is saying that you will receive a certain percent, you must ask, "Percent of what?" The *what* is the preferred stock's par value. Presuming that all the CYA issues had a $100 par value, you would calculate 7 percent of $100 ($7.00), 11 percent of $100 ($11.00), and 13.2 percent of $100 ($13.20). These issues' annual dividend rates would be, in order, $7.00, $11.00, $13.20. Their quarterly rates would be, respectively, $1.75, $2.75, $3.30. If the 7 percent preferred had a par value of $50, its annual dividend would be $3.50 (7 percent of $50). If the 11 percent preferred had a par value of $38, its annual dividend would be $4.18 (11 percent of $38).

Method 3. RFQ company uses only letters of the alphabet rather than dollar values or percentages. Now there is no way you can figure the amount of the dividend just from the security's name. You will have to look it up in one of the security industry's information service manuals such as Moody's, Value Line, or Standard & Poor's.

THE SENIOR ASPECTS OF PREFERRED STOCK

This type of equity security is called "preferred" for several reasons. For one, a company must pay dividends on all its preferred stock issues, in full, before it can pay anything to the common shareholders. Within a given company, its preferred issues are "safer" than the company's common stock, with respect to the payment of dividends. In a broad sense, preferred issues are purchased for fairly safe income and not for capital gain possibilities. They are "preferred" by the more conservative investor over common stocks.

TYPES OF PREFERRED STOCK

Cumulative Preferred. Virtually all preferred issues are *cumulative.* This means that, if the company skips a quarterly dividend, it is still owed to the preferred shareholder. If the company is struggling through bad times, they will almost certainly reduce or even eliminate the dividend on the common stock. If they get in a real cash bind, they will also skip the preferred stock dividend. While the "skipped" common stock dividend is gone forever, the preferred dividend becomes an arrearage and is still owed to the cumulative preferred shareholders. When the company ultimately recovers, all such passed-over preferred dividends must be paid before dividend payments to the common shareholders may resume. This is another example of the preferred stock's relative safety.

Callable Preferred. Some preferred issues are *callable.* This means that the issuing corporation reserves the right to retire the preferred issue by paying the stockholders a certain amount of cash. When a preferred issue is called, the shareholder has no other option than to surrender the stock. The minimum call price is par, which is the amount for which the issue was originally sold to the investing public. Callability is an undesirable trait for a preferred stock, at least insofar as the *shareholder is concerned.*

New preferred stocks are issued at the then-prevailing rates of return. If interest rates are high, then new preferred issues will also have a high return. If, sometime after a callable preferred issue is sold to the public, interest rates fall dramatically, then the company will refinance the existing issue by "calling" it and issuing other securities at a cheaper dividend payable rate. This saves the company money since they are replacing a high dividend rate with a lower rate, just as a homeowner refinances a mortgage when rates decline below the original mortgage rate. A shareholder who purchased a callable preferred when interest rates were high will have it called away just when things are getting good—when the return on the preferred purchased is higher than newly issued preferreds. Thus, with a callable preferred, an investor cannot "lock up" a high rate of return.

Callable preferreds are usually not callable immediately after issuance. There is traditionally a grace period during which the issue is not callable, the first five years after issuance being fairly standard. When the issue ultimately becomes subject to call, the company usually offers a few "extra" dollars over par as compensation.

Let's look at how a typical situation for a $100 par callable preferred might be. NFW seven percent preferred ($100 par) is offered at $100 per share in August of 2000. It is not callable until August of 2005, at which time the stated call price will be $106 per share. Beginning in 2006 the call price will be $104, reducing to $102 in 2007, and $100 beginning in 2008. The callable feature of this preferred stock might then be described as "noncallable for first five years, initially callable at a 6-point premium, scaled down to par in 2008." The issue may then be called, at the company's discretion, any time after August of 2008. If interest rates remain at the same level as they were when the preferred was issued, or go even higher, than the company will probably not elect to call the issue.

Convertible Preferred. Some preferred issues are *convertible*. This option feature permits the shareholder to exchange preferred shares for other securities, usually common stock of the same corporation. The preferred shareowner has complete control

over when, or if, he converts. You cannot convert back into preferred once you have exchanged your shares for common stock.
It's a one-time deal.

The number of shares of common stock that you will
receive for each exchanged share of preferred is known as the
conversion ratio. Financial publications usually express the
exchange feature as a *conversion price*. A conversion price can be
changed to a conversion ratio simply by dividing the issue's par
value by the conversion price. Thus a convertible preferred ($50
par) with a conversion price of $25 has a conversion ratio of 2. In
other words, each preferred share can be exchanged for two
shares of common stock ($50 ÷ $25). Most investors find it easier
to work with the conversion ratio.

Nonconvertible preferred stocks (known as *straight* preferreds) move up and down with changes in interest rates. They
go up in price when interest rates fall, and down in price when
interest rates rise. Bonds exhibit the same trait; it's a feature of all
fixed income securities. These straight preferreds, while sensitive
to interest rate changes, are relatively impervious to other market
forces such as reported earnings and the general business outlook.

That's both the good news and the bad news! Straight preferreds go their merry way, pricewise, even though the
company's business falls off. They are "safe" in this respect. But
what if the company does fabulously well? The common stock's
dividend, which is unfixed, may be raised dramatically and the
market price of the common stock may skyrocket. The straight
preferred stockholder is normally denied the opportunity for
large capital gain profits (other than by buying noncallable preferreds just before interest rates fall sharply). The capital gains or
growth profit is the province of the common stockholder, while
the preferred stockholder is normally only interested in yield.

Ownership of *convertible* preferreds permits the holder to
profit in both the preferred or the common stock market. If the
common stock doesn't rise greatly in price, you simply hold the
preferred and enjoy its relatively safe yield and price stability. If
the common stock does rise dramatically in price, the convertible preferred will keep pace with this rise. If, for example, a preferred stock has a conversion ratio of 4, then it will normally

always sell for at least four times the value of the underlying common shares. Therefore a convertible preferred stock offers capital gain possibilities referred to as Conversion Arbitrage, that is the conversion of the convertible preferred into the receivable common stock and the sale of the common at a profit, as well as being a fairly sure income producer.

Isn't this the best of all possible worlds? A corporation issues convertible rather than straight preferred shares for a good reason: to save money! When issued, convertibles pay less of a dividend than do straight preferreds. That's the "price" you pay for the convertibility feature—the lower return you must accept.

■ STOCK RIGHTS

Some common stocks may have a *preemptive rights* feature. This means that existing shareholders will be given the first opportunity to buy any new common shares that are sold to the public. The general rule is that "existing" shareholders are issued one right for each share they own. These rights may be surrendered, with a cash payment known as the *subscription price*, for the new shares. Shareholders not wishing to subscribe for the new shares may sell their rights in the open market. This feature permits shareholders to maintain their same proportion of ownership in the company, should they choose to do so. For example, Ms. Claudette Morgan owns 100 shares of XYZ. Since a total of 10,000 shares of XYZ are outstanding, she owns 1 percent of the company (100 ÷ 10,000). If another 10,000 shares were issued, and Claudette did *not* purchase any of these new shares, her ownership would be reduced to only 0.5 percent (100 ÷ 20,000). If the company had a preemptive rights feature, and Ms. Morgan chose to use her rights and subscribe to 1 percent of the new shares, she would then own 200 shares and would remain a 1 percent owner (200 ÷ 20,000). A rights offering lasts about one month. During this time, the rights are traded on the same exchange or marketplace as are the old shares of stock.

Because the subscription price is set somewhat under the current market price for the old shares, the rights have value.

After all, using them gives you the ability to buy stock at a discount, and thus save some money. It's similar to the value of a discount coupon. When a shareholder receives rights, she must determine whether to subscribe to the new shares. If the rights are *not* used, they should definitely be sold for their intrinsic value. It would be foolish neither to use nor to sell rights.

■ STOCK WARRANTS

Warrants are, essentially, long-term subscription securities and are usually issued on existing shares. At times warrants are issued as a feature of new offerings. Typically, they offer holders the right to purchase common shares at a fixed price (the subscription price) for periods of up to 10 years, sometimes even longer. They are sometimes issued as a "sweetener" on a new issue of stock to make the new offering more attractive to the investing public. While rights are issued with a positive value (they allow the purchase of stock at a price *less* than the stock's current market price), warrants are "out of the money" at the time they are issued. They permit the purchase of the company's stock at a *higher*-than-current price so that, at least at the time of the issuance, they have no value. What's their attraction? Because they have so long to run (up to 10 years or more), investors believe that *sometime* during their long life the underlying common stock's market price might rise to well above the subscription price, and thus the warrants would then have real value. Warrants are generally considered to be speculative. As we shall see in Chapter 9, they are very similar to a "deep out-of-the-money call." Warrants do not necessarily trade on the same exchange or marketplace as does their underlying common stock.

■ SUMMARY

In this chapter we have examined several of the investment products available in the stock market. Common and preferred shares are both equity securities. Common and preferred shareholders are considered owners of the corporation, even though only common shareholders ordinarily have the right to vote. The preferred share has many of the features of a bond: a fixed annual payment, a superior position over the common stock with respect to dividend payments, and possibly a call feature and/or a convertibility feature.

Most people think of common stocks when they speak about the "stock" market. Preferred issues are also stocks, although they don't enjoy the same press coverage. There are many more common stock issues outstanding than there are preferred issues. Common stocks are not callable and not convertible. Also mentioned were two financial instruments that are not *quite* stocks, at least not when they are purchased. Rather, they represent the right to *buy stocks. These are short-term (rights) or long-term (warrants). They have no voting privilege and do not receive dividends, but rights and warrants are also part of the "stock" market.*

Several later chapters will be devoted to other instruments of the stock market: closed-end and open-end funds in Chapter 9, and stock options in Chapter 10. The former represent a "package-plan" approach to investing, the latter a sophisticated way of investing in, speculating with, and hedging common stocks.

READING
THE FINANCIAL PRESS
Determining Share Value, Determining Your Investment Return

■ CASH ACCOUNTS

Individuals who purchase securities through a brokerage firm normally do so either in a cash account or in a margin account. Some customers utilize only one of these types of accounts; other clients have both.

SETTLEMENT DATE—REGULAR WAY

The *cash* account, by far the most common, calls for the customer to pay for any purchases, in full, on or before the transaction's *settlement date*. The settlement date (also known as the *due date or clearance date*) for most transactions falls three business days after the trade date (T+3). This is known as *regular way settlement*, used for the majority of all trades. Trades done on a Monday, for example, settle on the Thursday following; Tuesday's trades settle the following Friday; and so on. If any of the three business days after the trade date is a holiday, delivery is extended one day because three *business* days must be counted to establish the settlement date. This three-day settlement is used for almost all transactions except those in options and government securities. Trades in these investment products normally settle on the *next* business day after the trade (T+1). This is regular way settlement for trades in options and governments. A current major goal of the industry is to reduce the settlement period to T+1, the next business date after the trade.

When clients sell securities in a cash account, they are entitled to be *paid* by the brokerage firm on the settlement date, provided they have made *good delivery* of the securities sold. If the security that was sold is long in the customer's account (almost certainly in *street name)* at the time of the sale, there will be no problem with the delivery since the security is already in the firm's possession. If the security is not long in the customer's account, it must be delivered to the selling firm, in good form, on or before the settlement date.

The brokerage firm cannot pay out the proceeds of the sale before they have possession of the securities sold. A customer cannot demand payment unless the securities sold have been received into the account, in negotiable form (good delivery). Under unusual circumstances the customer may be unable to deliver on or before the settlement date. If the security hasn't been received by the firm, then the brokerage firm may have to *buy in* the security, thus flattening the account, and charge the customer for any resultant debit. This doesn't happen very often.

Many cash account clients leave their securities with their brokerage firm to avoid having to safeguard them in a safety deposit box. This is referred to as Street Name Stock. They are also saved the bother of sending their securities to their broker when they are selling, and thus they can always be paid on the settlement date. Since SIPC insures accounts for $500,000, there is very little reason for clients to be concerned about the safekeeping of their securities.

■ MARGIN ACCOUNTS

Just as you can purchase a home or an automobile by putting up only a portion of the purchase price and borrowing the remainder from a bank or other financial institution, you can also purchase most securities in the same manner. When investors make a down payment on securities and borrow the balance of the purchase price from the stock brokerage firm buying the securities for them, they are said to be buying *on margin* (in a margin account). You can therefore purchase twice as much market value of stock on margin as you can for cash. This is called leverage, where the investor uses borrowed money for a greater percentage of profit.

However, even though this affords the opportunity to make more money for a given amount of invested dollars, it also means that you will *lose* twice as much if a margin investment goes sour. Another consideration is that you must pay interest on the amount owed to the broker (the *debit balance*). This interest, charged monthly, is usually more than the amount of dividends and interest coming into the account from the securities purchased.

Although trading on margin provides *leverage*, it is considered a relatively sophisticated technique and is definitely not for the faint of heart. If the market value of your margined securities drops dramatically, the brokerage firm will demand that you deposit more money (a *maintenance call*). If you cannot (or choose not to) meet the call, then some or all of your securities will be sold to bring the account to a properly margined status. Unfortunately, such forced sales are normally executed in rapidly falling markets that are near their low point.

Stocks purchased on margin cannot be sent to you. They must remain in street name with the brokerage firm as collateral for your debit balance. Such securities will be in the broker's name, even though you are the true owner. You are the *beneficial owner*, but the brokerage firm is the *owner of record* (registered owner). Such securities, owned by you but held by the brokerage firm, are again said to be in *street name*. When you own stocks held for you by a brokerage firm, in cash and/or margin accounts, that firm will send to you, monthly, a statement of your account showing the securities and cash that they are holding for you. They will refer to your "positions" as either *long* or *short*. Interestingly, trades will be posted to your account on their *settlement* date rather than their trade date. You are considered the owner of the securities on the trade date, but the trades aren't posted to your account until settlement date. Some brokerage firms will show "pending" trades for securities with a trade date in a given month that do not settle until the following month. This avoids the anxiety of those customers who, for instance, buy or sell in late April but don't see the trades appear on their April monthly statement. Those late April trades won't be posted until early May. With the adoption of T+1 or next day delivery this will become rare.

■ SECURITY POSITIONS: LONG, SHORT, FLAT

A customer's security positions at the brokerage firm are said to be "long" in his account. To be *long* means to *own*, to have a positive (+) position. You are thus long any securities that your broker is holding for you. Should you order your broker to buy 100 shares of IBM for you, you "go long" immediately after the trade is executed for you. Your account will remain "long 100 IBM" until such time as you ask the broker to send you the stock certificate, or until you ask him to sell the shares.

If you sell the shares while they are with the broker, your account will then be *flat* (a zero position). The sell trade "flattens" the position. The position will also become flat if you, the customer, ask for physical delivery of the shares. The shares will be transferred to your name and shipped to you. Your account will say "delivered 100 IBM" (or simply "100 IBM del"), and this will also flatten the position. The word *flat* will not appear on your statement; it is simply the brokers' way of designating that they don't "owe" you any shares.

A partial reduction of the shares held by the brokerage house does not flatten the account. If you are long 250 XYZ and you sell only 100 XYZ, your long position will be reduced to 150 shares. If you are long 1,000 NFW and your broker delivers 300 shares to you, then your long position is reduced to 700 shares. Your long position reflects only your standing with the brokerage firm, since, they have no way of knowing what shares you might have at home, with other brokerages, or with banks. Only if you sell all your shares does your account go flat.

Should you send stock to your broker to be held in your account, the transaction will be posted as a *receive*. Purchases and receives will create or increase long positions; sales and delivers will reduce or eliminate long positions.

Your broker keeps all your positions separate. Should you own 300 shares of ABC, 400 shares of DEF, and 500 shares of GHI (a total of 1,200 shares of the three different stocks), your broker will show you not "long 1,200," but rather "long 300 ABC, long 400 DEF, long 500 GHI." When, as a customer, you wish to know which securities the broker is holding for you, you are most likely to ask, "What's my long position?"

After a short sale the customer's account will be *short* the stock borrowed to complete the sale. Since a short sale is the sale of something that you *don't* own, after the sale you *owe* (not *own*) the stock to the person it was borrowed from. This is a negative (–) position. The stock was borrowed and, until you return it (by a covering buy transaction), you will remain short. Some active trading accounts have both long positions (the customer is bullish and expects the long stocks to go up in price) and short positions (the customer is bearish on the short stocks and expects them to go down in price). Short sales may be executed only in a margin account!

Sometimes a short position is the result of an error. If you own 300 shares of XYZ that are long in your account, and you ask your broker to sell them, he should enter an order to sell 300 shares. But suppose he makes an error and instead sells 3,000 shares! After the incorrect trade is posted, the account will show a short position of 2,700 shares of XYZ. (You were long only 300 shares but 3,000 shares were sold, resulting in a short position of 2,700 shares.) The error will, of course, be corrected by the removal of the oversale of 2,700 XYZ and your account will then be, correctly, flat with respect to XYZ. Short positions may also result from the sale of the wrong security (ABC instead of ACB), an incorrect delivery (CAY

> *To be **long** means to **own** (+); to be **short** means to **owe** (–), to be **flat** means to neither own nor owe (0). We have all heard such expressions such as, "Don't sell him short!" Or "That's the long and the short of it." Now you know how such expressions came into use.*

instead of CYA), or other errors on the part of the brokerage firm's staff or the client herself. A short position that is not the result of a deliberate short sale is an indication of trouble in an account. The account should be researched immediately to find the source of the error so that it can be fixed as soon as possible.

■ PRICING STOCKS: POINTS AND FRACTIONS

Stocks, both common and preferred, are priced in dollars and in eighths and sixteenths of dollars. A stock trading at "26" is selling for $26.00 per share. The next higher price is 26 1/16 ($26.625 per share), the next lower price is 25 15/16 ($ 25.93 75 per share). The full range of prices for a stock trading between 26 and 27 would be: 26 1/16, 26 2/16, 26 3/16, 26 4/16, 26 5/16, 26 6/16, 26 7/16, 26 8/16, 26 9/16, 26 10/16, 26 11/16, 26 12/16, 26 13/16, 26 14/16, 26 15/16, 27. At times, depending on heavy market volume, and greater liquidity, stocks will trade at fractions smaller than a sixteenth. The complete fractional range appears in the schedule on the following page.

A *point* on a stock means one dollar per share. If a stock is trading at 94 ($94 per share) and it goes up 2 "points," the price will then be 96 ($96 per share). A stock at 46 8/16 ($46.50 per share) that goes down 3 "points" will decline to 43 8/16 ($43.50 per share). A price change of "one and one-half points" translates to a difference of $1.50 in the per-share price of the stock.

STOCK FRACTION	PER-SHARE VALUE
1/64 = .015625	33/64 = .515625
1/32 = .06125	17/32 = .53125
3/64 = .046875	35/64 = .546875
1/16 = .0625	9/16 = .5625
5/64 = .078125	37/64 = .578125
3/32 = .09375	19/32 = .59375
7/64 = .109375	39/64 = .609375
1/8 = .125	5/8 = .625
9/64 = .140625	41/64 = .640625
5/32 = .15625	21/32 = .65625
11/64 = .171875	43/64 = .671875
3/16 = .1875	11/64 = .6875
13/64 = .203125	45/64 = .703125
7/32 = .21875	23/32 = .71875
15/64 = .234375	47/64 = .734375
1/4 = .25	3/4 = .75
17/64 = .265625	49/64 = .765625
9/32 = .28125	25/32 = .78125
19/64 = .296875	51/64 = .796875
5/16 = .3125	13/16 = .8125
21/64 = .328125	53/64 = .828125
11/32 = .34375	27/32 = .84375
23/64 = .359375	55/64 = .859375
3/8 = .375	7/8 = .875
25/64 = .390625	57/64 = .890625
13/32 = .40625	29/32 = .90625
27/64 = .421875	59/64 = .921875
7/16 = .4375	15/16 = .9375
29/64 = .453125	61/64 = .953125
15/32 = .46875	31/32 = .96875
31/64 = .484375	63/64 = .984375
1/2 = .5	1 = 1

Most investors buy stocks in 100-share lots (*round lots*). Amounts of shares between 1 and 99 are referred to as *odd lots*. Here are some examples of the dollar values of various stock prices, both on a per-share basis (1 share) and on a 100-share basis:

SHARE PRICE	DOLLAR VALUE OF 1 SHARE	DOLLAR VALUE OF 100 SHARES
13 3/4 (12/16)	$13.75	$1,375.00
5 1/8 (2/16)	$5.125	$512.50
88	$88.00	$8,800.00
46 1/2 (8/16)	$46.50	$4,650.00
31 5/16	$31.3125	$3,131.25
128 5/8 (10/16)	$128.625	$12,862.50
1 1/4 (4/16)	$1.25	$125.00
22 3/8 (6/16)	$22.375	$2,237.50
42 7/16	$42.4375	$4,243.75
39 7/8 (14/16)	$39.875	$3,987.50
7	$7.00	$700.00

It is expected that within the next few years stocks will be priced in decimals. To implement this change many stocks are currently priced in trade variations of U.S. pennies (.01) and nickels (.05). Moreover, the financial press has taken the lead by pricing stocks in dollars and cents.

■ THE FIGURATION OF CURRENT YIELD

A stock's *current yield* is calculated by dividing its annual dividend per share by its current market price per share. It shows the percent of the current market price that is expected to be returned to a shareholder, as cash dividends, during the coming year. This is known as the investor's return. It takes into account only the current declared dividend and does not reflect any possible changes in the per-share price during the year. (A security's *total return* would reflect both dividend income and per-share price changes.)

For example, ABC common stock is currently trading at 46 3/8 or 43 6/16 and has an annual dividend rate of $2.60 (a *quarterly* rate of $0.65 per share). ABC's current yield would be 5.6 percent. The annual dividend is divided by the current price: 2.60 ÷ 46.375 = 0.056 or 5.6 percent.

Current yields on preferred stocks are figured in the same manner. Rights, warrants, and stock options do not pay dividends and so do not have a current yield. *The Wall Street Journal*, among other newspapers, shows each stock's current yield on a daily basis, figured on the "closing" price each trading day, adjusted for changing dividend rates on an ongoing basis.

■ NEWSPAPER LISTINGS

Investors can track the value of their stockholdings through the financial press, of which *The Wall Street Journal* is the most widely known and most widely utilized. Figure 2–1 shows a portion of the New York Stock Exchange stock price tables published in *The Journal* on Tuesday October 31, 2000. It shows prices for the previous trading day, Monday October 30, 2000.

In the figure, there are 12 headings across the width of each column. (They are shown "here" or "in the chart on page 29" with numbers in parentheses, which do not appear in the listings.)

(1)	(2)	(3)	(4)	(5)	(6)	(7)	(8)	(9)	(10)	(11)	(12)
52 Weeks					Yld		Vol				Net
Hi	Lo	Stock	Sym	Div	%	PE	100s	Hi	Lo	Close	Chg

(1) The *52 Weeks Hi* lists the highest price at which a round lot (100 shares or more) of that particular stock has traded during the previous 52 weeks, plus the current week, excepting only the trading day shown.

(2) The *52 Weeks Lo* shows the lowest round lot trade recorded during the same period, plus the current week, again excepting the trading day shown.

(3) The *Stock* column shows the security, with its name abbreviated to fit into the small space allotted. Also shown, if necessary, is whether the stock is a preferred issue or a different class of common stock. Enough information will be given, even if cryptically, to distinguish the security from all the other issues on that exchange.

Monday, October 30, 2000

	52 WEEKS				YLD		VOL				NET
	HI	LO	STOCK	SYM	DIV %	PE	100s	HI	LO	CLOSE	CHG

-A-A-A-

	HI	LO	STOCK	SYM	DIV	%	PE	100s	HI	LO	CLOSE	CHG
x	26⁵⁰	9⁷⁵	AAR	AIR	.34	3.2	10	1275	10⁵⁰	9⁸¹	10⁵⁰ +	0⁴⁴
	28	19²⁵	ABM Indus	ABM	.62	2.3	15	101	27³⁸	26⁸¹	27³⁸ +	0³⁸
	26⁵⁰	19³⁸	ABN Am ADR	ABN	1.28e	5.7	...	961	22⁵⁶	22⁰⁶	22³⁸ +	0⁴⁴
	23⁷⁵	19¹⁹	ABN Am pfA		1.88	8.4	...	356	22⁴⁴	22²⁵	22²⁵	...
	22⁶⁹	18⁸⁸	ABN Am pfB		1.78	8.4	...	364	21³⁸	21¹³	21¹⁹ −	0⁰⁶
n	26²⁵	20²⁵	ACE CapTr		1.73e	6.9	...	17	25	24⁶⁹	25 +	0⁵⁰
▲	40¹⁹	14⁰⁶♣	ACE Ltd	ACL	.52	1.3	19	13301	41	39²⁵	40⁶³ +	1³⁸
n▲	82⁷⁵	47⁶⁹	ACE LtdPRIDES		2.45e	3.0	...	190	83	80³¹	83 +	2⁵⁰
	8¹⁹	6³¹	ACM GvtFd	ACG	.78	10.3	...	782	7⁵⁶	7⁴⁴	7⁵⁶ +	0¹³
	8	6²⁵	ACM OppFd	AOF	.72a	10.0	...	120	7²⁵	7¹⁹	7¹⁹ −	0⁰⁶
	7⁶⁹	6¹⁹	ACM SecFd	GSF	.78	10.7	...	878	7³⁸	7²⁵	7³¹ +	0⁰⁶
	6²⁵	5¹³	ACM SpctmFd	SI	.60	10.0	...	342	6⁰⁶	6	6	...
	10²⁵	6⁸⁸	ACM MgdDlr	ADF	1.02	14.1	...	404	7³¹	7¹³	7²⁵	...
	8	4⁷⁵	ACM MgdInco	AMF	.63	12.9	...	155	4⁸⁸	4⁸⁸	4⁸⁸ −	0⁰⁶
	12⁶⁹	10¹³	ACM MuniSec	AMU	.87	6.9	...	67	12⁶³	12⁵⁰	12⁵⁶	...
s	72⁸¹	27¹⁶♣	AES	AES			...	45 19491	56³¹	53⁵⁰	55⁸⁸ ┃	1⁶³
	110	50	AES Tr		3.39e	3.9	...	211	86⁶⁹	83⁵⁰	86⁶⁹ +	1⁹⁴
▲	**68⁶³**	**33⁵⁶**	**AFLAC**	**AFL**	**.34**	**.5**	**31**	**21842**	**73²⁵**	**67⁸⁸**	**71⁵⁶ +**	**3⁵⁶**
	14⁵⁰	9⁹⁴	AGCO Cp	AG	.04	.3	dd	1823	11⁵⁶	11⁰⁶	11⁵⁶ +	0⁴⁴
▲	20⁶⁹	15⁵⁰	AGL Res	ATG	1.08	5.3	14	928	20⁹⁴	20⁵⁶	20⁵⁶ −	0¹³
	31⁵⁶	13⁷⁵	AgSvcAm	ASV	...	11	9	15⁰⁶	14³⁸	15⁰⁶ +	0⁴⁴
	20⁹⁴	9⁷⁵	AICI CapTr	pf	2.25	16.4	...	53	13⁷⁵	13⁵⁶	13⁷⁵ +	0²⁵
	31⁶³	15	AIPC	PLB	...	14	850	21	20²⁵	20⁵⁰ −	0⁵⁶
	20¹³	**7⁸⁸♣**	**AK Steel**	**AKS**	**.50**	**5.2**	**10**	**3531**	**9⁶⁹**	**8⁷⁵**	**9⁶⁹ +**	**0⁸⁸**
	25	18	♣AMB Prop	AMB	1.48	6.3	14	901	23³⁸	23²⁵	23³⁸	...
	24¹³	19¹³♣	AMB Prop pfA		2.13	10.2	...	37	20⁹⁴	20⁶³	20⁸⁸ +	0³⁸
s▲	**6³⁸**	**1⁸⁰**	**AMCOL**	**ACO**	**.04m**	**.6**	**1**	**1066**	**7**	**6²⁵**	**6⁷⁵ +**	**0⁶³**
	4⁴⁴	0¹³	AMF Bowl	PIN	...	dd	1765	0²⁵	0²⁰	0²³	...
	25³¹	19⁴⁴♣	AMLI Resdntl	AML	1.88f	8.1	6	159	23³¹	23	23¹⁹ +	0¹³
s	**39**	**20⁷⁷**	**AMR**	**AMR**	**stk**	**...**	**5**	**23494**	**34⁹⁴**	**31**	**33⁶⁹ +**	**2²⁵**
	23⁸⁸	19⁵⁶	AMR PINES		1.97	8.5	...	46	23⁵⁰	22⁸¹	23³¹ +	0⁴⁴
	24⁶³	20⁶⁹	ANZ pf		2.00	8.7	...	420	23	22⁷⁵	22⁸⁸ −	0⁰⁶
	25⁰⁶	20⁸⁸	ANZ II pf		2.02	8.7	...	192	23³¹	22⁸⁸	23²⁵ +	0²⁵
	9²⁵	**3¹³**	**APT Satellt**	**ATS**	**.41e**	**10.1**	**...**	**354**	**4¹³**	**4**	**4⁰⁶ +**	**0²⁵**
	21¹³	14¹⁹	ASA	ASA	.60	4.2	...	454	14⁵⁶	14³¹	14³⁸ +	0⁰⁶
	25²⁵	21⁶⁹	AT&T 8 1/4 PNS		2.06	8.4	...	170	24⁵⁶	24³⁸	24⁵⁰	...
	25⁸⁸	21⁵⁶	AT&T 8 1/8 PNS		2.03	8.5	...	572	?24³¹	23⁸⁸	24 −	0¹³
	61	21²⁵	AT&T	T	.88	3.9	13	270168	22⁸⁸	21⁹⁴	22⁶³ +	0⁶⁹
n	36	18⁰⁶	AT&T Wrls	AWE	...	...	35694	23³¹	22¹³	23⁰⁶ +	0⁸¹
s	50	19¹³♣	AVX Cp	AVX	.14	.5	12	11773	26⁵⁰	25⁷⁵	26¹³ −	0³⁸
	81⁵⁰	58²⁵	AXA ADS	AXA	2.16e	3.4	...	6742	63⁵⁶	62⁰⁶	63³⁸ +	0⁸⁸
	55	25⁹⁴♣	AXA Fnl	AXF	.10	.2	22	35066	53⁴⁴	52⁸¹	53⁰⁶ +	0¹³
	22⁹⁴	9	AZZ	AZZ	.16f	1.1	10	98	15⁵⁰	15	15¹³ −	0⁵⁰
s	8¹³	0⁴⁴	AamesFnl	AAM	...	dd	478	2⁰⁶	1⁷⁵	2 +	0¹⁹
	20	11⁴⁷	AaronRent	RNT	.04	.3	10	115	13⁸¹	13²⁵	13⁸¹ +	0²⁵
	20	14⁶³	AaronRent A	RNTA	.04	.3	14	2	15⁷⁵	15⁷⁵	15⁷⁵	...
	22²⁵	19	AbbeyNtl	SUA	1.75	8.2	...	88	21⁵⁶	21²⁵	21³¹	...
	23²⁵	19⁵⁰	AbbeyNtl 7 1¼%	SUD	1.81	8.1	...	214	22⁵⁶	22²⁵	22³⁸	...
	25⁵⁰	22¹³	AbbeyNtl pfA·		2.19	9.1	...	82	24¹³	23³¹	24¹³	...
▲	52⁷⁵	29³⁸	AbbotLab	ABT	.76	1.4	31	59793	54	51⁶³	54 +	2³¹
	32⁵⁶	8	Abercrombie A	ANF	...	16	14651	23⁷⁵	22⁶⁹	23 +	0¹⁹
	13⁶⁹	**7**	**Abitibi g**	**ABY**	**.40g**	**...**	**...**	**3626**	**8⁵⁰**	**7⁸⁸**	**8⁵⁰ +**	**0⁶⁹**
	6²⁵	4³⁸♣	AcadiaRlty	AKR	.48	8.3	15	44	5⁷⁵	5⁶⁹	5⁷⁵ +	0⁰⁶
	15¹³	2⁷⁵♣	AcceptIns	AIF	...	dd	127	5⁵⁰	5³⁸	5⁵⁰ −	0¹³
	19⁵⁶	8	AckrlyGp	AK	.02	.2	2	582	10²⁵	9⁸¹	10 +	0⁰⁶
	26⁸⁸	16³¹	ACNielsen	ART	...	24	1319	23³⁸	22⁷⁵	23³¹ +	0⁴⁴
s	5⁴⁴	1⁵⁸	Actuant A	ATU	...	5	1681	3⁷⁵	3⁵⁰	3⁵⁶ −	0¹³
	22⁸⁸	9⁸¹	Acuson	ACN	...	dd	586	22⁸⁸	22⁷⁵	22⁸⁸	...
s	27⁰⁴	19⁹²♣	AdamsExp	ADX	1.63	6.5	...	257	25	24⁵⁶	25 +	0¹⁹
	112	69⁵⁵	Adecco	ADO	.61e	.7	...	29	85⁵⁰	84⁹⁰	85⁵⁰ +	0⁶⁹
s	44⁵⁶	7⁵⁰	Administaff	ASF	...	79	2242	31¹⁰	28⁷⁰	30¹⁵ −	0⁴⁰
	22²⁵	17¹³	AFP Prov ADR	PVD	.91e	4.3	...	29	20⁹⁴	20⁹⁴	20⁹⁴	...
s	48⁵⁰	9⁹⁴♣	AdvMicro	AMD	...	8	67647	20⁸⁸	20	20²⁵ −	0¹⁹
n	**7**	**5³⁸**	**AdSemiEng ADS pf ASX+**		**...**	**...**	**314**	**6⁶³**	**6**	**6 −**	**0⁶⁹**
n	7¹⁹	5³¹	AdSemiEng ADS ASX		...	...	33	6⁶⁹	6³⁸	6³⁸ −	0³¹
	33⁹⁴	15⁶³	Advest	ADV	.24	.7	14	497	32⁴⁴	31²⁵	32²⁵ +	0⁴⁴
	45¹⁹	17⁵⁶	Advo	AD	...	16	686	36⁶³	36¹⁹	36⁶³ +	0¹³
s	49¹³	31⁵⁰♣	AEGON	AEG	.60	1.5	28	1684	39⁹⁴	39⁴⁴	39⁶³ −	0¹⁹
	73⁶⁹	38⁵⁰	Aetna	AET	.80	1.4	13	12291	59⁰⁶	56⁵⁶	56⁹⁴ +	0¹³
	57⁵⁰	31	AffilCmptr A	ACS	...	25	3005	55³⁸	55³⁸	54⁹⁴ −	0¹³

FIGURE 2–1 Stock Price Table from *The Wall Street Journal*

(4) The *Sym* column lists the security's trading symbol. Every stock is assigned a symbol consisting of 1, 2, or 3 letters of the alphabet. Each security's symbol is listed as a convenience to those who "watch the tape" and want to follow the price movements of their favorite stocks. Sales brokers enter customers' orders by stock symbol rather than by spelling out the entire name of the security they are buying or selling.

(5) The *Div* column shows the company's current *annual* dividend rate. Irregular payments, as well as special or extra dividends, are identified with footnotes.

(6) The *Yld %* column shows the stock's current yield, based on the dividend rate shown and the closing price, just as we described in the preceding section of this chapter.

(7) The *PE* column shows the stock's *price-earnings ratio.* This is calculated by dividing the closing price by the company's primary per-share earnings during the previous four quarters.

(8) The *Vol 100s* column called a round lot shows the total number of shares of that security traded that day, in hundreds.

(9) The *Hi* column shows the highest price at which the stock traded that day.

(10) The *Lo* column shows the lowest intraday price.

(11) The *Close* column lists the price at which the last reported trade took place on that day.

(12) The *Net Chg* column shows how the day's closing price compared with the previous day's closing price—how much the stock went up, or down, compared with the previous day.

Let's follow a complete line of information, from left to right, across the entire "New York Stock Exchange Composite Transactions" listing. We'll use AbbotLab (marked for you in Figure 2–1):

(1) The first figure, 52.75, signifies that AbbotLab sold at that price, and no higher, sometime during the previous 52 weeks, $52.75 per share was the "high for the previous 52 weeks, plus the current week."

(2) The next figure, 29.38 was the stock's preceding 52 week low. That gives us a trading "range" for the stock of 52.75 high–29.38 low, a variance of 23 dollars and thirty seven cents.

(3) Next is an abbreviation for the name of the corporation. Its full name is, of course, Abbott Laboratories.

(4) The ticker symbol assigned to Abbott Laboratories is ABT.

(5) The annual dividend is $0.76 per share.

(6) The current yield is shown as 1.4 percent. We can check this out by dividing the annual dividend ($0.76) by the stock's closing price (54): $0.76 ÷ 54 = 1.4 percent. It checks out! Yield is the dividend expressed as a percentage of the current market value.

(7) The price/earnings ratio is 31. This means that the stock is selling for about 31 times its diluted per share earnings over the last four quarters. This indicates that Abbott Laboratories' per-share earnings over the previous four quarters were about $1.74! Using a little algebra: if $P/E = 31$ and $P = 54$, then E, or earnings per share is $1.74.

(8) The trading volume for the day was 5,979,300 shares (59793 × 100). It was a very active stock that day!

(9) The day's highest trading price was 54 ($54 per share), which is also a new 52-week high for the stock indicated by the up arrow in the margin on the left.

(10) The intraday low price was 51.63 ($51.63 per share). Its "trading range" during the day was $2.37.

(11) The last trade of the day was at 54 ($54 per share).

(12) The price change from the previous closing price was up $2.31. This indicates that the previous closing price was 51.69. The stock gained $2.31 from the previous day's close.

See the ABBEY NATL PFA listed just before ABT. It is a preferred stock with a fixed yield.

See the n and s letters, which are sometimes included in the extreme left column. The "n" means that the stock has only been listed on the exchange within the 52 weeks. The "s" indicates that the stock has had a split, or a 10 percent or greater stock dividend, within the previous 52 weeks.

THE INITIAL
PUBLIC OFFERING
Getting the Stocks
to the Marketplace

Some 250 years ago, Wall Street was nothing more than a dirt path that started in front of Trinity Church and ran downhill toward the dockyards of Manhattan's East River.

There, on the piers, is where the stock market began. The original securities were actually bills of lading for the cargoes loaded off the inbound ships. No paper money was exchanged. The international unit of trade was silver, primarily the Spanish Dubloon, because gold was hard to come by. To make change, the coins were cut into pieces of eight, when necessary, to purchase shares in the cargo, which is the traditional reason why stocks are traded in eighths in the United States to this very day, reduced, of course, to sixteenths.

From such beginnings, securities trading flourished in this East River shipping center. In 1789, as a result of mounting war debts, Congress authorized the issue of $80 million in government bonds. A few years later, bank stocks were offered as a result of the establishment of the nation's first bank. Insurance companies began to appear, and an organized pattern of trading emerged. Although no formal stock market existed, there were securities to be traded. As they became more and more plentiful, securities were sold literally over the counter like any other product. This is how the so-called "over-the-counter" market of today initially developed.

In the spring of 1792, twenty-four men signed an agreement on Wall Street that, in effect, was the beginning of the New York Stock Exchange (NYSE). They agreed to sell securities only among themselves and established fixed commission rates—a policy that did not change until May of 1975, when rates were made negotiable. In the early 1800s, the members of this group—the New York Stock and Exchange Board—moved into what is now 40 Wall Street. In 1863, they moved again to the present site of the New York Stock Exchange, although the building occupied today was not completed until 1903.

With the advent of the Industrial Revolution, Wall Street exploded with activity. Issues that were deemed too speculative to trade by the Board were eagerly traded by non-members, often right in the street, because few non-members could afford office space. These traders became known as "curbside brokers" and the market as "The Curb." By the early 1900s the Curb had grown considerably and its brokers occupied offices on Broad Street. The system of trading by hand signals was developed by curbside brokers in an attempt to communicate over all the curbside shouting and confusion with their shouting clerks leaning out of upper-story windows. In fact, it came to be the exchange's trademark. In the early 1920s, the Curb Market moved indoors into its present location at 86 Trinity Place. Many years later, in

FIGURE 3–1   WALL STREET IN THE EARLY 1800s

1952, the so-called New York Curb Exchange adopted its present name, the American Stock Exchange (AMEX).

Today the stock market is worldwide. In addition to the New York and American exchanges, there are regional exchanges across the United States, as well as in London, Tokyo, Paris, and elsewhere around the globe. The American over-the-counter (OTC) market, which began as the "outsiders" trading circle, compares favorably with the exchanges in terms of the volume and quality of the securities traded.

The exchanges and the OTC market, together, make up what is known as the "secondary market." We will talk about the secondary market in Chapter 7. In this chapter, we will look at the primary market.

■ THE PRIMARY MARKET—HOW BUSINESSES ARE CAPITALIZED

There are several ways to buy ownership in a business. Perhaps the simplest way is to negotiate a one-on-one agreement with the business owner. For example, suppose your friend is opening up a small plant that manufactures candle figurines. He calculates that the money he intends to invest is not enough to cover the start-up period, when expenses typically outweigh revenues. To make up the difference, he asks you to invest in his business. You decide to do so, and a business agreement is drawn up, stating the terms and nature of your profit-sharing ownership. Since you know nothing about manufacturing candle figurines, the agreement stipulates that you do not become involved in the day-to-day affairs of the business. You have just become a part owner—a partner—in the business.

Although you share ownership, you will never see a stock certificate, because the business is not a corporation. When your friend owned it by himself, it was a sole proprietorship. When you invested, it became a partnership. But neither form of business is permitted by law to issue stock. To do that, the business must become a distinct legal corporate entity.

As time goes by, you and your friend might want to incorporate for one or more of several reasons. Suppose, over the first three to five years of the business, the candle figurines are so well accepted that it is time to expand. You want to open at least two more plants in different parts of the country and start a national marketing and sales campaign. To do this, you need far more money than you could hope to borrow from friends or relatives.

There are several possible sources of funds.

One source is a commercial bank, such as Citibank, Chase, and others. Any money you get from such a source would be borrowed and only on a short-term basis. The bank would become a creditor of yours, not an owner.

Another possibility is a venture capital firm, whose sole purpose is to invest in young, promising companies. To secure funds from such a firm, you would have to prepare a convincing business plan for the expanded operation, showing the return you expect on the investment—and how you intend to make it. Among other requirements, the venture capital firm will expect you to incorporate. What does the venture capitalist get out of investing in your company? A sizable percentage of ownership.

A third source of funds is the investment banker, who can help you raise the money through the sale of securities, *only* if the company is incorporated.

Before explaining what the investment banker, or underwriter, does for the company, let's see how the business becomes incorporated.

■ INCORPORATING THE BUSINESS

A corporation is a legal "person," separate and distinct from its owners. As a sole proprietor, or partner, an individual could lose his personal assets—the house, the car—if someone sued the business, and business assets were insufficient to satisfy the claim or other outstanding debts. When the business is incorporated, however, it becomes an entity on its own. If someone sues the business, only its assets are subject to loss. Your personal liability as a corporate shareholder is unaffected. Similarly, anyone who buys stock in a corporation (and who becomes a part owner) enjoys this same limited liability; owners may lose only what they invest, nothing more.

THE CERTIFICATE OF INCORPORATION (OR CHARTER)

The first step in forming a corporation is drafting a certificate of incorporation, or charter. This document contains all the information necessary to identify the corporation distinctly in the eyes of the law. One such piece of information, of course, is the company's name; no two corporations may have the same name. For example, if the company's name is Maxwell Manufacturing, no other company may incorporate under that name. Conversely, if another corporation has already incorporated under that name, the second proposed Maxwell Manufacturing must incorporate and do business under another name.

The charter contains, among other clauses, several elements of interest.

The purpose statement. This clause states what the corporation does for a business. In Maxwell's charter, the business could be as specific as the manufacture of candle figurines. This information is important to prospective shareholders, who need to know how the company is going to use their money. They might support the idea of candle figurines, but what happens if the acceptance of this new idea weakens in the marketplace? Maxwell might see an opportunity to make great profits by diversifying and making plastic chess pieces, but stockholders could take action—even sue—because the company is violating its original purpose statement of making candle figurines.

To avoid such situations, many states, led by Delaware, permit charters to have "general purpose clauses," that is, business as a corporation. This type of statement gives the company's management, that is the Board of Directors, the flexibility to diversify without fear of action from the shareholders.

The capital statement. This clause states the number of shares authorized for sale in order to raise capital. It also stipulates whether the company will issue common or preferred stock—or both. New companies preparing to go public usually issue common stock for several reasons. Common stock gives its owners equity through the use of voting rights, as well as the right to share in appreciation in value as the company prospers. But it does not obligate the company to pay regular fixed cash dividends, as does preferred stock—payments that a young company may not always be able to make, in as much as dividends may be paid only if there is sufficient surplus of earnings and profits. In addition, common stock can be priced lower than preferred stock when it is offered to the public and it therefore has a larger potential market.

The capital statement also states how many of the authorized shares the company will be issuing, that is, offering for sale. For example, if Maxwell's capital statement says that it has authorized 1 million shares of common stock for sale it may offer part or all of them in the primary offering. Let's say that you and your friend decide to issue about half—600,000 shares. The other 400,000 shares you decide to save for some future time when you might need additional capital. The 1 million shares are the "authorized stock." The 600,000 are classified for sale, and they are said to be "issued and outstanding," once they are sold. The "rainy-day" stock of 400,000 shares is said to be "authorized but unissued."

You and your friend, of course, would retain major percentages of the issued shares. If one or more of your employees made key contributions to the company's success during start-up and you want to reward them—keep them in the company—perhaps you would give them a percentage of the issued shares as well.

Or you might grant them an option to buy company stock at a specified low price at any time in the future. For instance, suppose that in the past three years Bill Wilson was a key person in figuring out ways to meet production quotas and deadlines. Without him your success would be doubtful. You grant Bill an option to buy Maxwell stock any time over the next ten years for $10 a share. Although you plan to publicly offer the stock at $15 a share in the primary offering, its value should increase steadily in the years to come. Should the stock's market value increase to

$20, $30, $40, or more, Bill need only exercise his option to buy at $10, and he has a built-in profit.

When the charter is filed with the secretary of state of the State in which you wish to incorporate, and all other legal requirements are met, Maxwell Manufacturing becomes Maxwell Manufacturing, *Inc.*, or *Corp.*, or *Corporation.*

GLASS-STEAGALL ACT

Now that Maxwell is incorporated, it has established the foundation for selling securities in the public market, referred to as the "issuance" or "underwriting" of securities. But how is the actual underwriting of securities to take place and the needed capital raised through the sale? Can either a brokerage firm or a commercial bank assist in this process?

Prior to the crash in 1929, banks were heavily engaged in the stock market. As the market plummeted, many banks went under. As a result, the Great Depression began. As President Franklin D. Roosevelt took office, Congress declared that the federal government should have regulatory powers over the financial securities markets (specifically the stock market) and, further, that commercial banks may not provide brokerage services involving corporate securities. This is the essence of the Glass-Steagall Act of 1933: Commercial banks may take deposits and issue loans; investment banks may be involved in the buying and selling of securities.

This dividing line was a clear one until the 1980s, when commercial banks began to successfully challenge the law. Nowadays, commercial banks may legally offer brokerage services and have time deposits whose rate of interest is pegged to a market index. Correspondingly, many brokerage houses offer the equivalent of checking and money market accounts to their investing clients.

Nevertheless, the line is still there, albeit not as distinct as in the past. Many banks provide distinct securities brokerage functions today. This type of service is often called "discount brokerage." Banks also deal in U.S. government bond and municipal bond securities in the primary market (bonds are debt instruments, unlike stocks); in this case, they do what investment bankers normally do for corporations issuing stock. In fact, many banks, such as Citicorp, and Chase, are bigger than most brokerage houses in the business of selling municipal bonds.

Governmental bonds were not a factor in the Great Crash of 1929. Recently, commercial banks were granted permission by the Federal Reserve to act as investment bankers, for example, to underwrite corporate bonds.

With banks in brokerage, with brokerage firms financing mortgages and maintaining checking accounts, how reasonable is it to maintain this line of demarcation between commercial and investment banking? The Great Depression is long over, and banks are continuing to vigorously push for the Glass-Steagall Act to fall, once and for all.

What all this means to Maxwell Manufacturing is that the company may borrow short-term funds from a commercial bank, but the loans have to be ruled out for four main reasons.

1. Banks are often unable or unwilling to lend a potential start-up business venture borrower the sizeable amount of money that it needs to borrow.

2. Banks are often unable to provide the terms that such a borrower wants. For instance, a company might want to borrow money at a fixed-rate for 20 years, whereas most banks will not make fixed-rate commercial loans for longer than seven years. There is usually the question of collateral.

3. Banks are often unable to lend to companies with low credit ratings, and a potential for great risk. New companies often do not have enough collateral to secure bank financing. Because banks have a duty to their depositors not to take excessive risks with their deposits, there is some truth to the adage that "the only way to get a bank to make a loan is to have so much money that you don't need one." Individual investors, on the other hand, are often willing to invest in risky situations if they feel the potential reward justifies the risk.

4. Banks often charge interest rates that translate into more dollars paid out than the company has to pay if it raises capital directly from investors.

The alternative to a commercial bank loan is to turn to an investment banker to help in offering shares of the company to the investing public. Companies that cannot be served adequately by commercial banks often turn to investment bankers for such help. These firms serve as intermediaries between potential investors and the companies wishing to raise capital. Because such firms, through their brokers, are in contact with thousands of investors, they can match issuers of securities with investors for whom the securities are appropriate.

For example, if a small growth company like Maxwell needs money for its new plants and inventory, an investment banking firm can line up the investors interested in the high-risk/high-reward stock like Maxwell's.

■ THE INITIAL PUBLIC OFFERING (IPO)

The first step to going public is to engage the services of an investment banking firm in order to sell (underwrite) the securities. The investment banker will have the necessary marketing contacts and skills, as well as the legal expertise to sell the securities in compliance with U.S. securities laws. When the terms of such an arrangement between the issuer and the banker are negotiated one on one, the underwriting is called just that—negotiated. This is in contrast to a "competitive" underwriting, in which a number of investment bankers may compete for the privilege of conducting the offering. Competition occurs for offerings by Coca-Cola, IBM, or General Motors. For a company like Maxwell, the deal is negotiated.

For a start-up company like Maxwell, the investment banker will probably distribute the stock on a "best-efforts" basis. The role of the investment banker, or underwriter, is simply to make the best effort it can to sell the stock. The risk remains with the issuer, and the underwriter takes a fee on whatever stock it sells. If the firm's investors do not express enough interest in the issue, the issuer has the right to call the whole thing off if it has reserved an all-or-none requirement. Hence, the name "all or none": the underwriter will sell all of the issue or none of it.

This type of underwriting contrasts with one that is conducted on a "firm" commitment basis. In this case, the underwriter actually buys or guarantees the stock from the issuer at one price and resells it to the public at another, slightly higher price. The profit to the underwriter is in the spread between the buy and sell price.

Given Maxwell's lack of track record, the underwriter will very likely offer management a best-efforts deal. And Maxwell would probably be wise to accept it.

THE REGISTRATION PROCESS

After the Crash of 1929, investigations led to the uncovering of a number of abuses in the securities industry. Prior to 1929, no law prohibited companies from issuing stock at liberty, without regard for the effect of unlimited issues on shareholders' interests, on the value of the stock itself, or, for that matter, on the economic system of the country. The Securities Act of 1933 was enacted, with the chief purpose of protecting the public in the primary, or new issue, market. Enforcement of the law is delegated to the Securities and Exchange Commission (SEC).

The chief tool of the SEC in this area is the "full disclosure statement," or registration statement that must be filed. This document is prepared jointly by the issuer and underwriter, and it tells everything there is to know about the issuer. (See Figure 3–2.) The Act—a lawyer's dream—runs about 80 pages with another 400 pages in regulations. Yet it can be basically summed up in three words: "Tell it all." If you need capital and are going public, tell it all—everything—in the disclosure statement. Some of the main items are:

■ Management aims and goals
■ How many shares the company is selling
■ What the issuer intends to do with the money

1. The name of the issuer.
2. The name of the state or sovereign power under which the issuer is organized.
3. The location of the issuer's principal office.
4. The names and addresses of the directors and other senior officials.
5. The names and addresses of the underwriters (if any)
6. The names and addresses of persons owning 10 percent or more of any class of issuer's stock.
7. The quantities of securities owned by the directors, senior officials, underwriters, and 10 percent or greater holders.
8. The general character of the issuer's business.
9. A statement of the issuer's capitalization.
10 A statement of securities reserved for options outstanding, with names and addresses of persons allotted 10 percent or more of these options.
11. The amount of capital stock of each class included in the offer.
12. The issuer's funded debt.
13. The purposes to which the proceeds of this offering will be applied.
14. Remuneration payable to the issuers directly, naming them specifically when annual payments exceed $25,000.
15. The estimated net proceeds to be derived from the offering.
16. The price at which the public offering will be attempted.
17. Commissions, fees and so on, to be paid to the underwriters.
18. An itemized detail of expenses incurred by the issuer in connection with this offering.
19. The net proceeds derived from any securities sold by the issuer in the preceding two years and pertinent details of those sales.
20. Any consideration paid to a promoter in the preceding two years.
21. The names and addresses of any vendor of property or goodwill to be acquired with the proceeds of this offering.
22. Full particulars of any dealings between the issuer and its officers, directors, and holders of 10 percent or more of its stock that transpired in the preceding two years.
23. The names and addresses of counsel passing upon the legality of the issue.
24. The dates and details of material contracts created outside the issuer's ordinary course of business within the preceding two years.
25. Certified financial statements of any issuer or business to be acquired with proceeds of this offering.
26. A copy of the underwriting contract or agreement.
27. A copy of the law firm's written opinion attesting to the legality of the issue.
28. A copy of all material contracts referred to in item 24.
29. A copy of the issuer's charter, bylaws, trust agreement, partnership agreement, and so forth, as the case may be.
30. A copy of the underlying agreement or indenture affecting any security offered or to be offered by the issuer.

FIGURE 3–2 SOME OF THE INFORMATION REQUIRED IN THE FULL DISCLOSURE STATEMENT

- The corporation's tax status
- Fallback plans in the event things don't go as expected
- The company's legal standing, such as any lawsuits
- Its income and expenses—its profit and loss
- Inherent risks of its enterprise

If something is held back in this statement, severe civil and criminal penalties can result, with the civil monetary damages often worse than the criminal consequences.

The disclosure statement cannot be used to sell securities; the firm's sales force may not show it to clients to get an "order." The reason is that the statement has to be accepted by the SEC. Until it is, it cannot be considered as having met legal requirements. To make that clear, the statement is printed, in red ink, on the side of the statement. With this red blurb, the registration statement is called the "red herring." (See Figure 3–3.)

The SEC does not "approve" the statement. The SEC may send the statement back to the underwriter more than once, requesting additional information or clarification. Once all the information required by law is included, the SEC may accept the statement and declare the offering effective. By accepting it, the Commission does not approve the offering; it merely affirms that the statement now meets legal requirements. It does *not* affirm that the company is well-managed, that it will be successful, or

FIGURE 3–3 THE STANDARD STATEMENT ON A "RED HERRING"

A registration statement in relation to these securities has been filed with the Securities and Exchange Commission, but has not yet become effective. Information contained herein is subject to completion or amendment. These securities may not be sold nor may offers to buy be accepted prior to the time the registration statement becomes effective. This prospectus shall not constitute an offer to sell or the solicitation of an offer to buy nor shall there be any sale of these securities in any state in which such offer, solicitation, or sale would be lawful prior to the registration or qualification under the securities laws of any such state.

that the stock will rise in value. All that information remains for the individual investor to determine.

Conversely, a rejection of a registration statement is not a condemnation of the company or the stock. It is only an indication that, for some reason, the underwriter is not supplying the information required by law.

Once the statement is accepted, the "red herring" statement comes off, and the statement becomes a "final prospectus." *Now* it may be used to solicit orders from the investing public. The prospectus offers investors the basic information they need at least to know that the company offering is in compliance with federal securities laws.

Finalizing agreements. Once the terms of the offering are settled among the underwriters, they have an agreement drawn up and sign it. This is the agreement among underwriters, which stipulates:

- Members of the underwriting group
- Members of the selling group
- Size of the underwriters' retention (the pot)
- How group sales will be conducted
- What the lead manager must do if the stock's price climbs or drops quickly in the after market

The next agreement is made between the underwriting group and the issuer—the "underwriting agreement" or "purchase agreement." This formalizes the negotiations leading up to this point. It is filed with the SEC and becomes part of the registration statement by amendment.

THE COOLING-OFF PERIOD

While the SEC is reviewing the statement, the IPO is said to be in the "cooling-off period," usually about 20 days. During this period, the underwriter's staff is busy doing several things.

Circling the stock. Stockbrokers (account executives registered representatives, stockbrokers) are busy calling the firm's present clients to solicit "indications of interest." The salespeople will speak about the stock in general, both risks and benefits, but cannot ask for an order inasmuch as the SEC has not declared the offering effective and a final price has not been established. Instead, they simply ask whether the client would be interested in buying such a stock and, if so, about how much. This is called "circling the stock."

The information gathered in this process is a solid indication of how successful the offering is likely to be.

Forming the syndicate. After the underwriting agreement is entered into in principle, between the investment banker and the issuing corporation, the investment banking group creates a syndicate, which is a temporary group of investment bankers, formed for the express purpose of underwriting the offering. Most firms do not try to sell an entire issue by themselves (unless it is a small one). Instead, they solicit the help of other firms to spread the risk and create a wider market for the stock. All of the firms involved in selling the new offering, acting as a group, form the syndicate. The firm that puts the deal together is called the "lead manager." In building a syndicate, a brokerage firm can play three different roles:

1. If the firm puts the deal together, it is the "lead manager" and runs the books.

2. If the firm does not put the deal together but is willing to commit its capital by joining the syndicate and buying some of the issue for resale (in a firm offering), the firm is simply called an "underwriter."

3. If it does not commit its capital but helps only to sell the securities, the firm is referred to as a member of the "selling group."

Each of these three types of participants shares differently in the spread, depending on the capital at risk and the responsibility undertaken.

EXAMPLE: Brokerage firm A takes on an offering of some 1 million shares and, assuming responsibility as lead manager, builds a small syndicate and selling group. Brokerage A pays the issuer $9.50 per share. It plans to resell the shares to investors for $10 a piece. The spread between $9.50 and $10.00 of 50¢ represents a 5 percent profit on the deal.

Given Maxwell's size and relative newness as a corporation, perhaps only one investment banker is interested in it. In this case, management would negotiate directly with the one under-writer over the price that Maxwell receives for the stock. If Maxwell cannot get what it thinks is a fair price in a firm offering, it simply does not sell its shares.

If no investment banking firm will make it a firm offer, Maxwell can resort to accepting a best-efforts offering. The disad-vantage is that an offering is an expensive proposition. If it does not go through to completion and success, the corporation can lose tens and sometimes hundreds of thousands of dollars in expenses.

Blue-skying. In the 1900s, the Kansas state legislature passed the country's first state securities law. One of the state law-makers quipped, "Now Kansas citizens will have more of a basis for making investment decisions than merely by the shade of the blue sky."

Today every state has its own securities laws, and, to do business in a state, the brokerage house has to comply with these laws. When a new issue of stock is coming to the market, the underwriter's legal staff gets to work on meeting such require-ments—state by state. They are said to be "blue-skying" the issue.

THE DUE DILIGENCE MEETING

At some time either before or during the cooling-off period, the lead manager assembles representatives from all the firms in the syndicate. This, the due diligence meeting, has a couple of purposes, in addition to ironing out any last-minute details.

Allocating the issue. Each underwriting firm indicates how much it will sell of the issue, depending on the information from the salespeople who circled the stock. This can be a ticklish job for the lead manager, who ultimately decides which firm gets what. The firms now have to make good on their commitments. The manager does the best job possible in allocating the issue, but holds back a portion, usually about 25 percent, for allocation to the selling group and sale to institutional clients. The held-back portion is known as "the pot."

Group sales are made out of the pot. If an institutional investor, such as a pension fund or a mutual fund, wants 50,000 shares, the manager will take those shares out of the pot, rather than glean them a little here and a little there from the underwriters. In turn, each member of the syndicate shares in the proceeds according to its percentage of sales in the overall issue.

When the members hear, "The pot is clean!" they know that institutional investors consider the stock a worthwhile one and their selling efforts get easier.

Setting the price. The new issue has no market value, since it has not yet traded on the open market. What price, therefore, is the "right" one?

To determine its fair value, the underwriters ask at a pricing meeting:

- How strong is the company fundamentally?
- How much demand is there for the stock?
- How strong, or weak, is the market right now?

Setting the price is a tightrope walk. The issuing firm, of course, wants as high a price as possible, and investors want as low a price as they can get. The underwriting firm, whose profit comes from the spread, has to set a price that is fair to the issuer but attractive to investors. Historically, a stock that is "priced right" rises slightly in value as it hits the market. If the market price drops slightly, the price was set too high. If the price skyrockets, investors win big, the issuer watches additional capital fly out the window, and the underwriter is left wearing only a sheepish grin.

By the end of the meeting, the syndicate has its price, and the lead manager notifies the printing company that it can start printing the final prospectuses with the price fixed.

THE EFFECTIVE DATE

The SEC has accepted the registration statement by declaring the offering effective and announcing an effective date. The time has come to see how the public receives the offering.

The salespeople now have a document that can be used to solicit and accept orders for the stock. The final prospectus has a consolidation of the information in the registration statement and *must* be given to anyone who buys the stock no later than with the customer confirmation statement. This is a customer's receipt of purchase and it occurs on the "effective date," the date on which the stock may be sold. (See Figure 3–4.)

The sales brokers start calling clients with the price information. As the orders are finalized, the underwriting firms keep the lead manager abreast of sales. The manager, whose job is to "keep the books" for the group, knows how the offering is going.

Stabilizing the market. As the issue is distributed, the reception among investors is sometimes not as great as expected. Maybe the price was set too high; maybe the company is just not strong enough in the eyes of the investing public. Whatever the reason, the offering is "weak." If new owners of the stock see the price drop in the marketplace, the danger is that they will start getting rid of their shares and start a sell-off. In such a case, the stock's price would drop sharply and the underwriters would stand to lose a bundle because they would own a substantial quantity at a lower price.

This is the one time the law allows a brokerage firm acting as underwriter to "fix" a market price. It may place a standing bid on behalf of the syndicate in the secondary over-the-counter or stock exchange market to buy the new stock at or slightly below the offering price. It may not be higher. The effect of this standing bid is that it prevents the market value of the stock from dropping far below the offering price. New stock owners are assured that speculators will not step in and render the market for the stock unstable. This measure taken by the lead manager is known as "stabilizing the market."

Hot issues. At other times, the issue sells vigorously—customers cannot get enough. The issue is "hot"! The syndicate members have no problem distributing the portions allocated to them. In fact, they want more.

Managers may deal with a hot issue in a couple of ways. They can oversell the issue by as much as 15 percent—legally—because historically they get that much in cancellations. If they

3,500,000 Shares

eBay Inc.

Common Stock
(par value $.001 per share)

Of the 3,500,000 shares of Common Stock offered hereby, 3,489,275 shares are being sold by eBay Inc. and 10,725 shares are being sold by a Selling Stockholder on behalf of a charitable foundation established by the Company. See "Principal and Selling Stockholders". The Company will not receive any of the proceeds from the sale of the shares being sold by the Selling Stockholder. Prior to the offering, there has been no public market for the Common Stock of the Company. For factors considered in determining the initial public offering price, see "Underwriting".

See "Risk Factors" on page 6 for material risks relevant to an investment in the Common Stock.

The shares of Common Stock have been approved for quotation on the Nasdaq National Market under the symbol "EBAY," subject to official notice of issuance.

THESE SECURITIES HAVE NOT BEEN APPROVED OR DISAPPROVED BY THE SECURITIES AND EXCHANGE COMMISSION OR ANY STATE SECURITIES COMMISSION NOR HAS THE SECURITIES AND EXCHANGE COMMISSION OR ANY STATE SECURITIES COMMISSION PASSED UPON THE ACCURACY OR ADEQUACY OF THIS PROSPECTUS. ANY REPRESENTATION TO THE CONTRARY IS A CRIMINAL OFFENSE.

	Initial Public Offering Price	Underwriting Discount (1)	Proceeds to Company (2)	Proceeds to Selling Stockholder
Per Share	$18.00	$1.26	$16.74	$16.74
Total (3)	$63,000,000	$4,410,000	$58,410,463	$179,537

(1) The Company and the Selling Stockholder have agreed to indemnify the Underwriters against certain liabilities, including liabilities under the Securities Act of 1933, as amended. See "Underwriting."
(2) Before deducting estimated expenses of $975,000 payable by the Company.
(3) The Company has granted the Underwriters an option for 30 days to purchase up to an additional 525,000 shares at the initial public offering price per share, less the underwriting discount, solely to cover over-allotments. If such option is exercised in full, the total initial public offering price, underwriting discount and proceeds to Company will be $72,450,000, $5,071,500 and $67,198,963, respectively. See "Underwriting".

The shares offered hereby are offered severally by the Underwriters, as specified herein, subject to receipt and acceptance by them and subject to their right to reject any order in whole or in part. It is expected that the shares will be ready for delivery in New York, New York on or about September 29, 1998, against payment therefor in immediately available funds.

Goldman, Sachs & Co.
    Donaldson, Lufkin & Jenrette
        BancBoston Robertson Stephens
          BT Alex. Brown

The date of this Prospectus is September 24, 1998.

FIGURE 3–4 A FINAL PROSPECTUS

are still short, they can go into the market and buy the stock back. This is not considered a stabilization measure because the manager is paying at least the offering price and probably more.

The manager can also ask for a "green shoe privilege." With the offering selling out quickly and customers asking for more, the lead manager asks the corporate issuer for an option to buy more of the stock at a price below the original offering price, and usually within 30 days after the effective date. Once the agreement is signed and filed by amendment with the SEC as part of the registration statement, the manager exercises the option, buys the additional shares, and uses them to cover the short positions created when they oversold the issue.

There's a downside to a hot issue. With demand for the stock so great, the aftermarket value is likely to increase sharply, as investors who could not purchase them in the offering seek them out in the secondary market. For this reason, anyone who is in a position to buy stock in the initial public offering is often guaranteed an instantaneous profit. Insiders could easily cash in on a hot issue. To prevent such an abuse, no one who works for one of the underwriters or who is related to an employee of the firms may buy these issues during the offering. That's the law.

THE TOMBSTONE

No doubt you have seen television advertisements for major brokerage houses. Whether it's Merrill Lynch's bull, investors smilingly thanking Paine Webber, Salomon Smith Barney earning money the old-fashioned way, or Charles Schwab telling you why it's a lot smarter to place your orders with a discount firm, securities firms advertise their services and names with all the sophistication that Procter & Gamble uses to sell its soap. They are allowed to.

But they are *not* allowed to use such techniques to sell securities. Securities may be sold only by prospectus—the final prospectus. The brokerage firm may not, by law, conduct a commercial ad campaign on behalf of a new issue of IBM, or of a high-tech stock, or of any stock.

What they are allowed to do is to place a somber ad in the financial news on the effective day of the offering. This ad does nothing more than convey basic information about the issue, the issuer, and the underwriting group. It is so understated an ad that it is called a "tombstone" and in fact looks like one. The double irony is that, by the time the ad appears and is read, the issue is very often sold out or nearly so since the indications of interest converted into orders on the effective date usually deplete the amount of available stock.

If the ad does not sell any stock and if it's too late to serve that purpose anyway, what reason does the syndicate have for placing it? Why spend the tens of thousands of dollars required to have it appear in *The Wall Street Journal* and/or *New York Times*, or other financial publications?

The reason is prestige. Investment bankers work according to an informal but very visible pecking order. Some syndicates are made up of firms that have done underwritings together for years. They are used to working together, and each firm knows where it stands in relation to the others. In other cases, the political maneuvering and dickering that go into the arrangement of the firms' names on the tombstone can be fierce.

Look at the tombstone in Figure 3–5, focusing for now on just the underwriters' names. The top five names, Donaldson, Lufkin & Jennrette, Banc of America Securities LLC, etc., are the five lead managers. How do you know that? Their names are at the top and on a bold descending pattern.

Syndicate members are arranged alphabetically by groups, and the alphabetical rule carries throughout the listing. In Figure 3–5, read from the next line—Bear, Stearns & Co. Inc.—down to C.E. Unterberg, Towbin. If you look at the "last" names of these firms, you will see that they are listed across each line alphabetically: Bear, Chase, CIBC, Edwards, and so on. The alphabetization starts all over again with Adams, Harkness & Hill Inc. because the next group represents a different bracket of underwriters, who received less stock for sale than the top bracket members. While Bear, Stearns and that group are in the "major" bracket (handling large portions of the underwriting), Adams and the others up to Wachovia are in a "submajor" bracket. They handle less than the firms in the major bracket.

The urgency with which higher standings are pursued arises from something other than prestige. As it is with most issues in the securities industry, the underlying motivation is to make money.

This announcement is neither an offer to sell, nor a solicitation of an offer to buy, any of these securities.
The offer is made only by the Prospectus.

July 18, 2000

12,650,000 Shares

 MSL

Manufacturers' Services Limited

Common Stock

Price $16.00 Per Share

Copies of the Prospectus may be offered in any State from such of the undersigned as may legally offer
these securities in compliance with the securities laws of such State.

Donaldson, Lufkin & Jenrette

Banc of America Securities LLC

Robertson Stephens

Thomas Weisel Partners

DLJ*direct* Inc.

Bear, Stearns & Co. Inc.	Chase H&Q	CIBC World Markets	A.G. Edwards & Sons, Inc.
Lehman Brothers	Merrill Lynch & Co.	Morgan Stanley Dean Witter	Prudential Securities
Salomon Smith Barney	SG Cowen	UBS Warburg LLC	C.E. Unterberg, Towbin
Adams, Harkness & Hill, Inc.		Advest, Inc.	Robert W. Baird & Co. Incorporated
William Blair & Company, L.L.C.	The Chapman Co.	FAC/Equities	Fahnestock & Co. Inc.
Gruntal & Co., L.L.C.		Johnston, Lemon & Co. Incorporated	C.L. King & Associates, Inc.
McDonald Investments Inc.		Needham & Company, Inc.	Pennsylvania Merchant Group
Ragen MacKenzie Incorporated		Raymond James & Associates, Inc.	Sanders Morris Harris
Sands Brothers & Co., Ltd.		Stephens Inc.	SunTrust Equitable Securities
Tucker Anthony Cleary Gull			Wachovia Securities, Inc.

FIGURE 3–5 A TYPICAL TOMBSTONE

The lesser-bracketed firms stand to make less money than the higher ones because they are generally allocated last and the least.

In a $1.1 billion Citicorp stock offering, for example, Merrill Lynch organized a syndicate of 110 underwriters and took 2 million of the 20 million shares in the offering. Institutional investor orders ran high, the pot was cleaned quickly, and four of the lowest-bracketed firms never received any stock at all to sell. At best, they were credited to their portion (however small) of the institutional sales.

In the words of a syndicate department manager at a major investment banking firm, "Tombstones have been, and remain, Wall Street's scoreboard. They provide a subjective measurement of a firm's strengths."

And that's not all they do. They also provide investors with some idea of the investment value of the issue. For example, Salomon Smith Barney will not underwrite a new company's issue unless the corporation has a sound financial track record and structure. It is not in the business of selling medium- or low-quality issues. If Salomon is part of the offering, you may assume that the issuer has met fairly stringent financial requirements.

Neither will you find a company like Salomon underwriting two-cent stocks, so-called "penny stocks." Such stocks are low-priced because they are *very* high-risk with little to no economic fundamentals, and a tremendous quality of stock authorized for sale available. Selling for less than a dollar, they even require special market making requirements.

This is the type of gamble you take when you invest in penny stocks. The potential is certainly there to win big, if the company is successful and the demand for the stock continues. But the success stories are few and far between, and you have to be willing to take your losses as part of the penny stock game. Before moving on, let's look at a few other items in the tombstone in Figure 3–5.

■ At the very top is a notice, as prescribed by law, indicating that the ad is "neither an offer to sell, nor a solicitation of an offer to buy." It also makes reference to the final Prospectus.

■ Immediately below the advisory is the number of shares being offered If you multiply that number by the offering price ($16, just a little farther down in the ad), you come up with the size of the offering: $202,400,000.

- The issuer is MSL, short for Manufacturers' Services Limited.
- Copies of the offering circular (final prospectus) may be obtained only in the states where the issue has been blue-skyed and where the underwriting firm is licensed to do business. In the case of the larger firms, that's all the states. For the smaller, regional firms, it might be just some.
- In the upper right-hand corner is the effective date, in this case July 18, 2000, the date on which the stock was first offered.

■ AFTER THE OFFERING IS COMPLETED

When the offering is completely distributed, the syndicate is disbanded, and the deal is said to have "broken syndicate." The stock may now be bought and sold in the secondary market, along with the thousands of other securities already there.

Some issues will begin trading immediately on an exchange, if the issuer is already listed—AT&T, IBM, General Motors, and the like, or if the company has completed its filing for listing on a national securities exchange.

If the issuer is not listed, the stock may begin trading in the over-the-counter market, and brokerage firms—most of them the original underwriters—may elect to become "market makers" in the stock. (I will explain more about market makers in Chapter 7 and Chapter 8.)

Whether the stock trades on an exchange or on the Nasdaq or in the OTC market, the underwriters relinquish their intermediary role between issuer and investor. The issuer has the capital it sought, and the investor can watch the stock's quotations every day in the financial news.

INSIDE THE BROKERAGE FIRM
Who Does What?

In a brokerage firm, the only person who takes an order from you, the customer, is the registered representative, also known as an account executive (AE), financial advisor, or, more commonly, a stockbroker. AEs are "registered" because the law requires them to pass an examination prepared by the New York Stock Exchange and administered by the National Association of Securities Dealers (NASD, called the Series 7 about which we will say more later). This examination contains questions on every aspect of the securities industry—the markets, the products, the back office operations, and the regulatory requirements. Having passed the exam, AEs are legally qualified to give clients investment advice and to take orders.

Investors should remember, however, that account executives are *sales* professionals. As such, their compensation is earned from commissions (that is, charges for the execution of transactions), not from fees. Here's how account executives earn their money. A client enters an order with the AE to buy 100 shares of Pinhole Enterprises. The broker then sends the order to the order room (or wire room, see Figure 4–1 on p. 59), whose staff forwards the order to the appropriate market where Pinhole is traded. If the order is executed—that is, the stock is purchased—at $17 per share, the client has just spent $1,700 (100 shares × $17). And the firm has just earned a commission. If the brokerage firm charges 1.96 percent on transactions, then the customer will be charged an additional $33.32 on the purchase ($1,700 × 0.0196). Of that $33.32, a percentage, usually between 20 percent and 40 percent, goes to

55

the AE; the balance goes to the firm itself. This is one way in which brokerage houses earn profits.

A couple of things become clear from this example. One is that both the AE and the firm make money on every purchase or sales transaction, whether or not it turns out to be a profitable one for the client. This is not to say that AEs do not care about the profitability of transactions. With few exceptions (which we read about in the papers), AEs *do* care very much for an easily understandable reason: As long as the AE continues to make profitable recommendations to clients, they will remain customers. Nevertheless, registered representatives—unlike other professionals, such as doctors or accountants—must be regarded as *sales*-oriented. Their compensation increases in direct proportion to (a) the number of times a client places orders to buy or to sell and (b) the size of the orders. The AEs who last in the business are the ones who make well-reasoned, suitable recommendations to their clients. Others sometimes let the sales orientation dominate their thinking. These seldom last in the business, which is why over 60 percent of all account executives have been in the business for less than five years.

Another question that arises from our example is, how does an AE, much less a large brokerage house, make money on small, single transactions? The answer is that it is very difficult. The "retail" portion of the securities business—the portion coming from individual investors—has shrunk over the years to a very small percentage of the total dollar volume traded in the stock market, approximating 20 percent. The other 80 percent comes from "institutional investors," such as pension funds, mutual funds, insurance companies, and other "big" players in the market. Obviously the commission on 5,000 or 10,000 shares of a blue-chip stock selling around the $100 mark is going to make the brokerage firm a great deal more money than the 100-share retail order.

Still another way that brokerage houses earn money is by buying and selling securities for their own inventory proprietary trading account. Professional traders employed in the trading department of the firm will buy and sell the stock and other securities.

How do the traders know what to buy and what to sell? They rely on their intuition and judgment, as well as on the reports and recommendations of the company's research department which supplies reports and other information to both the sales and trading areas. (See Figure 4–1 on p. 59.) In the research department are highly skilled financial professionals who follow the ups and downs of the market, analyze specific stocks, weigh the effects of outside influences on the market (interest rates, inflation, deficit reports, and the like), and ultimately make calculated projections as to what and when to buy and sell. Traders act on the information on behalf of the firm; account executives use the information to make recommendations to their clients.

For most of the U.S. stock market's history, a brokerage firm's commission was fixed. No firm could charge more or less than the industry-wide minimum. On May 1, 1975, sometimes called "May Day," this all changed when commission rates became negotiable. Competition among brokerage houses became keener than ever, and not long thereafter "discount houses" appeared on the scene.

■ FULL SERVICE VERSUS DISCOUNT

As the name "full service" implies, full-service brokerage firms supply clients with a wide range of service, including:

- *Investment research.* The brokerage firm's research department analysts watch market trends, search out future investment possibilities, and supply research reports.
- *Asset management.* A number of brokerage firms offer customers what are known as "management accounts," which serve as savings accounts, checking accounts, and investment accounts—all in one. For example, if you sold some stock but did not wish to immediately take or reinvest the proceeds, you could "park" the money in the firm's money market account until you made up your mind, as opposed to transferring it to demand or time deposit in a bank. You earn interest (probably more than you could from a demand

deposit), and the brokerage firm maintains control of your assets.

- *Investment advice.* While many investors do their own investment analysis, it cannot be compared to the millions of dollars spent on research by a full-service brokerage firm. For example, Morgan Stanley Dean Witter has spent up to $20 million per year on stock research alone! Spending that kind of money on research does not make the professional analysts right all the time, but if they were not right often enough, either they would not be employed by the firm or the firm would be out of business. When the AE makes a recommendation to a client, it is based on the same information given to the traders—who use the firm's money to buy and sell.

- *Order execution.* How would you buy or sell stock without the services of a broker? To sell stock, for example, you would have to locate a buyer who is willing to make the purchase at the price you want. You would have to certify to the buyer that you are the legal owner, and then you would have to make arrangements to transfer ownership. The brokerage house does all this for you.

- *Clearing.* After the order is executed, there is a long paper trail, in which each step meets a legal or regulatory requirement. (See Figure 4–1. Clearing will be explained further in Chapter 11.)

Firms that offer this full range of services fall into a number of categories.

"Wire houses" are large, diversified firms that are generally known to investors and non-investors alike: Merrill Lynch, Morgan Stanley Dean Witter, Paine Webber, Inc., and so on. They offer a wide array of investment vehicles and are very retail-oriented. They seek the individual investor's account.

While wire houses handle institutional accounts and trade for their own inventories, they also make money on the retail side by handling large volumes of transactions *efficiently*. In fact, their name derives from the fact that orders are entered, from all

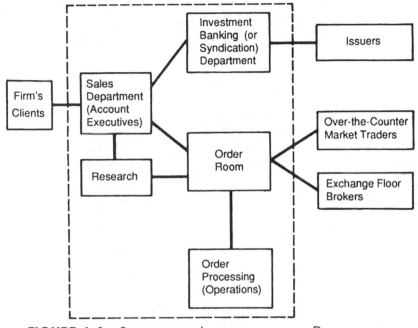

FIGURE 4-1 Some of the Interdepartmental Relationships in a Brokerage Firm

over the country, over the "wire"—that is, by means of highly automated systems that keep the cost of processing and clearing order transactions very low.

"Specialized" firms, unlike the wire houses, deal in only one investment vehicle, or a very few, such as government bonds. One widely known specialized firm is Lebenthal & Co., specializing in municipal bonds.

The "carriage trade house" is essentially a New York-based firm whose clients are well-heeled and select. Some traditional examples are Goldman, Sachs or Bear, Stearns. Their service is highly personalized and their research exceptional.

If you feel you would like to open an account with such a firm, you may find that you do not meet their customer requirements. These houses are very selective. Most new accounts are opened only on the recommendation of existing clients. More often than not, references are required.

"Boutique firms" also offer personalized service, but to the middle-income-bracket investor. They are also fairly diversified, and they therefore can offer the benefits of both a wire house and carriage trade firm. Such firms are A.G. Edwards & Sons or Gruntal & Co.

All these types of firms are considered "full service."

Discount firms such as Charles Schwab offer fewer services and charge lower commissions. When you place an order with a discount firm, you may receive only two services: order execution and clearance. You have to do your own research and analysis, pick your own stock, and decide on timing by yourself. Your AE, a person who probably works for a salary rather than a commission, takes your order and confirms its execution—without offering any investment advice, even upon request. Thereafter, the discount firm's back office clears the transaction. Some discount houses go so far as to offer newsletters or possibly money markets, but that's all.

In return for sacrificing services, you get commissions that are significantly lower than a full service broker firms. The exact commission amount should be discussed with the broker beforehand.

Discount commissions can take two forms:

■ *A percentage of the share's price.* If you sell 100 shares at $20.50 (for proceeds of $2,050), and if the firm charges a 1.1 percent commission rate, the commission in dollars would be $22.55 (1.1 percent × $2,050).

■ *A dollar amount based on the number of shares traded.* If you buy 100 shares, regardless of their price, the firm might charge a flat $0.20 per share for the transaction. You would pay $20 ($0.20 × 100 shares). Odd-lot transactions for less than 100 shares will probably cost you more; brokerage firms provide quantity discounts for higher-volume transactions.

Both full-service and discount firms offer benefits and have their drawbacks.

Which suits your purposes better? The real question is, how much help do you need in making your investment decisions? If you are confident in your investment choices, you can obviously save quite a bit in commission dollars with a discounter. However, if you do not have the time or resources to research a company thoroughly, you may wind up losing much more in poor investment choices than you would save by going with a discount house.

For example, suppose you buy 100 shares at $30 per share with a discount broker, and suppose the commission rate is 1.1 percent. You pay $33 in commission (100 shares × $30 × 0.011). If you bought the same stock through a full-service broker who charges 2.5 percent, you would pay $75 (100 shares × $30 × 0.025). That's a $42 saving if you go with the discounter—42¢ less per share.

If your stock is a good investment choice, it will rise in value, and your profit on it will be greater because of what you saved on commissions. As soon as the market value hits $30.33, you have broken even; any increase in value from that point is profit. If you had bought through a full-service firm, you would not break even until the stock hit $30.75.

On the other hand, if, without the benefit of investment advice from the AE, you buy a stock that turns out to be a poor investment choice, you could lose considerably more than 42¢ per share.

Another question to ask in deciding between discount and full service is, how frequently do you trade during the year? If you enter, say, a half-dozen orders over the course of a year, perhaps the savings do not represent enough to offset the risk of making investment decisions without expert advice. If you are an active buyer and seller of stock, the savings could be a considerable factor in your profits and losses over the year. (Of course, if you are an active trader, you are also probably an active analyst and don't need the advice as much as the "dabbler.")

Whether choosing discount or full service, always check into the firm's background and reputation.

■ SELECTING A BROKERAGE FIRM AND AN ACCOUNT EXECUTIVE

Should you elect to do business with a discount house, there is no need to "select" an AE. The salesperson at the other end of the phone line is there for one thing: to take your order and get it executed. Again, don't expect any small talk or advice.

One way to find a broker is to give an order or open an account with an AE who "cold calls" you right out of the phone book. That salesperson may or may not turn out to be the right one for you and your investment objectives. It's also possible that the cold caller is looking for a quick order. *Never* commit to a cold-calling securities salesperson unless you are satisfied that he or she is legitimate and sincere. For one thing, if all you hear and feel over the phone is pressure to place an order, hang up. If you are undecided about a caller's credentials, listen for the following signals:

- Does the caller ask leading questions? "As a provider, you *do* want the best for your family, don't you?"

- Is the appeal mainly to your "sense of greed" or "guilt" over missed past opportunities?

- Does the caller promise guaranteed results? "This stock is 100 percent guaranteed to double in value in less than six months!" (This type of selling is against the law.)

- Is the caller rushing you into making a decision without supplying you with answers to your questions? "If you wait for the prospectus or the annual report to arrive at your office, these valuable shares undoubtedly will be sold to other smart investors who are able to act quickly."

- Does the caller seem to care about whether the investment suits your financial means? "Don't worry about investing the money. You'll have it back *and more* within three months."

- Does the caller hedge when asked information about the brokerage firm or stock? "If you haven't heard of XYZ

Securities, sir, you can't have been investing for very long. We're one of the biggest names in brokerage."

■ Is the cold caller looking for a substantial monetary commitment way beyond your budget?

Any legitimate, reputable account executive will be more than happy to answer your questions straightforwardly—because your questions represent a glimmer of interest on your part. Look at the call from the cold caller's point of view. An AE may make as many as one hundred calls before anyone expresses interest in opening an account. That's the normal "batting average" for telephone sales in securities. In making those hundred calls, prospects hang up abruptly, waste the caller's time with questions and then don't place an order, and say no scores of times. By the time someone shows some interest—enough to ask questions—the caller is primed to provide all the information you want.

Here are some legitimate questions to ask:

■ Where did you get my name?
■ Why is this stock suitable for me?
■ What risks are involved?
■ Will you speak to my lawyer and/or accountant?
■ Where is the stock traded?
■ What are the market making sources?
■ Which regulatory agency governs your firm?
■ What if I want to withdraw from this investment in the future? Am I locked in, or is there an adequate resale market?
■ Where can I get references about your firm or you?
■ When can we meet to discuss things further?

You at least know whether you are dealing with someone who is legitimate and who has a sense of professional expertise. You can take things from there.

You can be more active in selecting a broker. You may decide to open an account with a particular firm and then try to find an AE within the firm. Or you might simply look for a broker who seems to be able to meet your investment objectives. In either case, you can start by asking friends, relatives, and business associates about their brokers. Particularly, you might ask:

- Have you been pleased with your broker?
- Have the recommendations, on the whole, worked out well?
- What are your investment goals, growth (short term or long), yield, diversification, Blue Chip, safety of principal, and is your broker responsive to them?
- Does the broker respond to your calls? Call back promptly? Do you get requested information quickly?
- What about the firm? How are your accounts handled? Are mistakes corrected promptly? Do you get your monthly statement on time?
- Do you think your broker would be able to handle the account?
- Are there monthly carrying charges?

Again, look at it from the AE's point of view. Most successful brokers, who have endured in the business for any length of time, rely on word of mouth for references. Sometimes they even actively solicit references from their existing clients. A good AE knows that the best kind of "prospecting" is to provide quality service to present customers. This is the type of broker you should seek out—one who will work with you on a professional level.

Once you have the names of several AEs, phone each of them. They will be happy to answer your questions if you express interest in opening an account. Nevertheless, have your questions ready. Since they work in a hectic environment, many handling up to 200 accounts, the AES may ask to meet with you after business hours.

Whether on the phone or face-to-face, here are some questions to have answered:

- How does the broker plan to handle your account, given your investment goals?
- Will you be notified promptly of favorable opportunities to buy and/or sell?
- Has the broker worked at any other firms? Which ones?
- What kind of services does the firm provide?
- What's the commission rate? When does an investor qualify for special rates? (Don't forget that rates are negotiable. You might be eligible for a special rate.)

And, if you wish, you can write the Securities and Exchange Commission (SEC) or National Association of Securities Dealers (NASD). These regulatory agencies will not endorse a person or an agency, but they can advise you as to whether a broker or firm is registered to do business and whether there have been any disciplinary proceedings. These addresses are:

NASD/NASD Regulation/Nasdaq
   Washington, DC Offices
   1735 K Street, NW
   Washington, DC 20006-1500
   Telephone: (202) 728-8000
   Inquiries: (301) 590-6500
   FAX: (202) 2936260

SEC Headquarters
   450 Fifth Street, NW
   Washington, DC 20549
   Office of investor education and assistance:
   (202) 942-7040

Once you get the right answers to your questions, determine your own investment objectives, and select an account executive, the salesperson will have some questions for you that probe your financial status. How much income you earn per year . . . how much money you have in accounts or other investments . . . how much you have to invest . . . and so on. These are questions that people don't normally ask of one another. Yet the AE is required to know everything possible about your financial worth, as well as your personal tolerance of risk: Are you a risk taker or risk avoider? Be prepared to make full disclosure to the AE. Doing so is in the best interests of both of you.

■ THE SALES ASSISTANT

In most brokerage sales offices, one person serves as an assistant to every two or three account executives. This person handles routine calls from customers, follows up on paper work, takes messages, keeps the files, and in general does the office work and, when necessary, is the back office liaison connected with securities sales. This person, known as the "sales assistant" is typically not registered, but like the AE, knows a great deal about investment products, the markets, and regulations.

When the account executive calls a customer to say that the missing dividend check has been located, it was probably the sales assistant who found it. When the AE explains how a margin error has been corrected in a customer's account, the assistant likely straightened things out. When the AE sends the client a corrected confirmation statement or monthly statement, the assistant made the call to the appropriate "back office" department to find out what happened.

These "behind the scenes" people can help you on many routine matters. They may *not* help you with investment advice, express opinions on a particular stock, or take an order. They may, however, help you get mistakes corrected and answer questions about the firm's policies, procedures, and current quotes and prices.

Customer brokers and sales assistants are the brokerage firm employees that the investing public know best. The rep takes investors' orders and passes them on to the "marketplace" where they are logged in and, forwarded to other firm employees who actually participate in the stock market. These are the traders who get the clients' orders executed in the over-the-counter market or the floor members who get the job done on an exchange.

THE SECONDARY MARKET
Executing Orders on the Exchange Floor

The client's order is passed from the sales desk to the order room, usually through a telecommunications link. From there, it is routed to one of two places for execution: an exchange floor or an over-the-counter trading desk. Although these markets share some characteristics, they are different in a number of ways. In this and the next chapter we will see how orders are executed on an exchange, with a focus on the New York Stock Exchange. (Executing orders in the over-the-counter market is the subject of Chapter 7.) Furthermore, with respect to the New York Stock Exchange, or NYSE, itself, we shall also discuss important aspects, such as the listing and maintenance criteria for companies.

■ THE NEW YORK STOCK EXCHANGE

To visitors at the New York Stock Exchange, the trading floor may seem a study in confusion: people taking calls at banks of telephones along the walls, crowds milling at trading posts, pages pushing through clusters of brokers, great electronic ticker tape screens suspended from girders along the ceiling and flashing coded trading information. Tens of millions of transactions take place here every trading day. Yet despite the hectic pace and apparent chaos, an organized and effective system is in effect and orders can be executed accurately here, in a matter of seconds.

While the New York Stock Exchange is not the only exchange in the country, it is certainly the oldest and, in terms of volume, the biggest. At the exchange are traded some of the largest corporations in the country: IBM, AT&T, General Motors, and the like. NYSE is therefore often regarded as the prototype of exchanges—the "Big Board." Furthermore, the New York Stock Exchange has traditionally been one that has attracted many of the so called blue chip securities. Among these include stocks of corporations, such as General Electric, Johnson and Johnson, and General Motors. Some technology corporations do trade on the NYSE, such as IBM, Hewlett Packard, and Honeywell. As such, the New York Stock Exchange is used as the model of exchange trading for this chapter.

■ LISTING REQUIREMENTS AND CRITERIA OF THE NYSE

For a company to become listed on the NYSE, there are certain minimum requirements that must be achieved. Some of these requirements (for U.S. companies) are as follows.

First, with respect to minimum quantitative criteria, any of the following:

a. $250 million in revenues of the past fiscal year, in addition to average $1 billion in global market capitalization; or

b. $25 million total operating cash flow for the three past years if the company exceeds $200 million revenue in the past 12 month period and exceeds $500 million global market capitalization. Note that there cannot be a negative cash flow in any of the individual three preceding years.

c. With regard to earnings before tax, there must be $6.5 million pretax earnings through any of the following combinations:

d. $2,500,000 earnings before tax in the most recent year, with $2,000,000 earnings before tax in each of the two most recent years; or

e. $4.5 million pretax earnings in the most current year. Note that the past three years must yield a profit.

Next, with respect to minimum distribution standards:

a. 1,100,000 outstanding publicly held shares,
b. $100 million market value in public shares of any public companies; and any of the following:
   (1) 2,000 round lot shareholders, that is, shareholders of minimum 100 shares;
   (2) 2,200 total shareholders having 100,000 shares average trading volume per month in the most current 6 months; or
   (3) 500 shareholders having 1 million shares average trading volume per month in the most current 6 months.

Some of the additional criteria for listing concern the relationship between the quantity of shareholders and trading activity.

It should be noted that if a company fails to strictly comply with the criteria set forth by the exchange, the NYSE may still consider the corporation for listing where other attractive qualities are present.

Foreign companies seeking to become listed upon the NYSE are subject to criteria which differ somewhat from the above requirements for American companies. Some of the criteria for listing for foreign companies are as follows:

With respect to standards concerning minimum distribution criteria:

a. $100,000,000 worldwide market value of public shares on a global scale;
b. 2,500,000 publicly held shares on a global scale; and
c. 5,000 shareholders of minimum 100 shares on a global basis.

In addition, with respect to minimum quantitative standards, any of the following:

a. $250 million revenues in the past fiscal year, with an average $1 billion in worldwide market capitalization;

b. $100 million total cash flow for the past three years with $25 million cash flow minimum for each of the two past years for a company in excess of $200 million revenues over the past 12 month period and in excess of $500 million worldwide market capitalization; or

c. $100 million total earnings before tax in the past three years, with at least $25 million pre tax revenues in the past two current years.

■ NYSE MAINTENANCE LISTING REQUIREMENTS/DELISTING FROM NYSE

It is very difficult for stocks that are listed on the NYSE to become delisted. Stocks, once listed on the NYSE, are subject to very stringent rules that discourage delisting from the exchange. Stocks which are normally delisted from the NYSE are those of companies that have undergone major corporate reorganizations, such as acquisitions, mergers, and restructuring. Other markets, such as The Nasdaq Stock Market, have taken issue with the fact that they have lost the opportunity for companies wishing to transfer the listing of their securities from the NYSE to Nasdaq because of the structure of the NYSE listing and delisting rules.

However, it is possible for a company to become delisted from the NYSE if it fails to comply with maintenance requirements for continued listing. In addition, the NYSE has the power and the right to delist a company's stock in certain situations that indicate that continuance of trading fails to serve the interests of shareholders and/or the public. Existence of any of the following conditions may result in delisting:

a. quantity of less than 400 total shareholders;

b. quantity of less than 1,200 total shareholders with an average of less than 100,000 shares of trading volume per month over the past 12 month period;

c. quantity of 600,000 or less shares held publicly;

d. regarding financial standards, that either:

    (1) the average worldwide market capitalization falls below $15 million over the past 30 days;

    (2) total worldwide market capitalization is below $50 million with shareholder's equity below $50 million; or

    (3) companies that fall under the original global market capitalization listing standard has either an average worldwide capitalization of less than $100 million over the past 30 days, or that generally such be less than $500 million with total earnings under $50 million for the past 12 months.

e. failing to adhere to requirements of the NYSE; or

f. failing to follow rules concerning disclosure of information—i.e., failure to distribute fiscal reports to shareholders both quarterly and yearly; failing solicitation of necessary and important shareholder proxies for voting.

Companies who are in danger of being delisted from the NYSE will receive notice of a hearing from the exchange so as to provide an opportunity to explain a violation of a NYSE requirement.

■ THE NYSE FLOOR

The exchange floor consists of separate trading rooms, all connected by passageways that allow members to walk from room to room to execute orders. Each room contains mechanical and electronic equipment for use in the transaction of business:

1. Most of the stock securities listed on the exchange trade in the *main* room.

2. The *garage* is a nickname for a smaller trading area located next to the main room. It was built many years ago when a lack of space became a problem. Why the "garage"? Because that was what it once was.

3. The *blue* room, even smaller than the garage, is on the other side of the main room. It was built in the late 1960s when the volume of activity on the floor increased rapidly. Why the "blue room"? That's the color of the walls.

Stocks are traded at specific locations on the floor called "trading posts." Each post is a horseshoe-shaped structure with an outside circumference of 26 to 31 feet. At each post a number of assigned stocks are traded in "round lots." (A round lot is 100 shares.) The only exception is that some stocks are traded in 10-share round lot units either because of their low volume or high price. An example is Berkshire Hathaway Class A currently selling at approximately $64,000 per share. At this large table-like structure, located in a corner of the garage, most of the inactive preferred stocks listed on the NYSE are traded in lots of 10 shares. Because of their inactivity, the trading unit assigned is 10.

Around the edge of the trading rooms are telephone booths, used by member organizations to:

- Receive orders from their offices
- Distribute orders to brokers for execution
- Transmit details on the executed orders and pertinent trading information back to their offices

THE PLAYERS ON THE FLOOR

Only members are allowed to do business on the floor. Membership, or "seats on the exchange," may be transferred or sold subject to the approval of the governing body of the exchange. The price of a seat, like that of a stock, depends largely on the forces of supply and demand. New York Stock Exchange

FIGURE 5–1. NYSE Floor Layout

FIGURE 5–1. NYSE Floor Layout

EXCHANGE PLACE

BLUE ROOM   BLUE ROOM

EXISTING TRADING FLOOR	EXISTING	
	BOOTH COUNT	LINEAR FEET
GARAGE	270	355
MAIN ROOM	749	1232
BLUE ROOM	187	393
OLD OPTIONS	–	–
TOTAL	1206	1980

N.Y. STOCK EXCHANGE   SK-36

members are usually categorized according to their activities. There are:

- Floor brokers
- Two-dollar brokers
- Competitive traders
- Competitive market makers
- Specialists

Each group is assigned a *primary* function.

Floor brokers, also known as commission house brokers, working on the exchange floor, execute the orders of public customers of their firm.

Very often, commission house brokers are unable to handle the volume of orders they receive. Even if these brokers receive only two orders at the same time, there can be a problem if the orders are for different securities. If the brokers try to execute two orders at different trading posts, they may miss the market in one or both. In such a situation, brokers may call upon the two-dollar broker.

Two-dollar brokers execute orders in any security for any organization and are paid a commission known as "floor brokerage" for their services. At one time the fee for these services was a flat $2 for each 100-share order executed. Now, however, the fee is fully negotiable according to the difficulty of the execution, the size of the order, and often the price of the security. These brokers are also known as "independent brokers" or "agents." (Commission house brokers with available time can also act as two-dollar brokers.)

Competitive traders buy and sell stock for their personal accounts and risk on the floor. To be allowed to do so, they must meet certain financial, trading, and reporting requirements, and their transactions are regulated to prevent them from conflicting with transactions initiated by public customers of member organizations.

Although they attempt to buy and sell profitably for their accounts, competitive traders frequently act as buyers when customers want to sell and as sellers when customers want to buy. In this capacity, they enhance the liquidity of the maker and, in so doing, assist the specialists, whose function will be described shortly. Competitive traders may also act as two-dollar brokers to earn brokerage fees, provided they have not traded the same stock for themselves on the same day.

Competitive market makers buy and/or sell stock in any NYSE-listed issue at the request of a floor official or another broker holding a customer's order. They can deal in any stock, which differentiates them from specialists who maintain markets in specific issues assigned to them.

Though competitive market makers may also act as two-dollar brokers for brokerage fees, they may accept only certain types of orders. Also, they may not act for themselves as principal and for others as a two-dollar broker in the same stock during the same trading day.

The *specialist* is the focal point of most of the activity on the exchange floor. Each stock listed on the NYSE is assigned to a specialist unit. For each stock assigned, specialists must maintain a "fair and orderly market" and an "orderly succession of prices." Specialists stabilize price variations and they may not let the price of a stock "run wild." When supply (sellers) greatly exceeds demand (buyers), specialists must act as buyers; they buy the stock with their own money and for their own accounts. When there are more buyers than sellers, they must act as sellers, again for their own accounts. In general, although specialists do not participate in every transaction, they manage the activities of the trading crowd.

Specialists therefore furnish a vital service to the exchange, and to the entire stock market, by providing liquidity and saving it from violent price swings that typically work against the interests of the investing public.

Specialists strive to achieve two things:

■ *Price continuity*, which is the degree of price change from one transaction to the next. For example, a stock that moves from 30 to 30 4/16 on one transaction has better continuity than one that moves quickly from 30 to 31.

■ *Market depth*, which is the number of shares associated with the price movement between two or more transactions. As an example, a stock that moves from 30 to 30 8/16 in five transactions totaling 5,000 shares has greater depth than one that moves from 30 to 30 8/16 in five transactions totaling 1,000 shares.

Specialists pool their financial resources and expertise to form "specialist units." Each unit is responsible for maintaining fair and orderly markets in the securities assigned to its members.

In the next chapter, the crucial duties of the specialist will be explained further.

■ THE DELIVERY OF ORDERS TO THE NYSE: SUPERDOT AND THE BROKER BOOTH SUPPORT SYSTEM

NYSE member firms who have orders to be delivered to the exchange can do so through the SUPERDOT system, the Broker Booth Support System, or, if the order needs special floor assistance, by directly calling the order to the floor. Orders can be also sent to brokers through high tech devices now available, including pagers, cellular phones and handheld PCs. The following describes the SUPERDOT and Broker Booth Support Systems, in addition to the utilization of modern communication technology.

A. NYSE SUPERDOT SYSTEM

SUPERDOT is an electronic system that manages many orders, specifically, limit and market orders, on the exchange. The limitation upon the quantity of these orders that the SUPERDOT system will accept are approximately 30,000 shares for market orders and under a million shares for limit orders.

The SUPERDOT system is used to transmit and deliver the orders from NYSE member firms to the specialists at the exchange. Specialists who are sent orders can find them in their Display Book available at the trading posts. The Display Book is an electronic workstation. It keeps a running account of all limit and market orders in the SUPERDOT system, and matches market order so that they may be executed immediately. The Display Book also performs a sorting function for orders and displays them on the screen. When execution of an order has occurred, an execution report message for each trade is sent to the investor.

The SUPERDOT system, in addition to limit and market orders in general, also receives good-till cancelled orders and pre-market opening orders. Pre-market opening orders that are no greater than approximately 30,000 share in size, are taken by the Opening Automated Report Service, or OARS, component of the SUPERDOT system. Basically, the function of the OARS, is to take these pre-market opening items, and match orders to sell and buy together. Then, until opening, the service notifies the specialist, who is deciding the opening price, of any imbalances in such orders.

The SUPERDOT system is available for orders that are both retail and institutional.

The SUPERDOT system of the NYSE is further discussed in Chapter 6.

B. NYSE Broker Booth Support System

The Broker Booth Support System, also referred to as BBSS, is another system used by the NYSE to transmit orders to the exchange. Member firms and brokers on the floor utilize the BBSS. The limitation upon the quantity of orders that the BBSS will accept are approximately 3 million shares for market orders and the same for limit orders.

The BBSS is a system that manages orders which generally are greater in quantity. Specifically, orders can be entered into the system and through it are delivered to NYSE. Orders can be routed to any of the following: (1) BBSS terminals of brokers, located at the broker's booth; (2) portable high tech communication devices, for example, handheld computers and cell phones; (3) Display Books of specialists at their trading posts; and (4) the Crossing Session.

The BBSS is a full system that is able to provide users with in depth summarizations of items, for example, average order price, recaps, and displays or orders. Its users are able to contact other users through the e-mail component of the system.

C. ORDERS THROUGH HIGH TECH COMMUNICATION DEVICES

In addition to the above, there are other means by which brokers can receive orders on the floor straight from NYSE members. With the advent of high tech communication devices, including handheld PCs, cellular phones, and beepers, for example, brokers can now be notified of new orders. In addition, the same technology also enables them to communicate with the trading booths and send information to them. Furthermore, brokers, using these devices, can also contact the member firm that requested the order so that they can be informed of the execution and circumstances surrounding it.

■ NYSE'S ONLINE COMPARISON SYSTEM

Another feature that the NYSE has to offer is the Online Comparison System, or OCS. What the OCS provides is the opportunity for those who are clearing members of the NYSE to compare real time trades. It also allows these members and specialists a means to be used that can help answer and resolve problems and issues concerning trades after the execution date.

Most executed trades are sent from Display Books, high tech communication devices, and the BBSS to the OCS after no more than three hours has passed after trade execution occurred.

■ THE AUCTION SYSTEM

The exchange market is known as an "auction market" because trading takes place by open outcry and exchange members call out bids and offers to determine prices and offers. This is just another way of saying that trading takes place at prices determined by supply and demand.

Along the walls of the exchange are telephone clerks who are employed by member firms and who take orders from the order room or trading areas of the firm. They pass the orders along to the firm's commission house brokers who then take the order to the trading post, where the stock specified in the order is traded. At the trading post, the members of the exchange who are involved in the purchase and sale of the particular issue are referred to as the trading crowd.

Arriving at the post, the member broker first asks for the current market in the security but does not reveal the terms of the order. This request is actually for the *quote*, which consists of the bid and offer prices, as well as their *size* (that is, how many shares are being quoted). The size is always in round lots. The "bid" is the highest price that brokers are willing to pay for a number of shares. The "offer" is the lowest price at which brokers are willing to sell. The difference between the bid and offer prices is the "spread." Only the highest bid and the lowest offer may be quoted. It is the responsibility of the specialist acting as on-floor market maker to maintain the quote. Each and every stock is assigned to a specialist.

- 27 8/16 bid—27 10/16 offered, 2 by 1. This quotation means that 2 lots, or 200 shares, are wanted at 27 8/16, and 1 lot, or 100 shares, is being offered for sale at 27 10/16. The spread is 2/16 (27 10/16 less 27 8/16) and is expressed as "twenty-seven and eight-sixteenths to ten-sixteenths, two by one."

- 63 14/16 bid—64 2/16 offered, 2 up. This quotation means that 200 shares are wanted at 63 14/16 and 200 shares are offered at 64 2/16. The spread is four-sixteenths (64 2/16 less 63 14/16).

The specialist, acting as a market maker, supplies the quotation at the request of the broker. If the broker has an order that can't be executed at the specialist's bid or offer, he can (depending on the type of order he is holding) start bidding (if buying) or offering (if selling), as long as his prices are either equal to the price of the bid or offer, or better. This means bidding or offering "inside" the spread. For example, the specialist is quoting the market at 42 8/16 bid and offered at 42 12/16. If a broker is holding an order to buy at 42 10/16, he can start bidding in the trading crowd. The same rule applies to sellers. Brokers cannot offer stock for sale in the crowd unless their price is equal to or lower than the prevailing offer. Remember that the quote consists of the best (highest) bid and the best (lowest) offer.

The trading crowd uses a language all its own. To avoid confusion and misunderstandings, brokers must state their bids and offers as prescribed by the exchange. Bids are announced as "price for size." When bidding for a stock, a broker says something like the following:

- 35 8/16 for 2...,   meaning a price of 35 8/16 for 200 shares
- 35 7/16 for 2...,   meaning a price of 35 7/16 for 200 shares
- 12 10/16 for 7...,   meaning a price of 12 10/16 for 700 shares
- 12 9/16 for 7...,   meaning a price of 12 9/16 for 700 shares
- 54 for 3...,   meaning a price of 54 for 300 shares
- 54 1/16 for 3,   meaning a price of 54 1/16 for 300 shares

The word "for" indicates that the broker is buying. Similarly, an offer is announced as "size at price." The word "at" means that a broker is selling as follows:

- 2 at 28...,   meaning 200 shares offered at 28
- 2 at 27 15/16...,   meaning 200 shares offered at 27 15/16
- 10 at 15 4/16,   meaning 1,000 shares offered at 15 4/16
- 10 at 15 13/16...,   meaning 1,000 shares offered at 15 13/16
- 6 at 43 8/16,   meaning 600 shares offered at 43 8/16
- 6 at 43 7/16...,   meaning 600 shares offered at 43 7/16

Notice again that size is quoted by lots and not by shares. Accepting a bid or offer also requires a certain wording. To accept, or "hit," the bid, the broker says "Sold!" This one word finalizes a transaction and can cause a change in the market through the entry of a new series of bids and offers in the stock. To accept an offer, the broker says "Take it!" As long as brokers and traders accept bids and/or take offers, stock prices are constantly fluctuating.

■ HOW ORDERS ARE EXECUTED IN THE CROWD

Three basic types of orders are allowed on the exchange floor.

1. A *market order* is to be immediately executed as soon as the broker enters the trading crowd at the best available price. A market order to buy stock requires a purchase at the lowest, meaning the best, offering price available at the time the broker enters the crowd. A market order to sell stock that is owned by a customer (meaning "long stock") requires a sale at the highest "best" bid price available at the time of entry.

If brokers fail to carry out the instructions of a market order, they have "missed the market." Their firm may be required to reimburse the customer promptly for any loss resulting from the error. But brokers don't miss the market often. When they do, their error is usually caused by their misplacing the order after receiving it from the telephone clerk, or by accepting too many market orders in different securities at the same time.

2. A *limit order* sets the maximum price that the customer is willing to pay as a buyer, or the minimum price that he or she is willing to accept as a seller. A member cannot disobey the customer's instructions by paying more to buy or by selling for less than the specified price.

A price limitation, however, always includes an "or better" qualification. That is, if members can buy the stock below the limit or sell it for more, then they have to do so immediately. If brokers fail to finalize an order that can be carried out according to the customer's wishes, they may be held financially responsible for missing the market. If on-floor commission brokers get to the crowd and cannot execute a limit order right away because a customer's requested limit price is currently unavailable, they generally cannot wait at the post very long. Other orders may be coming in—maybe orders for other stocks trading at other posts. In these situations, the order is left with the specialist who puts the order "on the book" and executes it for a fee, called "floor brokerage," when the market permits. The broker is then free to get on to other business.

3. A *stop order* is a "memorandum" that becomes a market order only if a transaction takes place at or through the "stop" price stated in the memorandum. That transaction is called the *electing* or *activating sale*. Stop orders may be entered for a variety of reasons as "buy stop" or "sell stop," depending on their purpose.

A buy stop order is placed above the present market level for one of the following reasons:

■ To reduce a loss on an existing short position. (This subject is discussed further later in the chapter.)

■ To purchase a security if a transaction at the stated price creates a technical buy signal.

■ To preserve a profit on a previously established short position.

For example, a customer sells a stock short at 28, anticipating a drop in value. (A short sale is a sale of stock that the seller does not own in the expectation of a drop in prices.) She can suffer a substantial loss if the price rises higher than 28 contrary to her original expectations. To protect herself against loss caused by an upward move in price, she can enter a buy stop order at a price higher than 28, for instance 28 8/16. If the price rises to 28 8/16 or above, the memorandum becomes a market order to buy, and the broker purchases the stock immediately at the best available price. The exact best available price, however, is unknown until the stop order is activated and becomes a market order and is actually executed. It is therefore impossible to determine the exact loss until the purchase is carried out.

A sell stop order is placed at a price below the present market level for one of the following reasons:

- To preserve a profit for a stock previously purchased at a lower price.
- To initiate a short position by a short sale (but only if a transaction at the stated price creates a technical sell signal).
- To reduce a loss on a present stock holding.

EXAMPLE: A customer purchases a stock at 35 and watches it rise to 43. As it continues to move higher, he will most likely want to hold onto that security. But if it begins to drop, the paper profit will soon disappear and a sharp decline could lead to a loss. So the investor enters a sell stop order at a price below 43, at 42 8/16 for example, and tries to preserve most of his paper profits in the event of a rapid decline in price. If the price falls to 42 8/16 or lower, his stop memorandum is activated and becomes a market order to sell at the best available price. The exact profit can be determined only when the actual sale takes place.

Limit and stop orders may be qualified by additional instructions that can affect the tactics and/or timing of the brokers in the trading crowd.

Day order. This is valid only for the trading day on which it is entered. All orders are automatically regarded as day orders, unless specified differently.

Good-till-cancelled (GTC). A GTC order, or "open order," remains valid until the customer cancels it or until it is executed.

Some brokerage firms accommodate their customers by accepting orders good through the week, through the month, or through a specified day. Because these orders may not be entered on the trading floor, they must be entered as straight GTC orders. The member firm assumes responsibility for canceling the order if it cannot be executed by the close of business on the specified date. If the firm fails to do so, it must accept any financial liability resulting from its error.

Not held (NH). This allows a floor broker to use personal judgment in determining the price and the time of execution of an order, although sometimes the discretion is for only a 2/16 or 4/16 point. Brokers are not held responsible for missing the market if their judgment proves to be wrong. Specialists can never accept this instruction from a broker or enter the order on their "book" as agent, because their primary responsibility is to maintain a fair and orderly market, not to trade on behalf of customers.

Participate but do not initiate (PNI). Institutional customers may use the PNI instruction to buy or sell large orders of stock as long as such activity does not create a new price. This type of transaction allows buyers or sellers to accumulate or distribute shares without disturbing the market forces.

All or none (AON). This customer wants to buy (or sell) a sizable quantity of stock at one time and at a designated price. Brokers are prohibited from announcing this instruction in the trading crowd. For the purpose of obtaining on-floor standing and capturing the market they must inquire about the quotation and quality and watch market conditions carefully, until *both* the price and quantity available can satisfy the order. It's all or none. Only then may the brokers execute the order. Normally, AON orders are left with the specialist, and are normally large in size and are used by institutions to test the available depth and liquidity of the market.

Fill or kill (FOK). This instruction calls for the immediate and complete purchase or sale of a specified amount of stock, or no execution at all. If the broker cannot fill the order immediately upon entering the crowd, the order is automatically canceled (that is, "killed"). The order is an immediate depth tester and often used to obtain a better price inside the spread on a here and now basis.

Immediate or cancel (IOC). The customer wants all or part of the order executed promptly, as soon as it is entered in the trading crowd, with the unexecuted portion of the order cancelled immediately. When the floor broker makes the bid (or offer):

■ If someone responds but only partially fills the order, the broker accepts, cancels the unsatisfied portion of the bid (offer), withdraws from the trading area, and reports partial success to the customer.

■ If no one responds, the broker withdraws the bid (offer), leaves the trading area, and reports to the customer that the order has been cancelled. The order is similar to the "fill or kill" except that the customer is willing to accept less than all.

Scale order. Scale orders are multiple limit orders that are entered at various prices but at the same time. Multiples of round lots (100 shares) may be either bought at prices called down from a given value or sold at prices scaled up from a given value. Let's say that the customer places a scale order to buy 400 shares, the first 100 at 51, and then each 100 of the remaining shares at execution prices that are successively 2/16 point lower. This order means that 100 shares are to be bought at 51, 100 at 49 14/16, 100 at 49 12/16, and 100 at 49 10/16. This is an example of scaling down. Another customer places a scale order to sell 300 shares, 100 at 15 8/16, "scaled up" 4/16 point for the remaining 200 shares. With this order, 100 shares are sold at 15 8/16, 100 at 15 12/16, and 100 at 16.

In either case, the purpose is to obtain a favorable "average" purchase or sale price. That's the advantage. The disadvantage is that the entire order may never be carried out unless the stock fluctuates in a wide enough price range.

At the close. On the stock exchange, this type of order is executed at the close of the trading day. The end of trading is signaled by the ringing of a bell for 30 seconds. However, this may not be the final trade in that security; another broker could have better timing during those last 30 seconds.

Alternative (either/or). The broker has been furnished with two alternatives: either to buy at a limit as soon as possible, or to buy the same security at market. Execution of one part of the order automatically cancels the other. With this type of order, a customer is trying to buy at a given price, if possible, and, if not, to purchase the security regardless.

Sell plus. The broker has either a market or a limit order to sell a security at a price higher than the previously priced transaction for the stock. For example, if the previous price was 36, then the current sale price for a sell plus order would be 36 2/16.

Buy minus. The broker has a market or limit order to purchase a security at a price lower than the previously priced transaction for that stock. For instance, if the previous price was 54, then the current execution price for this order would be 53 14/16.

Switch (contingent or swap) order. The customer enters a limit order to sell (or buy) one stock. When it is executed, he or she enters a limit or market order to buy (or sell) another stock. The transaction may also be called a "proceeds sale" if the proceeds of the sell order are used to make the purchase on the buy order.

Cancellation. Although a cancellation is not really an order, it can significantly influence floor-trading activities. A cancellation is the revocation or modification of a buy or sell order, an action that is allowed at any time before the execution of an order.

■ CROSSING STOCK

To "cross stock," a broker combines, or pairs off, a purchase order with a sell order in the same security at the same time and same price but for different customers. Let's look at an example. Customer A enters a market order to buy 2,000 shares of Chrysler at the same time that customer B enters a market order to sell long 2,000 shares of Chrysler. Both orders are given to the same floor broker, who carries the orders to the Chrysler crowd. Each stock trades in its own designated location, at a post, referred to as "the crowd," which is of course managed by its assigned specialist. The broker, if market conditions permit, may cross the orders—that is, execute both orders at the same time—by having customer A buy from customer B. The purpose of the cross is to permit both A and B to obtain a better price inside the spread, that is the difference between the bid and the offer. To cross stock, the broker must make certain of three things. First, the stock has to be crossed at its assigned trading post and within the quotation prevailing there. Second, the spread must be at least a 2/16 point when the broker enters the trading area; a 1/16 point is not large enough for crossing within the spread. The broker must pair off the orders at a price within the quotation. If the stock were quoted 13–13 4/16, the intended cross would occur at 13 2/16, not at 13. A quotation of 13–13 1/16 doesn't leave any room between the bid and offer prices to arrange a cross, because the trade has to be made at either 13 or 13 1/16; it cannot be made within the quotation. Third, the broker must give either customer a brief opportunity to improve on the price at which the orders are to be crossed or paired off. To do so, the crossing broker momentarily either bids 1/16 point lower or offers 1/16 point higher than the crossing price.

■ AFTER (OFF) HOURS TRADING— A/K/A CROSSING SESSIONS

For almost a decade, the NYSE has conducted two crossing sessions, which are after hours, or off-hours, trading sessions. The purpose of these special trading sessions is to promote and make available the crossing of portfolios and stocks for its members and potential new investors. Furthermore, another goal of the NYSE in providing these sessions is to promote the future development of a 24 hour and possibly a 24/7 ongoing market of NYSE securities.

A. NYSE CROSSING SESSION I: FIXED PRICE SESSION

The first crossing session, known as "Crossing Session I", occurs from 4:15 to 5 PM Eastern Standard Time. Availability of the session is limited to member broker-dealers of the NYSE who are SUPERDOT subscribers. Orders may be placed only in the SUPERDOT system. Specifically, during Crossing Session I, also known as the "Fixed Price Session," NYSE members can enter orders for execution of specific stock securities at 5 o'clock P.M. New York time. During this first session, the matching and execution of orders occurs at the closing price of the regular session of that day for that specific stock. A printout of these orders appears and is available on the consolidated tape.

B. NYSE CROSSING SESSION II: BASKET SESSION

The second crossing session, commonly referred to as "Crossing Session II", or the "Basket Session," starts at 4 P.M. and ends at 5:15 P.M., Eastern Standard Time. This session is again open to every NYSE member and allows "baskets" of multiple securities to be traded. Each basket that can be crossed during this session must meet the minimum requirements of having at least $1 million in cumulative market value and possessing at least 15 different stocks that are listed on the NYSE. Prices are established in aggregate combined totals. At the end of the session, information concerning every basket order that was executed, specifically, the totals of dollar value and quantity of shares executed is made available. Furthermore, after the trades are made, the NYSE Daily Sales Report makes available a printout three days later of the individual securities, which comprised the executed baskets, with volume.

The volume of shares traded in both of these crossing sessions is substantial. In fact, at the end of the 1990s, the volume of shares during Crossing Session I had been averaging approximately 2.5

million shares each day. Similarly, in Crossing Session II, the average daily volume of shares was over 7.5 million. It is much higher today.

■ THE SHORT SALE

A short sale is the sale of a stock that the investor does not own. Accordingly, the seller is considered to be "short" the security. The principle of the successful short sale is to "sell high and buy low" at a later date, typically in anticipation of a price decline. The seller's brokerage firm borrows stock for delivery to the buyer's firm. The selling firm can arrange this "stock loan" by borrowing the stock from its own vault or from another firm. The selling investor pays interest on the borrowed stock, just as he or she would on the loan of money. When the customer closes the short position by buying the stock in the open market, the stock is given back to the lender. To insure that the stock borrowed is returned, a short sale can only be transacted in a margin account. Of all transactions, short sellers assume the most risk.

An example will clarify how a short sale works. A customer sells 100 shares of Hitek short at 30 2/16, expecting it to drop in price. Her brokerage firm takes 100 shares of Hitek from its vault, or borrows it from another firm to make delivery to the buyer firm on settlement day.

A week later, Hitek's price has dropped to 27 4/16. Patel places a market order to buy 100 shares, which she uses to close the open short position. The shares are returned to the brokerage firm vault. This order closes the short position profitably. Patel received $3,012.50 on the short sale, bought the stock at $2,725.00, and closed the position at a profit of $287.50. Even deducting commissions, fees, and interest charges, the short sale is a success.

Not all short sales are so successful. If the stock should rise in price after the short sale, the short position becomes more and more of a losing situation.

Again, all short sales must be executed in a margin account (which is explained in Chapter 11). Also, short sales may not be executed when they are likely to increase the momentum of a down trading market. The SEC requires that a short sale has to be executed on a "plus tick" or "zero plus tick," referred to as "upticks." That is, the trade must be made at a price that is higher than the last different regular-way sale of the security.

For example, if the last transaction in Hitek was at 30, the customer's short sale order could not be executed at a lower price. A transaction at 30 2/16 would, of course, constitute an uptick.

The short sale can also be made on "zero plus tick," which is a price equal to that of the preceding transaction but higher than the last different price. Let's say that two round lots of Hitek trade at 29 14/16 and 30, in that order. A short sale may be executed on the next trade at 30 or higher. The first trade at 30 is a plus tick; it represents an advance in the price. The second trade at 30 is a zero plus tick, and the seller in that trade is permitted to have been a short seller.

You'll recall that stock from the vault was given to whoever bought it from the short selling. A question might arise as to whether the lender is entitled to receive dividends that may be declared on the stock. The answer is yes. Securities lenders are still entitled to receive any dividends paid during the time the securities are loaned. The short seller is responsible for protecting the lender's interests, and paying dividends personally, even when the lender's certificates are re-registered into the name of the new buyer.

To ensure this protection, the lending firm must maintain accurate records of all securities loaned. If the issuing corporation declares a cash dividend, the borrowing firm sends the lending firm a check for the dividend amount. The customer whose certificates may have been loaned never realizes that the broker/dealer no longer possesses the security. The short seller's margin account is debited with the actual amount of the dividend or interest on the "record date," the day the short seller becomes liable for that payment. (More about dividends is to be found in Chapter 11.)

■ INSTITUTIONAL TRADES

Selling or buying a large block of stock—such as 100,000 shares or more—by an institutional investor could be an upsetting influence on the market depending on the stock. In such a case, the brokerage firm may request permission from the NYSE to use one of the following special block procedures:

- Exchange distributions or acquisitions
- Special offerings or bids
- Secondary distributions

Let's use an example to explain an *exchange distribution*. An institutional client of a brokerage firm, a pension fund, intends to sell 100,000 shares of CNF. The seller certifies in writing to the NYSE that it owns all the shares and that the amount in question represents all of the security to be marketed for a reasonable period. The brokerage firm, rather than going directly to the floor, asks other firms (generally one or two) to canvass their clients for offsetting purchase orders (which are not binding). Once the selling member firm is assured of sufficient purchasing interest, the large sell order and all the buy orders are sent to the floor of the exchange, where they are officially "crossed at the current market price." The pension fund pays everyone's "special commission." The transaction is printed on the ticker tape and identified by the letters "DIST" preceding the security symbol and volume.

If the pension fund wanted to purchase a large block of stock, the transaction is called an *exchange acquisition*. The fund's brokerage firm would solicit buyers, the stock would be crossed, and the letters "ACQ" would identify the transaction on the ticker tape.

A *secondary distribution* involves an amount of listed stock so very large that it cannot be normally handled on the exchange. It is better handled "off the floor," that is, over the counter. Often the distribution is handled collectively by a number of brokerage firms, acting either as dealers (buying and then reselling the stock as in a firm underwriting) or as brokers (selling on behalf of the institutional customer and taking commissions). Since the block is sold off board by a group of firms, somewhat similar to a primary offering, the transaction is called a "secondary distribution."

Such an enormous transaction has to meet a number of requirements:

- The selling brokerage firm must obtain the permission of the exchange.

- The fixed price of the distribution may not be higher than the last security transaction on the exchange at the point that the offering commences.

- The seller absorbs all commissions.

- All buy orders on the exchange floor whose prices are equal to or higher than the offering's price must be satisfied first.

- If the offering starts (as if often the case) after exchange trading hours, the distributor must make the special price available for at least 30 minutes after the close.

Although the ticker tape does not show the actual transactions in such an offering (they are "off board"), it announces its completion or continuance from day to day, as the case may be.

All the rules and regulations—whether required by the SEC, the exchange, or the firms themselves—have one thing in common: to maintain just and equitable principles of trade. For the market to be *fair* for everyone in it, the forces of supply and demand have to be allowed to determine prices. But it's not a perfect world. Given the liberty, some market participants would orchestrate transactions so as to manipulate prices. Others, in sincere attempts to protect their interests, might place orders that would work against stability. Therefore, for even a free market to be orderly, you need rules and regulations.

But you also need something else. Every second of the trading day, the buy orders and sell orders exert pressures on the price of a stock to go up or down. What rule or regulation can dictate what is to be done in every fleeting situation? When, at any given moment, is the market stable and when is it threatening to become volatile? What is needed is someone on the trading floor whose primary duty is to watch each stock, moment to moment, and to do instantly whatever is necessary to maintain a fair and orderly market. That person is the specialist, who is the subject of the next chapter.

■ DECIMALIZATION

Presently, many newspapers have begun to convert fractions such as 1/16 of a point to the nearest penny. It is also an early reporting stage of the NYSE and Nasdaq to begin trading stocks in decimals with an early implementation for some stocks of fractional variations of nickels and pennies. The exact decimal has yet to be determined. Stay tuned.

CONVERSION CHART FROM FRACTIONS TO DECIMALS

Fraction	=	Price		Fraction	=	Price
1/16	=	.0625		9/16	=	.5625
2/16	=	.125		10/16	=	.625
3/16	=	.1875		11/16	=	.6875
4/16	=	.25		12/16	=	.75
5/16	=	.3125		13/16	=	.8125
6/16	=	.375		14/16	=	.875
7/16	=	.4375		15/16	=	.9375
			16/16	=	1.000	

■ OTHER IMPORTANT FEATURES OF THE NYSE

A. NYSE AND THE INTERMARKET TRADING SYSTEM (ITS)

For over two decades, the intermarket trading system (ITS), often referred to as the National Market System, is an order routing and tape reporting system that has been available to traders. The purpose of the ITS is to connect the exchanges in an effort to promote trade data dissemination to all market participants and encourage a competitive atmosphere among the individual exchanges on a national level. Through ITS, a wider selection and marketplace is made available for fulfilling investor's orders, thus raising the chances that an order will be executed at a better price. By providing competition and a larger forum, ITS aims to expand an increased market opportunity for investors.

The ITS presently electronically links the NYSE, the Chicago Board of Option Exchange (CBOE), the NASD, along with the Chicago, Cincinnati, Boston, Philadelphia, and Pacific Exchanges. The ITS also links the American Stock Exchange (Amex) with each of the above markets, depending on whether the stock or option in question is listed on the NYSE or the Amex. When the Consolidated Quotation System displays a more desirable stock price in an ITS affiliated market or exchange, traders can participate and trade in that other exchange through the ITS.

The ITS gives the best quoted prices and the most recent sale prices of the linked exchanges. ITS routes orders automatically to the market with the most desirable execution. So even though an order may be entered with the member firm of one exchange, the execution of the order may occur at a different exchange.

At the end of the past decade, the average daily share volume of executed trades exceeded 21 million shares.

For a further discussion of the ITS, refer to Chapter 6.

B. THE NYSE COMPOSITE INDEX

For approximately three and a half decades, the NYSE Composite Index has been a prominent and well-known measure of general market performance of NYSE. Common stocks are a major source of NYSE stock price movement. The NYSE Composite Index reflects price changes in the total market value of all common stock listed on the NYSE. The index is calculated by multiplying the per share market price by the quantity of listed shares for the common stocks of every single NYSE company. Thus, ultimately, price changes and market movements are measured in dollars and cents.

The NYSE Composite Index also takes into account certain adjustments. Adjustments include those for common stocks, such as whether stocks become newly listed or delisted, in addition to changes in capitalization. Furthermore, another adjustment to the index that must be accounted for is a base value factor also used to determine the current value of the index.

It should be noted that subcategory indexes, such as Finance, Industrial, Transportation, and Utility Indexes are also published by the NYSE in addition to the Composite Index.

C. NYSE RULES 80A AND 80B: COLLAR AND CIRCUIT BREAKER RULES

New York Stock Exchange Rules 80A and 80B are individually known as the "Collar" (80A) and "Circuit Breaker" (80B) rules. These set forth certain restrictions to be imposed in certain circumstances in which the Dow Jones Industrial Average (DJIA) experiences certain price movements. These restrictions concern index arbitrage trading and halts in stock trading. The reason the New York Stock Exchange implemented these rules was to manage volatile market action during turbulent times. These rules arose after strong market downturns in October 1987, which is described in Chapter 15.

(1) NYSE RULE 80A: COLLAR RESTRICTIONS

New York Stock Exchange Rule 80A, also known as the collar restrictions, set forth restrictions that apply to index arbitrage trading of orders for component stocks of the S & P 500 Stock Price Index. Under Rule 80A, when a collar restriction becomes effective due to the fact the DJIA experiences a significant advance during the trading session, then it is mandatory that every index arbitrage order to buy a component stock in the S & P 500 is marked as "buy minus."

"Buy minus" means at a price lower than the last sale on a minus or zero minus tick.

If a collar restriction under Rule 80A is effective because the DJIA has significantly declined, then every index arbitrage order to sell a component stock in the S & P 500 is to be marked "sell plus."

"Sell plus" means at a price higher than the last sale on a minus or zero minus tick.

Rule 80A restrictions become effective in circumstances where the DJIA has approximately a minimum 200 point variance above or below its previous trading day's closing value. These restrictions are lifted when the variance increases or decreases so that the DJIA is within no more than approximately 100 points or less of its previous trading day's closing value.

The specific threshold of 200 and 100 point changes in the DJIA that either trigger or remove these restrictions, respectively, are set for a three month period or quarterly by the NYSE and may be amended thereafter. These revisions usually go into effect on the first of every January, April, July, and October.

2) NYSE RULE 80B: CIRCUIT BREAKER RULES

New York Stock Exchange Rule 80B concerns circuit breakers that are implemented during extremely volatile market periods. In cases where Rule 80B circuit breakers become effective, trading in NYSE stocks will experience a temporary halt because of the drastic drops in the DJIA in the same trading day.

There are three levels of circuit breakers that set forth how long the trading halt will last. For each of three trading halt levels to be applicable, there is a specific threshold of market movement by which the DJIA must decline below its previous trading day's value. These thresholds are in effect for a quarter, that is, three month period and are continually revised for the first of every January, April, July, and October. The threshold of point levels is based upon the prior month's average closing value of the DJIA.

For a Level 1 Halt in trading to be effective, the DJIA must decline by approximately a minimum of 1,000 points below its previous day's trading value. A halt at this level that occurs before 2 P.M. lasts an hour. If a Level 1 Halt begins between 2 to 2:29 P.M., then the halt lasts a half hour. At 2:30 P.M. and afterwards, there will be continuous trading for the rest of the day unless a Level 2 Halt goes into effect, which is explained in the next paragraph.

For a Level 2 Halt in trading to be effective, the DJIA must decline by approximately a minimum of 2,000 points below its previous day's trading value. A halt at this level that begins before 1 P.M. lasts two hours. If it occurs between 1 to 1:59 P.M., then the halt lasts one hour. Where a Level 2 Halt occurs at 2:00 P.M. and after, then trading halts for the rest of the day.

For a Level 3 Halt in trading to be effective, the DJIA must decline by approximately a minimum of 3,000 points below its previous day's trading value. A Level 3 Halt, which occurs at any time in the trading day, will result in a trading halt that lasts the rest of the day.

D. NYSE TECHNOLOGY: NETWORK NYSE

In its quest to keep abreast of and provide to its members and investors the latest technological developments in the trading world, the NYSE is introducing Network NYSE. Network NYSE is a high-tech platform of products and services designed to provide advanced dissemination of market data in addition to stock trading.

Network NYSE will seek to offer traders advantages akin to those available via the computerized trading systems known as electronic communication networks, or ECNs. The ECNs present competition against NYSE. However, the NYSE is more attractive to many traders as ECNs have experienced problems of lack of liquidity in trading. The NYSE, on the other hand, provides a very liquid market for its traders. In fact, just under 3,000 stocks listed on the NYSE trade daily at approximately one billion share volume.

(1) NYSE DIRECT+

Through the NYSE Direct+ component of Network NYSE Some of the ECN-like benefits that the Network NYSE will offer traders include immediate electronic trades through NYSE Direct+. Through NYSE Direct+, the NYSE will enable its member firms to link electronically to the exchange floor. This will allow them access to very fast-paced immediate execution of customer limit orders of less than 1,100 shares in size. Additionally, Network NYSE will allow traders, both large and small, to place trades directly themselves without broker assistance. However, if an investor desires broker intervention, then such help will also be available. This is a benefit attractive to smaller traders.

With Network NYSE, anyone placing a trade order on Network NYSE can preserve anonymity. This anonymity is attractive to trades as it will help avoid a situation in which others attempt to trade first before very sizable orders that can impact the market.

(2) NYSE MarkeTrac

Through Network NYSE, the exchange is planning to also provide NYSE MarkeTrac. Through the NYSE internet site on the world wide web, NYSE MarkeTrac will display the exchange floor in a very clear, 3-D (that is, three dimensional) format. Furthermore, it will be interactive for internet users accessing the web site. Not only will viewers be able to see various aspects of the exchange floor, but they will have a realistic look at the Display Book of the specialist, along with particular stocks provided by the book. Furthermore, NYSE MarkeTrac takes another step in breaking down barriers to information disclosure by enabling anyone with internet access, and not just market professionals as was the case in the past, to receive real time market data and other related trading information.

(3) Institutional XPress

Aside from the Network NYSE and features that it will provide, the NYSE also tries to maintain itself as a technologically modern exchange via Institutional XPress, which is a combination of services and products for firms that are members of the NYSE. Another recent development of the NYSE is that it now provides Institutional XPress. Basically, Institutional XPress has three parts: XPress Information, XPress Orders, and XPress Routing. These are described as follows.

A) XPRESS INFORMATION. NYSE XPress Information is a service that provides firms, which are members of the exchange, with a continuous feed of market information. Furthermore, XPress Information allows these firms to send such data to their customers. XPress Information is available to member firms via Internet access.

B) XPRESS ORDERS. NYSE XPress Orders allows execution of certain orders for institutions through the SUPERDOT system without the possibility of others splitting it up. For orders to qualify for this treatment, they must be institutional orders of minimum 25,000 shares whose quotations are shown for a minimum 30 seconds.

C) XPRESS ROUTING. NYSE XPress Routing service, which is anticipated to begin in Spring 2001, will provide privacy to institutions as their brokers will not have access to information concerning the source of their orders.

(4) NYSE E-BROKER

NYSE e-broker is a development which allows brokers on the floor to better handle orders with respect to executions and organization. It also is helpful in raising the quality of data flow and exchange for its customers.

■ AMEX—THE AMERICAN STOCK EXCHANGE

In addition to the New York Stock Exchange, another leading exchange also located in New York City is the American Stock Exchange. The American Stock Exchange, commonly referred to as the Amex, historically began in the late 1700's as a market of curbstone brokers. Even today, the Amex is affectionately called "the Curb." It has since evolved to become the second largest floor-based exchange in the United States, offering a variety of securities such as common stocks, options, derivatives, and index shares. The Amex conducts trading through the specialist system. This, in conjunction with market liquidity and the fast paced order delivery via computers, makes trading possible on the Amex.

Specialists have a very important role at the Amex. Every specialist is responsible for handling all sell and purchase orders of the securities for a particular company in which he is registered. In doing so, the specialist ensures a market that operates in a fair and orderly manner. In essence, the specialist is an on-floor market maker who provides liquidity, continuity, and stability to the market. Each company listed on the exchange has a minimum unit of three specialists to handle trades of stocks assigned to them by the exchange. The unit is located at a post on the exchange floor. The specialist system is described in greater depth in Chapter 6.

Basically, customers have a buy or sell order for a stock that is sent to a specialist. The specialist's role is to match up buy and sell orders, and execute them. In addition, specialists on the Amex are allowed to handle customer orders that are entrusted to them (referred to as placing an order on "the Book") as broker agents. In addition, specialists trade for themselves as principals. Allowing specialists to trade on their own behalf as market makers is beneficial to the market, as the specialist becomes another factor helping to create and maintain market liquidity for the stock. Liquidity, of course, is another term for "ease of buying, ease of selling." Furthermore, in such an instance, a specialist is setting forth a specific price quotation in the market for a particular security at prices close to or equal to the last sale. This last process is referred to as market continuity.

Specialists, in addition to maintaining order in the market, also ensure the execution of limit orders. Limit orders are specific price orders away from the current market at lower bid or higher offer prices.

The Amex, like so many of the competing exchanges today, has implemented stock trading in 1/16ths. In addition, the Amex performs surveillance functions to help ensure fairness

FIGURE 5–2. AMEX FLOOR LAYOUT

in trading. Specifically, through its Market Surveillance and Trading Analysis sections, market trading is monitored and regulated. Typically, Amex staff gathers market data, such as filings by Amex members, and prepares reports on market activity. They question suspicious trading activity that may be illegal or violate rules and regulations. Furthermore, they analyze specialist's trading performance to assure that all transactions are executed in a fair and orderly manner, with tight price variations.

THE SPECIALIST
Riding the Bulls and Bears

On the exchange floor, the forces of supply and demand take the form of orders to sell and orders to buy, respectively. When the sell orders outnumber the buy orders, stock prices tend to go down. With more buy orders at the trading post, prices tend to rise. The greater the preponderance of one type of order over the other, the faster and farther prices can move. When there is excessive, one-sided buying or selling volume, this is when you see dramatic price fluctuations, that is, great volatility.

The psychology of buying and selling stock—of supply and demand—is such that lopsided volume spurs more volume. As holders of a stock see prices dropping sharply, they decide to sell—selling tends to cause more selling. As would-be owners of a stock see prices rising, they decide to buy—buying tends to cause more buying. Either way, as they enter their orders, they create more volume on one side of the market and increase the force of supply or demand. This increased volume draws more orders to sell or to buy, thus creating even faster price movements. It's a self-perpetuating cycle of more volume, bigger price movements, still more volume. This is when prices move too quickly for investors to react properly—to sell a stock that is losing value rapidly, for instance. And this is when investors get hurt in the stock market. Left unchecked, the cycle can lead to precariously high-priced stocks and, worse, to selling panics and crashes.

On the other hand, if a stock is not trading at all—that is, if volume is zero—it would draw very little investor interest. Such a lack of liquidity would cause prospective owners to buy at much higher-than-normal prices and to sell at much lower-than-normal levels. Many a stock would not trade at all under such conditions.

A specialist is a stock exchange member who is a market maker in each stock assigned to him or her by the exchange. Every listed stock is assigned to a specialist.

The role of the specialist is to provide liquidity and eliminate the temporary disparities between supply and demand. When, for instance, sell orders outweigh buy orders, specialists must and will buy stock to absorb the sales. They'll also take the sell side, given a greater number of buy orders. Either way, they put a brake on the cycle. Similarly, if an order comes in for a stock that no one else is buying or selling, the specialist must fill the order and become the "other party," or "contra," to the transaction, just to "make a market" in the stock. In either case, specialists do not dictate or change market direction. They simply allow the market value of a stock to rise or fall in reaction to the forces of supply and demand without large or unreasonable price fluctuations. Specialists maintain the "fair and orderly market" which is their responsibility at minimum to no change in price; this is referred to as market continuity.

■ THE SPECIALIST'S ROLE: AS DEALER, AS BROKER

Specialists on the NYSE fulfill their responsibilities in two capacities: To begin with, once a corporation lists its stock on either the NYSE or the American Stock Exchange, it is assigned to a specialist by the Allocations Committee of that Exchange. Specialists are registered broker-dealers, and the concept is a unique American institution practiced nowhere else.

Specialists provide two main functions:

- As agents or brokers, they execute orders on behalf of other floor members and charge a commission for this service, called "floor brokerage." In this capacity, they are acting as agents on behalf of the public customer orders that are left with them. Normally, orders left with the specialist are limit orders, stop orders and other non-market order types that are "away from market" and cannot be immediately filled. This process of entrusting an order to a specialist is referred to as placing an order "on the book."

■ As *dealers* (or *principals* or *market makers*), they buy and sell stock for their own accounts and with their own money to provide liquidity to the marketplace. In this capacity, they take no commissions; instead, they expect to profit on what they buy and resell.

When floor brokers cannot execute an order immediately, such as in the handling of a limit order that is "away from" the current quote, they may leave the order with the specialist in that stock for execution at a later time. The specialists file all such orders in their book, which is a lot of all limit and stop orders left with him or her for execution. When specialists eventually execute these orders, they do so as agents of the entering brokers on behalf of their customers, and they charge the brokers' firms a commission. This is called Floor Brokerage.

The "book" referred to that the specialist uses consisted of paper in the past but now is available electronically. Basically, at the trading posts, the book is a display of information shown on a terminal. Orders that floor members place with the specialist for execution are displayed on the electronic book. Limit, stop, and stop-limit orders are the most common. Most of the orders, especially small round lot orders, in the NYSE are transmitted through the SUPERDOT system to the trading post of the specialist. Most brokerage firms utilize the services of floor brokers for complex orders or orders big in size.

Even as agents, however, specialists must act in the best interests of the market. Given several limit orders for the stock, specialists are always checking the book and will quote the highest bid or lowest offer, as appropriate; that is, the highest price anyone is willing to pay for the stock or the lowest price at which anyone is willing to sell the stock. If these prices are no more than 1/16 or 1/8 point from the last sale price when a floor broker enters the trading crowd with a market order to buy or sell a stock, then the specialist executes the limit order and tells the broker the name of the firm that entered the limit order in the book. If all the limit orders are more than 1/16 or 1/8 point away from the last sale price, or if there are no limit orders logged in their books, then specialists may execute trades for their own accounts. Under no circumstances may specialists compete with orders in their books, that is, by selling at the same price ahead of orders entrusted with them.

When specialists buy or sell for their own accounts, they are acting as *dealers* or *market makers*. Although the specialists' passive role as brokers' agents is an important one, their active role as dealer/market maker is critical to the maintenance of a fair and orderly market and to the proper functioning of the auction market.

When a market order arrives at the post and none of the "book" orders is near the last sale, specialists are expected and are required to bid for or offer stock from their own accounts at a price variation reasonably close to, or at, the last sale. In so doing, specialists prevent wide price fluctuations, provide liquidity, and assure that each transaction bears a price relationship close to the prior transaction. Again, this is referred to as maintaining price continuity. (Actual price variations will depend on the size or volume of the transaction.)

For example, the last sale in CMF stock was 50, the best public bid on the specialist's book is 49 8/16, and the best public offer in the book is 50 8/16. (Assume that there is no other broker in the crowd.) A broker who wants to buy 100 shares at the market in this instance without a specialist would purchase at 50 8/16, the offer price. Similarly, a broker seeking to sell 100 shares without a specialist would receive 49 8/16, the bid price. The specialist, who must provide price continuity with reasonable depth and limit price fluctuations, is expected to narrow the quote spread and is obligated to improve the market by making a better (higher) bid and/or a better (lower) offer for his own account. A one-point spread between 49 8/16–50 8/16 is excessively wide and will cause wide price variations. The narrowest spread is one-sixteenth. For a stock that is bid 49 8/16, if the stock is reasonably active and liquid, the widest spread you should expect is one-quarter of a point.

The price and size of specialists' quotations, either for orders on the book or for their own accounts, must be firm. Again, specialists may not compete at the same price with public orders on their books.

Supply and demand cause price movements; specialists do not establish price. They adjust their bid and offer prices depending on the size, prices, and types of orders logged in their books and/or executed at the post. The aim of the specialists' trades is to "stabilize" the market by counterbalancing the force of supply and/or demand. In fact about 95 percent of all specialists' transactions as dealers (or "principals") are aimed at stabilizing the market trend. But how do specialists know the trend? They watch the price of the last sale.

- *They sell on a plus tick (+) or a zero plus tick (0+).* A plus tick is a sale made at a price higher than the previous sale. For example, if the last sale was at 50 3/16 ($50.1875), a plus tick sale would be at 50 4/16 ($50.25) *or higher*. A zero plus tick is a sale at the same price as that of the previous sale but higher than the last different price. For instance, let's say that sales occur at 50, 50 2/16 (50.125), and again at 50 2/16. The second sale at 50 2/16 is a zero plus tick because it is the same as the prior sale but higher than the last different sale of 50.

- *They buy on a minus tick (–) or zero minus tick (0–).* A minus tick is a price lower than that of the last sale. If the price moves from 50 2/16 to 50, the second sale is a minus tick. A zero minus tick is the same price as the last sale, but lower than the last different price. In a series of transactions at 50 2/16, 50, and 50, the second sale at 50 is a zero minus tick.

Here is a series of transaction prices and the corresponding indicators:

50 1/16	Initial sale
50 2/16 +	Plus
50 2/16 +	Zero plus
50 4/16 +	Plus
50 4/16 +	Zero plus
50 3/16 −	Minus
50 3/16 −	Zero minus
50 2/16 −	Minus
50 3/16 +	Plus

Accordingly, to counterbalance selling in the market, which will cause a price drop, the specialist is expected to purchase stock to stabilize the selling trend on downticks. Similarly, to stabilize an uptrend caused by buying, specialist dealer sales activity should be on upticks.

■ THE ROLE OF AUTOMATION AND TELECOMMUNICATION

As a result of increased activity and volume over the years, all exchanges have had to speed up order handling to provide efficient and prompt execution. So the exchanges developed computer-assisted order routing systems, permitting member firms to transmit small orders directly to the specialist post without intervention by the floor broker. These systems therefore enable member firms to use their floor brokers more efficiently to handle larger orders.

To accommodate small round-lot market orders, the NYSE makes use of an automated system known as *Super Designated Order Turnaround* (SUPERDOT). The American Stock Exchange uses a similar system called Post Execution Reporting (PER). SUPERDOT is a computerized, message-switching system connecting subscribing member firms with the trading posts on the exchange floor. Orders can be entered through the system and be received within seconds at the appropriate trading post for immediate execution by the specialist. Bypassing the firm's telephone clerks, the SUPERDOT system eliminates the need for commission house brokers or two-dollar brokers to physically transport orders and execute them at the trading posts. The system thus saves precious time in processing small market orders. Transaction reports are routed back to the originating firm through the same system.

This system also handles odd-lot orders of up to 99 shares, either separately or simultaneously with round-lot orders. Over the years, more and more firms have come to use such systems, and technological enhancements have improved them. Gradually, the systems have been upgraded to accept larger market orders, limit orders, and odd-lot orders. Today, exchanges and their members can guarantee one-price executions up to certain limits on system-generated orders. Telecommunication is also having an effect on exchange floor activities, particularly those of the specialist. Congress saw the need to connect other market centers that traded the same securities as the NYSE or Amex, such as the Boston, Cincinnati, the Chicago, Pacific, and Philadelphia Stock Exchanges, as well as NYSE-listed stocks that are traded also in the OTC market. The latter is referred to as the third market. The intent of Congress was to provide public customers with the best price regardless of the exchange and the OTC market on which a stock is traded. From this need evolved the *Intermarket Trading System* (ITS), a linkage of all exchanges and OTC Markets that trade the same stocks.

While this system certainly benefits public customers by fostering competition, it has its complications. One is that professional market makers in other parts of the country can access the primary market on the floors of the NYSE and Amex, and NYSE and Amex specialists are afforded access to regional markets as well. Another complication is that the floor brokers and specialists on the NYSE or Amex are obligated to comply with additional rules and procedures.

Foremost among the rules is the one that requires *pre-opening notification*, whereby specialists must solicit interest, whether among public customers or principals, from other market centers when the opening price of an ITS stock is expected to exceed agreed-upon guidelines. Not to do so would cause wide variations between the exchanges in dually listed stocks. Other rules prohibit:

■ Trading through and honoring better bids and/or offers that are away from the market.

■ Causing a locked market, either by posting a bid in an ITS security at a price equal to or higher than a published offer on another market center, or by offering it at a price equal to or lower than a published bid on another market center.

The linkage of market centers within the United States has prompted some exchanges to explore international connections and continuous after hours trading. With the demand for increased order flow and volume, longer trading hours, and improved automation through computerization, the NYSE and Amex are continually seeking to tap underused resources and find other ways to expand business.

The SUPERDOT and ITS systems are more fully discussed in Chapter 5.

■ OTHER DUTIES OF THE SPECIALIST

It is fair to say that the specialist is involved, not always directly, but at least indirectly, in just about every kind of transaction on the exchange floor. To manage the crowd properly, specialists must be aware of every trade in the assigned stock. In addition to holding and executing limit and stop orders, and otherwise acting as a contra to the market, specialists are involved in

■ Opening of the market
■ Short sales
■ Stopping stock
■ Block sales
■ Odd-lot trading

OPENING OF THE MARKET

One of the functions of the specialist is to open the market at a price that is as close as possible to the closing price of the previous trading day. This can become somewhat challenging where there are many orders at the opening of the market as a result of late breaking news the prior day. In situations where the orders to sell vastly outnumber the orders to buy at the market opening, the specialist must purchase enough shares in his or her own account to help make the opening price be fair and reasonable. Specialists are not obligated to purchase every offered share. Furthermore, specialists are allowed to open the market at a different price from the last transaction. However, if the opening price vastly differs from the prior day's closing price, a floor governor must give his or her permission to the opening price as a prerequisite.

The NYSE specialist can use the Opening Automated Report Service (OARS) of SUPERDOT. This service receives all orders received *before* opening. It then matches and instantly executes sell and buy orders. Finally, the report service helps the specialist to decide on a price at opening by laying out any imbalances concerning the orders.

SHORT SALES

Specialists may sell stock short when necessary to maintain a fair and orderly market. Specialists must sell stock to meet demand whether they have a long or short position in the stock. But the same rule applies to them as to investors: short sales may be executed only on plus or zero plus ticks. This rule prevents short sellers from driving the stock down, creating public sell interest, and then covering their positions at artificially depressed prices—thus reaping huge profits.

Although short selling seems like a negative force in the marketplace—a downward influence of a stock price—it may actually cause a stock to rise higher. This is called the "cushion" or "short interest" theory. Eventually, short sellers must become buyers to return the stock to the lender; they must re-enter the marketplace to cover their initial short sales and realize their profit or limit their loss. In so doing, they exert demand pressure thereby causing upward influence on the stock price.

STOPPING STOCK

By "stopping stock," specialists guarantee a price on a customer's order, thereby allowing the broker to try to improve on the price without fear of missing the market. Specialists may grant such a privilege (though they are not obligated to do so) under the following conditions:

■ The buy or sell order must be for a public customer's account, not for an exchange member's account.

■ The broker must ask for the stop. The specialist cannot solicit such requests from the broker.

■ The spread must be at least a 2/16 point when the request is made.

■ The specialist must be willing and able to trade as principal if necessary to avoid defaulting on the guarantee.

Once a floor broker obtains a stop grant from the specialist, he or she becomes free to perform his or her duties away from the trading post with confidence that the market will not be missed. The customer is protected in that the guarantee stop price is the worst possible price at which the stock could be executed.

Specialists, by stopping stock on request, contribute to maintenance of a fair, liquid marketplace. Specialists who grant stops and, therefore, act the role of agent for the broker benefit as they receive a floor brokerage fee for this. More importantly, the spread on the quote is narrowed. Note, however, that a specialist cannot grant a stop for an order that is nonpublic, for example, a specialist's order.

Let's look at an example. Assume a broker, entering the trading crowd with a market order to buy 100 shares of Hitek, is informed by the specialist that the quotation is 42 bid to 42 2/16 offered. Ordinarily, the broker is obliged to buy Hitek at 42 2/16 or face the risk of having someone else take it, in which case he or she is guilty of missing the market.

To avoid missing the market, he or she asks the specialist to "stop" 100 shares at 42 2/16, which assures her a price no higher than that. If the specialist agrees to stop the stock, the broker has a chance to acquire it more cheaply by trying to buy the stock at 42 1/16 inside the quote spread without potential financial liability. To improve the price for the customer and to narrow the spread in the quotation, he or she bids 42 1/16 for the 100 shares. The market is now quoted 42 1/16—42 2/16. If another broker brings a market order to sell into the crowd soon afterward, the broker buys 100 shares at 42 1/16 because his or her bid of 42 1/16 is the highest prevailing bid.

If another broker with a buy order arrives and purchases the stock offered at 42 2/16 before the seller appears, then the broker seeking to "stop" the stock is not only "stopped out" and forced to pay the price of 42 2/16, guaranteed by the specialist, but he or she has also not missed the market while trying to do better for his or her customer.

BLOCK SALES

Specialists also act as a conduit for putting together buyers and sellers of large blocks of stock. A block is generally defined as a trade of 10,000 shares, or more. As central figures in the marketplace, they usually are aware of selling and buying interest expressed to them in their specialty stocks. To minimize a large sell order's impact on the price of the stock, the specialist contacts other brokers who have expressed a buy interest. If unable to locate enough interest on the opposite side to handle the whole order, the specialist may negotiate a suitable purchase bid with the seller and buy the balance for his or her own account.

There are about 600 specialists on the floor of the exchange, each assigned to one to five stocks on average. This kind of activity goes on in each of the approximate 3000 trading crowds all day long.

■ ODD-LOT TRADING

An odd lot is an amount of stock smaller than the normal trading unit. The normal trading unit, or "round lot," is 100 shares. However, as previously mentioned, a relatively few inactive stocks have been assigned a trading unit of 10 shares. Any trade of 100 shares is a round lot. A trade of multiple of 100 shares involves more than one round lot. For example, a 1,000-share trade in a stock would be considered to be ten round lots or trading units.

Although most odd-lot orders are processed through the exchange's computerized facilities, they are executed by specialists who are the designated odd-lot dealers in their stocks. In addition to maintaining an orderly round-lot market, specialists also accommodate odd-lot customers by acting as dealers and filling odd-lot orders. Brokerage firms, acting as agents for their customer, transmit the odd-lot orders to the specialists, who execute the orders as principals. Specialists must buy when a customer wants to sell, and sell when a customer wants to buy. And they must do so at the first possible opportunity after receiving the odd-lot order.

The customer pays two types of charges on odd-lot orders. One is the commission charged by the brokerage firm for its services for processing the order. The commission appears as a separate charge item on the customer's confirmation statement. The second charge is known as the "differential," which is paid to the specialist odd-lot dealer for executing the order.

Let's look at an example. Customer Jones enters a market order to buy 50 shares of B&D. Jones' brokerage firm telecommunicates the order directly to the trading post and charges a commission. When the specialist gets the order, he watches for the next sale in B&D, which is known as the "effective sale." If the next B&D trade takes place at, say, 30, the specialist sells Jones 50 shares of B&D, out of his own inventory, at 30 2/16. The 2/16 point tacked on to the effective sale price is the differential and it goes to the specialist as compensation for filling the order. On Jones' confirmation statement, the execution price is

"30 2/16." The differential is not itemized. While the normal differential is 2/16 point, it may vary.

If Jones had put in an odd-lot sell order, the specialist would have deducted a 2/16 point from the effective sale price. Jones' confirmation would have read "29 14/16" and the 2/16-point difference would, again, go to the specialist.

Specialists are not obligated to charge a differential, and often they do not. Usually, no differential is charged to odd-lot orders entered in the following ways:

- At the beginning of the trading day, on the opening transaction in the issue.
- Through the off-the-trading-floor facilities of a few large member organizations.
- Through the NYSE Super Designated Order Turnaround (SUPERDOT) system, if entered as part of a round-lot order.

Neither is the differential charged when a customer enters separate odd-lot orders, all with the same terms and conditions, which add up to a round lot. In such a case, the orders *must* be combined, or bunched, into the trading unit, thereby eliminating the odd-lot differential. Odd-lot orders for separate customers may be bunched as long as the consent of each customer is obtained.

TYPES OF ODD-LOT ORDERS

All of the following may be entered as day or good-till-canceled orders.

Like round-lot market orders, *odd-lot market orders* require execution at the best available price. Because odd-lot orders may not be bid, offered, or used to initiate transactions, they must wait for an effective round-lot execution.

To sell short on a market order, the effective sale must be higher in value than the last round-lot transaction at a different price. For example, with the last sale on CMF at 40 4/16, trades occur at 40 and then 40 2/16. Because the trade at 40 2/16 is at a higher price than that of the previous price of 40, it qualifies as the effective sale for an odd-lot short seller. (This is basically the same requirement as for short sellers of round lots.)

Odd-lot limit orders must all be executed on the first eligible effective sale. Because odd lots are never represented in the quotations, they do not have to wait their turn for execution. And they do not actively compete with one another, as do round-lot orders.

In an *odd-lot limit order to buy*, the effective sale is the first round-lot transaction in that stock that is *below* the limit. When the differential is added to the round-lot price, the execution price may not exceed the customer's maximum price limit. For example, an odd-lot limit order to buy Hitek Industries at 30 must be executed as soon as a round-lot trade in Hitek takes place at 29 14/16 or less. When the 2/16-point differential is added to the execution price of 29 14/16, the odd-lot trade appears on the customer's confirmation as 30, the same limit designated by the customer.

For a *limit order to sell long*, the effective sale is the first round-lot transaction *above* the limit. When the differential is subtracted from the round-lot price, the execution price may not be below the customer's designated minimum price. For example, an odd-lot order to sell Hitek at 31 must be executed as soon as a round-lot transaction takes place at 31 2/16 or higher. When the 2/16-point differential is deducted from the execution price, the odd-lot trade appears on the confirmation as having been executed at a price of 31, as requested.

For a *limit order to sell short*, the effective sale is the first round-lot transaction that is both higher in value than the last different price (that is, an uptick) *and* above the limit stated in the order. Let's say that the last round-lot trade in Hitek was at 30 12/16, a minus tick, and a customer enters an odd-lot limit order to sell short at a price of 30 10/16. If the next round-lot trade in Hitek is at 30 12/16, the broker may not execute the order. The sale is higher than the odd-lot limit but not higher than the last transaction. If the next round-lot trade is at 30 14/16 or higher, the order may be executed because the price is higher than the limit *and* the previous trade. (This rule prevents a short sale from being executed on a downtick, that is, a lower effective sale price.)

The *odd-lot stop order* is a notice addressed to the specialist to buy or sell the odd lot at the market, if and when a round-lot transaction occurs at or through the stop price. The round-lot transaction that activates an odd-lot stop order is called the *electing sale*, and the effective sale is the first transaction following the electing sale. For example, the specialist has an odd-lot stop order to buy Hitek at 29 8/16. The first round-lot transaction at 29 8/16 is the electing (or activating) sale. The stop order is executed, however, on the next round-lot transaction, at *any* price, which becomes the effective sale. The differential is then added to the effective sale price.

The *stop limit order* is treated as normal limit order after the stop is elected, but the next round-lot transaction is not necessarily the effective sale. If the next round-lot transaction is not at least 2/16 point better than the customer's limit, the odd-lot order cannot be executed. If the market moves continuously away from the customer's price, the order may never be executed. As an example, with Hitek at 29 10/16, the specialist has an odd-lot sell stop limit order for 29 12/16 stop, 29 12/16 limit. A round-lot trade at 29 12/16 or higher activates the order by electing the stop. If the market moves higher on the next trade, then the order may be executed. If it backs off to 29 10/16 or lower, the order may not be executed—and it will not be executed as long as the market moves away from the limit in that direction.

The *on-the-quotation order* is for customers who insist that their odd-lot order be executed immediately. The price is based on the existing round-lot quotation, not the transaction, on the floor of the exchange. The customer can buy at the prevailing offering price plus the differential or sell long at the prevailing bid price minus the differential.

The *at-the-close order* is for customers who wish to buy or sell their stock as near the end of the trading day as possible. An at-the-close order to buy or sell is executed not on the last round-lot sale of the day but on the quotation prevailing when the closing bell stops ringing. Customers may buy at the offering price plus the differential, or sell long at the bid price minus the differential. With a *basis price order*, specialists may execute odd-lot orders at "basis" price, which is a fictitious round-lot price, somewhere within the prevailing bid and offering. This price is used when the issue doesn't trade throughout the day, and when the spread between bid and offering is at least two full points. Basis price executions are available only to customers who deal in stock that trades in 100-share units by the exchange, and they must enter their orders at least 30 minutes before the market closes.

■ ASSIGNING SECURITIES TO THE SPECIALIST

Specialists lose assigned stocks because issuing companies merge, acquire one another, or delist their stocks. As a result, the competitive environment among specialist units for new listings is fierce. Whenever a qualified company becomes listed on the NYSE, the Allocation Committee of the exchange decides which specialist unit can best service this newly listed corporate stock.

Of great importance in this decision are floor brokers' evaluations of the specialist unit and their past performance. The exchange requests floor brokers to evaluate specialists' performance quarterly in a number of critical categories, such as the quality of their principal marketmaker activities, service, staffing, and brokerage function. On the basis of the floor brokers' evaluations and disciplinary actions in the specialist units' files, the Allocation Committee assigns a unit to specialize in the stock. While the committee considers other factors, such as the units' capital, manpower, and expertise, the decision is weighted heavily on performance. The better a particular unit's performance, the more likely it is to be selected by the Allocation Committee.

Given the competition among market centers to attract new listings, listed companies have tremendous input into the selection of its specialist unit. The company may be given a list of units that are performing equally well, along with the opportunity to interview them. The persistent fact remains that the only way for a business—and a specialist unit is a business—to survive and grow is to involve itself with new listings.

The specialist system is unique and is used on the Amex and on the regional exchanges across the country. The Chicago Board Options Exchange (CBOE) also employs a market-maker system. Unlike the specialist on the CBOE, members classified as "market makers" are charged with maintaining a fair and orderly options market. (Other exchange employees, called "board brokers," maintain the public order book.) On the floor of the CBOE, screens display the book market and the market maker's market. Through their competitive bids and offers, the best available market is displayed.

Market makers, whose activities must be conducted at least partially in person, may trade in other than their assigned options—unlike specialists, who are restricted to their assigned stocks. As a result, market makers compete among themselves for executions, and the board brokers make sure that executable book orders are satisfied.

The fact is that in any market in which supply and demand determine prices, a moderating influence is needed. In the over-the-counter market, that influence is exerted by the market makers whom we will meet in the next chapter.

■ CONCLUSION

Specialists perform an important integral part of stock exchange trading. Their market maker function of providing a fair and orderly market, and maintaining liquidity, minimum price fluctuations, narrow quote spreads, and stability in market prices is literally the heart of stock exchange market operations in the United States.

THE SECONDARY MARKET
Over-the-Counter Trading

Forty, fifty stories or more above the sidewalks of Manhattan, an open office floor covers the area of half a city block. Inside are paneled and carpeted offices, whose windows command views that extend for miles. Outside these offices are first the assistants' desks and then banks of desks whose main features are computer terminals. Clerks hurry amid the desks, dropping off orders and picking up execution slips.

This is a trading room for a major brokerage firm.

In the middle of the floor, a clerk drops off an order ticket at one of the traders' desks to buy 100 shares of Safeco, Inc.

The trader calls a market maker in Safeco. He obtained the name and telephone number of the market maker from the "pink sheets." Named for their color, these sheets contain an alphabetical list of stocks traded over the counter. They include the names of market-maker brokerage firms in each stock and, of course, the telephone numbers. The pink sheets are published daily.

The trader first attempts to obtain a quote from the market maker, since all trading in every market begins with a quote. The quote consists of the bid, the offer, the size of the bid, and the size of the offer. The bid is the highest purchase price; the offer, the lowest selling price.

"How are you quoting Safeco?" the trader asks, or "What's the market in Safeco?" The inquiry could be as simple as, "How's Safeco?" The market maker on the other end of the phone responds, "Twenty-four and eight-sixteenths bid, twenty-four and twelve-sixteenths offered, five by five."

By the time the trader hangs up, only a few seconds after, he is very likely to have executed the order to buy Safeco over the counter for his firm's customer by negotiating the most favorable price available.

This is how an over-the-counter trade for a non-Nasdaq or Bulletin board stock is executed.

The OTC market has no trading centers, no geographic boundaries. Instead, it consists of hundreds of brokerage firms located throughout the country and doing business by telephone. These are very often the same brokerage firms that underwrote the issues in the primary offering as the selling syndicate, now acting as "market makers" for the stock in the secondary market. That is, they publish their bid-offer quotations and buy or sell the stock for their own account. In short, they "make a market" for the stock. They are willing to buy or sell the stock at their quoted prices and in round lots. Orders of individual investors to buy or sell the stock are usually filled out of a market maker's inventory.

Firms in the OTC market are generally referred to as "broker/dealers," because they can buy and sell securities either as brokers (agents) or as dealers (principals). As *market maker* (or dealer or principal), the firm can sell the customer stock from its own inventory or buy the security from the customer for its own account. As the customer's *agent* (or broker), the firm can buy the stock from or place the stock with another broker/dealer who is a market maker. Whether acting as an agent or principal, broker/dealers must tell their customers in what capacity they acted in filling an order.

When acting as a broker or agent, the firm must disclose to the customer the actual dollar amount of the commission charged.

When trading from the firm's own account, a broker/dealer who fills a customer order directly, as a principal, tries to make a profit on either a markup or markdown. A markup is the difference between what the firm pays for a security and what it charges the customer. Conversely, if the customer is a seller, the markdown is the difference between the firm's bid price and what it actually pays the customer.

Sometimes a broker may receive orders from different customers of the firm for both the buy and sell sides of a transaction. This is called a *riskless transaction,* because the broker/dealer is not subject to any risk but has only to cross the two orders. In such a case, each customer sees only his or her part of the commission, markup or markdown.

The OTC regulatory agency, the NASD, has declared a 5 percent charge guideline applicable to markups and markdowns. Its purpose is to assure that member firms' profits and commissions are fair, equitable, and proportionate to current market prices. The NASD has issued a number of determinations with respect to this guideline:

- The 5 percent is to be used as a guide, not as a rule, in conjunction with the fair and reasonable requirements of the rule.
- A NASD member cannot justify markups on the basis of excessive expenses.
- Current market prices should be used in determining markups.
- Even a markup of 5 percent or less may be considered unfair in some cases.

The key message is that markups and markdowns must not be unfair, regardless of the guideline percentage.

How does a broker/dealer know what is fair? The NASD board believes that, in determining fairness, NASD members and committees should consider the following:

- *Type of security.* Stocks are typically marked up more than bonds.
- *Availability of the security.* An inactive security is harder to buy and sell and therefore might justify a higher markup or markdown.

- *Price of the security.* The lower the price of the security, the higher the percentage of markup or markdown.
- *Size of the transaction.* A relatively small transaction might justify a higher markup or commission.
- *Disclosure.* Merely disclosing an unfair charge to the customer does not make it fair.
- *Pattern of markups.* The percentages of charges should be consistent and justifiable.
- Nature of the member's business. A broker/dealer who provides better service and facilities than competitors might be justified in charging a higher markup or commission.

The 5 percent guideline applies to all securities in the over-the-counter market, including the following:

- Riskless, or simultaneous, transactions in which the NASD member has a buy and sell order for the same security and simply crosses the orders
- Trades from the member's inventory
- Purchases of securities from customers
- Agency trades, in which commissions must be fair in light of all relevant factors
- Proceeds transactions, in which a customer sells securities and uses the proceeds to buy securities

The guideline does not apply to:

- Sales or purchases of new issues
- Transactions that require the delivery of a prospectus or offering circular, such as those for mutual funds
- Sales or purchases of listed securities

With so many securities trading over the counter, broker/dealers typically make markets in many of them. In their role as market makers, broker/dealers may deal with many kinds of customers, depending on the size of their firm. Some are whole-salers who deal only with other dealers in what is often called the "inside market." Some deal only with large institutions, such as pension funds or insurance companies. Some smaller firms buy from wholesalers and sell to individual investors.

The market makers *are*, for all practical purposes, the OTC market. This is the basic difference between exchange and OTC trading. Whereas listed stock transactions take place amid a trading crowd on the floor of an exchange, OTC trades are nego-tiated, trader to trader, over the phone. One is considered an "auction" market, in which bids and offers are made in open outcry, and the other is "negotiated," in which securities are traded one-on-one, on the phone.

■ FOLLOWING AN ORDER BEING EXECUTED OTC

OTC orders enter the firm through the customer's broker, or account executive, who forwards them to the order room. From there, the order in an OTC-traded stock is passed on to the firm's OTC trading desk. There the traders may act in one of two capacities: "as agents" (or brokers) if the firm is not a market maker in the stock, or "as principals" (or dealers) if the stock is in the firm's inventory.

If the firm is a market maker, the trader may simply execute the order "as principal" at the firm's quoted bid or offer. For a buy order from the customer, the trader adds a markup to the price; for a sell order, the firm deducts a markdown from the price. In either case, the size of the markup or markdown is gov-erned by the 5 percent guideline, just explained.

If the firm is not a market maker, the trader has to locate one. On the Nasdaq system, which means the National Association of Securities Dealers Automated Quotations system, it is a simple matter.

As previously mentioned, the Nasdaq system which is described in greater detail in the next chapter, is an electronic communication and trading network with hookups for market makers, registered representatives, and regulators. Market makers can enter their quotations for display on terminals throughout the system.

Three levels of service are available on Nasdaq:

- *Level 1* is used by registered representatives whose terminal screens reflect the highest bids and the lowest offers available for NASD securities.
- *Level 2* is used by retail traders. This service not only provides current quotations, it also identifies market makers and provides for order execution capability within the system.
- *Level 3* is used by market makers. For each security, the system provides current quotes and identifies all market makers. Level three also allows users to enter, delete, or update quotations for securities in which they are making a market. To be an authorized subscriber to level three, a NASD member must meet certain net capital and other qualifications.

More and more trades are being executed by means of computer. The NASD uses the Small Order Execution System (SOES), which executes agency orders for 1,000 shares or less on the current inside market for National Market System stocks. This system frees the Level 3 Nasdaq machines and brokerage firms' computers to transact orders for customers, with market makers participating through the NASD.

Nasdaq has currently about 5,000 stocks in the system. Some of the larger companies that are traded have as many as 40 market makers or more, such as Microsoft and Dell Computer.

If the price from one market maker is not right, it is easy enough for a trader to shop around. If the order is for Dressbarn, for example, the trader keys in the Dressbarn symbol and gets all the quotations—sizes and prices—for this stock. Perhaps Bear Stearns shows a 16 6/16 bid and 16 10/16 offered, 5 by 5. That means Bear Stearns is ready to buy up to

5 round lots at 16 6/16 and/or sell up to 5 round lots at 16 10/16. The quotation shows both the "price" and the "size." At the same time, Merrill shows 16 6/16 bid, 16 8/16 offered 10 by 5. Paine Webber shows 16 4/16 bid, 16 8/16 offered, 15 by 15.

This is why Nasdaq is so successful. It is a computerized, real-time, video display screen "trading crowd," in which the market makers publish their bids and offers (their quotes), with, as always, the forces of supply and demand constantly nudging prices up and down. The execution of the trade occurs at the screen by a flick of the hand.

The National Market System consists of a growing list of stocks for which more information is available than is for other OTC stocks. For most stocks traded over the counter, the newspaper listing shows the name, dividend, volume, bid/asked, and day-to-day price changes. National Market System stocks—approximately 5,000 currently—meet guidelines set by the National Association of Securities Dealers (discussed earlier in this chapter). In addition to the normal information, listings for these stocks also include high and low prices for the previous 52 weeks and high and low prices for the day. Trades in NMS stocks are reported within seconds.

With non-Nasdaq-traded stocks, the trader must call several market makers to obtain the best quote. To know that, he has to make at least two calls. Once he has the best offer, he enters into a quick negotiation with the other trader. This method, called "shopping the street," means that a trader might have to redial a market maker. But what if the quotation has changed in the ten seconds or so that it takes the trader to get back? Shopping the street depends on a number of OTC rules and conventions that provide for this and similar contingencies. Let's look at these before seeing what the trader does next.

While on the phone with the market maker, the trader may obtain one of several types of quotes. *Firm bids* or *firm offers* are prices at which the broker/dealer is committed to buy or sell a stock right away. A firm bid or offer is usually good for the moment that the quote is given, but it may also be firm for a longer period. Also, unless otherwise stated, it is good for one round lot. In other works, the broker/dealer's commitment to buy or sell at the quoted price is limited to 100 shares of stock or 10 bounds at the quoted price.

Broker/dealers can give a firm quote in a number of different ways:

- "The market is 10–10 8/16."
- "It's 10–10 8/16."
- "We can trade it 10–10 8/16."

A firm quote of "10–10 8/16" means that the quoting broker/dealer stands ready either to buy at least 100 shares at $10 a share or to sell at least 100 shares at $10.50 a share.

The prices quoted in the NQB pink sheets are not firm quotes. Firm quotes, sometimes referred to as the "actual market," must be obtained verbally from the market maker or through Nasdaq.

If the broker/dealer gives a "subject" quote, the quote is subject to confirmation; it is not firm. Generally, the broker/dealer has to have more information before making the quote firm. Subject quotes should be expressed as follows: "It's 10–10 8/16 subject." Sometimes the broker/dealer gives a quote with a very wide spread and follows it by the word "workout." A workout quote is not firm. Instead, it provides a range in which the dealer believes a price can be worked out. These quotes are typically used for infrequently traded securities.

Occasionally, a broker/dealer wants to buy or sell but receives no bids or offers. In such cases, the market maker hangs something like a "for sale" sign on the security by advertising the would-be transaction in the National Quotation Bureau sheets. The term "bid wanted" (BW) in the sheets tells other broker/dealers that the stock is for sale and that the advertising market maker is looking for bids. "Offering wanted" (OW) means that the market maker wants to buy the security and is soliciting offers.

■ THE OVER-THE-COUNTER BULLETIN BOARD: OTCBB

In 1990, the NASD brought forth the OTC Bulletin Board, a service whose objective is to provide investors with data concerning non-listed Nasdaq market securities. It is not part of the Nasdaq nor of the Amex. However, it is relevant to this discussion as the OTCBB provide investors with data, such as pricing, of non-Nasdaq listed securities. In addition, like the Nasdaq Stock Market, the OTCBB is regulated by NASD.

The OTCBB service electronically provides for its subscribers real time stock quotes. In essence, it provides Pink Sheets in computerized form for non-Nasdaq securities. However, it is not the same as Pink Sheets. Pink Sheets, overseen by the NQB, or National Quotation Bureau, provides both paper and electronic quotes to broker/dealers.

In addition to listing real time prices, the OTCBB provides volume data and last sale prices. The OTCBB is not, however, an issuer service. Through the OTCBB, market maker participants are able to provide and change stock quotes for which they are making a market. Such quotes include firm, non-firm, and non-priced interest indications. In addition, they can receive other market makers' quoted prices and provide phone numbers at which they may be reached. The OTCBB is accessible via Nasdaq Levels 1, 2, and 3. Level 3 can be utilized to enter and modify quoted prices.

Generally, OTCBB listed stocks are over-the-counter equities of companies not large enough to meet the listing and trading requirements of the Nasdaq Stock Market. In addition, they include stocks not traded nor listed on national securities exchanges. Presently, there are over 6,500 OTCBB stocks, which include Direct Participation Programs (DPPs), American Depository Receipts (ADRs), foreign equity issues, units, and warrants.

Investors should also be aware of EDGAR. EDGAR, which is a database of the SEC for companies that have made filings, is a source of information for investors seeking to obtain data of companies who are listed on the OTCBB.

Variances exist between the Nasdaq Stock Market and the OTCBB. First of all, the OTCBB, unlike the Nasdaq Stock Market, fails to have the following features: minimum listing standards, same rules for market makers, relationships with issuers whose securities are listed, and automated executions for trades; listing and maintenance fees charged to issuers. However, like the Nasdaq, the OTCBB does require certain criteria to be adhered to for maintenance of listing and quotations and also provides electronically real time quotes for U.S. securities. Furthermore, there are rules aimed at protecting customers investing in the markets. Some rules are exclusive to each individual market; others are the same between the two.

The rules which provide safeguards for investors in the Nasdaq Stock Market but not the OTCBB are (1) the limit order display rule, and (2) manning/limit order protection rules.

The limit order display rule concerns situations where a Nasdaq investor has placed a limit order. If the price of the limit order is either the same or better than the market maker's current quotation and there is not immediate execution of the order, the maker is required to display the limit order to the entire market on the trading screen. The effect of this is that displayed to the market are the limit orders with the best prices. The maker could instead, for display, send this order to an ECN or a different market maker.

In addition to the limit order display rule, the manning or limit order protection rules designed to give security to Nasdaq investors mandate that NASD member firms cannot trade ahead of them at the same price.

On the other hand, there are some rules for the OTCBB market, and not the Nasdaq Stock Market, which give investors some degree of protection. These are: (1) SEC risk disclosure rules, and (2) penny stock rules.

SEC risk disclosure rules set forth requirements that the broker/dealers obtain from investing customers at writing. This writing must acknowledge that the investors have a Risk Disclosure Document, which states the meaning of "penny stock" and also some of the risks of penny stock investing.

Under the penny stock rules, broker/dealers must do two things before executing an investor's penny stock order. These are: (1) approve the account of the investor for penny stock, and (2) give the investors important information, including market information.

Rules which give protection to investors of both the Nasdaq Stock Market and the OTCBB are: (1) best execution rule, and (2) firm quote rule.

The best execution rule mandates that reasonable diligence to get the best price possible be used by brokers/dealers when executing a trade for customers. If the stock is an over-the-counter market stock, the broker/dealer must get quotes from at least three dealers. If there are fewer than three dealers available, then quotes must be obtained from all dealers.

Under the firm quote rule, brokers/dealers generally must offer to sell or purchase at a stated price and for, at minimum, their stated size. However, a broker/dealer can make this offer only if he or she has made preparations to trade at the stated price under the terms and conditions stated when the offer is made. Furthermore, under the firm quote rule, a broker/dealer must correctly set forth and specify the details, i.e. nature, concerning quotes that others may obtain. Brokers/dealers must also prepare to handle questions during the business day.

Another difference that existed in the past between the OTCBB and the Nasdaq Stock Market regarded mandatory SEC filings. All companies listed on the Nasdaq Stock Market must comply with certain SEC reporting requirements in addition to the qualitative and quantitative listing standards of the Nasdaq; on the other hand, the companies listed on the OTCBB are required to only file regular financial reports with the SEC.

Recently, the NASD has created a rule which gives it permission to require that all OTCBB companies file updated reports. Under the rule reports must be filed with regulators in banking or insurance, or with the SEC. In January 1999, this rule was approved by the SEC and, by mid-2000, applied to all OTCBB companies. Additionally, with respect to rules affecting the OTCBB and Nasdaq, as of mid-2000, the Nasdaq Stock

Market has authority, granted by the SEC, to activate halts for both quotes and securities trading in certain instances. Situations under which these halts go into effect are as follows. The first situation is where a halt goes into effect because an issuer of an OTCBB security fails to comply with the submission to the NASD of information required by SEC Rule 10b-17 by the deadline date. The second situation is that a halt in the OTCBB goes into effect for a security when such security is also either registered with a regulation authority that is foreign or listed on a foreign market, and such foreign entity also has a halt in effect. Similarly and finally, a halt also goes into effect for an OTCBB security that is a component or derivative of, a security listed on another exchange or the Nasdaq Stock Market, and such other market halts trading in the security.

■ TYPES OF ORDERS

The most common types of order entered by customers in the over-the-counter market are market orders and limit orders. Like its counterpart in an exchange, a market order must be executed as soon as possible and at the best possible price. A limit order specifies the price at which the security must be bought or sold. Limit orders may be entered for the day or be marked good-till-canceled (GTC).

Regardless of the type of order entered, the broker must always attempt to get the best possible price for the customer. Let's see how the trader negotiates that price. When asked, "What's the market in Safeco?" or "How are you quoting Safeco?," the market maker does not know whether the inquiring trader wants to buy or sell. The market maker responds with a quote, that is, his current bid, offer, and size: "Twenty-four and four-sixteenths bid, twenty-four and twelve-sixteenths offered, five by five." This is an abbreviated way of saying "Twenty-four and four-sixteenths bid for five round lots, and twenty-four and twelve-sixteenths asked for five lots on the sell side." Note that the quotation handles both the "size" and the "price." This means that the market maker is willing to *buy* up to 5 round lots at 20 4/16 or *sell* up to 5 round lots at 20 12/16. The size of the bid and offer will vary.

This quotation is what the trader was listening to on the phone.

If the terms get mixed up, thousands of dollars will be spent in error and a fair amount of time will have to be spent on undoing and minimizing the damages. This type of mistake can be one of the most common trading errors made. Traders have to be clear and alert on the phone.

Usually a negotiated trade will occur within the spread. The quote given to the trader in this transaction is 8/16 "wide." The tighter the spread, the better (that is, the more liquid) the market. A tighter spread would be 24 4/16 bid and 24 6/16 offered.

Given the spread of 8/16, the trader might say to the market maker "Twenty-four and eight-sixteenths for one." Now, for the first time, the market maker knows that the trader is buying. It's up to the market maker to either come down with a new offer or stand firm.

If the market maker comes back and says, "Sell one at twenty-four and eight-sixteenths," the market maker has "hit" the broker/dealer's bid. Safeco now has been bought for the customer at 24 8/16.

If the market maker says, "One at twenty-four and ten-sixteenths," a counteroffer has been made. The trader now knows that the market maker will not come down to 24 8/16. Now it's up to the trader either to accept the stock offered at 24 10/16 or, if he feels he can get a better price, to call another market maker.

Let's look at another example. An order to sell 1,000 shares of Panhandle Enterprises is transmitted to the order room, where it is sent to the OTC trading room. A trader telephones a market marker for a quote and obtains a market of "22 8/16, 23, 10 by 5." In other words, the market maker is ready to buy 10 round lots at 22 8/16 or sell 5 lots at 23.

The trader executing the sell order has several options. He can execute the order right away and sell at 22 8/16. He can also try to negotiate within the bid and offer (the spread) by saying something like "Offering ten at twenty-two and twelve-sixteenths." If the market maker takes the offer, the order is executed. Still another option might be to offer to sell 5 at 22 12/16, 3 at 22 14/16, and 2 at 23. If the market maker accepts the offer, the sale is made at "staggered" sizes and prices.

Obviously there is no magic number or formula. Other traders might have handled each of the preceding orders differently. Much depends on traders' expertise as negotiators and their understanding of not only the stock but what the market will bear.

In addition to orders for individual investors, over-the-counter trades may include certain stocks listed on the New York Stock Exchange (or on any other national stock exchange). Again, such trades are called "third-market transactions," that is, OTC trades of an exchange-listed stock.

"Fourth-market transactions" also take place on the over-the-counter market. These trades are made directly between large institutional investors, such as mutual funds, insurance companies, pension funds, and bank trust departments. Broker/dealers are not involved in these trades and obviously no commissions are involved.

■ COMPLIANCE REGULATIONS OF THE NASD

The NASD was organized under the Maloney Act, an amendment to the Securities Exchange Act of 1934. Although established by Congress and supervised by the SEC, the NASD operates not as a government agency but as an independent membership association that sets operating standards to promote commercial honor and integrity. (See Figure 7–1.)

The NASD's power to regulate is based upon its ability to suspend the membership of—or to fine or censure—any broker/dealer operating in an unethical or improper manner. Because only NASD members have the advantage of price concessions, discounts, and similar allowances, the loss of membership privileges all but prevents a firm from competing in the marketplace. In addition, NASD members are permitted to do business domestically only with other members.

To promote the investment banking and securities business.

To standardize principles and practices.

To promote high standards of commercial honor.

To promote the observation of federal and state security laws by members.

To provide a medium through which members may consult with government and other agencies.

To enable members to cooperate with governmental authority in the solution of problems affecting the securities of industry and investors.

To adopt and enforce rules of fair practice.

To promote just and equitable principles of trade for protection of investors.

To promote self-discipline among members.

To investigate and adjust grievances between the public and NASD members, as well as between NASD members.

FIGURE 7-1. OBJECTIVES OF THE NASD

Nonmembers are therefore severely restricted in the business they can do.

Membership in the NASD is open to all properly qualified brokers and dealers whose regular course of business is transacted in any branch of the investment banking or securities business in the United States. All broker/dealers must be registered with the SEC and the state authorities, as required by law, to be eligible for membership in the NASD. By definition, banks are not broker/dealers and are therefore not eligible for NASD membership.

Some broker/dealers may not become members of the NASD if they:

■ Have been suspended or expelled from any regulatory association.

■ Have had their SEC registration revoked or denied.

■ Employ individuals who have been convicted for securities-related crimes or who otherwise do not qualify for registration.

■ NASD RULES OF FAIR PRACTICE

The Rules of Fair Practice are a part of the NASD bylaws designed to promote and enforce the highest ethical conduct in the securities business. The most basic of the rules is Section 1, Article III, which states the fundamental philosophy of the NASD: "a member, in the conduct of his business, shall observe high standards of commercial honor and just and equitable principles of trade."

Following are several rules that directly affect the relationship of NASD member firms with their customers:

- It is a violation of the rules for a member to publish, circulate, or distribute any advertisement, sales literature, or market letter that it knows to contain untrue, false, or misleading statements. Similarly, no material fact or qualification can be omitted from advertising material if the omission causes the material to be misleading. In short, all advertising, sales, and market literature must be fair and in good faith.

- So that all customers may benefit from a free and open market, NASD members must use "reasonable diligence"— that is, after considering all pertinent factors—to make sure that the customer gets the best possible price under prevailing market conditions. The rules also state that a member's obligation to do the best for customers is not fulfilled by channeling business through another broker/dealer, unless using a third party reduces costs to the customer.

- No member may accept a customer's purchase order for any security without first making sure that the customer agrees to receive those securities against payment. On the sell side, no member may sell securities for a customer without being reasonably sure that the customer possesses the securities and will deliver them within five business days. To satisfy the requirement of "reasonable assurance," the broker/dealer or registered representative should note on the order ticket the present location of the securities to be sold.

- When securities are held for a customer by a brokerage firm, they usually are held in "street name" (that is, in the name of the broker/dealer). In these cases, the issuer of the security sends all literature, including reports and proxies, to the brokerage firm, not to the customers. If NASD member firms do not promptly forward such material to customers, their conduct can be regarded as inconsistent with high standards of commercial honor.

■ All recommendations to customers to purchase, sell, or exchange securities must be based on reasonable grounds and be suitable for the individual customers. In all recommendations, the controlling factor is the best interest of the customer. To determine suitability, the registered representative of the member firm is expected to learn about the specific financial condition and needs of each customer. (See Figure 7–2.)

Members should not recommend low-priced, speculative securities if they do not know the customer's other holdings, financial situation, and other relevant information. For example, a low-priced security may be suitable for a wealthy investor with large holdings who understands the risks. The same investment would not be suitable for a person of modest means on a fixed income with no other investments.

Creating excessive activity in a customer's account to generate commission is a violation known as "churning" or "overriding."

Trading in mutual fund shares is a violation of the Rules of Fair Practice. Mutual fund shares are considered long-term investments, and many of them charge a sales commission (or "load") on purchase. They are therefore clearly not trading vehicles, and trading these shares does not benefit the customer.

Members may not establish fictitious accounts to execute trades that would otherwise be prohibited, such as purchases of hot issues.

Members may not execute transactions that are not authorized by the customer.

Members may not use or borrow customers' securities without authorization from the customer.

Registered reps may not conceal transactions from the member firm that employs them.

FIGURE 7–2. VIOLATIONS OF THE SUITABILITY RULE

OTC and exchange trading make up the large, active secondary market that many regard as "the stock market." This market is so visible to so many people—in the daily newspapers and in the TV and radio newscasts—that it is regarded almost as something with a life of its own. "The stock market edged up on heavy trading today." "The stock market recovered from morning losses, making substantial gains before the closing bell." The stock market "did" this or that.

Anyone who stops to think about it, of course, will see that the market really doesn't "do" anything. In fact, it is a very passive thing. If it is anything, it is merely an arena in which two fundamental forces constantly interact: the forces of supply and demand. If someone could analyze how these forces interact so as to predict precisely how they would affect prices in the future, that person could make a great deal of money. That is what stock market analysis and Chapter 12 are all about. Before getting to the subject of analysis, however, we need to see how transactions are "cleared" in the brokerage firm's back office. This is the focus of Chapter 11.

THE NASDAQ
Ongoing Changes

The Nasdaq is the National Association of Securities Dealers Automated Quotation service. In 1990, its official title was changed to the Nasdaq Stock Market. This market was originally formed in 1971 for trading OTC stocks in an automated system.

The Nasdaq Stock Market (or just Nasdaq) is a market competitor that strives in its efforts to bring quality in investing for investors and attract technologically oriented companies.

At present, the Nasdaq Stock Market is the home of most tech and computer stocks. Companies, such as Microsoft and Intel, have settled in the Nasdaq Stock Market whereas a few, such as Hewlett-Packard and International Business Machines (IBM), are traded on exchanges such as the New York Stock Exchange.

In addition, the Nasdaq Stock Market is seeking to globalize and expand its market worldwide.

This chapter shall discuss the nature of the Nasdaq Stock Market, how it functions, and the developments that have taken place within this market.

■ NASD: NATIONAL ASSOCIATION OF SECURITIES DEALERS, INC.

A. The Structure of the Nasd and Its Subsidiaries

The National Association of Securities Dealers, Inc., known as the NASD, is a self-regulator in the securities that has been in

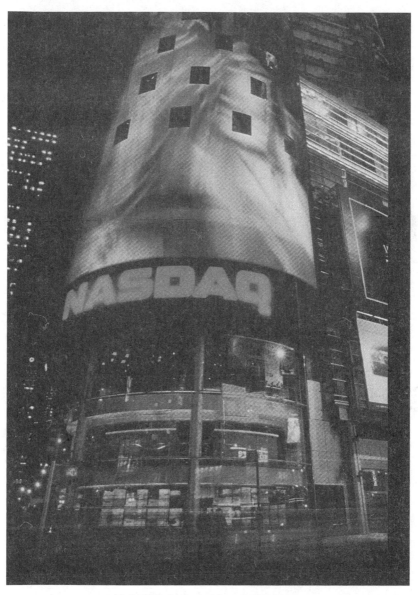

FIGURE 8–1. Nasdaq Photo

existence since 1939. It is the largest self-regulator in the securities industry in the United States. The NASD and its subsidiaries establish and enforce standards of conduct for its members. These standards seek to make the securities business fair and honest for investors. Virtually every securities firm that sells securities to the public is a member of the NASD.

In 1999, there were 33 members on the Board of Governors of the NASD. Represented are staff and industry members. Also represented are public, nonmember individuals.

The NASD is the parent of many organizations, including subsidiaries: (1) the Nasdaq, (2) the American Stock Exchange, Inc. (Amex), and (3) the Nasdaq Stock Market, Inc.; and (4) NASD Regulation, Inc. NASD, as the parent corporation, coordinates, supervises, and evaluates its subsidiaries' plans and policies.

B. NASD REGULATION, INC.

Although operation of the Nasdaq Stock Market and its subsidiary organizations are overseen by their parent NASD, the individuals and brokerage firms who are active within these markets and are members of NASD are regulated by NASD Regulation, Inc.

NASD Regulation, Inc. was formed as a subsidiary of NASD in 1996. Its purpose is to regulate securities firms, of which there are now over 5,500 with over 50,000 branches, and provide protection for investors. It also regulates over 500,000 securities professionals who are registered. Activities of NASD Regulation, Inc., include governing and enforcing rules which deal with qualification requirements of these professionals and firms. It also deals with rules aimed at protecting investors.

■ REQUIREMENTS FOR SECURITIES TO BECOME LISTED ON NASDAQ

The Nasdaq Stock Market includes two different and separate markets: (1) Nasdaq National Market, and (2) the Nasdaq SmallCap Market. Companies that seek to have their shares listed on either of these two markets within the Nasdaq Stock Market must adhere to certain financial requirements to become initially listed and maintain such status. The requirements of each market differ. However, the corporate governance standards are the same.

A. Nasdaq National Market

Currently, there are near 3,800 different corporate common stocks listed on the Nasdaq National Market. It requires that listed companies adhere to the same corporate governance standards as those who are listed on the Nasdaq SmallCap Market.

(1) Initial Listing Requirements

The current Nasdaq National Market Listing Requirements provide three different options under which a company may initially list. These are as follows.

Option # 1: A company seeking to become initially listed within this first option is required to have:

1) $6 million in net tangible assets,
2) $1 million in pretax income in either the latest fiscal year or in two of the last three fiscal years,
3) 1.1 million public float shares,
4) $8 million market value of the public float shares,
5) $5 minimum bid price,
6) 400 round lot shareholders,
7) 3 market makers, and
8) corporate governance.

In addition, for option # 1, there are no rules for market capitalization, total assets, total revenues, and operating history.

Option # 2: A company seeking to become initially listed within this second option is required to have:

1) $18 million in net tangible assets,
2) 1.1 million public float shares,
3) 2 years operating history,

4) $18 million market value of the public float shares,

5) $5 minimum bid price,

6) 400 round lot shareholders,

7) 3 market makers, and

8) corporate governance.

In addition, for option # 2, there are no rules for market capitalization, total assets, total revenues, and pretax income.

Option # 3: A company seeking to become initially listed within this third option is required to have:

1) either $75 million market capitalization, or $75 million total assets and $75 million total revenues,

2) 1.1 million public float shares,

3) $20 million market value of the public float shares,

4) $5 minimum bid price,

5) 400 round lot shareholders,

6) 4 market makers, and

7) corporate governance.

For this third option, there are no rules for net tangible assets, pretax income, and operating history.

(2) CONTINUED LISTING REQUIREMENTS

The following are continued listing requirements for companies who became initially listed under either of the first two options.

1) $4 million net tangible assets,

2) 750,000 public float shares,

3) $5 million market value of public float shares,

4) $1 minimum bid price,

5) 400 round lot shareholders,

6) 2 market makers, and

7) corporate governance.

For continued listing of such companies, there are no requirements for market capitalization, total assets, total revenues, pretax income, and operating history.

The following are continued listing requirements for companies who became initially listed under the third and last option.

1) Either $50 million market capitalization, or $50 million total assets and $50 million total revenues,

2) 1.1 million public float shares,

3) $15 million market value of public float,

4) $5 minimum bid price,

5) 400 round lot shareholders,

6) 4 market makers, and

7) corporate governance.

For continued listing, there are no requirements for these companies with respect to net tangible assets, pretax income, and operating history.

B. THE NASDAQ SMALLCAP MARKET

The Nasdaq SmallCap Market lists over 1,200 issues. The securities of a company listed on the Nasdaq SmallCap Market may grow to eventually qualify to become listed on the Nasdaq National Market. Since amendments to the Nasdaq Stock Market listing requirements approved by the SEC in 1997, the Nasdaq SmallCap Market became subject for the first time to the same corporate governance standards that apply to the Nasdaq National Market.

There is one set of initial listing requirements for the companies seeking to have their securities listed on the Nasdaq SmallCap Market and are as follows.

1) either $4 million in net tangible assets, $50 million market capitalization, or $750,000 net income (net income requirement applies to the latest fiscal year or two of the last three fiscal years),

2) 1 million public float shares,

3) $5 million market value of the public float shares,

4) $4 minimum bid price,

5) 300 round lot shareholders,

6) 3 market makers,

7) one year operating history or, if history is less than a year, then minimum $50 million market capitalization, and

8) corporate governance.

The requirements for continued listing on the Nasdaq SmallCap Market are as follows.

1) either $2 million in net tangible assets, $35 million market capitalization, or $500,000 net income (net income requirement applies to the latest fiscal year or two of the last three fiscal years),

2) 500,000 public float shares,

3) $1 million market value of the public float shares,

4) $1 minimum bid price,

5) 300 round lot shareholders,

6) 2 market makers, and

7) corporate governance.

There is no requirement for operating history for continued listing.

■ NOVEMBER 1998 MERGER WITH THE AMERICAN STOCK EXCHANGE

On November 2, 1998, NASD and the American Stock Exchange (Amex) merged. The end result of this merger was to make the Amex a subsidiary of the NASD, just like Nasdaq is one of NASD'S subsidiaries.

Although this merger occurred, the Amex will continue operations as an individual market separate from the Nasdaq market.

Each of the markets retains its own set of financial requirements for companies to be eligible to list their securities. In June 2000, Nasdaq held a private placement through which it sold Nasdaq shares. The placement was available to companies listed on the Nasdaq, institutional investors, and members of the NASD. In the latter part of 2000, another private placement will be held for more shares in Nasdaq, after which the NASD shall be 25% owners in the Nasdaq. Next year, the investing public may have an opportunity to acquire shares in Nasdaq via an IPO (initial public offering).

■ NASDAQ-100 INDEX TRACKING STOCK (AMEX SYMBOL QQQ)

The Nasdaq-100 Index Tracking Stock began trading on the American Stock Exchange in March 1999. This product is based on the Nasdaq-100 Index. Although it functions as an index fund, it is treated as a stock, traded in the Amex under the ticker symbol QQQ.

QQQ represents Nasdaq-100 Trust ownership. The Nasdaq-100 Trust is a unit investment with a portfolio of stocks that make up the Nasdaq-100 Index. The Nasdaq-100 Trust seeks to produce results that are related to the Nasdaq-100 Index performance. Since its introduction, the Nasdaq-100 Index Tracking Stock has experienced a two-for-one stock split and increases in price and share volume to high levels. For instance, the stock price increased almost 80% in 1999 alone.

■ THE MAJOR NASDAQ STOCK MARKET INDEXES

There are many indexes for investors to choose from which are traded in the Nasdaq Stock Market. Indexes are based on the performance of a particular group of companies, which have some common characteristic, such as industry sector. Indexes of the Nasdaq Stock Market include the Nasdaq Composite, eight industry-specific sub-indexes, Nasdaq National Market

Composite Index, the Nasdaq-100 Index, and Nasdaq Financial-100 Index. Although all are important, the two we shall focus on are the Nasdaq Composite Index and the Nasdaq-100 Index.

A. THE NASDAQ COMPOSITE INDEX

The Nasdaq Composite Index is a very popular, major market index that was introduced in 1971. It is based on the financial success and market valuation of all common stocks, both foreign and domestic, which are listed on the Nasdaq Stock Market. Since its inception, its value has multiplied more than 20 times its original value.

The value of every stock included in the Index has a bearing on the index value. As each stock price varies, the Index will increase or decrease proportionate to the market value of the stock.

Approximately, five thousand companies of various industries stock comprise this Index. The Nasdaq Composite Index is more comprehensive than either the Dow Jones Industrial Average (DJIA) or the S & P 500 indexes. Indeed, it is often utilized as a measure of market movement in the technological sector, because it is comprised of hundreds of technological corporations.

B. THE NASDAQ NATIONAL MARKET INDEX

The Nasdaq National Market Index is similar to the Nasdaq Composite Index. It includes all Nasdaq National Market listed companies that are part of the Nasdaq Composite Index.

C. THE NASDAQ-100 INDEX

The Nasdaq-100 Index was introduced in 1985. It represents one hundred of the biggest Nasdaq, non-financial companies with the greatest growth throughout major industry sectors. All the companies that make up this Index are listed on the Nasdaq National Market. Securities participation requires a company to have a minimum market capitalization of $500 million. In addition, the average trading volume of the companies is a minimum 100,000 shares.

Options based on this Index are traded on the Chicago Board Options Exchange. STRIDES, which are Merrill Lynch's Stock Return Income Debt Securities, are traded on the Amex. These debt securities are related to the Nasdaq-100 Index. Also based upon the Nasdaq-100 Index is the newly developed Nasdaq-100 Index Tracking Stock. As mentioned previously, this tracking stock trades on the Amex under the symbol QQQ.

■ EXPANSION OF NASDAQ WORLDWIDE: GLOBALIZATION OF STOCK TRADING

The Nasdaq Stock Market is expanding into other countries. In June 2000, the National Association of Securities Dealers (NASD), the parent of the Nasdaq Stock Market opened Nasdaq Japan in conjunction with Softbank Corp., a prominent Japanese investor in the Internet. Nasdaq Japan lists the shares of a limited number of companies, and plans to gradually and consistently increase the number of corporations listed on that exchange. Similarly, Nasdaq Canada is a similar effort on behalf of NASD and the Quebec government for a Montreal-based exchange, and will be the next foreign Nasdaq exchange to open. In addition, it is also expected shortly thereafter that a Nasdaq merger or bid to take over the London Stock Exchange (LSE) will occur.

A. NASDAQ INTERNATIONAL, LTD.

The Nasdaq Stock Market, Inc. has a subsidiary located in Europe known as Nasdaq International, Ltd. This subsidiary is a corporation in the U.K. Its focus is on globalization and helping to develop and market to the world services and products of Nasdaq.

Some of the duties of Nasdaq International, Ltd. include working to encourage other markets around the globe to allow multiple market listings of American stocks. In addition, it has the responsibility for listings of companies not in the United States. Also, it is making efforts to encourage foreign businesses to invest in stocks listed on the Nasdaq market.

■ MONITORING THE MARKETS

In order to oversee the market, it is necessary that there be some form of surveillance. The Nasdaq Stock Market relies on the Nasdaq Marketwatch Department and NASD's Market Regulation to monitor the markets.

The Nasdaq MarketWatch Department was formed in 1996 because the Nasdaq Stock Market needed the power to monitor the market, handling issues with real time trade reporting and halting trading when necessary. Before the development of Nasdaq MarketWatch in 1996, these responsibilities were substantially performed by the NASD. The duties of the Nasdaq MarketWatch Department consist of only online, real time surveillance responsibilities separate from those of the Market Regulation Department and includes TradeWatch and StockWatch.

TradeWatch monitors, on a real time basis, trading in the Nasdaq Stock Market. It is responsible for checking overrides in prices and trade reports with errors. In addition, it handles and provides resolutions for issues concerning real time trade reporting.

StockWatch monitors, on a real time basis, issuers in the Nasdaq Stock Market. It is responsible for watching volume and prices of stocks. In addition, StockWatch is concerned with press releases of companies that are listed on the Nasdaq Stock Market. It watches for important news that can result in a halt in trading.

The other body that the Nasdaq Stock Market relies upon for surveillance over the market is Market Regulation of NASD. Market Regulation Department is responsible for automated surveillance over stock trade activity within the Nasdaq Stock Market and Nasdaq Intermarket for trades in securities that are exchange listed by members of the NASD. Its three components are Compliance and Surveillance, Quality of Markets, and Trading and Market Making Examination/Market Integrity. This department strives to provide investors with protection while preserving an equitable marketplace at the Nasdaq Stock

Market. The department also prosecutes violations and imposes sanctions, and works in conjunction with other agencies to enforce laws, such as SEC.

In order to effectively and efficiently monitor the market, Market Regulation utilizes SWAT, which is the StockWatch Automated Tracking System. This is an automated system that profiles, on an individual basis, each security. Data that is used to create stock profiles include news, industry trends, and price and volume data. Furthermore, RADAR, the Research and Data Analysis Repository, has been used by Market Regulation since 1995. It is an advanced technological computer system enabling instant access to information concerning the market available for analysis. Furthermore, Market Regulation provides guidance on rules (SEC and NASD rules) and problem areas to participants in the Nasdaq Stock Market.

■ OTHER MAJOR DEVELOPMENTS WITH THE NASDAQ

A. GENERALLY

Today, the Nasdaq Stock Market, Inc. is the leading American market with respect to the dollar volume and daily shares traded. As far back as 1994, its annual share volume exceeded that of the New York Stock Exchange. It continues to do so today. In fact, the Nasdaq Stock Market has become such a popular choice of investors that, in 1997, it became the first stock market that traded one billion shares within one day. The market capitalization of institutional holdings of companies listed on the Nasdaq National Market has grown to an amount over two trillion dollars.

B. TECHNOLOGICAL DEVELOPMENTS

The Nasdaq Stock Market has made continuing efforts to stay abreast of current technological developments with respect to the stock market.

(1) SMALL ORDER EXECUTION SYSTEM: SOES

In 1985, the Small Order Execution System, known by the acronym "SOES," was created by the NASD. SOES is an automatic, electronic order execution system. Its purpose is to help foster only small public market orders and limit orders executable at a maximum of 1,000 shares.

Under the SOES, market makers are required to buy at the bid price and sell at the asking price. The system obliges them to execute the first order that matches either their asking or bidding price. This automatically happens under this electronic system. Market makers cannot pass over any order at the price and quantity they had quoted. As orders are executed, the SOES system provides confirmations to both parties to the transaction.

The SOES system is beneficial, especially for E-DAT traders and small investors, because it enables them to exit or enter quickly into a stock position, even in times of economic crisis.

(2) NASDAQ WORKSTATION

In 1987, a PC based platform called the Nasdaq Workstation was introduced to benefit traders. It provided speedy, customized services for traders. However, presently the Nasdaq Workstation II, which is more advanced than the Nasdaq Workstation, is being utilized.

(3) ADVANCED COMPUTERIZED EXECUTION SYSTEM: ACES

In 1988, the Nasdaq Stock Market introduced ACES, the Advanced Computerized Execution System SM. Its purpose is to allow market makers to have automatic execution of trades.

(4) AUTOMATED CONFIRMATION TRANSACTION SERVICE: ACTS

In 1989, the Nasdaq Stock Market began implementing the ACT Service, that is, the Automated Confirmation Transaction Service. This is an online reconciliation and matching system useful for trades placed by either telephone or electronic means. (Note that the majority of Nasdaq trades are electronically placed.) The ACT Service is useful to confirm trades, and allows reporting and comparisons of trades within the same day.

Specifically, this is how the system works. Market makers have 90 seconds to report a Nasdaq transaction. Such an order is matched online after both parties have reported the transaction. In the case where only one of the two parties has reported the transaction, the non-reporting party has 20 minutes within execution to respond via acceptance, rejection, or provide its facts of the transaction. Acceptance of the report results in a confirmation. Rejection results in dropping from ACT the transaction.

(5) SELECTNET

In 1990, introduced on the Nasdaq Stock Market was SelectNet. It is a service providing online screen negotiation and execution of trades. SelectNet is an electronic routing system provided by the NASD in addition to the Small Order Execution System (SOES). Its purpose is to execute trades that are greater in quantity than SOES or help facilitate trades at better prices. There is no obligation on the part of market makers to use SelectNet in trading stocks. Furthermore, SelectNet assists makers with electronic communications.

With the SelectNet system, an E-DAT trader can buy and sell like a market maker, that is, sell at the asking price and buy at the bid price. Essentially, the E-DAT trader directly transacts with market makers.

Orders transmitted over SelectNet can only be executed by market makers and have no access to limit order protection. Additionally, all investors wishing to see them can view these orders. Furthermore, orders can be entered into the SelectNet system by all members of the NASD for either themselves or their customers.

(6) NASDAQ WORKSTATION II AND RADAR

Later, in 1995, the Nasdaq Stock Market introduced and implemented both the Nasdaq Workstation II, which is more advanced than Nasdaq Workstation, and RADAR for surveillance purposes.

(7) New SEC Rules

In 1997, the Nasdaq Stock Market began implementation of new rules from the SEC concerning handling orders, especially limit display orders (which are discussed in Chapter 7), and quotations via the quote rule. Under the quote rule, the most competitive price quotations of market makers must be displayed. As a

Nasdaq Workstation II

Setup Order Report Scan MarketMaking InfoServices Tools Supervisory Utilities Help

Sec:	MCIC	Comb	NM10 S1		M C I COMM CP ##
Last:	43 5/16	Q +5/8	01:57 Vol: 3811500	PCL: 42 11/16	OP
HiLo:	43 3/8	42 3/4		PCL:	
Ins:	43 1/4 ■	Q 43 5/16	Q 10 - 10	Ins:	

Your:

Quick Update — up — 1/8 — (h)
○ QuickReport ○ NPRV
◉ QuickOrder ◉ SeNT
Send Clear

p	MLCO	43 1/4	43 3/8	10-10		p	INCA#	43	43 5/16	29-3
p	DLJP	43 3/16	43 9/16	10-10		p	SBSH	43 1/8	43 5/16	10-10
p	OLDE	43 3/16	43 9/16	10-10		p	ISLD#	42 1/2	43 5/16	1-10
p	KINN	43 1/8	43 1/2	10-10		p	DMGL	42 13/16	43 5/16	10-10
p	NITE	43 1/8	43 1/2	10-2		p	BTAB	42 7/8	43 3/8	10-10
p	TSCO	43 1/8	43 5/8	10-10		p	OPCO	42 7/8	43 3/8	10-10
p	MASH	43 1/8	43 3/8	10-12		p	RAJA	42 3/4	43 3/8	5-10
p	CANT	43 1/8	43 1/2	10-10		p	HRZG	42 7/8	43 3/8	2-5
p	SHWDL	43 1/8	43 3/8	10-10		p	JPMS	42 3/4	43 3/8	10-10
p	SBSH	43 1/8	43 5/16	10-10		p	MLCO	43 1/4	43 3/8	10-10
p	GKMC	43 1/8	43 7/16	10-7		p	TNTO#		43 3/8	-50
p	MADF	43 1/16	43 1/2	10-1		p	MASH	43 1/8	43 3/8	10-12
p	BTRD#	43		20		p	SHWDL	43 1/8	43 3/8	10-10
p	JBOC	43	44	3-10		p	GKMC	43 1/8	43 7/16	10-7
p	PRUS	43	43 1/2	10-10		p	SELZ	42 1/2	43 1/2	10-10
p	AGED	43	43 1/2	10-10		p	PERT	42 3/8	43 1/2	10-2
p	FBCO	43	43 1/2	10-10		p	PRUS	43	43 1/2	10-10
p	BEST	43	43 1/2	10-41		p	PWJC	42 3/4	43 1/2	30-10
p	JEFF	43	43 1/2	10-10		p	AGED	43	43 1/2	10-10

Sec:	WCOM	Comb	NM10 S1		WORLDCOM INC ##
Last:	32 1/2	Q +1 1/16	01:57 Vol: 7132000	PCL: 31 7/16	OP
HiLo:	32 1/2	31 11/16		PCL:	
Ins:	32 7/16 ■	Q 32 1/2	Q 10 - 50	Ins:	

Your:

Quick Update — up — 1/8 — dn
○ QuickReport ○ NPRV
◉ QuickOrder ◉ SeNT
Send Clear

p	JOSE	32 7/16	34 13/16	10-10		p	SALB	31 3/4	32 1/2	10-10
p	INCA#	32 7/16	32 1/2	10-50		p	JEFF	32	32 1/2	10-10
p	DLJP	32 3/8	32 3/4	8-10		p	CHGON	31 1/2	32 1/2	10-36
p	HMQTN	32 3/8	32 7/8	10-10		p	UBSS	32	32 1/2	10-10

| 1QkTS | 2TenAct | 3Vol | 4DirReq | 5FrmLst | 6NsdNws | 7Symb | 8NsdPhn |

FIGURE 8–2. Nasdaq Workstation II Screen

result, an investor will be aware of what the best price is that market makers will trade the stock both privately and publicly. This rule will help investors receive a trade execution at the price most desirable in either a private or publicly traded system.

(8) ELECTRONIC COMMUNICATIONS NETWORK AND THE INTERMARKET

In addition to the above, the Nasdaq Stock Market is currently utilizing electronic communication networks (ECNs) in addition to its system of using market maker NASD member firms to participate in trading in the market. ECNs are types of alternative trading systems (ATS) which offer trading opportunities beyond the formal exchanges. ECNs, such as Reuters Instinet, are networks of semi-exchanges that are computerized. Some, such as NexTrade and Archipelago, even offer continuous 24-hour trading of stocks listed on the OTCBB and Nasdaq, an aspect which encourages globalization of the securities market. As ECNs are increasingly being used as an alternative means of trading, many of them have formed partnerships with various financial management companies and brokerages. Some of these ECNS, such as MarketXT, Bloomberg Tradebook, BRUT, REDIBook, Island, and Archipelago, have teamed up as partners with such firms as Bear Sterns, Merrill Lynch, Goldman Sachs, TD Waterhouse, Salomon Smith Barney, and Morgan Stanley Dean Witter, to name a few.

ECNs show one or two side quotations that represent real orders. They allow offers by sellers and buyers to be matched up without the need for a market maker or middleman to make the match. In short, through an ECN, customers can trade directly with other customers. Orders to buy and sell Nasdaq securities via ECNs are orders which are typically placed by subscribers, such as: (1) institutions, or (2) broker/dealers on behalf of the public. Depending on the particular ECN, those allowed accessibility to the trading system varies. For instance, although most ECNs allow orders to be *directly* placed only by broker/dealers and institutions, others also have expanded *direct* access to include the retail market and market makers. Individual retail customers can directly trade on some ECNs, such as Archipelago, Instinet, and, in certain instances, MarketXT. Market makers also have access to some ECNs, such as Instinet, MarketXT, and Island, for example.

ECNs can also be utilized by market makers. When this occurs, ECN is used to search for a matching order. Thereafter, an unmatched order, labeled as an ECN quotation, is sent to and posted on the Nasdaq. Execution of this order can occur either via the ECN or Nasdaq itself.

A common ECN phrase, "top of book," refers to orders with the best-priced sell-offers and buy-bids of a particular stock. All members of the NASD who access SelectNet can look up the top of book prices.

ECNs offer many advantages for traders. First of all, ECNs provide investors with an opportunity to trade before, during, and after the regular trading day. Secondly, ECN subscribers can trade while not having to disclose the entire amount of securities holdings he has. Thirdly, ECNs charge lower costs to execute trades than do the traditional brokerage firms. Furthermore, one can enter orders through an ECN anonymously, a benefit well appreciated by traders of very large stock holdings. Also, ECNs encourage market makers to compete.

If an ECN system meets and fulfills certain rules, then it becomes a "qualified ECN." A qualified ECN is one that is eligible to post quotes on Nasdaq alongside market makers and other ECNs. The rules that an ECN must meet in order to become a qualified ECN are as follows:

(1) be a NASD member;
(2) be a registered broker/dealer;
(3) receive SEC approval as an ATS; and
(4) agree to the contractual terms of Nasdaq with respect to operating the ECN's link into Nasdaq's network.

Currently, many ECNs are taking steps to obtain official recognition by the Securities and Exchange Commission as securities exchanges. Some ECNs have also begun to work in conjunction with one another so that customers will be able to trade after hours. Furthermore, by being connected, the ECNs are attempting to avoid commission costs charged by SelectNet, increase liquidity, and lessen the time it takes to execute orders. With respect to recent developments of Nasdaq with ECNs, the Nasdaq Stock Market, Inc., in June 2000, has made separate agreements with three ECNs in which each shall be linked to the Nasdaq Intermarket.

The Nasdaq Intermarket is market that brings together members of the NASD using Nasdaq technology, proprietary systems, and Intermarket Trading System (ITS) for the quotation and trading of exchange listed securities. These Nasdaq participants are linked to one another and with the ITS through CAES, the Computer Assisted Execution System. This helps with ordering and execution of trades for all securities listed on the exchange. Ordering and execution is accomplished through API, an application programming interface, or NWII, Nasdaq Workstation II. The ITS makes possible a linkage between participants to the national exchanges. It also enables them to obtain listed exchange quotes in cases where it improves the CAES' best consolidated quote.

The ECNs involved in the June 2000 agreement involving the Nasdaq Intermarket include BRUT, MarketXT, and Bloomberg Tradebook. Through these agreements, each ECN shall be posting stock quotes and shall perform execution of trades within the Nasdaq Intermarket. The ECNs will have the opportunity to match orders of their customers both internally and with others participating in the Intermarket. Especially important is the fact that this will be the first time that an ECN can post these orders and trade through a compact, national quote system.

(9) Trading in 1/16's and Decimals

In 1997, the Nasdaq Stock Market received SEC approval to quote in 1/16^{ths} of a dollar for securities whose price trades higher than $10. Also, with this new method of quoting prices, the Nasdaq Stock Market began utilizing new rules in 1997 for order handling, which helped lessen the spreads on prices.

Securities listed on the Nasdaq Stock Market will soon be priced under a decimalization system because the NASD is planning for the conversion to decimal pricing. Implementation will occur in a period starting later in 2000 through the first quarter of 2001.

(10) AFTER HOURS TRADING SERVICES

In addition to its normal trading hours of 9:30 A.M. to 4:30 P.M. EST, the Nasdaq Stock Market offers certain after hours trading services from 4 P.M. to 6:30 P.M., Eastern Standard Time, for any members who are interested. Included in such services are SelectNet, dissemination of quotes, and ACT. The purpose of providing these services after the regular trading day is to help broaden accessibility of the market to investors both locally and globally.

In addition, the Nasdaq Stock Market, Inc., which was the first electronic stock market, continues to update its services with the latest market technological advances available to keep pace with the competition provided by the other stock exchanges. Presently, over half a million computer terminals across the globe have simultaneous access to Nasdaq stock data.

■ CONCLUSION

As you can see, the Nasdaq has undergone many structural and technological changes and developments. These developments have greatly contributed to the success and growth of the Nasdaq both domestically and internationally, not only as an automated stock exchange, but as an indicator of the new technological economy.

INVESTMENT COMPANIES
Closed-End and Open-End Funds—The "Package-Plan" Approach

Mutual funds, which are offered by management investment companies, are portfolios that may consist of any one or a variety of securities, such as stocks and bonds. Management of these funds is performed by either an individual professional or even a group. Mutual funds are subject to certain rules and registration requirements. Inclusive of this are statutory laws that set forth mutual fund requirements; for example, the Investment Company Act of 1940. Also inclusive are regulatory bodies that require registration by mutual funds; for example, the SEC (Securities and Exchange Commission).

We have made the case that investing in stocks is considered almost a necessity for many people. Of the many hurdles to overcome before you can begin investing, the most daunting is selecting the stocks to be purchased. Many investors are fully aware that they should not put all their investment funds into just one stock. If you could somehow know what the single "best" stock was, there would be no problem. Clearly, that is an impossibility.

Assume an investor wishes to diversify and could afford to buy a large selection of securities representing many different industries. He or she might include in his or her *investment portfolio* the securities of older, fairly stable companies, those of newer companies believed to be in a growth phase, income stocks, technology stocks, and venture capital shares. He or she might include in his or her portfolio common stocks, straight preferreds and convertible preferreds, warrants, investment-grade and speculative bonds ("junk" bonds), and other investment instruments. Spreading investments and risk among many different securities is the principle of *diversification.*

Another consideration is the *maintenance* of the portfolio after it is put together. Even if the investor is interested only in the longer term, the investments must be constantly monitored to ensure that they are still in line with his or her overall objectives and the degree of risk that he or she is willing to assume. For example, some poorly performing stocks might have to be weeded out and replaced with others in more progressive industries, or the balance between fixed-income (preferred) and fluctuating-income (common) stocks might have to be altered. An investor needs skill, patience, and time to devote to this activity.

Dividends, if they are not being spent as received, should be reinvested. This has a *compounding* effect, over time, similar to leaving interest in a savings account to earn "interest on interest." This presents other problems: how to invest these relatively small amounts as they are received, and what to invest them in. Many hundreds of thousands of investors have chosen an investment medium that relieves them of many of these anxieties and problems—the *investment company.*

The objective of fund investing is, of course, to reap profits upon a given amount of capital. Individual funds, however, can be structured so as to achieve a particular goal, that is, capital gains and/or income. Funds, which are oriented toward producing capital gains, invest in securities, such as bonds and stocks, for the purpose of producing wealth based upon the increase in the market value of such instruments. On the other hand, funds that are oriented toward producing income focus upon investing which results in a continual stream of dividend and interest income. In addition to these objectives, some funds also focus on such goals as maintenance of principal and preservation of capital.

■ INVESTMENT COMPANIES

There are three types of investment companies that were specified within the Investment Company Act of 1940. These are the face amount certificate, the unit investment trust, and the management company. Each of these three types is briefly set forth as follows.

A. FACE AMOUNT CERTIFICATE COMPANIES

Face amount certificate companies are few and far between. These certificates are contracts in which investors make one or periodic payments, the total of which are less than the face amount the investor receives in return upon maturity.

B. UNIT INVESTMENT TRUSTS

More popular than face amount certificate companies are Unit Investment Trusts (also known as unit trusts or UITs). UITs are securities portfolios that make it possible for investors to have diversity with a smaller investment. UITs are also chosen by individuals whose goal is to produce income.

Each UIT is structured by a management firm. However, UITs are not managed but rather consist of a fixed set of investments with a fixed expiration date. Upon the creation of a UIT, a sponsor sets up the securities for the trust. During the life of the UIT, a trustee, such as a bank, manages the fund, secures the securities, and receives the principal and income.

Popular among investments made by the UIT include municipal debt. Principal from debt invested in by the UIT is distributed to the UIT investors upon maturity, selling, or calling of the debt. However, this principal and any interest earned cannot be reinvested into the same UIT.

Distribution of UIT assets to holders occurs on a specified date. Furthermore, generally preceding liquidation of the UIT is the maturity of all the debt investments which the trustee has invested in.

C. MANAGEMENT COMPANIES

Management companies are comprised of open-end and closed-end funds. These funds have managed portfolios that can vary day to day. The portfolios are diversified. The funds also may reinvest distributions and dividends.

The main type of investment company that this chapter will focus on is the management company and the funds that it can offer.

■ MANAGEMENT COMPANIES: CLOSED-END AND OPEN-END FUNDS

Several thousand *investment companies*, which are management companies, pool the investment funds of many different investors into a single portfolio of securities, with individual investors sharing the risks and returns of the complete "package" of securities, in proportion to their individual holdings. The people managing these investment companies are financial professionals. As such, they are presumably better qualified to choose the specific securities to be invested in, and to constantly monitor these investments, than is the average investor. The general idea is to "leave it to the pros." The professionals will:

- Select the securities to be invested in.
- Buy and sell other securities as they deem appropriate.
- Collect dividends and interest payments.
- Safeguard the securities.
- Arrange for investors either to invest more money in the pool, to cash in some or all of their investment, or to reinvest their dividends and capital gains, if they so choose, in an attempt to compound their investment gains.

These professionals manage many different types of pooled investment funds, with many different investment objectives. The people investing in a given fund will have a similar overall objective—either conservative growth, speculative growth, income, preservation of capital, or a combination of these aims. Furthermore, management companies offer common stock in themselves. However, their difference in pricing is essential.

■ PRICING A CLOSED-END FUND

Some investment companies make a one-time offering of shares, invest the money received in a portfolio of securities, and thenceforth monitor the portfolio, making sales and additional purchases as they see fit. Investors who did not buy shares on the original offering can only purchase them, in the secondary market, from current shareholders. The investment company is not involved in this secondary market trading of its shares. This type of company is known as a *closed-end fund* or *publicly traded fund.*

The financial press regularly publishes the actual "worth" of a single share of each of these funds. It is called the fund's *net asset value per share.* To determine this value, the fund's total assets are added together (the current market value of their entire portfolio) and then the fund's liabilities are subtracted to arrive at *net* asset value. The net asset value is divided by the number of outstanding shares (that is, the shares of the fund itself, *not* the number of shares of other companies that they own for investment purposes). The result is the net asset value per share. This is, at least in theory, the *liquidating value* of a share of the fund: what the owner of a single share would receive, in cash, if the investment company were to be liquidated.

Many of the larger closed-end funds are listed on stock exchanges while some trade over the counter (OTC). After the initial offering, which is at a set price, the funds' shares trade in the open market at prices set by the investing public (that is, by supply and demand). Sometimes the funds trade at a price that is *higher* than their net asset value per share—*premium* prices. More often than not, however, they trade at a price *lower* than their liquidating value—*discount* prices. Secondary market trades are effected just like trades in other stocks, and a buyer can usually expect to pay "standard" commission rates.

■ PRICING AN OPEN-END FUND

Open-end funds called (*mutual* funds) are *initially* offered in the same manner as closed-ends. But the market for mutual funds is dramatically different in that the funds continually offer new shares to interested investors. Mutual funds are essentially a perennial new issue!

How they are sold is also very different. The mutual fund redeems outstanding shares upon request, effectively permitting fund shareholders to "cash in their chips." A mutual fund can be purchased at its offering price (asked price), which is always at least equal to the actual net asset value per share. Unlike closed-end funds, mutual funds are never available at a discount from net asset value. True "no-load" mutual funds do not charge a commission and are thus both bought and sold (redeemed) at their then-current net asset values. Some funds are "loaded" and their offering prices may include a sales charge (the *load*) of up to 8 1/2 percent of the amount invested.

Reading from left to right in Figure 9-1, the various columns indicate:

(1) *The name of the fund.* Notice that the first three funds listed are under their "family" name of AAL Mutual. The second and third fund families (AARP Invst and ABN AMRO Funds) have many different funds each. But then API Gr appears by itself, without a family name, indicating that there is only one fund under supervision by that particular group of organizers.

(2) *The fund's investment objective* (the newspaper listings currently list over two dozen different objectives). This indicates whether the fund is investing for conservative growth, aggressive growth, income, or some other objective (or combination of objectives), or whether it is specialized so as to be invested exclusively in bonds or "small capitalization" stocks. A list of objectives for stock and equity funds are as follows:

(a) index funds, which aim to resemble performance of a particular index, such as the S& P 500 stock index fund that duplicates the performance of the S & P 500 stock index.

(b) sector funds, which focus on specific sectors of the market;

Ranges for investment companies, with daily price data supplied by the National Association of Securities Dealers and performance and cost calculations by Lipper Inc. The NASD requires a mutual fund to have at least 1,000 shareholders or net assets of $25 million before being listed. NAV-Net Asset Value. Detailed explanatory notes appear elsewhere on this page.

NAME	NAV	NET CHG	YTD %RET	NAME	NAV	NET CHG	YTD %RET
AAL Mutual A:				LrgCpGr t	16.62	−0.50	+ 20.5
AggGrth p	8.84	−0.09	NN	LrgCpOpp t	13.25	−0.26	NS
Balance p	12.57	+0.12	+ 2.1	MdCpOpp t	22.40	−0.32	+ 9.9
Bond p	9.50	...	+ 6.4	MidCpGr t	13.59	−0.25	− 0.8
CGrowth p	39.22	+0.67	− 0.8	SelGrth t	27.12	−0.28	+ 10.5
EqInc p	14.88	+0.26	+ 5.2	SmCpGr t	33.86	−0.88	+ 9.5
HiYBdA	6.88		− 5.3	SmCpOpp t	24.78	−0.54	+ 21.1
Intl p	12.49	−0.04	− 16.4	Valu t	41.93	+0.42	− 11.2
MidCap p	18.29	−0.01	+ 17.0	Weing t	25.49	−0.46	− 11.7
MuniBd p	10.78	...	+ 8.4	**AMF Funds:**			
SmCap p	15.20	+0.04	+ 14.0	AdjMtg	9.85	...	+ 5.5
TechStk p	8.31	−0.36	NN	IntMtg	9.33	−0.01	+ 6.4
AAL Mutual B:				ShtUSGv	10.33	−0.01	+ 5.4
Balance t	12.51	+0.12	+ 1.2	USGvMtg	10.28	...	+ 7.2
CGrowth p	38.12	+0.65	− 1.7	**AMIDEX35 p**	17.61	−0.68	+ 23.2
EqInc p	14.86	+0.26	+ 4.3	**AMIDEX35A p**	13.77	−0.52	+ 23.2
HiYBdB p	6.88		− 5.9	**API Gr fp**	13.61	+0.14	− 7.4
Intl p	12.14	−0.04	− 17.2	**ARK Funds:**			
MidCap	17.62	−0.01	+ 16.0	Balanced	16.29	+0.09	+ 2.1
SmCap p	14.75	+0.04	+ 13.0	BalancedA p	16.22	+0.09	+ 2.0
AAL Mutual Inst:				BalancedB	16.20	+0.09	+ 1.4
Bond	9.50	−0.01	+ 6.8	BlChpEqA p	22.25	+0.36	− 0.8
CGrowth	39.28	+0.68	− 0.5	BlChpEqB p	22.01	+0.35	− 1.5
LgColdx	9.64	+0.13	NN	BlChpEqI	22.28	+0.36	− 0.7
AARP Invst:				CapGr	23.62	+0.14	0.0
Balanced	20.61	+0.15	NN	CapGrB p	23.17	+0.13	− 0.6
CapGr	71.05	+0.40	− 2.1	CapGrwthA p	23.40	+0.14	0.0
GNMA	14.61	−0.01	+ 7.1	EmMktEqA p	9.11	−0.04	− 32.7
Global	25.91	+0.13	NN	EqIdxA p	14.28	+0.18	− 4.0
GroInc	27.11	+0.45	NN	EqIdxI	14.31	+0.18	− 3.8
Income	12.28	−0.01	NN	EqInc	12.48	+0.28	+ 10.8
Intl	52.12	+0.09	NN	Income	9.66	−0.01	+ 6.1
MgdMuni	8.73	...	NN	IntlEq t	10.90	+0.01	− 19.9
PthwyCnsv	12.14	+0.06	NN	IntmFixI	9.58	...	+ 5.5
PthwyGro	15.07	+0.15	NN	MidCEq	17.96	+0.02	+ 13.3
S&P500	18.65	+0.25	NN	MDTxF A p	9.73	...	+ 6.8
ShtTmBd	10.43		NN	MDTxFree	9.73	...	+ 6.9
SmCoStk	17.23	+0.03	− 4.2	PATxFBd	9.68	+0.01	+ 7.1
ABN AMRO Funds:				SmallCapA	17.29	+0.12	− 10.1
AsiaTCm	7.02	−0.09	− 35.7	Small CapI	17.45	+0.13	− 10.0
Bal Cm	11.12	+0.10	− 2.9	STBond	9.77	...	+ 4.3
FixIncCm	9.75	...	+ 6.7	STTreasI	9.96	...	+ 4.9
Gwth Cm	17.34	+0.11	+ 0.9	USGvtBd	9.46	−0.01	+ 5.5
IntlEqCm	19.22	−0.05	− 22.1	ValEq	13.62	+0.21	+ 0.3
LatinAm	11.76	+0.14	− 15.8	**AXA Rosenberg:**			
SmCpCm	13.97	−0.08	+ 6.8	IntSmCp	10.74	+0.04	− 1.2
TE FICm	10.23	...	+ 7.5	MktNeut	7.68	+0.05	− 6.3
ValueCm	11.68	+0.36	− 0.9	SSMktNeu	9.97	−0.06	NN
AFBA Five Star Funds:				US SmCp	9.54	+0.07	− 1.3
Balanced	11.46	+0.14	+ 11.2	**Accessor Fd:**			
Equity	15.40	+0.35	+ 18.6	Growth	30.59	−0.15	− 12.7
USA Gbl	16.03	+0.28	+ 10.1	IntEq	15.26	−0.06	− 23.6
AHA Funds:				IntFxIn	11.38	...	+ 6.3
Balan	13.24	+0.20	+ 6.1	Mortg	12.25	−0.01	+ 7.6
DivrEq	22.18	+0.43	+ 4.0	ShtIntFx	11.84	+0.01	+ 5.2
Full	9.82	−0.01	+ 7.9	SmMidCp	21.91	−0.23	− 12.6
Lim	10.18	...	+ 5.8	Value	21.01	+0.55	+ 3.5

FIGURE 9-1. MUTUAL FUND PRICE DATA

(c) international funds, which invest in foreign stocks; similarly, funds focusing on a specific country, range or region of foreign countries (i.e. an entire continent), and emerging or developing markets of foreign countries;

(d) global funds, which are similar to international funds, but invest in a mix of domestic and foreign companies;

(e) equity funds, which focus the production of income from dividends on stocks;

(f) growth funds, which aim at capital growth over a long period of time;

(g) aggressive growth funds, which aim at quick capital growth;

(h) growth and income funds, whose objective is growth and dividend income over a moderate long term period and base investment in large, successful companies;

(i) multifunds, which are arrangements of different mutual funds within a mutual fund type;

(j) specialized funds, which focus on a particular industry or area;

(k) balanced funds, which aim at income and growth on a moderate level; and

(l) asset allocation funds, which are similar to balanced funds; also known as flexible funds.

(3) *The fund's net asset value per share.* This is calculated by "netting out" the fund's assets (subtracting liabilities from assets) and dividing by the number of fund shares outstanding. This is the price a shareholder would receive when *redeeming* (selling) shares of the fund. Occasionally a fund will charge a redemption fee, but most such charges are relatively modest, and they are reduced or eliminated for investors who have held the shares for a fair length of time.

(4) *The day's change in price (the NAV price) from the previous day.*

(5) *How the fund has performed.* The "% Ret YTD" column assumes that all distributions (dividends and capital gains) have been reinvested.

The commissions on loaded funds can be reduced through a number of techniques. Most loaded funds offer reduced sales charges for relatively large orders. For example, a fund might charge 8 1/2 percent for orders under $5,000, but might reduce the sales charge to 7 percent or so for orders between $5,000 and $10,000, with further reductions at $25,000, $50,000, and beyond. These dollar levels are referred to as *breakpoints.*

It is possible, through the use of a *letter of intent*, to be charged one of these reduced commission rates even if you don't purchase the required total dollar amount all at once, but rather in a series of smaller purchases spread over 13 months.

Most funds offer a *withdrawal plan*, a popular feature for retirees. If an investor follows the plan and has achieved a certain dollar amount of the fund, usually $10,000 or more, he can direct the fund to send him a regular monthly or quarterly payment. The fund liquidates just enough of your fund shares to make the requested payment. If you ask for a relatively large amount, and/or if the fund's portfolio does not perform well, you may well exhaust your entire investment. On the other hand, it may be possible to "have your cake and eat it too" if the fund does well with its investment portfolio. Your gains might very well be great enough to replace the amounts of your withdrawals. Withdrawal plans are sometimes described as *self-directed annuities.*

The typical mutual fund holds dozens of different issues. Buying a fund ordinarily provides purchasers with "instant diversification" since they effectively own a great number of different securities wrapped up in a single package. The promoters of the fund will collect all dividends and interest payments and (after deducting expenses) will distribute them or reinvest them in additional fund shares, as the shareowners direct. The fund's managers make all portfolio buy and sell decisions, and they attend to all security-related matters including redemptions and conversions. These are some of the reasons that investing in mutual funds has become so popular. They provide diversification, convenience, and professional management.

Most mutual fund organizations will open an account for those who are making initial investments of as little as $500. Additional investments in any dollar amount of $50 or more may be made at the client's discretion. The fund will hold your shares, freeing you of the responsibility for safeguarding them. There are several thousand different funds to choose from. They are offered with a wide variety of different investment objectives, and different degrees of risk, to suit almost any investment situation. They bring together the assets of many different investors who share a common investment objective.

■ VARIETY OF TYPES OF OPEN-END (MUTUAL) FUNDS FOR BONDS

There are a variety of bond mutual funds that are available on the market. These include:

(1) short-term corporate bond funds, which invest in bonds that mature within five years;

(2) corporate bond funds, which invest in long term corporate bonds that mature in 10 year or longer periods;

(3) convertible bond funds;

(4) high-yield bond funds, which are junk bonds with risk oriented higher rates of return;

(5) GNMA funds, or Government National Mortgage Association—Ginne Mae;

(6) U.S. government bond funds;

(7) municipal bond funds, which are tax free because of their municipal status; and

(8) international bond funds, which focus on government and corporate bonds of foreign countries.

The category of money market funds provides investors with an opportunity to invest their money in a fund that is limited to purchasing short term money market instruments.

■ CONCLUSION

In summary, individuals have a wide variety of investment choices, some of which include fund investing. Funds are particularly helpful to individuals with specific profit objectives and who wish to diversify their portfolio risk through professional management.

STOCK OPTIONS
Multipurpose Instruments

In the world of financial investments, stock options serve a great variety of investment purposes.

Options are basically contracts where the buyer obtains, from the option seller, the right to sell a predetermined amount of stock shares at a preset price. The buyer may exercise this right for a limited and specific time span. Furthermore, options are derivative investment instruments, that is, their worth depends on and are derived from the worth of the underlying stock.

Options are used for leverage, the protection of profits, the prevention or hedging of losses on other investments, and the production of income. Yet, options can be very speculative as well.

Trading options makes it possible for individuals to structure their investment portfolios in such a way that they can modify upwards or downwards the level of risk willing to be taken while simultaneously increasing the opportunity to reap great profits. There are many different approaches to accomplish this objective. Some approaches allow an investor to profit on options during times when the market value of the underlying stock remains constant. Others make money by generating high gains on a low risk investment of a minimal amount of money. This is known as leverage and is the essential foundation of all options trading. The fact that an option will cost less than its underlying stock provides investors with another trade mechanism. This involves different risk and capital considerations apart from the more traditional forms of investment established in the stock market.

Trading options is very attractive to investors as these derivatives provide a multitude of advantages and benefits. As this chapter will demonstrate, options provide the investor with the following advantages. First of all, option trading allows investors to raise income from their stocks within a preset period of time. Secondly, it gives the investors protection over their stock portfolios in the event a downfall occurs in the market. Thirdly, options let investors purchase stock at lower prices at a limited risk. This is due to the fact that the cost of options is much lower than the cost of the underlying stock. Finally, trading options enables investors to gain wealth from the increase or decrease in the market value of a stock even though they do not own the stock or sell it.

■ THE OCC AND THE EXCHANGES THAT OFFER OPTION TRADING

Trading exchange option contracts became available to investors in the market back in 1973 with the opening of the Chicago Board of Options Exchange, more commonly known as CBOE. The CBOE offers to investors a marketplace where only option orders are placed and executed. The CBOE provided liquidity, for the first time, in the trading of options contracts. That is, options contracts could be purchased and sold. In addition, options contracts could be sold (short) and purchased and covered. This liquidity was accomplished by providing for standardization of options contracts and their issuance and guaranty by the Options Clearing Corporation known as the OCC.

Today, besides the CBOE, there are many different exchanges where investors can trade options. These exchanges, which, unlike the CBOE, are not limited to options trading, include such major players as the American Stock Exchange, or AMEX, Pacific Stock Exchange, and Philadelphia Stock Exchange. Until the past few years, the New York Stock Exchange had also participated in the world of options but has since excluded itself and dropped all options trading. All option exchanges are members of the OCC. Again, the purpose of the OCC is to secure and guarantee every option contract that is traded as options on exchange, especially with respect to issuance and pricing of options contracts.

■ OPTIONS: A DEFINITION AND EXPLANATION OF HOW STOCK OPTION CONTRACTS GENERALLY FUNCTION

A. GENERALLY: STOCK OPTIONS

Stock options are contracts or legally binding contracts involving sellers, who are also known as writers, purchasers, and the OCC. These option contracts can be structured as two option types: puts and calls. (There may be a great number of puts and calls outstanding on a single stock, all at the same time.) Underlying an option contract is the common stock of a specific company. Generally speaking, one hundred shares of stock (the basic round lot) are represented by the options contract unless otherwise adjusted.

A put is an options contract in which the purchaser obtains the right to sell, at the strike price, the underlying stock of the option. A call is an options contract in which the seller becomes obligated to sell the underlying stock of the option to the purchaser if the latter exercises the right to buy that stock.

Under an option contract, a buyer pays an amount called the premium to the seller for the right to exercise an option, that is, either to purchase, in the case of a call, or to sell, in the case of a put, the underlying stock of the contract at the exercise or strike price. The contract lasts until an expiration date, after which it can no longer be enforced by the purchaser nor traded on the market. In addition, the option contract is supported by the OCC as it gives assurance that the terms of the contract will be adhered to between seller and buyer. These elements of the option contract are more fully described as follows.

B. THE PRICE OF ENFORCING OPTION RIGHTS: STRIKE OR EXERCISE PRICE

Within a contract between an option buyer and seller is a price called the strike price, which again is also commonly referred to as the exercise price. If an options purchaser exercises his options contract, the strike price is the price at which such exercise shall be carried out.

More specifically, strike or exercise price is the price at which the two individuals and/or entities will exchange the stock that underlies the contract if the purchaser of the option decides to exercise his rights under the contract if the expiration date has not yet come to pass. In other words, the strike price is the "per share" price to have an option exercised, that is, to have the underlying stock bought or sold.

Uniformity and standardization of stock option exercise prices have been established in the marketplace and generally appear within ranges that can vary based upon what the value is of the stock that underlies the option contract. The actual strike prices are established by the stock exchange on which the option trades according to the following parameters.

ILLUSTRATION OF EXERCISE PRICES

Incremental Change of Exercise Prices	Current Market Prices of Stock
2 1/2	$ 5 To $ 25
5	$ 25 To $ 200
10	Above $ 200

According to the above chart, depending upon what the current market value of the stock is, the increments in strike prices will be either 2 1/2, 5, or 10. Therefore, if the market price of the underlying stock per share is valued:

a. from $5 to $25, then the increments in strike price are set at 2 1/2; for example, if the underlying stock is trading at $18 per share, then the exchange will create strike prices at the $15, $17 1/2, and $20 levels.

b. from $25 to $200, then the increments in strike price are set at 5; for example, if the underlying stock is trading at $67 per share, then the exchange will create strike prices at the $60, $65, and $70 levels.

c. above $200, then the increments in strike price are set at 10; for example, if the underlying stock is trading at $222 per share, then the exchange will create strike prices at the $220 and $230 levels.

In addition to the above, keep in mind that in the event the market value of the underlying stock increases or falls to the next incremental change, brand new exercise prices will be established by the exchange.

C. THE EXERCISE OF AN OPTION: THE EXCHANGE OF STOCK

There is no mandatory requirement that a purchaser exercise his option rights. The decision to exercise is purely optional, no pun intended. However, whenever a purchaser does choose to exercise his rights under the option contract, that is, enforce the right to have the seller transfer the stock underlying the contract, the broker-dealer firm representing the seller contacts the current seller of the option with a twofold purpose. The first objective is to make him aware that the purchaser indeed is exercising his option rights. The second goal is to make the seller aware of the assignment to him of the duty, that is, the obligation to carry out the exchange of stock as specified in the contract.

The options seller, according to the following synopsis, will fulfill the assigned duty to exchange stock at the exercise price.

RIGHTS AND OBLIGATIONS UNDER THE OPTION CONTRACT FOR:

Option	Buyers	Seller
Put:	—buyer has the right to *sell* 100 shares of stock at the strike price if he or she exercises the put option	—seller is obligated to *buy* 100 shares of stock at the strike price if he or she is assigned the obligation to purchase the stock upon buyer's exercise
Call:	—buyer has the right to *buy* 100 shares of stock at the strike price if he or she exercises the call option	—seller is obligated to *sell* 100 shares of stock at the strike price if he or she is assigned the obligation to sell the stock upon buyer's exercise

When the exercise and the obligations applicable to the option contract are fulfilled, the buyer and seller have no more duties or rights under the contract as it then ceases to exist.

(1) EXERCISE OF THE OPTION BY THE PURCHASER: AN EXAMPLE

So, for example, if underlying the option contract are one hundred shares of ABC stock that have not been modified for a stock dividend, and the purchaser exercises option rights, then for every contract that is exercised, one hundred shares of ABC stock will be transferred between the parties. Furthermore, the buyer who exercised the option will pay the excrcise price for the stock as originally specified in the option. In this example, if the exercise price is $50, then the exercise will require a payment of $50 × 100 underlying shares of ABC, or $5,000 total per option contract.

D. LIQUIDATING THE OPTIONS POSITIONS

During the period that the option contract is viable, an options contract holder may liquidate his or her options position. This is the liquidity created by the CBOE and the key to the success of the options program, that is, the ability to liquidate your options position. In a case where a purchaser has not yet exercised his option position, either an options purchaser or options seller (writer) holding an open position can sell or cover (repurchase) the contract at its current trading value.

E. DURATION OF THE CONTRACT AND THE EXPIRATION DATE

The life of the options contract is predetermined by the creating exchange. The date at which the contract ceases to have force is known as the expiration date. Options can be exercised and/or traded until and including the expiration date. Once the expiration date comes to pass, the option contract can no longer be exercised or traded. Furthermore, if an option contract is exercised before the expiration date, the contract ceases to exist once such exercise is complete.

There are uniform months at which the options expire for options listed on the exchanges. Furthermore, the expiration date must fall on the third Friday in the month the contract expires. So a January option will expire on the third Friday of January, a February option will expire on the third Friday of February, etc. The exception to this rule applies where a holiday recognized by the market falls on such Friday, in which case the business day immediately prior to the holiday will be deemed the expiration date.

The expiration date is displayed as the month in which the option contract ceases, as apparent within the contract's description. For example, if there are November options in ABC stock, accordingly a November 50 option in ABC will be expressed as ABC Nov 50.

■ TYPES OF OPTION CONTRACTS: PUTS AND CALLS

In the previous section, we discussed the basic general elements that comprise all stock option contracts. These elements are universal and apply to the two basic kinds of stock option contracts: put option and call option contracts. The following sets forth explanations of what both of these types of option contracts are.

A. PUT OPTIONS

Puts, or "put options" as they are otherwise termed, are option contracts that enable the purchasing put option holder to effectively sell his underlying stock at a predetermined price. Put option holders anticipate a decline in the price of the underlying stock. To take advantage of the expected decline in stock, the investor purchases a put option for the right to sell or exercise it, only hopefully, after the stock turndown has occurred. If, however, the value of the underlying stock rises after the put option has been purchased, the losses for the investor are limited and he cannot lose more than the premium price he or she paid for the option.

Generally speaking, the values of the underlying stock and put option contract are related as follows. The put option contract's value rises as the underlying stock's value drops. So the opposite is also true. The value of the put option shall fall as the underlying stock value increases.

Those who engage in put writing, by selling the put and naturally getting paid for it, try to take advantage of their expectation that, after such sale, the value of the underlying stock will rise. If the stock does rise in price, then the put will not be exercised and the put writer profits.

(1) Puts: An Illustration

Here's an example of how an investor's XYZ put positions and how they might be reported:

(1)	(2)	(3)	(4)	(5)	(6)
5	XYZ	April	60	puts	@ 2 1/2

In this case, the customer is long "5 XYZ April 60 puts" at a put price of 2 1/2 per contract.

(1) *The number of puts.* The customer has 5 puts, each of which gives the holder the right to sell 100 shares of XYZ common stock. The person owning these puts would thus have the right to sell 500 shares of XYZ. One put would entitle the holder to sell 100 shares, 2 puts control the sale of 200 shares, and so on.

(2) *The "underlying" stock.* The put holder has the right to sell a total of 500 shares of XYZ *common stock,* the underlying stock. He is not *obligated* to do so, but he *may* sell 500 shares of XYZ if he chooses to.

(3) *The month of expiration.* As mentioned earlier, all options have a limited life, with the longest currently offered options expiring at terms of 3, 6, and 9 months after they are first traded. The vast majority of "listed" options expire in less than one year. This option, an *April* option, will expire on the third Friday in April, the expiration month.

(4) *The strike price.* Also known as the *exercise* price, this is the price at which the put holder can sell [at 60 ($60) per share] in this example.

(5) *The type of option.* In this case, the option is a put.

(6) *The premium*. This is the option's price in the open market, set by supply and demand. The options illustrated were purchased at 2 1/2. Since each option controls the sale (put) of 100 shares of the underlying stock, the option's price must be multiplied by 100. The premium of 2 1/2 thus translates to a total dollar cost (excluding commissions) of $250 per option (2 1/2 × 100), or a total of $1,250 for all 5 puts (5 × $250).

That's what this customer, that is, put option buyer has purchased. But what is he hoping for? How much can he make? How much can he lose?

The purchaser is hoping for XYZ to decline; he is *bearish* on XYZ stock. He thinks it is too highly priced at its current trading market value of $61 a share and that it will drop substantially between January (when he bought the puts) and the third Friday in April when the puts expire. He expects that XYZ common stock will decline.

How much can the purchaser make? How far can any stock decline? That's right, to zero. It's improbable, but at least in theory it could happen. If XYZ stock goes bankrupt, the purchaser will be a very happy person. He can then buy 500 shares of XYZ in the open market—essentially for close to nothing— and then "put" the stock by exercising his option to sell 500 shares at $60 per share. Some unlucky person has to honor that put exercise (the loser is the one who sold the put), and pay $60 a share for all 500 shares. The purchaser will then make the difference between what he bought the shares for—zero—and $30,000, the amount he will receive when he exercises his puts by selling 500 shares at $60 a share. His net profit will be $28,750 [$30,000 - $1,250 (the cost of the put contracts)].

How much can the purchaser lose? The stock might "go the wrong way" (as far as the purchaser is concerned) and *rise* substantially in price to, say, $75 per share and stay at that price until the puts expire. Then it will not be to the purchaser' advantage to buy stock in the open market at $75 a share and sell it through exercising his puts at $60 share. That would give him a large loss. He would certainly be much better off simply *not* exercising the now- worthless put options and letting them expire. In that case, all he loses is the premium of $1,250. It's important to remember that when you buy an option—any option—the most you can lose is what you paid for it, the premium. That's one of the advantages of buying options—the fact that your maximum loss is limited to the price you paid, and never any more.

But what if XYZ did not go all the way down to zero? Suppose it went down to, say, $54? Then the purchaser could buy XYZ at $54 a share and exercise his "60" put, making a profit of 6 points (buying at 54 and selling at 60). The profit of 6 "costs" the purchaser 2 1/2 because that's what he paid for each put. His net profit (excluding commissions) will then be 3 1/2 on each put, for a total of $1,750. That's not bad for an initial investment of only $1,250! It illustrates the tremendous *leverage* that options afford.

This is an illustration. Remember, the put purchaser can simply sell the put contract without buying the underlying stock at $54 per share and still greatly profit by doing so. Later in this chapter, information on pricing options will be provided.

Note: If the purchaser, being bearish on XYZ, had instead sold 500 shares short, his potential loss would have been unlimited! That's one good reason for buying a put, to profit from a downward movement in the price of a stock: your loss is limited rather than unlimited.

B. CALL OPTIONS

Calls, which are synonymous with the phrase, "call options", are option contracts that allow the option holder to purchase from the writer, at the strike price, a security for a predetermined amount of time. If the buyer exercises his call option, then the seller must sell to the buyer the underlying stock at the strike price. The seller is obligated to do this if the exercise demand is made by buyer, even without regard to what market value the underlying stock is currently trading at the time of the exercise.

The trading position of one buying an option, in which case would make the individual a call option holder, is long. On the other hand, the writer or seller of an option has a short account position.

Generally speaking, the call option contract's value will decrease as the underlying stock value also decreases. The opposite is also true, that a call option's value will increase in value as the underlying stock value also increases.

A seller (writer) of a call anticipates that the underlying stock value will fall or remain constant. Call writing can be either covered or uncovered.

Covered call writing is the common form of option writing that attracts both the regular public and institutions. This type of option writing is call option selling against common stock and convertible equivalents. Many institutions and substantial investors sell *(write) covered calls,* that is, they receive premiums for selling calls on the stocks that they own. These premiums are paid by call buyers. If the underlying stock fails to rise above the strike price, the call expires and the seller keeps the premium. The premiums from expired calls provide income in addition to any dividends received. The downside is that, if the underlying stocks sell above the strike prices, the call writer will be "called" upon and will have to surrender the stock at the strike price. Writers of covered calls are in an odd position in that they don't want their stocks to go up until *after* the call options expire! If the calls they write, that is, sell expire unexercised, they will keep the premiums and will perhaps then sell another call for further income.

With respect to uncovered call writing, the writer sells to the buyer the right to purchase stock that the writer does not own. For instance, assume that a call is sold at a premium of $4. The call has a $35 strike price as the underlying stock is trading at $33. Assume that the call writer receives a premium of $400 ($4 × 100 underlying stock shares) for each call option. The writer will gain the $400 premium even if the stock's market value remains below the $35 strike price of the call and the option is worth nothing at its expiration.

Calls: An Illustration

Here's an example of a call position:

(1)	(2)	(3)	(4)	(5)	(6)
1	RFQ	July	35	call	@ 3 1/2

(1) *The number of options held.* One option entitles the holder to buy 100 shares.

(2) *The underlying stock.* In this case, the underlying is RFQ common stock.

(3) *The expiration month.* The option will expire on the third Friday of July.

(4) *The strike price.* The option can be exercised at $35 per share.

(5) *The type of option.* This is a call option.

(6) *The premium.* This is the cost of the option in the open market. A 3 1/2 premium means the option costs $350, which is calculated as follows. The option's price must be multiplied by 100; therefore, a premium of 3 1/2 times 100 equals $350 per option, that is, the total dollar cost (excluding commissions) per call option. In this case since there is only one call option, the total cost for all options is $350.

The holder of the call enjoys the upside profit potential and movement of the stock and, as a result, may either exercise the call or sell it at a profit before the option contract expires. The call option holder is bullish and wants the underlying stock to increase in price. As with a put, the holder's maximum loss is the cost of the option, in this case, $350. There's the leverage: a relatively small cost, upside profit potential, and limited exposure to loss. If RFQ goes up sharply in price, the holder of an RFQ call option will gain substantially more, percentage-wise, than a holder of the stock itself.

Of course, keep in mind that the option will only last until the expiration date, and that the stock must increase in price before the option expires. As a result, timing is more important with an option than it is with outright stock purchases. Another negative feature of call options is that they don't generate income in the form of dividends as do long stock positions.

■ OPTION PREMIUM: THE PRICE OF THE OPTION CONTRACT

Although exercise price is a necessary component of the option contract, another important figure to the contract is the premium, which is the price the buyer pays the seller for the option contract. (Remember that an options purchaser can never lose more than the premium.) It is based upon both time value and intrinsic value. The formula to calculate the option premium is:

Intrinsic Value Plus Time Value = Option Premium

To more fully understand what the option premium is, we shall now explore these underlying value concepts more deeply.

A. Whether the Option Is "In" or "Out" of the Money: The Concept of Intrinsic Value of the Option Contract

The first valuation concept is that of intrinsic value of the option. Intrinsic value is what the actual value of the option would be upon exercise. More plainly stated, intrinsic value is how much the option contract is "in the money". However, where there is no intrinsic value, the option contract is either "at the money" or "out of the money", depending on whether the exercise price and underlying stock prices are equal or not. An option that fails to be "in the money" is one in which there would be a waste for the purchaser to exercise the option.

The intrinsic value or "in the money" amount is determined by finding the variance between the strike and stock prices. If the option is "in the money", then the variance will result in a number that, when multiplied by the standard 100 underlying shares per contract, equals the total intrinsic dollar or actual value of the contract.

(1) Is the Put Option Contract "In the Money"?

Specifically, to calculate the intrinsic value of a put, from the strike price subtract the underlying stock's current per share market price. The excess of the exercise price over the stock's current market price share is the option contract's "in the money" amount. As long as the subtraction results in a positive number, the put option is "in the money". This number, multiplied by 100 underlying shares per contract, equals the total dollar intrinsic value per put contract. However, if after subtracting current market price from the exercise price, if the result is either zero or a negative number, then intrinsic value of the put does not exist. In that case, the put is "at the money" in the case of a resultant zero, or "out of the money" if the resultant is a negative number.

In short, for a put, calculate the following:

Exercise Price

Less: Underlying Stock Current Per Share Market Price

Equals = "In the Money" Amount [or, if negative or zero, "out of" or "at the money"]

If the result is an "in the money" amount, then multiply the following:

"In the Money" Amount × 100 Underlying Shares = Total Dollar Intrinsic Value Per Put

For example, assume that a purchaser buys a put option contract that has a strike price of $115. If the stock's current market value equals $110/share, then the intrinsic value equals 5 ($115 less $110), which is $400 (4 × 100 underlying shares) total "in the money" or intrinsic value amount per put option contract.

If a purchaser, on the other hand, buys a put with an exercise price of $150, and the underlying stock's current market value is also $150/share, then the put has no intrinsic value as the excess of exercise over market value ($150 less $150) is zero, making each put contract "at the money".

Likewise, if the purchaser buys a put with an exercise price of $150, but the market value of the underlying stock is trading at $153 per share, then the put has no intrinsic value as the excess of exercise over market value is a negative 3 ($150 less $153), as each put is "out of the money".

(2) Is the Call Option Contract "In the Money"?

Conversely, to calculate the intrinsic value of a call, from the stock's current market price per share subtract the strike price per share. The excess of the stock's current market per share price over the exercise price per share equals the "in the money" amount. As long as the subtraction results in a positive number, the call option is "in the money". This number, multiplied by 100 underlying shares per contract, equals the total dollar or actual intrinsic value of the call contract. However, if after subtracting the exercise price from the current stock per share market price, the result is either zero or a negative number, then intrinsic value of the call does not exist and the call is "at the money" or "out of the money", respectively.

In short, for a call, calculate the following:

$$\frac{\text{Underlying Stock Current Per Share Market Price}}{\text{Less: Exercise Price}}$$

Equals = "In the Money Amount" [or, if negative or zero, "out of" or "at the money"]

If the result is an "in the money" amount, then multiply the following:

"In the Money" Amount × 100 Underlying Shares = Total Dollar Intrinsic Value Per Call

For example, assume that a buyer purchases a call option contract that has a strike price of $125. If the stock's current per share market value equals $129/share, then the intrinsic value is 4 ($129 less $125), which is $400 (4 × 100 underlying shares) total intrinsic value or "in the money" per call option contract.

If, on the other hand, a buyer purchases a call option contract with a strike price of $90, and the current market value of the underlying stock is also $90 per share, then the call option has no intrinsic value as it is "at the money" at zero ($90 less $90).

Similarly, if a buyer purchases a call with an exercise price of $145, and the underlying stock is trading at $139, then the call option has no intrinsic value as it is "out of the money" by negative 6, that is, the excess of market value over strike price ($139 less $145).

B. The Concept of Time Value of the Option Contract

Once the intrinsic value of the option contract is determined, the second valuation concept of time value can be determined. The forces of supply and demand determine the time value of an option contract. Because options are valued in time, they are referred to as a transfer of volatility representing the market influence of supply and demand on price fluctuations. Also, there are mathematical formulas that have been developed to calculate the theoretical value of an option. One example of such a mathematical formula is the Black-Scholes Option Pricing formula.

Regardless of whether the option contract is a call or put, time value is determined as follows. From the option premium subtract the intrinsic value to arrive at time value. The time value formula is as follows:

Option Premium Less Intrinsic Value = Time Value

Time Value × 100 Underlying Shares = Total Dollar Time Value Per Contract

An example illustrating the calculation of time value is as follows. Assume that the option premium of a call contract is 7 and the intrinsic value is 5. The difference of 2, multiplied by one hundred shares of underlying stock, equals a total dollar time value of $200 per call contract. Puts are also similar to calls in this regard. Assume that the premium of a put is also 7, but the intrinsic value is 2. Then the time value of the put contract is 5 which, multiplied by one hundred shares of underlying stock, represents a total dollar time value of $500 per put contract.

C. RECAP OF TIME VALUE AND INTRINSIC VALUE

As we have shown, the value of the option depends greatly on its relationship to the market price of the underlying stock. (Remember, transfer of volatility.) Is the strike price of the options greater than, equal to, or less than the underlying stock's market price? In one of the prior examples, the put customer was long "5 XYZ April 60 puts" at put contract price of 2.5:

(1)	(2)	(3)	(4)	(5)	(6)
5	XYZ	April	60	puts	@ 2 1/2

The put purchaser was bearish on XYZ, which was then selling at $61 per share. That was the price of the "underlying" when the put purchaser bought his "60" puts. At that price level ($61 per share), it would not, of course be profitable to buy XYZ in the open market and sell at $60 per share by exercising the put. In situations like this—when exercising an option is not profitable—the option is said to be *out of the money*. Out-of-the-money options have no *intrinsic value*. This is illustrated by applying the **put option formula:**

Exercise Price	$60
Less: Underlying Stock	
Current Per Share Market Price	Less $61
Equals = "Out of the Money" Amount	= −1

Because the result is not a positive number but is −1, a negative number, the put option is "out of the money" and thus has no intrinsic value.

Should XYZ decline below the $60 per share strike price, then it would be advantageous to put the stock. With XYZ at a current market value of $54 per share (as in our example), the put holder would make 6 points by exercising the option at $60 per share. Note that he would also profit by selling his put contract. With XYZ at $54 share, the option is *in the money* by 6. This positive value of 6, or $600 actual dollar value, is the option's *intrinsic value*. This intrinsic value is calculated applying the following **formula for put options:**

Exercise Price	$60
Less: Underlying Stock	
Current Per Share Market Price	Less $54
Equals = "In the Money" Amount	= 6

Because the result is a positive 6, the put option is "in the money" and thus has a positive dollar, that is, intrinsic value. This equates to $600 total intrinsic value per put option, calculated by multiplying the 6 times 100 underlying shares of stock, which is demonstrated as follows:

"In the Money" Amount × 100 Underlying Shares
= Total Dollar Intrinsic Value Per Put

6 "In the Money" × 100 Underlying Shares
= $600 Total Intrinsic Value Per Put

Assume that the stock's current market value is $60 per share. **Apply the put formula:**

Exercise Price	$60
Less: Underlying Stock	
Current Per Share Market Price	Less $60
Equals = "At the Money" Amount	= 0

Should XYZ trade at $60 (at the same level as the put strike price), then the option would be trading *at the money*, and again it would have no intrinsic value.

Why would the put purchaser buy an option with no intrinsic value, one that was out of the money? He knew that the option had additional time to run—from the purchase date to third Friday in April when the puts expire—and he believed that during those months the stock would go down below 60. When he purchased the option, with the underlying stock above his put strike price by 1, the option was out of the money by 1. Since the option has no intrinsic value, but was trading in the open market at 2 1/2 (the premium), the entire premium price consisted of *time value*.

To recap, the price of an option consists of two elements: its intrinsic value and its time value. The difference between an option's intrinsic value and its premium (if there is any) is its time value.

For example, CYA is trading at 48.75 while its 50 puts are selling for a premium 3, or $300 per put (3 multiplied by 100 underlying shares per put). Each put is "in the money" by 1.25, or $125 total intrinsic value calculated as follows:

Exercise Price	$50
Less: Underlying Stock Current Per Share Market Price	Less: 48.75
Equals = "At the Money" Amount	= 1.25

Because the result is a positive 1.25 and each put contract is "in the money", perform the following multiplication:

"In the Money" Amount × 100 Underlying Shares
= Total Dollar Intrinsic Value Per Put

1.25 "In the Money" × 100 Underlying Shares
= $1.25 Total Intrinsic Value Per Put

If the put option has a premium of 3 and an intrinsic value of 1.25, the option thus has 1.75 time value calculated as follows:

Option Premium	Less	Intrinsic Value	=	Time Value
3	Less	1.25	=	1.75

Time Value × 100 Underlying Shares = Total Time Value Per
Option

1.75   × 100 Underlying Shares = $175 Total Time Value
Per Put

In this instance the premium consists of two elements: 1.25 intrinsic value and 1.75 time value. You can check the accuracy of these calculations by adding the time value and the intrinsic value. They should add to the premium: 1.25 + 1.75 = 3. It checks out!

Similarly, assume that ABC stock is trading at $75 per share while its 70 calls are selling for a premium of 6, or $600 per call (6 multiplied by 100 underlying shares per call). The calls are "in the money" by 5, or $500 total intrinsic value, calculated as follows:

Underlying Stock Current Per Share Market Price	$75
Less Exercise Price	Less: 70
Equals = "In the Money" Amount	= 5:

"In the Money" Amount × 100 Underlying Shares = Total
Dollar Intrinsic Value Per Call

5 "In the Money" × 100 Underlying Shares = $500 Total Dollar
Intrinsic Value Per Call

If the call option has a premium of 6 and an intrinsic value of 5, the option thus has time value of 1, which is calculated as follows:

Option Premium Less Intrinsic Value   =   Time Value
6   Less   5   =   1

Time Value × 100 Underlying Shares = Total Time Value
Per Option

6   × 100 Underlying Shares = $100 Total Time Value
Per Call

Here, the premium consists of: intrinsic value of 5 and time value of 1. Verify the accuracy of these calculations by adding the time value and the intrinsic value. Added together, the result is the premium of 6, that is, 5+ 1 = 6.

At-the-money and out-of-the-money options have no intrinsic value, and so their premiums consist only of time value. Options are called *wasting assets* because each has a termination, that is, expiration date. As an option's expiration date approaches, its time value will be reduced since people are naturally unwilling to pay "extra" for an option that only has a short time to run. Time values are higher for options that have a long period of time until expiration, and for those whose underlying stocks are volatile (that is, vary greatly in price over time).

■ OPTIONS AS A HEDGING TOOL

Assume that an investor has a profit on his 100 shares of NFW common stock, having purchased them at $32 per share and watched them rise to their present price of $56. He is reluctant to sell, even though he could lock in a capital gain of $24 per share ($56 less $32) because he believes that NFW will continue to rise in price. The investor knows he has a "sure" profit of $24 per share, but he wants an even larger profit. What should this investor do? Should he hold or sell the NFW common stock?

One solution is for the investor to purchase an NFW 55 put as "protection" for his gain. Assuming that NFW 55 puts were trading at 2, the investor would continue to hold his 100 NFW common shares and also own an NFW 55 put, which cost him a total of $200. (Note that while NFW stock is trading on the market at $56 per share, the put is "out of the money" as the excess of $55 exercise price less $56 market value is negative 1.)

The investor is really hoping that his NFW will continue to rise in price and that he will never exercise his put. Buying the put is like buying life insurance; you want to live, but have the policy as protection. In this case, the investor hopes never to use the put and that it will expire unexercised, even though it cost him $200. However, if the trading value of NFW stock drops below the put's exercise price of $55, the investor can exercise his put. In such case, he can sell the underlying NFW stock at the strike price of $55 per share.

While the put is "alive", the investor has guaranteed himself a net profit of $21 on each NFW share (that is, $55 exercise price, for a subtotal of $23, less $32 stock purchase price less $2 put purchase price), or $210 per put (21 × 100 NFW shares underlying each put contract) —until the put expires—even if NFW goes bankrupt!

The following shows how it works step by step:

(1) The investor is long 100 NFW and can extend his gain if it goes even higher. This is what he wants, that is, for NFW to continue to increase in price. The put merely acts as "downside insurance."

(2) If NFW stock falls sharply in price to, say, $38 per share or so, then the investor will exercise his put and sell his stock for $55 per share, which is the strike price of the put.

(3) While the put is alive, the worst the investor can do on the sell side is to sell NFW stock at $55 per share. Thus, at a minimum, he will be to exercise the put at $55 per NFW share, after having bought originally for $32 per share, for a gross profit of $23 and a net profit of $21 per NFW share as the put (his downside insurance policy) cost $2 for each of the 100 NFW shares underlying each put, or $210 per put contract. In other words:

Exercise Price Per Put	$ 55 per NFW stock share
Less: Stock Purchase Price	32
Subtotal	23
Less Put Purchase Price	2
Equals Net Profit per NFW =	$ 21 Net profit per NFW
Upon exercise of put	share, that is $2,100 per put since each contract is for 100 hundred stock shares

(4) As long as the put is alive, the investor still has the opportunity for further profit, but has protected himself against losing most of his accumulated gain.

Most investors buy put options for one of two reasons: because they are bearish on a stock and hope to profit through a decline in the stock's value; or because they want to protect a profit or guard against a large loss.

Conversely, the seller of a put expects the price of a stock to rise and sells the contract for the premium earned. If the stock does increase in price, then the put contract will never be exercised and the put seller will keep his premium as his profit.

■ MISCELLANEOUS OPTION TOPICS:

A. Option Positions

There are different option positions that involve unique combinations of puts and calls.

(1) Straddle Position

A straddle position consists of a put and call for a security with identical features and terms, such as strike (exercise) price and expiration.

(2) Combination or Combo Position

In a combination, the options have expirations and/or exercise (strike) prices which vary. A typical kind of combination position in which there are identical calls with different puts.

B. Spreads

Spreads enable investors to make money on the variance of the prices of two options as the prices of the underlying shares change or remain constant. Although there are many types of spreads, two basic ones are the bull and the horizontal (calendar) spreads.

(1) BULL SPREADS

Bull spreads exist where there are two put or call options for the same underlying stock. The two options have different exercise prices while maintaining identical expirations.

(2) HORIZONTAL SPREADS

Horizontal spreads, also known as calendar spreads, are the inverse of bull spreads. Here, in this case, there are also two options. However, there are different expirations while exercise prices are identical.

■ CONCLUSION

The study of option trading is important for investors to know. It is a fascinating subject. Option trading is very commonplace today and is accessible to investors on a variety of exchanges. With options, investors have the opportunity for leverage of their capital investment, but also the advantage of liquidity. As we have seen, options can also provide investors with a mechanism for hedging against potential losses of a stock investment and insure loss damage control for negative market movement. Options are an exciting component of the marketplace and should be seriously considered by all investors before making significant decisions for growth and preservation of profits. However, before investing in options, they must be studied and understood. Once an option position is established, the investor must keep himself focused on the price of the underlying stock and the volatility of market forces.

For further information on the subject of options, see another book in this series, *How the Options Markets Work.*

THE BACK OFFICES
Following the Long Paper Trail

Whether on an exchange or in the OTC market, a trade can take place in seconds. Yet because the stock market is so highly regulated, and because money and stock are to be transferred, every aspect of a sale has to be documented and checked. As a result, behind every transaction is a long paper trail that winds through many departments in the brokerage firm. Collectively, these departments are known as "operations" or, more colloquially, "the back office." (See Figure 11-1.) Here is where trades are "processed" or "cleared."

On any given trading day, the typical back office processes a huge volume of transactions, day in and day out, with astonishing accuracy. This is particularly remarkable given the detailed nature of regulatory requirements of the stock market.

While the back office has always striven for great accuracy, the volume it could handle took a quantum jump in the late 1960s. Up to that time, stock trades were handled on a "cash-and-carry" basis. Before 11:30 A.M. on the settlement date, usually the fifth business day following the trade (T+5), a messenger, sent by the selling firm, carried the stock certificates to the offices of the purchasing firm. The messenger was given a receipt for the securities and then moved on to the next delivery.

The receiving firm then checked the certificates to make sure that they were the same ones that were purchased and that all of the other paper work was complete. Once it was determined that everything was in order, the purchasing firm "cut a check" to the selling firm and arranged for the securities to be re-registered in the new owner's name.

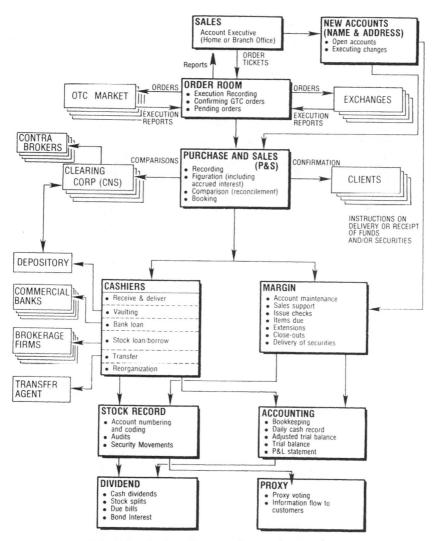

FIGURE 11-1. TYPICAL BACK OFFICE SETUP

Around 2:30 P.M. the same day, the delivering firm's messenger came back, presented the receipt, picked up the check, and returned it to the selling firm. That firm then verified that the check was for the correct sum and deposited it in the bank.

This system left very little time for trades to be verified in detail for accuracy and for errors to be corrected. Also, every trade required separate paper work, messenger pickups, check cutting, and stock re-registrations (or transfers). No matter how hard the brokerage firms' employees worked, there was a limit to how many transactions they could correctly process in a day. This became abundantly clear in the late 1960s when the New York Stock Exchange had to shorten its trading hours and finally take every Wednesday off in an attempt to reduce the number of transactions occurring in a day—to permit the firms to keep up with the paper work. During this time, many firms went out of business due to the financial strain of keeping up with the mountains of paper work created by the cash-and-carry system of settlement.

Clearly, a new system was needed, and one evolved that is still used today.

■ THE DEPOSITORY AND CLEARING HOUSE

The cornerstone of the system is a *securities depository* that acts as a central depot for most firms' securities. In the depository's vaults are most of the actual stock certificates owned by the firms that use the depository's services, and by those firm's clients. Most brokerage houses also maintain a cash balance at their depository. A second key player in the system is SIAC, the Securities Industry Automation Corporation, which is a processing facility jointly owned by the NYSE and ASE that provides a matching comparison service for all trades. For example, brokerage firm A buys 200 XYZ stock at 43 8/16 from firm B. At the end of the trading day, firm A reports to SIAC that it bought 200 XYZ at 43 8/16 from B. Firm B reports that it sold 200 XYZ at 43 8/16 to firm A. SIAC "pairs off," or compares, the trade as reported. If there is no disagreement between the two reports, there is no problem; the trades compare with each side knowing the other.

However, after most of the trades are paired off, usually some trades are left over with no identical countertrade. For example, if firm B reports a purchase of 200 shares of XYZ at 43 6/16 and there is no reported countertrade, most likely one firm or the other made a price error. In this case, both firms are notified that their trades do not match up, that is, there is a "break." It is left to them to resolve the error. Perhaps one firm can prove to the other that it is right by comparing the price at which the transaction occurred to the price at which the stock was trading in the market at the time the order was executed. Or maybe one firm finds that it made a paperwork error and corrects the report it sent back to SIAC. If neither firm can prove it is right, then the two traders of the firms involved may negotiate a settlement between themselves.

It's important to note that the firm, not the client, suffers the loss resulting from an error. To take an example, a firm reports a purchase to a client at 43 6/16 when it actually bought the stock for 43 8/16 The client pays only 43 6/16. The extra eighth of a point is absorbed by the firm.

SIAC therefore verifies that the details of the transaction, as reported by the two parties to it, agree in all respects. SIAC does this for the millions of trades that take place every day in the stock market—and does it with amazing reliability. Each exchange, as well as the OTC market, has its own clearing agency, and compared trades are forwarded to the clearing corporation for settlement. That is, payment and delivery.

With the physical stock certificates in one place, all a selling firm has to do is to electronically instruct the clearing house to transfer the securities from its account at the depository to the purchasing firm's account there. The purchasing firm notifies the clearing house to pay the selling firm from the cash reserve in its account. When the clearing house has instructions from both firms, it verifies that they are correct and then transfers the securities and the money. With this system, no messengers need to be sent and no checks need pass between firms. Let's take a look at an example of how this works. For their respective clients, firm A sells 100 shares of XYZ, Inc. to firm B, and firm B sells 100 shares of XYZ to firm C. The total for firm B does not change because it has both bought and sold 100 shares of XYZ; therefore, these trades can be paired off internally by journal entry at the cashier department. The clearing house simply instructs firm A to deliver 100 shares to firm C to settle all three transactions, thus reducing the number of transfers from three to one. Any price differentials are subtracted from, and/or added to, the firms' cash accounts, and each firm has the securities re-registered in the new owners' names.

Thus the time-consuming, labor-intensive tasks of delivering securities, transferring ownership, and issuing checks for payment can now all be done by means of telecommunicated instructions instantaneously. Only because of the automated depository/clearing house arrangement can brokerage firms process today's incredible daily volumes of transactions.

But these tasks are only part of the paper trail. Many other steps have to be taken before the trade is legally "cleared."

■ THE ORDER DEPARTMENT

The trail begins as soon as a sales representative opens a new account for a client. To do that, the rep has to have a number of forms filled out and sent to the new accounts (or name and address) department. The chief form is the *new account agreement*, which contains information on where the client's statements are to be sent, the client's investment objectives, and financial net worth, usually some information about the client's employer, and/or some credit references. The client who wishes to open a margin account has to sign a *margin account agreement*. To authorize the broker to make the decisions on what to buy and sell, and/or when to buy or sell, without first having to check with the client, the client also has to sign a *discretionary account agreement*. If the client is a corporation, partnership, charity, or any entity other than an individual, still more forms need to be completed.

When all these forms are sent to the new accounts department, the people there check to be sure the forms are completed properly; they store the paper work, and open an electronic file for the client on the firm's computer system. They also make sure that the information is kept up-to-date, changing the file information whenever the client moves, gets a new phone number, changes employer, and so on.

With the account opened, the client is now ready to have the brokerage firm execute trades. Any orders that the client sends or calls in to the account executive are passed on to the order department, often called the order room or wire room, which acts as a "go-between" for the firm's salespeople and its traders. In a small firm, the orders may simply be carried to the order department as they are received.

In a large firm, with offices all over the country, the brokers forward their orders via an electronic mail system, or wire. If a branch office sends an order to the order room via this system, the order quickly prints out in the order room on a teletyper. The order department staff checks the order for obvious errors (missing account numbers, missing office numbers, and the like). Then, because speed is of the essence, it immediately forwards the order (either electronically or via a phone) to the exchange or to the OTC trading department for execution. In the meantime, the order department keeps a copy of the order in its file. When the trade is executed (which may take seconds or months depending on the type of order), the floor clerk or trader then sends back an execution report to the order department.

The people in the order department then record the price on the execution report on the order copy and notify the broker (via the wire system) of the execution and the execution price. The broker, in turn, notifies the client. All this activity, however, serves only to get the trade executed. It is only the beginning of the paper trail.

■ P&S DEPARTMENT

After the order has been filled, the order department personnel notify another department, known as the purchase and sales (P&S) department, whose personnel do basically three things.

1. They "record" the trade—that is, they book it on the firm's master records. Because these records are the basis for later notifying SIAC of which securities have been bought and sold by the firm, accuracy is a must.

2. They do the "figuration," that is, the calculation of all other charges related to the trade. For a purchase order, the initial step in this process is, of course, to determine how much the client owes the firm for buying the stock. For a sell order, the computation is for how much the firm owes the client selling the stock. In addition, however, they compute commissions (added to a buying client's bill and subtracted from a client's sales proceeds), "ticket charges" (processing fees that some firms charge), and any applicable state or federal transfer taxes.

   The P&S department clerks then, *usually on the same day as the trade,* mail the confirmation statement to the client. This statement contains the details of the trade and shows what the client owes the firm or what the firm owes the client.

3. The P&S staff compares the details of the trade, from its firm's point of view, with the P&S department of the contra firm, to be sure that both firms agree. Because of the sheer speed at which orders are executed and the number of trades performed each day, some misunderstandings are inevitable. For example, firm A may think it sold firm B 200 shares of a stock, whereas firm B thinks it bought only 100 shares of the stock from firm A. It's important that these disagreements be discovered, resolved, and corrected prior to settlement day. Otherwise the trade will not settle and a costly error could occur.

Given the average daily volume in today's stock market, confirming each trade with every other firm would be an overwhelming task for any P&S department. So catching most of these disagreements prior to the settlement date is an important responsibility.

When P&S sends the confirmation notice to the client, it also sends a copy of the statement to the cashier department. This area of the back office is sometimes referred to as "the cage" because it is frequently enclosed in a floor-to-ceiling protective enclosure. The reason for the security is that here is where the firm's vault (or "box") is located.

In the cage are personnel with a number of duties:

1. The receive and/or deliver section of the cashiering department takes or makes delivery of stock certificates from customers, other firms, or depositories. The actual deliveries take place at a counterlike window in the cage. When receiving or delivering the certificates, the firm must make sure that they are in negotiable form. That is, the back of the certificate has to be signed by the owner. If a stock has more than one owner (such as a husband and wife), both must sign the certificate just as their names appear on the front of the certificate. Without the appropriate signatures, the securities cannot be delivered to the new owner. If the stock actual physical certificates registered in the customer's name are being held by the broker, clients must sign a separate form (called a "stock power"), which the firm attaches to the certificate.

2. Every time a stock changes hands, it has to undergo "transfer." That is, the existing certificate, which carries the name of the former owner, must be canceled and a new certificate, which reflects the name of the new owner, must be issued. This is the job of the *transfer agent,* usually a commercial bank or other organization outside the brokerage firm. Another outside agency, often a trust company or bank, acts as registrar. Its duty is to keep track of the number of shares or bonds an issuer has in circulation and to maintain the record owner list. It verifies that no more shares are issued than are destroyed, so that the total number of outstanding shares remains constant. (Often, the transfer and register duties are handled by the same bank or agency.) When a firm receives securities that have been sold, it passes them on to the transfer agent so that they can be re-registered in the name of the new owner. If the firm has the

old certificates at a depository, the depository sends them to the transfer agent to be re-registered.

3. When the cashier department gets back the re-registered certificates, it forwards them to the new owner if the client wishes to hold the securities. If not, then the firm holds the stock for the client in the firm's name (or "street" name). In this case, the certificates are placed either in the company's vault, but more likely in the depository.

   Whether held at the depository or in the vault, the certificates must be divided into the two groups: (1) securities that are owned outright by the firm's clients and (2) securities that the firm itself owns or that the firms' clients have borrowed against (that is, margined). By law, securities that are owned outright by the firm's clients must be segregated from the other securities, regardless of whether the certificate is registered in the client's name or in the broker's name. For that reason, these securities are said to be "in seg" (short for segregation).

4. The securities that the firm owns, as well as the margined securities owned by clients, can be lent out by the firm to short sellers to enable them to complete delivery. The short sellers can be clients either of the same brokerage firm or of other firms. The stock loan clerk arranges to lend surplus securities and to borrow, from other firms and sources, the securities that the firm's clients want to sell short.

5. The bank loan section of the cashiering department arranges to borrow money from the firm's commercial banks, either to finance the purchase of securities for the firm's own account and/or to provide funds for margin loans to customers.

Investor Jane Jones has analyzed XYZ stock, selling at $25 per share, and has concluded that its market price will go down over the next few weeks. Given her expectations, she reverses the time-honored dictum to "Buy low, sell high." Instead, she sells high and then hopes to buy low. She does that by selling short.

Jane calls her broker to place an order to sell 100 shares of XYZ short at $25. Again this can only be done in a margin account. The brokerage firm executes the order, selling 100 XYZ to another firm at $25. The difference between a long sale and a short sale, as previously described, is that Jane does not own any shares of XYZ, which she has sold short.

The buyer's brokerage firm delivers $2,500 ($25 x 100 shares), but how does Jane deliver securities to her brokerage firm for delivery to the buyer's firm? The answer is that, because Jane entered an order for a short sale, she indicated to the broker that she does not intend to furnish the certificates. (The reason may be that she does not own them, but it might also be that she owns them and does not want to surrender them as a tax hedge.)

For a short sale, therefore, the cashier department in the seller's brokerage firm borrows 100 shares of XYZ, either from another firm or from one of its other customers, and delivers the borrowed securities to the buyer (in return for the $2,500 pur-

FIGURE 11-2. How Cashiering Handles a Short Sale

chase price). The lender of the stock is paid for the "use" of the stock, and the short seller pays interest on the "margin" loan. (See Figure 11-2.)

Several weeks later, XYZ stock drops to $18 per share—this is as low as Jane thinks the stock will go. She calls her broker again, this time to buy the 100 XYZ at 18, referred to as a short cover. This stock is then used to close out her short position: The 100 shares are paid for by deducting $1,800 ($18 x 100 shares) from the $2,500 proceeds of the short sale, and the certificates are "paid back" to the lender.

Jane's gross profit is $700 (not counting commissions and other expenses)—$2,500 less $1,800. As you can see, a short sale eventually has to be offset by a purchase.

The reorganization (reorg) department handles a number of duties relating to changes in the status or structure of an issuing corporation.

A *redemption call* is the exercise by the issuer of a call privilege on a bond or callable preferred stock. An absolute, or full, call requires all holders to submit their bonds or shares for redemption. In a partial call, only the holders of specific certificate numbers must respond; these certificate numbers are chosen at random by the company, often by electronic means. If the called securities are held in safekeeping and segregated by owner through individual identification methods, reorg simply submits the appropriate certificates to the company and credits the customer with the cash received. But if the securities are segregated in bulk form, the firm must either (1) record the specific certificate numbers for each customer account, or (2) adopt an impartial lottery system.

In conversions, the reorganization department processes requests to convert convertible bonds into the underlying common stock, which sometimes results from a full or partial call in a convertible issue. The issuing company forces the holders to exchange their securities for the common stock or accept the call price, which is typically lower than the market value of the comparable common shares.

In such a typical bond call, the bondholder is advised that, unless some personal action is initiated before the close of business on a given day, (1) the conversion privilege is revoked, (2) accrued interest on the bond ceases, and (3) the holder must accept the redemption price. In the meantime, the reorganization department must contact the beneficial bond owners and solicit instructions from them.

Reorg also handles *exchanges*, of which there are a couple of types. When one class of security is exchanged for another of the same issuer, it is called reorganization. Sometimes, if a corporation is in dire financial straits, its bondholders may accept stocks in exchange for their bonds to avoid prolonged and expensive bankruptcy proceedings. Or such an exchange may result from a decision in bankruptcy court. Either way, the reorg department submits the old certificates on behalf of the owners and accepts the new ones in satisfaction. If the exchange is voluntary, reorg needs a voluntary exchange request, that is, written instructions from the beneficial owner. In an involuntary exchange, no instructions are needed. Another type of exchange results from a merger, which is when one company's stock is exchanged for that of another. In a merger, reorg submits its customers' shares for shares in the surviving company or for shares of a newly organized third company. When the exchange is complete, reorg adjusts the records of the holdings of the firm and its customers. If the merger is an outright acquisition for cash, the customers' accounts are credited with the funds received after the reorganization department submits the old shares and obtains payment.

In a *preemptive rights (subscription privilege) offering,* a corporation offers its existing stockholders the right to purchase additional stock from an upcoming primary offering at a favorable price prior to the offering's effective date. The right to "subscribe" to the offering permits the owner to purchase the new stock at a "discount" price. As such, the right itself has a dollar value and can be bought or sold until its expiration date, after which it is worthless.

The reorg department handles the disposition of the rights for the firm's clients. If the beneficial owner of the rights wants to purchase stock (that is, "exercise" the rights), the reorg staff uses funds from the customer's account and the rights to subscribe to the new offering. If additional rights are needed to satisfy the customer's written instructions, reorg purchases them, either from the issuing company's agent or in the open market. Conversely, if certain customers decide not to subscribe or if they own rights in excess of the amount needed to subscribe for the number of shares they want to buy, the reorganization department disposes of the extra rights before they expire. It may either sell them to the company's agent bank or standby underwriter, or accept someone else's bid in the open market. Either way, the appropriate customer accounts are credited with the net proceeds of that sale.

Reorg provides a similar service for *warrants*, which are also subscription securities to buy the corporation's stock, but whose expiration dates are often years in the future. A few have no expiration dates. When the warrant holder exercises the purchase option, reorg handles the procedure but needs written instructions from the beneficial owner before taking action.

Reorg staff handles all the paper work in a *tender offer*, which is a formal solicitation to induce shareholders to sell their shares. A tender offer can be a successful method for acquiring large amounts of stock. It is often used by corporations or large institutions to effect a merger with, or to gain control of, another "target" company. If not enough shares are submitted for sale, the offering company is denied its objective. Under these circumstances, the offerer usually reserves the right to refuse the purchase of any shares tendered—a valuable privilege not available in open-market transactions. Similarly, if a tender offer produces more than enough shares to satisfy the offerer, the offerer can accept all the shares, any portion of them, or only the amount specified in the proxy statement. If only some of the shares are to be purchased, they can be bought either on a first-come/first-served basis or on a pro-rated basis.

■ MARGIN DEPARTMENT

At the same time that P&S sends a copy of the confirmation to the cashier department, it sends a copy to the margin department. The name of this department, however, is a bit of a misnomer. Staff members do handle all the calculations relating to margin transactions, but they also do a whole lot more. In fact, they are responsible for ensuring that *all* the firm's accounts—margin or other types—meet all the financial requirements of the various regulatory bodies.

Before listing their other duties, however, let's see how a margin account works. Customers may buy stocks in two types of accounts. In a *cash* account, they pay for the securities in full no later than the settlement date. For example, a client buys 100 shares of ZAP at 42. The market value of the securities is therefore $4,200 (100 shares of ZAP x $42). (Ignore commission and other expenses.) The client pays for the purchase in full, and the equity in the account is therefore $4,200. If ZAP rises to $60 per share, the market value becomes $6,000 (100 ZAP x $60), and the client's equity becomes $6,000.

In a *margin* account, the customer puts up a percentage of the sale price, and the brokerage firm puts up the rest. The cash that the client places into the account is the "equity," and the brokerage's part is called the "margin" or "debit balance," which is just another name for loan. The firm borrows the margin amount from a commercial bank at one rate and lends it to the client at a higher rate. (The customer pays an interest charge.) The firm keeps the purchased stock in its vault as collateral for both loans: the one to the customer and the one from the bank.

How much cash does the client have to pay to buy stock on margin? The percentage is determined by the Federal Reserve Board in its Regulation T. (Although Fed writes the regulation, the NYSE and NASD enforce it.) "Reg T" currently requires customers to initially put up at least 50 percent of the purchase price. The Fed has the authority to change the requirement. For example, a customer who wants to purchase $10,000 worth of stock on margin must put $5,000 (50 percent of $10,000) into the account. The brokerage firm lends the customer the other $5,000. Disregarding, for the sake of simplicity, commissions and other charges, this account now looks like this:

Current market value	$10,000	(100 shares x $10)
Less: Debit balance	$5,000	
Equity	$5,000	

As we know, however, stock prices generally do not remain the same for very long. Let's assume that the market price of ZAP rises to $12 per share. In that case, the account looks like this:

Current market value	$12,000	(100 shares × $12)
Less: Debit balance	$5,000	
Equity	$7,000	

Because the market value of the stock rose, the client's equity increased. There is no question that the client's account meets the 50 percent requirement: $7,000 is greater than the initial $5,000 equity (50 percent of $10,000). The account is said to have "excess equity" of $2,000 ($7,000 less the initial requirement of $5,000).

But suppose the market value of ZAP declined to $8 per share. Now the account looks like this:

Current market value	$8,000	(100 shares × $8)
Less: Debit balance	$5,000	
Equity	$3,000	

Now the equity ($3,000) is considerably less than the 50 percent requirement of $5,000 (50 percent of $10,000). As you can see, equity decreases with market value. But that's all right because the 50 percent requirement no longer applies; it is only an *initial requirement*.

The current market value of a margined stock may drop somewhat without the firm having to "call" the client for additional money. In fact, the market value may decline without a "margin call" until the equity is less than one-third of the debit balance as established by the brokerage firm. This is called the "maintenance" requirement. In the example, the equity is $3,000 and the debit balance, $5,000. This account is still adequately margined. If the market value drops to, say, $6.50, then the account is in need of more money:

Current market value	$6,500	(100 shares × $6.50)
Less: Debit balance	$5,000	
Equity	$1,500	

Equity is only $1,500—less than twenty-five percent of the $6,500 current market value. When this happens, the brokerage firm issues a "maintenance" or "margin" call. The call would be for at least another $125.00 enough to bring the equity up to $1,625, which is twenty-five percent of $6,500. If the market value drops again, another call would go out.

Again the minimum maintenance requirement established by the NYSE is 25 percent. If an account of position equity is less than one quarter of the current market value, the firm must issue a mandatory call to bring the account into compliance.

Note: While the Fed sets the initial requirement of 50 percent (which is subject to change), the exchanges and other regulatory bodies are allowed to—and do so—set higher requirements, both for initial and maintenance margin. The brokerage firms themselves often set even higher requirements for the sake of self-protection. Just as customers have to deposit "call" money if the stock's market price goes down, they are entitled to use any excess equity in the account if the price goes up. For example, when the price of ZAP rose to $12, the account had excess equity of $2,000. The customer may withdraw that money or apply it toward the purchase of more stock.

Let's say the customer wants to buy ABC stock, on margin, with that $2,000. How much stock can the customer buy? That is, what is the "buying power" of the excess equity? To answer that question, you need a simple formula:

Buying power	= Excess equity ÷ Margin rate
	= $2,000 ÷ 0.50
	= $4,000

This customer can buy up to $4,000 worth of ABC, currently at $40 per share, with the excess equity ($2,000) on a loan from the brokerage firm ($2,000). If both ZAP and ABC increase enough in value, whatever excess equity develops can be used to purchase still more stock. As you can see, buying on margin is an excellent leverage technique—a way of controlling as much stock as possible with the dollars available for investment. As long as stock prices keep rising, as in a bull market, the leveraging of excess equity can go on forever. The opposite is true when prices decline. As the current market value of the stocks drops, so does equity. As price declines continue, more and more margin calls go out, and stock owners have to decide whether to keep meeting those calls or just to sell some of the stock and take their losses. In a bear market, therefore, two things happen: margin calls and sell-offs increase in frequency. The sharper the drop in price, the faster the calls and sell-offs.

In addition to supervising cash and margin accounts, the margin staff:

■ Instructs the cage to issue checks or to deliver securities
■ Notifies account executives of "items due," such as cash or securities due from clients
■ Files for extensions on payment of margin calls
■ Closes out positions when necessary

■ STOCK RECORD DEPARTMENT

During the course of trading each day, the status of the securities under the firm's care changes constantly. Certificates arrive from and go out to customers and other brokers. Others go to the transfer agent, and still others come back. Book-entry changes of ownership occur, even though the certificates do not change hands. Separate logs of activity are maintained in the dividend, proxy, and reorg departments, but some kind of central control and reference source is needed.

The stock record department keeps track of all the securities for which the firm is responsible (bonds too, despite the department's name). For financial and regulatory reasons, the individual record of each issue must be unquestionably current and accurate.

The position lists used by the dividend, proxy, and reorganization departments are a part of the records that are prepared and maintained by the stock record department. This part of operations serves as a control and reference source for monitoring securities under the brokerage firm's jurisdiction. An individual record is maintained for each issue. The stock record ledger shows the following:

- Name of the security
- Owner of the security
- Location of the certificate

In terms of location, the stock record also has to identify whether that security is in one of the following:

- Safekeeping (the "box")
- Segregation
- Pledged in a loan arrangement at a bank
- Pledged in a loan to another broker/dealer
- In re-registration proceedings at the transfer agent
- In transit to the customer's agent bank or broker versus payment
- In fail-to-receive status from a contrabroker/dealer or customer

Throughout all the changes within a given day, the stock record has to remain balanced. A *break* in the record indicates that a mistake has been made. Given the amount of activity surrounding this document, errors must be corrected immediately—or they might never be corrected at all.

To ensure that record books are kept to a minimum size and corrected as soon as possible, the stock record department issues a daily report and a weekly report. The *daily stock record* reports the movement of all securities involved in any kind of movement: sale, purchase, transfer into or out of the vault, received from a customer, and so on. The *weekly stock record* is a balance sheet of all securities under the supervision of the firm, whether or not they were involved in a transaction the preceding week. Both of these reports must balance—like a balance sheet. Stock may not be removed from a part of the record without being accounted for in some way or another.

■ ACCOUNTING DEPARTMENT

The accounting department in a brokerage firm performs all the tasks that it would in any other type of company. However, in addition to its quarterly and annual reports to stockholders, the accounting department also issues special reports for regulatory bodies such as the SEC or NASD. Sometimes the regulatory authority calls for a report as the result of a special audit.

Other reports are generated periodically, such as the Financial and Operational Combined Uniform Single (FOCUS) Report. This statement gives regulators vital information about the financial health of the brokerage firm, because it demonstrates the firm's financial ability to carry on its business. The report discounts all nonliquid assets by 100 percent (that is, ignores their value completely). Then it reduces the value of other assets according to the amount of "prudent risk" they represent. Liabilities are carried at full exposure; only those that are 100 percent covered are excluded. Total liabilities are then divided by total assets. The ratio resulting from this test dramatizes the firm's strength in the face of adversity. Under this rigid test, liabilities usually exceed assets. Ratios of 4 to 1, to 8 to 1 are normal. The various self-regulatory organizations monitor firms and grow suspicious of those whose ratios reach 10 to 1 or 12 to 1. The rule is that a firm's ratio may not exceed 15 to 1. At this point, a firm usually goes out of business anyway.

The *15c3-3 report* is another responsibility of the accounting department. Under this SEC rule, the brokerage firm has to maintain a free credit balance in a "special reserve bank account for the exclusive benefit of customers." The 15c3-3 report compares this cash credit balance with the total of all customers' debit balances. If the total customers' credit balances exceed their debit balances, the firm has to deposit cash in a bank account. If total customer debit exceeds credit, the deposit is not necessary.

This rule denies the brokerage firm the right to use these funds in the speculative conduct of its own business. The accounting department, employing a formula approved by the stock exchange or the NASD, supervises the firm's compliance with this rule and ensures that customer money is used only for customer purposes.

The accounting department is also involved in the very last step in customer operations activity—the preparation of the statements of account. Under federal law, if there has been any transaction activity, security position, or money balance in an account within the preceding calendar quarter, the customer must receive a statement of account. Many firms comply by sending their customers (particularly margin account customers) monthly statements instead of the mandatory quarterly report.

Whether monthly or quarterly, the statement summarizes all that has occurred in the customer's account during the period. All purchase expenses are debited to the account, and sales proceeds are credited. However, each purchase and/or sales transaction is posted on the contract settlement date, whereas all other activities are posted on the day they occur. For example, a check received from a customer is credited to the account on the day it is received, and money delivered out of the account is debited on the actual day of reimbursement. But a regular-way sale of a corporate security on June 26 is not posted until July 3, five business days later. This difference is often a point of confusion for customers, especially when they receive their monthly statements of account without certain month-end trades posted on it.

Despite the best efforts and intentions of the accounting department, mistakes occur. Perhaps an issue is not carried forward to the following month's position listing, or duplicate entries are processed accidentally and both items are posted in the account. A typical customer statement, therefore, carries a self-protective legend, "E&OE," which means, "errors and omissions excepted." This statement allows the brokerage firm an opportunity to correct the mistake without legal liability.

■ DIVIDEND DEPARTMENT

Many people have their stocks registered not in their own name but instead in the name of their brokerage firms (or "street" name). By so doing, they do not have to worry about signing the securities or a stock power when they want to sell. Instead, all they have to do is call their broker and say "sell," and an officer of the firm endorses the certificate. The issuing corporation, however, may not know who those clients are. As a result, it sends the firm corporation anything that it would normally send to the stockholder, such as annual statements, proxy statements, and other company-related information. One of the things that the corporation sends the brokerage firm is a check for any dividends due on preferred and common stock held in street name. But those dividends rightfully belong to the "beneficial" owner of the stock, the client. For example, if 100 clients, each of whom owns 100 shares of a given stock, should decide to register their stock in their broker's name, then the company's books show that the firm "owns" 10,000 shares. When it's time to pay a dividend, the company makes one check payable to the firm, because the company has no way of knowing the actual beneficial owners. The firm, when it receives the check, then distributes the proceeds on a proportional basis to all of the actual owners.

This task falls to the dividend department employees, who are responsible for checking every security in every account to make sure that all clients receive the dividends to which they are entitled (and to make sure clients do not keep any dividend to which they are not entitled). Their work, however, is complicated by the dividend-paying process.

For cash dividends, the process hinges on four dates. First, on the *declaration date,* the company's board of directors announces that the company will pay a dividend of a certain size. On the second date, the *record date,* the company asks its registrar to provide a list of its current shareholders so that it knows who is entitled to the dividend checks. *To receive the dividend, the stockholder has to be on the company's books as a shareholder as of this date.* Third, on the *payment date,* the company actually cuts the dividend checks, usually about two weeks after the record date.

Many investors don't understand this cycle, and they angrily call their stockbrokers to demand dividend checks to which they are *not* entitled. Generally, the reason is that they were not the holders of record on the record date, but they don't understand why.

Hence, the fourth date, known as the *ex-dividend date.* Most stock trades take three business days (t+3) to be cleared, that is, they settle "regular way". Someone who buys the stock three business days before the record date will be the holder of record on that date. But a regular-way (that is, three-day settlement) trade made two or fewer business days before the record date will not be settled when the corporate registrar takes the list of stockholders. Therefore the purchaser receives no dividend. *Ex* means *without.* Buy on an *ex* date and you will receive no dividend. Why? Because the regular-way trade will settle after the record date. You are a record holder on the date the trade settles. The dividend will therefore be mailed (rightfully) to the seller of the stock. (Note: At printing the Exchanges and NASD have proposed that T + 3 be changed to T + 1.)

Something else happens on the ex-dividend date. Would-be purchasers of the stock know that they are not going to get the dividend as of this day. As a result, the market value of the stock generally drops by the value of the dividend when it opens for trading on the ex-dividend date.

Let's look at an example which involves the following calendar:

			MAY			
S	M	T	W	T	F	S
1	2	3	4	5	6	
7	8	9	10	11	12	13
14	15	16	17	18	19	20
21	22	23	24	25	26	27
28	29	31				

The board of directors puts out a press release on May 2 saying that it will pay a $0.50 dividend to the owners of record as of May 17, with checks to be mailed as of May 26. May 2 is the declaration date, May 17 is the record date, and May 26 is the payment date. To be a holder of record on May 17, the purchaser would have to buy the stock no later than May 12, regular way T + 3. The ex-dividend date is therefore May 15. If an investor buys the stock on May 16 for regular-way settlement, the trade does not settle until May 19. The investor is not recorded as the owner of the stock on the company's books until May 19. Thus, the seller is still entitled to receive the dividend. May 15 and 16 are also declared to be ex dates.

Sometimes the dividend check is mailed to the wrong person. Either the firm does not get the information about the new owner to the registrar in time, or the registrar does not process the information in time, or someone commits an error somewhere along the line. If the dividend check is inadvertently mailed to the wrong party, that party must return it so it can be correctly routed.

Stock dividends work a little differently. "Small" stock dividends (less than 25 percent) are handled like cash dividends. For large stock dividends (25 percent or larger) and all stock splits, the sequence of the dates is different. The ex-dividend date, now called the ex-distribution date, comes after the payment date instead of after the declaration date. Thus the sequence for a stock distribution is as follows:

■ Declaration date
■ Record date
■ Payment date
■ Ex-distribution date

The ex-distribution date is usually the business day following payment by the corporation. For example, using the same calendar:

			MAY			
S	M	T	W	T	F	S
	1	2	3	4	5	6
7	8	9	10	11	12	13
14	15	16	17	18	19	20
21	22	23	**24**	**25**	26	27
28	29	31				

If the company declares a 25 percent stock dividend on May 2, for payment on May 24, then the stock starts to trade ex-distribution on May 25. Anyone who buys the stock so as to receive delivery before May 25 is entitled to receive the stock dividend.

If someone buys the stock before the record and payment dates, it is possible that the stock could be delivered without the stock dividend. So, from the second business day before the record date until (and including) the payable date, all trades in a stock-dividend-paying security carry *due bills*, which are IOUs for the stock to be issued on the payable date.

For example, RIP is undergoing a two-for-one split. A client buys 100 shares of RIP at 50, so that the purchase settles before the record date. But delivery of the stock to the brokerage firm occurs after the record date. The receiving firm pays $5,000 to the delivering firm (100 shares x $50) and demands a due bill for the additional 100 shares that will result from the split. On the day following the payable date for RIP's two-for-one split, the shares are worth only $25 each. Now the dividend department has to claim the second 100 shares with the due bill. In return for the due bill, the dividend department receives the second hundred:

■ Client buys	100 RIP @ 50 = $5,000
■ Client receives	100 RIP @ 50 = $5,000
■ Value of stock after split	100 RIP @ 25 = $2,500
■ Client's account after due bill is satisfied	200 RIP @ 25 = $5,000

■ PROXY DEPARTMENT

In addition to dividend checks, firms receive proxy statements for any stocks they hold for their clients. Proxies, or "advisory and voting solicitations," give shareholders the right to elect members of the corporate board of directors and to decide on other important matters brought before an annual or special meeting of the stockholders.

Handling these proxies is the job of the proxy department. To allow the beneficial owners of the shares to vote, the proxy department sends a request form, called a proxy, to each of the beneficial owners. As the owners return their proxies, the firm tallies the votes and reflects the owners' wishes when it votes its shares at the annual meeting.

As an example, two owners leave their stock in street name. The first owner has 200 shares, and the second has 100 shares. The firm receives the right to cast 300 votes at the annual meeting. The firm sends proxies to the owners, collects their responses, and votes as they would have voted if they had actually attended the annual meeting and voted for themselves. If investor A votes yes and investor B votes no on a certain proposal, then 200 votes, one vote per share, are counted as "yes" votes and 100 shares are counted as "no" votes at the annual meeting.

Sometimes the beneficial owners do not bother to advise the proxy department about their preferences. Exchange regulations prevent a firm from voting on crucial issues unless it receives instructions from its clients. (However, firms can vote unreturned proxies on routine matters.)

The proxy department also acts as agent for any person or group wishing to communicate with the beneficial owners whose shares are in the firm's custody. The group, however, must have registered its proxy statement or solicitation with the SEC, per Section 14 of the Securities Exchange Act of 1934, and must agree to reimburse the brokerage firm for postage and other out-of-pocket expenses connected with a mailing.

A stockholder solicitation may be a simple plea for a vote to effect a reform or to change the company's present management. Or it may be a request for the beneficial owners to tender their shares in response to a purchase proposition. The latter, in larger firms, is often assigned to the reorganization department. Finally, the proxy department distributes corporate publications (including financial reports), notices of meetings, and voting information to the beneficial owners who have their securities in street name.

When they think of the securities industry, many people call to mind the busy floor of the stock exchange, the electronic trading screens, and the Wall Street area. Not many can picture the sometimes feverish back office work that is necessary to keep the records and books straight, to comply with regulations, to protect the interests of customer and firm alike, and through it all, to make a profit.

Never, however, were modern stock market mechanisms tested more than on Monday, October 19, 1987. On this day, the volume of trading reached levels unprecedented up to that time, while prices dropped out of control. What happened that day on the exchange floors, at the trading desks, and elsewhere is the subject of Chapter 14. Before getting to the events of so called "Black Monday," however, the next chapter covers market theories—how analysts try to predict market movement.

STOCK MARKET THEORIES
Can Prices Really Be Predicted?

Like so many simple-sounding maxims, "Buy low, sell high" is far more easily said than done. Living and profiting by this dictum means predicting the highs and lows of stock prices. It entails knowing when and for how long buyers will outnumber sellers and vice versa. Anyone who could accurately foresee bull and bear markets would never have to work another day and could live like a monarch. So the search for highs and lows goes on and on.

According to some market observers, however, that search is just about futile. Their reasoning is based on the assumption that any influence on supply or demand is already reflected in stock prices. For example, if a company is rumored to be going bankrupt, if an arms manufacturer is about to be awarded a large defense contract, or if a corporation is a takeover target—these and other influences must have been considered by reasonably well-informed investors before they placed their buy or sell orders. The market is regarded as "efficient," that is, it takes into account—or "discounts"—all the conditions affecting supply and demand.

A corollary of this theory is that the conditions resulting in stock prices are so complex and, for the most part, patternless that predicting them is all but impossible. No one can say with any great certainty where prices will be tomorrow, next week, or next year. That is, stock prices are said to take a "random walk." That's the "efficient market" or "random walk" theory.

Many professional traders make a great deal of money on "inefficiencies" in the market. For one thing, not all investors are equally well informed, nor are they all informed at the same time. The law prohibits this transmission of secret "insider" information. Most brokerage firms have securities systems and procedures, collectively known as a "Chinese Wall," to keep such information secret. Further, each investor may react differently to the same information. For example, some risk-aversive investors might regard a downswing of prices as a good reason to sell off stocks and get out of the market. More speculative market participants might look upon the same downturn as an opportunity to sell short and reap profits. Long-term buy-and-hold investors might dismiss the drop as a temporary setback in a trend that will not fail to turn upward again presenting them with an opportunity to buy low. These individuals would buy. Different investors, different investment objectives, different reactions.

Inefficiencies resulting from either varied investor reactions or the delayed diffusion of information are opportunities for profit for those who watch the stock market closely. Arbitrageurs are market watchers who are quicker to capitalize on such inefficiencies. Suppose, for the moment, that a stock is selling at a significantly lower price on one exchange than it is on another. Arbitrageurs might buy the stock at the lower price and simultaneously sell it at the higher price. To make money from such fleeting aberrations, arbitrageurs must have on-line access to information from many exchanges, a large amount of capital to work with, and the ability to get orders executed on a moment's notice. Inefficiencies do exist, and some market participants make money on them. Nevertheless, the efficient market—or random walk—theory does not sit well with most analysts. It implies that prices cannot really be predicted other than to say that, for as long as prices have been charted, they have worked their way generally upward. (Also by implication, the only viable strategy is to "buy and hold.") Yet to make real money, which is what brokerage firms are in business to do, you have to be able to predict prices more precisely and on a shorter-term basis.

■ THE FIRST AMERICAN ANALYST

The theoretical futility of analysis did not prevent a 31-year-old man from co-founding a financial information service company in 1882. The co-founders were Charles Dow and Edward Jones, and the company was the Dow Jones Company. The purpose of the company was to provide information and news that affected the stock market. Over 100 years later, the name "Dow Jones" has become associated with the financial newspaper (*Wall Street Journal*), a major publishing firm (*Dow-Jones Irwin*), and the most widely quoted and followed stock market averages in the world.

Only two years after founding the company, Charles Dow devised a method by which the prices of 11 railroad company stocks were averaged out and used as an indicator of prices in the railroad industry. In 1896, he created an industrial stock average, comprised of 12 such stocks, which by 1929 was enlarged to 30 stocks, and has remained at a component base of 30 stocks ever since.

Today, the financial news is not complete without a report on the three Dow Jones averages: 30 industrials, 20 transportation, and 15 utilities. Millions of newspaper readers and newscast viewers and listeners know about "the Dow."

Yet some critics say the Dow Jones average does not represent American industry today because the issuing corporations represented in the averages are "big cap." Their research and development projects are big-budgeted and long-term, unlike those of younger, emerging growth corporations, such as "hi-tech" computer systems or software companies. As a result, they argue that their successes or failures are "lag indicators," that is, they occur long after the rest of the market has moved.

Other averages are available, and they serve as indicators along with the Dow. Yet the Dow persists as the first, the oldest, and the most widely recognized of averages. The Dow averages are *the* key indicators used to interpret the so-called *Dow Theory*. Charles Dow never formulated a theory in a single writing but his successors attempted to organize his work into a coherent system, which today is normally called the Dow Theory.

According to this theory, these types of price movements are at work in the stock market at the same time:

- The "narrow movement" consists of day-to-day fluctuations.
- The "short swing" is made up of trends that last from two weeks to a month or a little more.
- The "main movement" is the long-term trend—bull or bear—that lasts four years or more.

The following expands on the Dow Theory. According to the theory, there are market trends that last over many years; however, such movements may be temporarily interrupted by corrections during intervals. The order or sequence through which a trend occurs begins with investors acquiring the stocks when they are priced at or near their low. However, as the price swings upward, additional investors become bullish as they rush in to purchase the stocks to participate in the upward move until the price has reached its peak, at which time a selloff of the stock occurs and investors become bearish. However, if the market exceeds its peak, or high, then an aggressive upward move is apparent and will continue higher as investors continue to buy in a market that has broken out of its selling resistance. Likewise, in reverse, if the market sells below its previous low, then a downward move will continue as investors aggressively sell in a market that has broken its support. This Dow Theory is not perfect; no theory is, but nevertheless it is utilized by many with their wallet on the line.

Perhaps the greatest criticism of this three-part theory, however, is that it is not intended to predict the duration of a trend. Rather it is intended only to *mark* trend reversals. The theory is therefore a market-following system (or lag indicator), not a market-predicting system (or lead indicator). It tells, supposedly through the Dow averages, only where the market's been, not where it's going.

Indexes, on the other hand, are also constructed to reflect American industry and the stock market. Indexes are generally

THE DOW JONES AVERAGES

Actual High
Close
Actual Low

Industrials

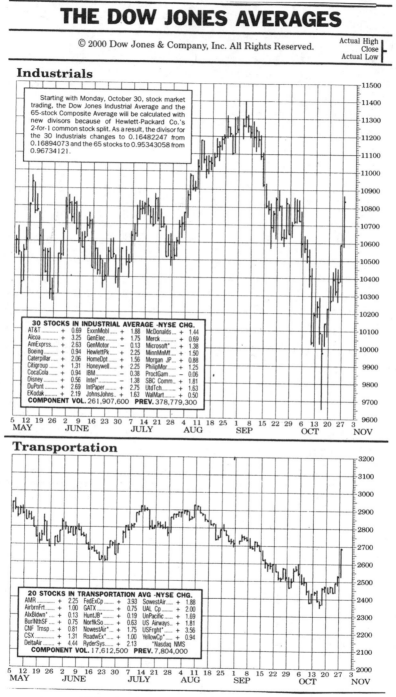

Starting with Monday, October 30, stock market trading, the Dow Jones Industrial Average and the 65-stock Composite Average will be calculated with new divisors because of Hewlett-Packard Co.'s 2-for-1 common stock split. As a result, the divisor for the 30 Industrials changes to 0.16482247 from 0.16894073 and the 65 stocks to 0.95343058 from 0.96734121.

30 STOCKS IN INDUSTRIAL AVERAGE -NYSE CHG.

AT&T	+	0.69	ExxnMobl	+	1.88	McDonalds... +	1.44
Alcoa	+	3.25	GenElec	+	1.75	Merck +	0.69
AmExprss.	+	2.63	GenMotor	–	0.13	Microsoft* +	1.38
Boeing	+	0.94	HewlettPk	+	2.25	MinnMnMf. +	1.50
Caterpillar	+	2.06	HomeDpt	+	1.56	Morgan JP. +	0.88
Citigroup	+	1.31	Honeywell	+	2.25	PhilipMor.... +	1.25
CocaCola	+	0.94	IBM	–	0.38	ProctGam... –	0.06
Disney	+	0.56	Intel*	–	1.38	SBC Comm.. +	1.81
DuPont	+	2.69	IntPaper	+	0.75	UtdTch........ +	1.63
EKodak	+	2.19	JohnsJohns.	+	1.63	WalMart....... +	0.50

COMPONENT VOL. 261,907,600 **PREV.** 378,779,300

5 12 19 26 2 9 16 23 30 7 14 21 28 4 11 18 25 1 8 15 22 29 6 13 20 27 3
MAY JUNE JULY AUG SEP OCT NOV

Transportation

20 STOCKS IN TRANSPORTATION AVG -NYSE CHG.

AMR	+	2.25	FedExCp	+	3.93	SowestAir.... +	1.88
AirbrnFrt	+	1.00	GATX	+	0.75	UAL Cp ...... +	2.00
AlxBldwn*	+	0.13	HuntJB*	+	0.19	UnPacific..... +	1.69
BurlNthSF	+	0.75	NorflkSo	+	0.63	US Airways.. +	1.81
CNF Trnsp	+	0.81	NowestAir*	+	1.75	USFrght*..... +	3.56
CSX	+	1.31	RoadwEx*	+	1.00	YellowCp*... +	0.94
DeltaAir	+	4.44	RyderSys...	+	2.13	*Nasdaq NMS	

COMPONENT VOL. 17,612,500 **PREV.** 7,804,000

5 12 19 26 2 9 16 23 30 7 14 21 28 4 11 18 25 1 8 15 22 29 6 13 20 27 3
MAY JUNE JULY AUG SEP OCT NOV

FIGURE 12–1. DOW JONES AVERAGES

Utilities

15 STOCKS IN UTILITY AVERAGE -NYSE CHG.

AEP............	+ 1.88	DukeEngy.....	+ 2.63	PubSvcEnt ...	+ 1.25
AES............	+ 1.63	EdisonInt......	+ 0.81	ReliantEn.....	+ 0.69
ColmEngy.....	– 0.06	EnronCp	+ 1.81	SouthernCo...	+ 0.88
ConEd..........	+ 0.88	Exelon...........	+ 2.75	TXU	+ 1.13
DominRes	+ 1.63	PG&E...........		WillmsCos....	+ 0.75

COMPONENT VOL. 15,949,100 **PREV.** 20,927,600

(chart y-axis: 410, 400, 390, 380, 370, 360, 350, 340, 330, 320, 310, 300, 290, 280)

x-axis: 5 12 19 26 | 2 9 16 23 30 | 7 14 21 28 | 4 11 18 25 | 1 8 15 22 29 | 6 13 20 27 | 3
MAY — JUNE — JULY — AUG — SEP — OCT — NOV

NYSE Volume In Millions (9:30 a. m. to 4 p. m. EST)

(chart y-axis: 1800, 1600, 1400, 1200, 1000, 800, 600, 400, 200, 0)

x-axis: 5 12 19 26 | 2 9 16 23 30 | 7 14 21 28 | 4 11 18 25 | 1 8 15 22 29 | 6 13 20 27 | 3
MAY — JUNE — JULY — AUG — SEP — OCT — NOV

THE DOW JONES AVERAGES HOUR BY HOUR

DATE	OPEN	10 AM	11 AM	12 NOON	1 PM	2 PM	3 PM	CLOSE	CHG		% CHG	HIGH (THEORETICAL)	LOW (THEORETICAL)	HIGH (ACTUAL)	LOW (ACTUAL)
30 STOCKS INDUSTRIAL AVERAGE: (divisor: 0.16482447)															
Oct 30	10588.06	10692.06	10756.90	10737.56	10747.80	10799.37	10827.81	10835.77	+ 245.15	+	2.31	10944.98	10506.25	10869.52	10578.49
Oct 27	10381.60	10392.33	10426.36	10529.58	10509.14	10551.41	10548.08	10590.62	+ 210.50	+	2.03	10696.43	10296.70	10590.62	10380.86
Oct 26	10330.18	10343.86	10303.54	10320.93	10339.06	10295.03	10333.04	10380.12	+ 53.64	+	0.52	10563.25	10128.18	10454.85	10265.06
Oct 25	10395.66	10338.78	10408.61	10401.21	10388.63	10379.75	10370.50	10326.48	– 66.59	–	0.64	10563.99	10170.08	10461.97	10306.59
Oct 24	10273.57	10361.99	10407.87	10426.73	10394.18	10370.13	10320.56	10393.07	+ 121.35	+	1.18	10583.96	10136.69	10439.31	10273.57
20 STOCKS TRANSPORTATION AVERAGE: (divisor: 0.20890294)															
Oct 30	2529.87	2564.61	2600.37	2606.39	2619.51	2634.70	2658.93	2686.61	+ 157.64	+	6.23	2720.29	2517.26	2692.32	2525.98
Oct 27	2492.20	2483.33	2484.29	2510.33	2509.84	2509.29	2513.70	2528.97	+ 37.07	+	1.49	2550.89	2456.00	2535.40	2478.42
Oct 26	2440.31	2445.69	2447.14	2455.82	2478.06	2461.67	2469.45	2491.90	+ 53.09	+	2.18	2514.96	2420.05	2492.67	2436.42
Oct 25	2470.49	2456.63	2462.07	2446.63	2443.72	2449.58	2451.42	2438.81	– 32.28	–	1.31	2489.26	2409.19	2471.69	2435.40
Oct 24	2439.85	2458.38	2466.99	2461.63	2466.28	2470.82	2457.28	2471.09	+ 34.23	+	1.40	2519.90	2405.78	2475.03	2439.85
15 STOCKS UTILITY AVERAGE: (divisor: 1.8686694)															
Oct 30	382.12	386.34	389.72	391.59	390.45	391.32	391.29	392.06	+ 9.97	+	2.61	394.97	382.09	392.46	382.12
Oct 27	373.86	369.92	374.83	379.35	378.58	379.01	379.85	382.09	+ 8.09	+	2.16	384.03	368.18	382.26	369.31
Oct 26	380.55	378.31	374.16	375.97	375.47	375.60	373.43	374.00	– 5.48	–	1.44	382.89	369.71	380.82	372.83
Oct 25	386.84	387.51	386.10	380.89	381.45	380.15	380.72	379.48	– 7.36	–	1.90	392.12	375.33	388.81	378.21
Oct 24	389.78	393.70	389.98	386.94	385.23	386.50	385.74	386.84	– 2.94	–	0.75	396.14	382.39	394.36	384.93
65 STOCKS COMPOSITE AVERAGE: (divisor: 0.9534306)															
Oct 30	3133.40	3167.58	3193.51	3194.96	3197.18	3211.26	3221.48	3230.30	+ 96.45	+	3.08	3262.26	3116.69	3233.26	3131.88
Oct 27	3073.70	3065.55	3081.49	3113.83	3108.71	3116.61	3118.79	3133.85	+ 60.41	+	1.97	3160.80	3039.87	3133.91	3062.99
Oct 26	3063.85	3065.46	3050.53	3059.19	3066.19	3055.35	3059.22	3073.44	+ 10.24	+	0.33	3127.59	3005.65	3089.39	3044.40
Oct 25	3096.47	3084.77	3095.56	3080.59	3079.12	3076.06	3076.07	3063.20	– 32.82	–	1.06	3140.00	3021.48	3103.87	3059.56
Oct 24	3073.44	3101.03	3103.35	3100.05	3092.07	3091.37	3078.43	3096.02	+ 22.90	+	0.75	3157.86	3028.55	3109.11	3073.26

a-Actual high or low exceeds theoretical value due to computational method. c-Corrected. r-Revised.

FIGURE 12–1. *CONTINUED*

composed of many more stocks than are averages, which are composed of few stocks, and those stocks make up a more representative array of American business.

Indexes are usually weighted according to float, that is that part of the total shares outstanding held by the investing public and not by management, so that each stock is represented proportionately in the resultant figure. Let's look at how Stocks A–D might be used in an oversimplified index:

	Market Price	Number of Shares Outstanding (Float)
1. Stock A	$50.00	10,000,000
2. Stock B	$45.00	2,000,000
3. Stock C	$55.00	3,000,000
4. Stock D	$60.00	1,000,000

To prepare a weighted index, multiply each stock price by the number of shares outstanding and add up all the totals:

	Market Price		Float		
1. Stock A	$50.00	×	10,000,000	=	500,000,000
2. Stock B	$45.00	×	2,000,000	=	90,000,000
3. Stock C	$55.00	×	3,000,000	=	165,000,000
4. Stock D	$60.00	×	1,000,000	=	60,000,000
Total					815,000,000

To this total is applied a divisor, which might be the total weighted value of the stocks in the index at the time the index was created. For example, suppose the baseline value, or divisor, is 125,000,000). This index value would be 6.52 (815,000,000 divided by 125,000,000. Naturally, actual indexes are much more complicated than this. Our illustration is a grossly oversimplified view of both averages and indexes. In truth, some averages are weighted and some indexes are not. In addition, both averages and indexes undergo adjustments for stock splits, companies that "disappear" due to mergers or other reasons, and other changes.

Indexes are a relatively new development in the securities industry, and they have become very popular as indicators. Some of the widely used indexes are:

- The New York Stock Exchange Composite Index of all of the common stocks listed on that exchange, approximately 3,200 corporate common stocks grouped as industrials, transportation, and financial/utility, with market movement measured in actual dollars and cents.

- The American Stock Exchange Market Value Index of all 800 or so common stocks listed on that exchange.

- Nasdaq Composite Index, comprised of approximately 5,000 stocks organized as industry, bank, insurance, other financial companies, transportation, utilities, and heavily inclusive of technology stocks.

- Standard & Poor's, 500 Common Stock Index, which includes different market sectors-industrials, consumer cyclicals, health care, transportation, public utilities and technology. (Standard & Poor's also publishes an index of 100 stocks and other indexes as well.)

- The Russell 2000 is composed of 2000 stocks.

- The Wilshire 5,000 Equity Index is perhaps the broadest index available, comprising 5,000 stocks for which daily quotations are available.

In addition to acting as market indicators, indexes have been widely adopted as underlying instruments for futures. The seller of a futures contract agrees to sell an underlying commodity or instrument at a specified price and time. The "underlying" interest can be anything from farm products to precious metals or Treasury bonds. The buyer of the futures contract, of course, agrees to buy the underlying commodity or financial instrument on the same terms.

Historically, the futures contract grew out of the agricultural economy of the past. Farmers needed to lock in a profitable price for their crops, that is, they needed to "hedge" their risk of losing money if the crop did not command a profitable price at the market. To assure a profit, they agreed to presently sell their future crops, when harvested at some specific future date, at a profitable price. Speculators entered into these contracts with the expectation of reselling the crops at even higher prices, thereby making a profit for themselves. In addition to speculators, processors bought such contracts to lock in the cost of raw materials. For example, a baked goods company might buy wheat contracts to lock in future expected wheat costs at a level that enables it to make a profit on the end products—bread, cakes, rolls, and the like.

What has all this to do with indexes? Over the years, the futures contract has become a trading vehicle on its own. Futures contracts are traded not only on the traditional agricultural commodities (soybeans, sugar, and the like), but also on precious metals, U.S. government securities, currencies, and a host of other underlying interests, including stock indexes.

Indexes, however, present a wrinkle. Implied in a futures contract is the actual delivery of the underlying commodity or instrument if the seller decides to "exercise" the contract. In practice only a few percent of futures are exercised, so delivery is not likely. Nevertheless, when a contract is exercised for actual delivery the seller's duty is to delivery soybeans, wheat, orange juice, or whatever. What does the seller deliver when an index futures contract is exercised? The answer is cash.

Here's how a futures contract on an index works. Let's say that you own—that is, if you are "long"—one December S&P 500 Stock Index futures contract. Assume that the current market price for the contract is 129, which is the "index number." If you exercise the contract—that is, demand delivery—you will be paid $64,500, which is the index number (market price) times $500, the contractual value of each point in the index number. If you paid less than 129 ($64,500) for the contract, then you make a profit. If you paid more, you lose money.

Who trades index futures? Among others, anyone who needs to protect a large position in stocks—pension funds, insurance companies, banks, brokerage firms, and other institutional investors. The portfolios for these investors typically include large positions in many different stocks. By diversifying their stock holdings, they hedge the risk of loss if one or another stock drops in value. The gains on other stocks in the portfolio generally more than offset such a loss in value. This type of risk is referred to as "specific," "non-systematic," or "diversifiable" risk.

Harder to hedge is the risk of an across-the-board loss, in which all or most of the securities in a portfolio take a nosedive due to a downturn in the market itself. This is called "market," "systematic," or "non-diversifiable" risk. Very little can be done to protect against losses due to this kind of risk other than to watch the market very carefully.

This is where index futures come in. By buying futures contracts on an index whose composition resembles the mix of stocks in their holdings, portfolio managers can limit their losses due to market downturns. For example, a mutual fund portfolio manager controls $500 million in stock values, and foresees a sharp near-term drop in the market. Trying to sell $500 million quickly at reasonable prices would be technically very difficult, and probably an undesirable course of action anyway, if the long-term prognosis is bullish. The stock market futures contract offers downside protection without exposure. The portfolio manager becomes a farmer with a silo jammed full of stock certificates rather than with ears of corn. A short futures position may be used by each as a hedge against the loss of inventory value. Speculators and others may likewise attempt to profit by taking outright long or short positions, thus providing the same type of risk transfer mechanism that has worked so well previously with farm products, industrial goods, and other financial instruments.

Here's an example. An investor holds a diversified portfolio of blue-chip stocks worth $250,000. The investor fears a sharp setback could occur prior to the resumption of a long-term bull market. Because of its greater concentration of blue-chip issues, the S&P 500 is the best hedge vehicle for its portfolio and the investor sells short three contracts at an assumed current price of $168. With each contract worth $500 x $168, the short position's dollar value is $252,000 ($500 x $168 x 3), hedging the entire portfolio value and then some.

If the value of the portfolio declines by 10 percent, the shares will be worth $225,000. However, if the portfolio's actual decline is 10 percent, the S&P futures position would have had a similar decline, possibly 9 percent, to 152.90. If the three futures positions are closed out at this price, the profit is $22,650, largely offsetting the loss in value on the portfolio. The futures profit is computed as follows:

	$	Points/Contract
Sold 3 contracts @ 168	$252,000	168.00
Loss: Covered short @ 152.90	$229,350	152.90
Profit	$ 22,650	15.10

As you can see, this is basically the same type of arrangement as that between the farmer and the speculator or processor. The manager needs to hedge the future value of the portfolio, and other stock market participants are willing to "speculate" that the market will not decline. Options are also traded on indexes. An option is the right to buy or sell an underlying instrument at a specified price (the strike price) by a certain time (the expiration date). An option to buy is a "call"; an option to sell is a "put."

While the first options were based on stocks, today options are traded, like futures, on a number of instruments, such as U.S. government securities, currencies, and, of course, indexes. Like futures, options imply the "delivery" of the underlying interest, whether it is IBM stock or deutsche marks, except in the case of indexes, where exercising the option results in a cash payment. While options are very different from futures in many ways, they are also used by portfolio managers to hedge market risk.

To further highlight the flexibility and application of options, they are also traded on futures, including index futures. When an option on a futures contract is exercised, the option holder takes delivery of the futures contract. To take delivery of the cash, the manager then has to exercise the futures contract. Many institutional investors maintain huge positions in index futures and in options in index futures, for the sole purpose of protecting their holdings against market risk.

Needless to say, these positions can become extremely complicated, very often far too complex for any one person to control without the aid of computerized trading programs. The manager of such a program calculates the size of the futures and/or options position necessary, specifies the stock price levels at which the contracts should be exercised, and then leaves it to the computers to enter the orders necessary to exercise the option and, if necessary, the futures. Such trading programs are therefore set like mousetraps, to go off when the market declines to a certain level.

These programs also have created a stock market phenomenon known as the "witching hour." Both options and futures have expiration dates, at which time the contracts must be exercised or be allowed to expire. At these expiration dates, the volume of exercised contracts has increased drastically. This sudden surge of volume can, and often does, upset the market values of the underlying stocks and indexes. The result is a brief period of high volume and volatility, which runs counter to the essential principle of maintaining a "fair and orderly" market.

Of even greater concern are the "triple witching hours," which will occur on the third business Friday of the month, when the expiration dates of futures, options contracts, and index contracts coincide. When this happens, the resultant volatility is synergized, playing havoc with the stock market. This represents such a threat to the market that stabilizing regulatory requirements have been implemented. The modern stock market is therefore much more complicated than in years past. It is an arena in which many institutional investors, both domestic and foreign, participate by means of sophisticated program trading systems.

For a further discussion of options, refer to Chapter 10.

▪ THE ANALYSTS

Into this crowded and fast-paced trading stage, enter the analysts, of whom there are two basic types. Some analyze the stock itself in terms of the issuing company, the industry, the stock market, and relevant economic conditions. On the basis of their analyses, they attempt to predict whether there will be enough interest among investors—both individual and institutional—to drive the price of the stock upward. These economic areas of analysis are known as "fundamentals," and these analysts are called "fundamentalists."

The basic principle underlying fundamental analysis is that the quality of a stock with respect to investment should be evaluated based upon a combination of economic factors. These factors include the performance of the company as compared to its competitors, in addition to industry and global economic conditions. Measurement devices such as ratio analysis, earnings, projected earnings, financial statements, interest rates, yield analysis, financial indexes, to name a few are the tools of the fundamental analysis to determine the quality of stock under consideration for investment.

Fundamentalists look for "what" to buy or sell based on economics and economic principles. Generally at odds with fundamentalists are "technical analysts." Although their aim is to predict stock prices, technical analysts dismiss the likelihood that accurate forecasts can be made by analyzing fundamentals. Instead, their approach is to closely follow price movements, analyzing supply/demand forces, the assumption being that *any* influences on prices are already reflected in these movements. Therefore, you do not need to gauge investor motivations and market conditions—just follow the prices themselves. To follow price movements, technicians use different types of charts: bar charts, point-and-figure charts, and line charts, which to be discussed later in this chapter. (See Figures 12–2 and 12–3.) For this reason, these analysts are also known as "chartists." In following price movements on their charts, technicians look for patterns. They are primarily concerned with "when" to buy or sell based on market timing. (See Figure 12–3.) Once they can identify a pattern, they will try to predict the direction of prices for a stock or for the market as a whole. Technical analysis is discussed more in depth further on in this chapter.

At any given time, many influences are at work on stock market prices: budget and trade deficits, fear of inflation or

Charting

The technician uses two types of charts: the bar chart and the point (P&F) chart.

Point and Figure (P&F) Chart

The Bar Chart

Constructing a bar chart is simple. At the top of the chart, enter the name of the stock (industry, index, market, or whatever you are charting). To the vertical axis assign a price scale, such as points or ⅛-points. On the horizontal axis, mark off the calendar time scale—days, weeks, or months. On a daily bar chart, every five-day period (a trading week) may be marked by a vertical line that is heavier than the others. For each day, the high, low, and closing prices are plotted. Vertical line, or *bar*, connects the high and low prices. A horizontal tick to the right of the bar indicates the closing price. A tick mark on the left side of the bar marks the opening price for the day. With so many chart services available, however, plotting one's own charts is often an unnecessary and unprofitable way to spend time.

a: The high price for the day, 32⅞ ($32.875).
b: The low price for the day, 32 ($32.00).
c: The opening price (not always on the bar chart), 32⅝ ($32.625).
d: The closing price, 32¼ ($32.25).

FIGURE 12–2. CHARTING

Point and Figure (P&F) Chart

Unlike bar charts, point and figure charts record only price movements; if no price change occurs, the chart remains the same. Time is not reflected on a P&F chart, although time reference points, such as "Mon," are sometimes used. Volume is indicated only by the number of recorded price changes, not as a separate entity.

25⅛	25⅜	25⅛	24¼
25⅛	25	25	
25¼	25½	24⅞	
25⅜	25⅛	25⅛	

Box Size. In a P&F chart, a rising price change is represented by an X, a declining price movement by an O. Each X or O occupies a box on the chart. One of the first decisions in constructing a P&F chart is therefore how great a price change each box should represent. For example, a chart might have a box size of a ¼-point ($0.25). On a less sensitive chart, a box might equal a point ($1); price movements of less than $1 would not be registered. On a more sensitive scale of, say, ⅛-point per box, more detailed price action would be visible. Obviously, the smaller the value assigned to the box, the movement the chart will reflect—and the more tedious it is to construct.

Reversal Criterion. On a P&F chart, the analyst moves one row of boxes to the right every time prices change direction. The question is what constitutes a reversal? If prices move ⅛-point against the trend, is that a significant enough reversal to warrant recording? Or is a 1-point reversal sufficient? Whatever the chartists decides to use as the occasion to move to the next row becomes the *reversal criterion* for the chart.

Example: A stock trades at the following prices:

If we want to chart these movements, the box size should probably be equal to ⅛-point. A box size that is only slightly larger—¼-point—would not include most of these movements. The reversal criterion should probably be ⅛-point also; otherwise, again, most of the reversals would not be reflected on the chart. The movements, as charted, would look like this (the dot represents the first transaction):

```
25½        X O
25⅜    X O X O
25¼    X O X O
25⅛  ● O X O X O
25     O X O X O
24⅞       O X O
24¾           O
24⅝           O
24½           O
24⅜           O
24¼           O
```

As you might suspect, box size and reversal criterion play a great role in how sensitive the chart is to price movements and in how the price movement data is represented. A "1x1" chart, for example, presents data so that every box is equal to a point and every point reversal is recorded. This would be a much more sensitive—and very different-looking chart—than a "2x3" chart, in which only two-point price changes and three-box reversals are reflected.

FIGURE 12–3. POINT-AND-FIGURE CHART

recession, rumors of, or the reality of, interest changes, and good news or bad news about a company, such as earnings forecasts. The fundamentalist's task is to assess the effect of each of these factors and then, in light of those assessments, predict what the price of a stock or the market itself will do. To simplify things, the analyst categorizes influences into two groups. One group consists of business fundamentals that have to do with the issuing company. The other is made up of economic fundamentals that relate to the economy and the market.

One type of business fundamental consists of a company's earnings. The assumption is that if management is capable of producing high earnings in the future, the company is likely to grow considerably. When all that happens, the stock generally appreciates in value because it draws investor demand interest, increasing numbers of buy orders, thereby "bidding up" the price in the marketplace. "Growth stock," as this kind of investment is called, offers an opportunity for significant increases in value over the original investment.

To measure earnings objectively, fundamentalists apply something known as a price–earnings (P/E) ratio. It is a useful measure for evaluating the quality of a stock investment is price earnings ratio. Price–earnings ratio is an indicator of money. This ratio is calculated as the stock price divided by the corporate earnings for the fiscal year that is most currently reported. In other words, this ratio, as its name implies, compares a stock's price with the company's earnings per share, by means of a very effective formula P/E. Current market price per share of the stock divided by the company's earnings per share equals ratio or relationship between P over E. Generally, earnings per share (EPS) is basically corporate net earnings, less any preferred dividends, divided by outstanding common stocks and dilutive securities.

Within the EPS calculation, dilutive securities represent those securities have the potential to become common shares, that is, those that potentially can be converted into common stock. Examples of such dilutive securities include convertible preferreds, bonds, or exercisable warrants, all of which are convertible into common stock. The term "dilutive" refers to the ability of the security to either decrease the earnings per share or increase the loss per share. This meaning is consistent with the calculation as outstanding dilutive securities increase the denominator.

The price–earnings ratio can only be calculated based on positive actual dollar and cents earnings. There cannot be a negative P/E ratio, as losses and zero earnings are excluded from the calculation. Furthermore, the P/E ratio is a relationship of price per share and earnings per share. A high ratio is often interpreted as an overvalued stock. In the long run, any market sell off would result in a downward spiral. Such a downward spiral has been illustrated by the example of the recent technology downturn.

Companies with low price–earnings ratios also present a safer investment because the company has a strong earnings base and would most often be a less volatile stock. In fact, the stock may be undervalued. Of course, other market indicators have to be considered, such as the book value of a company in addition to its yield, debt, and source of earnings.

For example, suppose a company earns a net profit of $500,000 and it has 1 million common shares issued and outstanding for the entire time period that is being analyzed. There are no preferred dividends nor dilutive securities outstanding in this example. The company's earnings per share are 50¢ per share, or $500,000 divided by 1 million shares. Suppose further that the stock is selling for $10. To calculate the P/E ratio, simply divide the market price by the earnings per share: $10 divided by 50¢ equals 20 to 1. What does that number tell the analyst? For one thing, this ratio is on the "high" side, indicating that this might be considered a growth stock. The rationale is that earnings heavily outweigh the current market price of the stock (by 20 to 1) and that the price is likely to rise dramatically as the company's earning power is recognized. This is one approach.

It also might be that the market is generally in an uptrend and that this stock is simply being swept along with the market. For example, in the bull markets of early 1929, 1938, 1946, and 1998, the Dow Jones Industrial companies had P/E ratios of 19 to 1, 25 to 1, and 20 to 1, and again 20 to 1, respectively. In the bear markets of 1942 and 1953, P/E ratios were closer to 10 to 1.

As a rule, P/E ratios are "bid up" during bull markets and "sold down" in bear markets. Investors evaluating a stock for its growth potential must distinguish how much of the ratio is due to the stock's potential and how much is due to the excessive demand in the market, to repeat a recent phrase of note, "Irrational Exuberance."

The P/E ratios of large, established companies tend to be lower. The reason is that their growth phase is largely over, and so the market value of their stock reflects their actual current earnings rather than potential future earnings. There is therefore a closer correlation between price and earnings than in more speculative stocks. Usually, in this category of low P/E ratios, for example, are the "bid cap" (that is, large, well capitalized) companies of the Dow Jones averages.

In addition to growth, investors also buy stocks for yield, or income, in the form of dividends. Yield is measure of the dividend payment as a percentage of the current stock price. The formula to calculate the current yield is the dollar and cents dividend per common share divided by the current market value of the stock.

Expressed in terms of dollars, however, a dividend is not a very good indicator. If the holder of preferred stock is paid, say, $5 per share, how good a return is that on the original investment? How can it be compared fairly with yields on other investments? To make such evaluations and comparisons, a share is expressed in terms of a percentage. For example, if a stock is purchased at a price of $100 and is paying $5 in dividends, the yield is 5 percent, calculated by the $5 per share dividend divided by $100 per share market value. But 5 percent on a yield basis can be an unappealing yield when other instruments, such as bonds, are paying 8 percent, 9 percent, or 10 percent. Suppose the price of the stock drops from $100 to $52. At that price the yield increases, because at a price of $52 for the stock the dividend of $5 will calculate a yield of 9.6 percent, calculated as $5 divided by $52. Given that yield, called the "current" yield, which is now competitive with other instruments yielding 8 to 10 percent, overlooks the nearly 50 percent drop in the stock price.

The instruments that compete chiefly with stocks for investors' dollars are bonds, which, like preferreds, pay a fixed income. For example, a bond with a $1,000 face value and an 8 percent yield pays an annual yield of $80 ($1,000 × 0.08).

The traditional assumption is that, when stock yields are lower than bond yields, investors' money "migrates" to the bond market. Yet history repeatedly has gainsayed this dictum. In early 1929, during the stock market's heyday, and again from 1959 to the crash in October of 1987, stock yields were lower than bond yields. Conceivably the lure of large gains during a bull market outweighs the "wisdom" of opting for the higher, fixed yields of the bond market.

In evaluating the investment-worthiness of a stock, a fundamentalist employs many more analytical tools than the P/E ratio and percentage of yield. Using information in a company's financial statements, security analysts (as fundamentalists are known in this role) make many financial comparisons or ratios: debt to equity, earnings to sales, book value per share or net asset value per share as it is sometimes called. This book value (B.V.) is calculated by subtracting liabilities (L) from assets (A), and dividing the difference by shares outstanding:

$$\left(\text{B.V.} = \frac{A - L}{\text{Shares outstanding}} \right)$$

If a stock is trading below book, it is fundamentally said to be "cheap," meaning it's a bargain. They also compare the company's ratios with accepted industry standards: is the company doing better or worse than the industry norms? They further try to establish trends in the company's progress from year to year. Are earnings up from last year? Has management put the company deeper in debt? Have increased sales yielded higher profits, or have increased selling expenses offset the gains? These are the types of questions asked by the fundamentalist when analyzing a particular stock.

Beyond evaluating the merits of a single stock as an investment, fundamentalists face a broad array of market fundamentals, including prevailing interest rates, trade and budget deficits, the value of the dollar, and program trading. Chief among market fundamental factors, interest rates are thought to affect the stock market in several ways. First, when interest rates rise, they represent an increase in the "cost" of money borrowed by corporations. As such, they act as a damper on expansion and on stock market prices. On the other hand, "cheap" money (low interest rates) is typically expected to be anti-recessionary because it encourages corporations to undertake large, capital-intensive projects. Low rates therefore are thought to create jobs, increase the demand for raw materials, and generally stimulate the stock market. Second, fluctuations in prevailing interest rates alter the relationship between stock and bond yields. As interest rates rise, investors can get better yields on short-term instruments like certificates of deposit. Two things then happen: the prices of bonds and preferred stock with lower yields begin to drop, so as to increase their current yields, and new issues of bonds start to carry higher coupon, or nominal, yields. The net effect is that money tends to flow out of the market for common stock by aggressive selling and into the bond market. As we've seen, however, this is not always the case when a bull market is in motion.

Finally, higher interest rates mean that investors have to pay more for margin, that is, for the funds they borrowed from their brokerage firms to buy stock. Escalated interest expenses eat into earnings, thereby cutting down on the number of would-be stock buyers. Demand is thus decreased, with a deflating effect on prices.

Compared to interest rates, the effect of budget and trade deficits on the stock market is not as clear. There certainly seems to be a negative psychological impact of the word "deficit." Beyond that, however, budget deficits mean that our government owes money, and in fact the amount owed is measured in the trillions of dollars. That debt is represented by the bonds, notes, and bills—the IOUs—issued by the Treasury. Much of these securities are being bought by financial institutions. Every time the U.S. government issues more Treasury debt securities, they are there to buy. To many observers, this arrangement represents fearful dependence on the affluence of other countries.

Should foreign holders opt to stop buying U.S. debt, the overall economic effect could be catastrophic. Although this situation remains basically the same on a day-to-day basis, most market participants do not include it in their considerations, except in times of market crisis, when the sensitivity to this precarious arrangement rises dramatically.

The trade deficit is more of an ongoing and immediate consideration, because it means that American industry, as a whole, is paying more money to overseas companies than those companies are paying to their U.S. counterparts. Thus, capital is leaking out of the country, capital that could be fueling growth in stateside firms, with concomitant activity in the stock market.

Yet, neither type of deficit seemed to hamper the raging five-year bull market that preceded the crash of 1987. Although these deficits should have starved the bull market of 1982–1987 of capital, their "predictable," "logical" effects simply did not happen. In the aftermath of "Black" Monday (October 19, 1987), analysts became more concerned with these presumably negative influences. In fact, the deficits commanded newspapers' headlines for weeks thereafter.

Also in the headlines, with suddenly stepped-up emphasis, was the falling value of the dollar. The fears were threefold. First, foreign investors would be discouraged from buying U.S. stock because stock prices are generally expected to fall with the value of the dollar. Second, inflation would start up again, the norm being that 1 percent of inflation can be expected for every 10 percent drop in the value of the dollar. Finally, the prices of foreign goods would increase, in terms of dollars, thereby drawing capital out of the stateside market.

As it turned out, the Fed eventually let the dollar float according to the push and pull of supply and demand. The thinking is that two things should happen. One, buying of American goods by both domestic and foreign companies should pick up. Second, given a floating U.S. dollar, the Fed can allow a decline in interest rates, thereby forestalling the recession that many analysts expected. By the end of 1987, the dollar had indeed lost some value, but the United States was getting the cooperation of other governments in stabilizing the trend.

Interest rates were holding steady, and economic analysts were becoming slightly more optimistic in their forecasts. Again, the expected effects of the loss in value did not come to pass.

As you can see, the fundamentalist approach is fraught with complicated and perhaps ambiguous cause-and-effect relationships, as well complex interrelationships among the many influences on the market. One wonders whether, beyond selecting a suitable growth or income stock, anyone can foresee the effect of these many causes in any accurate, coherent way. In fact, some critics maintain that one solution to the complexity of modern analysis—automation—is in itself a self-defeating approach. If the market is for the most part efficient, then the automated trading programs of institutional investors, and brokerage firms, both in the United States and abroad, may be considered just one more factor in a market that discounts all factors. From this point of view, automation only makes the market *more* efficient, and certainly more explosively volatile, and therefore the task of predicting future price movements all the *more* difficult and complex.

■ THE TECHNICAL APPROACH

In the world of stock trading, many investors find it necessary to rely on reports and analyses upon which they try to make intelligible decisions as to what stock should they risk their money. To help respond to these needs of investors, stock analysis has provided a way for traders to make their determination. Analysis is all about prediction, that is, trying to forecast the direction that a stock price is moving. As discussed earlier, fundamental analysis is a technique that enables stock market investors to make informed, rational decisions for investment. While fundamental analysis provides a valuable mechanism for investors, it should be used not solely but rather in conjunction or in addition to other types of analyses. Well, another important form of analysis upon which this chapter is based in addition to fundamental analysis, and whose use has spread throughout the marketplace, is technical analysis. Technical stock analysis, which is one of the oldest kinds of analyses for stocks, has been integrated, to some degree and extent, in the strategies and plans of many investors that help assist them in making investing choices in the market.

In a nutshell, technical analysis focuses upon searching for trends and patterns to help predict stock price activity. Basically, technical analysis is an approach to following the price activity, more specifically, the direction in which a price of a security moves. In short, it is an analysis of the supply and demand of a stock. It is also a chart study of trends, both upward and downward, price movements, break outs, breakdowns, and reversals.

To detect and follow trends and patterns for prediction purposes, technical analysis utilizes charting and enables investors to identify signals as to when to sell and purchase. It is essential that one using technical analysis be able to create charts and understand the information displayed. Technical analysis, however, is a technique that requires one seeking to benefit from it to become skilled in its art.

Technical analysts, referred to as chartists, sidestep the whole question of "calibrating" an efficient market. They do not attempt to relate economic causes to effects. Instead, they study the effects of many inscrutable influencing factors and follow price movements by analyzing market forces of supply and demand. In effect, they navigate the market, analyzing and predicting trends based on a belief that history will always repeat itself.

The utilization of technical analysis through charting is based on certain precepts regarding the market. Technical analysis is based on the belief that because human mentality and action based upon it is repetitious, market movement can be predicted based upon how people react under certain financial conditions. In addition, technical analysis functions upon the precept that prices move in a constant direction until an event or external condition occurs to disrupt the price movement. Finally, market news or conditions that affect the value of a stock are already accounted for and built into the price of the stock once these become public knowledge.

Furthermore, the school of thought behind technical analysis has also been influenced and shaped in part by principles of the Dow Theory, which was discussed earlier.

How do present price movements indicate future levels? The primary approach of technical analysis is that certain patterns of price movements repeat themselves. If you can correctly identify the pattern early in its development, you can then foretell future prices. As mentioned earlier, technical analysts believe that history will always repeat itself in their search for continuing patterns.

In addition to price patterns, technical analysts also keep an eye on a number of indicators, such as trading volume, breadth of the market, and new highs/lows. With respect to trading volume, the working assumption is that light volume means that the accompanying pattern will not gather a lot of momentum due to lack of demand; on heavy volume, it will. A lot of trading means that many investors are involved in the price movement and that the movement is not likely to peter out easily.

The "breadth" of the market also counts. This represents the number of issues advancing or declining. If more issues are being bought than sold, count the up-ticks versus down; the market is said to be "technically strong." If more stocks are being sold than bought, it is "technically weak." This makes sense. Whereas volume does not indicate which or how many issues are trading, breadth does. If a handful of "big cap," high-priced stocks have an active day and pull the Dow Jones averages upward slightly, a technically weak report on breadth would indicate technically a very weak market, despite volume.

Another indicator for technical analysts is the number of new highs or new lows. This is not to be confused with stocks that advance or decline. A "new high" or a "new low" is a price level not achieved by a stock in the prior 12 months. A series of new highs or lows is taken to indicate an up-or-down trend. So, if many more stocks are reaching new highs than are dropping to new lows, this is considered a bullish sign. Many more new lows than new highs are looked upon as a bearish indicator.

Volume, breadth, and new highs or lows are all grouped under the heading "technical indicators." Another group consists of "sentiment indicators." Short interest—or the amount of short selling in the market—is one type of sentiment indicator. By going short, people in the market are saying that they expect prices to go down.

But remember that, built into short sales, however, is their own undoing. "He who sells what isn't his'n, gives it back or goes to prison." Sooner or later, short sale positions have to be closed out. The only way to do that is for the short sellers to deliver the stock to the lending brokerage firm—and so they must buy it back in order to return the stock to the lender. Once the buying starts, the buy orders infuse demand—upward pressure—into the market. Prices stop dropping and may even start to climb a bit. The point at which prices start turning upward again is called a "support level." This is a level below which prices should not drop because of purchase interest at that price. The reason could be that short sellers are covering their positions, but there are other reasons as well, most of them having to do with investor psychology.

Let's look at an example. Suppose the market is "overvalued" (that is, people are paying more for stocks than they really should because of a generally bullish but speculative air in the market). A technical statement is that buying will always cause more buying; selling will always cause more selling. Sooner or later, holders of stock will start selling off, expecting a downturn. Those who do not own stock, with the same expectation, will start to sell short. Before long, the market has indeed turned downward. As prices drop off, more "longs" sell off and more "shorts" are created. Again, selling always causes more selling. When that happens, other longs, hoping perhaps to salvage some portion of their investment, sell off, driving the prices down again. At a certain point, the remaining longs start to sell to the shorts who are covering their positions. Perhaps others are buying the stock simply because its price is low. At this point, the buy orders are starting to offset sell orders, and prices edge upward again. Those who've been waiting for the turn, start to buy, thus accelerating the move upward.

Support is a price floor. Resistance is a ceiling. Perhaps a stock is attracting a lot of investors, demand is high, and the price is being bid up. At some point, the market runs out of buyers, the buy orders dry up, and the price rise shows. Some stockholders will begin to wonder whether the stock is about to drop in price, and some will sell off. Now there are more sellers than buyers. The price backs off and there are more sellers than buyers. The price backs off and may rise again to the same level, only to back off once more. Thus a resistance level—a price ceiling—has been established.

What are the reasons for it? There is no formula that tells you exactly what a stock is worth. The market price is certainly the result of the issuing company's performance and profitability. But that's not all. A price can be driven up just because the corporation is in a "popular" industry among investors. The current technology craze for example, because the market "looks strong," or because of any number of other reasons. The answer to the question why is largely psychological.

While fundamentalists might try to analyze why prices move as they do, technicians simply accept such movements and chart them.

In contrast, contrarians do not seek such answers. Instead, they simply determine what the market is doing—and do the opposite. The assumption is that most market participants are doing the opposite of what they should be doing. The thinking is still followed by many today, and is known as the "contrarian opinion" theory. Indeed, the theory might have merit at times, but it's all theory, yet many individual investors, acting on old information, wind up buying when they should be selling and vice versa.

Another theory that takes a contrarian view of the individual investor's ability is the "odd-lot theory." Small investors often deal in odd-lots (trades involving 1 to 99 shares), and odd-lot activity can therefore be taken as a gauge of what the small investor is doing. According to this theory, you should always take positions opposing those and contrary to the odd-lot trend. In other words, if odd-lotters are on balance buying, "sell"; if odd-lotters are selling, "buy."

As mentioned earlier, technical analysis is made possible through charting. Charting plays a major part in technical analysis, regardless of the stage of technology presently available to investors. Charting encompasses a variety of time periods, that is for example, day to day or month to month. Charting can utilize different financial indicators, such as price, ratios, interest, and volume, to name a few. They are used to help investors map out the market. Common forms of charting used by investors and traders are the bar charts, point and figure charts, and line charts.

Bar charts are often more advantageous than point-and-figure charts and are the most popular form of charting. A bar chart is present where the y-vertical axis reflects the price and the x-horizontal axis reflects time, with dates indicated along the bottom of the chart. (See Figures 12–2 and 12–4.) Bar charts are used to show day to day, week to week, or month to month activity, indicating the close, low, and high prices or averages. A bar chart, unlike the point-and-figure chart to be discussed next, enables investors to display more information and utilizes more financial indicators for analysis. Furthermore, in addition to prices, periods of time are shown and accounted for on the bar chart, but not on point-and-figure charts.

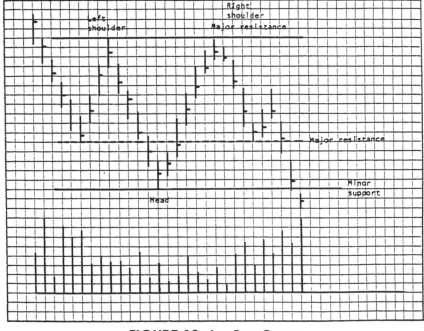

FIGURE 12–4. Bar Chart

A point-and-figure chart demonstrates price movements through x's and o's that alternate. In a point-and-figure chart, an "x" column means prices are rising whereas an "o" represents a fall in prices. (See Figures 12–2, 12–3, and 12–5.) In a point-and-figure chart, an "x" or "o" is not entered until there is a movement of at least one point in either direction. Also in a point-and-figure chart, each column shows a trend or indication of which the direction the price is moving.

As said earlier, point-and-figure charts do not account for time periods. Point-and-figure charts are not as popular as the bar charts, as they require more time and effort to create and maintain. However, a point-and-figure chart does enable investors to detect signals to buy and sell with more ease and efficiency than a bar chart. Also, point-and-figure charts are useful for securities that are active as they plot a minimum change of a point.

Another important kind of chart used by technical analysts is the line chart. (See Figure 12–6.) Line charts are utilized to show the pattern or trend of one statistic, such as price. Within a line chart, indicators such as relative strength and moving averages may also be evident.

FIGURE 12–5. POINT-AND-FIGURE CHART

FIGURE 12–6. LINE CHART

As a side note, for an investor wishing to manually perform line or bar charting, the graph paper used should have either one of two scales: (1) the semilog, that is, geometrical delination scale, or (2) arithmetic scale. Semilog scale is preferable for investors wishing to make their analysis with percentages or even on a long-term basis. On the other hand, arithmetic scale is preferable for investors wishing to analyze over the short term or even, instead of using percentages, follow prices on a point basis.

Besides charting, another major aspect of technical analysis is the concept of the trend. There is no question that trends play an important role to all kinds of investors in technical analysis, from the most amateur to even the most sophisticated and experienced of market players. Trends are studied to help investors make determinations as to what phase of activity the market is currently experiencing and what the future possibly holds. Trends help investors from jumping into or out of a position too soon or too late.

Trends can be detected on the various types of charts and are identified as uptrends or downtrends. Uptrends occur when there is a pattern in which each trough/peak is higher than the previous one. Lows counterbalance the trend. (See Figure 12–7.) Downtrends occur when each trough/peak is lower than the previous one. (See Figure 12–8.) However, in the absence of uptrends and downtrends present, there is a horizontal, or sideway, market. In this kind of market, prices fall within a trading range, in which prices are relatively constant and hard to predict which direction they are going. (See Figure 12–9.) Furthermore, trends of individual securities and of the market, in general, encounter high and low extremes. For instance, a high extreme can indicate that a price has reached its peak—that the price has topped out. Likewise, a low extreme can indicate that a price has fallen to its floor—that it has reached its bottom. These tops and bottoms are indicative of human psychology. A peak can represent greediness, seeking the maximum price but there is no one else to whom this can be sold. A bottom can represent fearfulness in the market, in which the value hits its lowest point as there are no more sellers of the security at hand.

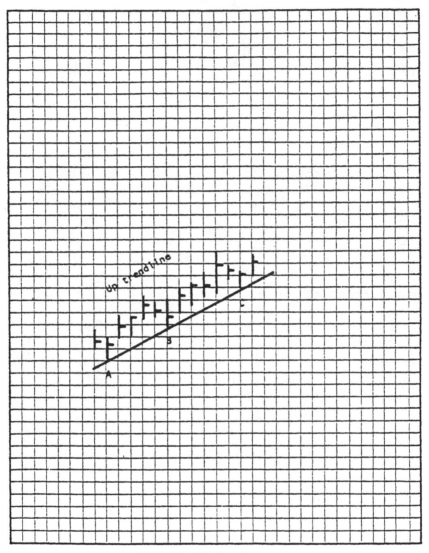

FIGURE 12-7. UPTREND

To help detect trends, investors often utilize the moving average based on a determined number of days, i.e. 10, 20, 30 days. To illustrate this concept, a 30 moving day average, for example, is calculated by dividing the numerator of the total of

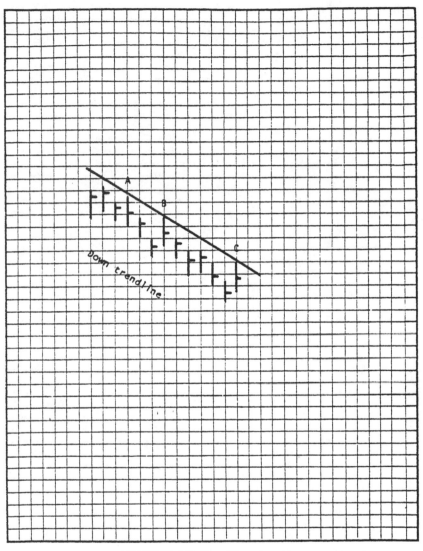

FIGURE 12–8. Downtrend

the closing prices of the most recent 30 days by the denominator of 30. This is a moving average because it ensures that the result will be updated by adding the price of the newest closing price while simultaneously disposing of the oldest closing price. It is

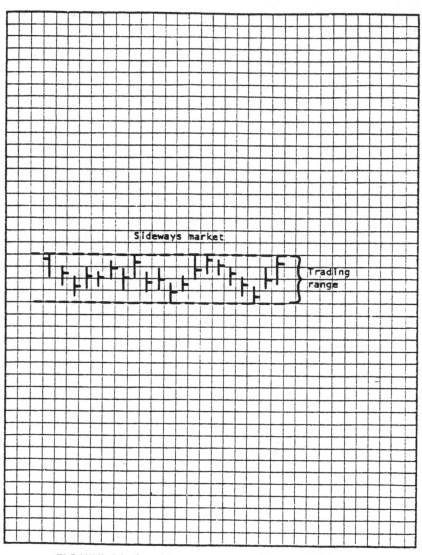

FIGURE 12–9. Horizontal, or Sideways, Market

up to the chartist to decide what the best terms are for him to base upon in order to detect a trend.

Technical analysis also maintains there are different concepts that encompass the reasons for price movements. For instance, according to support and resistance principle, which is integral to technical analysis, prices that fall on its demand but swing back up reached support level, a point at which the interest of investors to purchase can defeat pressures to sell. This causes a price fall known as a reaction low or trough. On the other hand, the resistance level, or supply level, is the point at which the interest of investors to purchase is defeated by pressures to sell. This is indicated where an upswing then fall in the price is demonstrated, and is known as a reaction high or peak. The occurrence of support and resistance situations is many times influenced by the amount of trading volume present (Figures 12–10 and 12–11). Furthermore, support and resistance may either represent levels based on either actual price activity or human psychology. For instance, they represent levels based on actual price activity when the focus of the study is a particular stock. This is due to the fact that this is based on the actual sell/buy transactions occurring among investors in the market. However, if the focus is an average of some aspect of market activity, then they represent levels based more on human psychology; this is due to the fact that averages are not directly traded in the market. Support and resistance levels are often analyzed on both bar charts and point and figure charts.

An example illustrating support and resistance is the model of a rectangular base pattern. (See Figure 12–12.) In such a pattern, in a tight trading range, there are alternating peaks and bottoms over several months. There is much volume until prices begin to go up and down. This is followed by a combination of falling prices and high volume with a possible heavy volume in price advances. This combination of activity signals a sell off in stocks. Rising prices are then accompanied by heavier trading volume which eventually go in sync with a movement in prices; this demonstrates resistance.

Another important model of trading activity is called a "head and shoulders top" pattern, and it signals a reversal, that is, an upward to downward trend, or vice versa, in the market. This pattern is so named because of the shape of a head and shoulders outlined on the chart. (See Figure 12–13.) In a head and shoulders model, prices begin to rise again after retracing

FIGURE 12–10. SUPPORT/RESISTANCE

only a third of the previous rise. The head and shoulders model is consistently repetitive enough for chartists to predict the drop. Chartists who correctly identify this pattern can buy at points B–D and sell at points A–C–E. That is buying low and selling

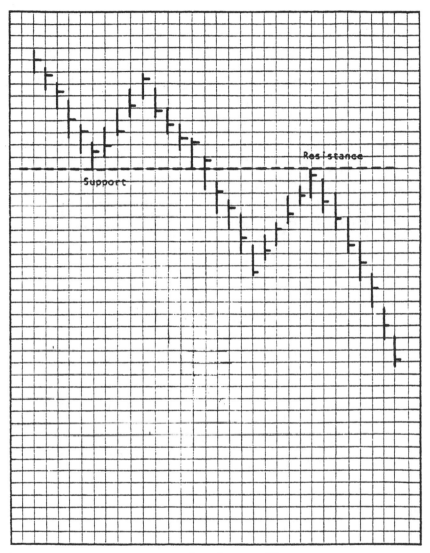

FIGURE 12–11. Support/Resistance

high in its most efficient form. Like the maxim itself, however, it is often easier said than done. (See Figure 12–14 for another head and shoulders pattern. Also refer back to Figure 12–3 for some of the many other price patterns in charting.)

FIGURE 12–12. RECTANGULAR BASE PATTERN

256

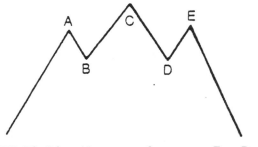

FIGURE 12–13. HEAD AND SHOULDERS TOP PATTERN

Other important aspects of technical analysis include relative strength and analysis of the market as a whole. Relative strength concerns the performance and activity of a particular stock or category of stocks relative, that is, as compared to the performance and activity of the entire market. The purpose of relative strength is to make a determination as to whether the movement of stock(s) is(are) consistent with the rest of the market, and to what degree of upward or downward variance there exists. In addition to relative strength, analysis of the overall, general market itself is something that is accomplished through the use of averages and indexes. Popular among such indicators include the DJIA, or Dow Jones Industrial Average. How heavily a stock weighs within such an average depends on the present trading value of the stock.

With respect to structuring a complete investment decision-making plan, investors should utilize both technical and fundamental analysis. By limiting themselves to only one form of analysis, investors may still make profitable decisions. However, they may increase the chance of subjecting themselves to immediate stock losses by ignoring valuable information of the second analysis. For example, an investor using fundamental analysis exclusively may purchase securities of a corporation with very good economic potential; the fundamentals for the stock are very positive stock. However, the investor may lose capital fast. By ignoring technical analysis, he is unaware that the short-term price of the stock is too high and a fall is coming. The investor ends up buying the stock too high before the decline. This down-

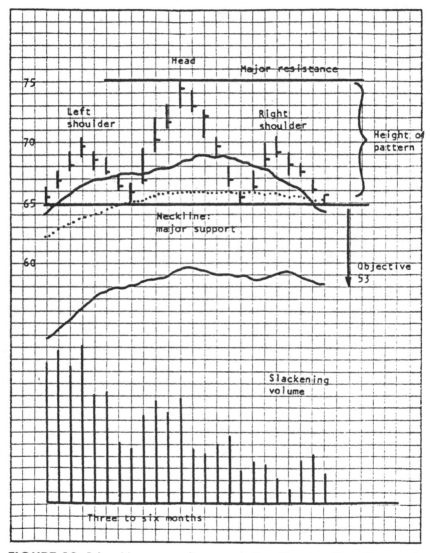

FIGURE 12–14. HEAD AND SHOULDERS TOP PATTERN (2ND EXAMPLE)

turn activity could have been foreseen had the investor implemented technical analysis techniques, in which case he would have waited for the stock price to fall before making the purchase. Likewise, investors who limit themselves to only technical analysis, while ignoring the economic information that fundamental analysis has to offer, increase the risk for immediate stock losses. In a word to the wise, both types of analysis should be known and utilized by the investor.

In sum, technical analysis and its utilization of charts provides investors with an important approach to decision making in the world of securities investing. Without technical analysis, investors may deprive themselves of an advantageous tool. Lack of this tool may, in turn, limit their ability to reap capital gains.

ANALYZING STOCKS
The Corporation's "Report Card"

Most people measure their personal financial success by the amount of their earnings and by the amount of their accumulated assets. Everyone wants to earn a decent salary and hopes to get an increase each year. We also strive to provide for a better life style, with a graceful retirement, by putting our "extra" earnings aside. We hope that our "nest egg" increases over time. It is a fairly simple matter to estimate our income each year. In fact, we *have* to, because we owe part of this income to the federal government, and possibly another portion to our home state and/or city, in the form of taxes. Not too many people keep track of their accumulated assets on a continuing basis, although it is a very good idea to do so.

Corporations *do* track their income and assets on a regular basis. Their income is reported at least annually in the company's income statement, also known as its *P&L* (*profit and loss statement*). The corporation's assets (and liabilities) are also carefully tracked and reported, at least annually, in its *balance sheet*. A corporation's balance sheet and income statement show its earnings and its assets. The publication of these statements is looked forward to eagerly by security analysts and the investing public. These reports are the company's "report card." They show its progress, with respect to how much they are earning for their shareholders—how much the company is actually worth, at least with respect to assets.

Every publicly held corporation strives for growth in earnings, dividends, and assets. While a single balance sheet or income statement might not be all that informative, the *trend* of earnings and asset growth is important. Analysts and individual investors attempt to spot companies that are in a growth phase, and they pore over corporate reports looking for such "buys." Serious investors should be able to read and interpret these statements. They may not have the same thoroughness and degree of professionalism as an accountant or securities analyst, but they should at least know how to apply some of the more common "tests" of corporate well being. We'll just do a few simple applications in this chapter, but a number of excellent texts develop these issues further, such as *The NYIF Vest-Pocket Guide to Stock Brokerage Math.*

■ CURRENT ASSETS AND CURRENT LIABILITIES

A corporation's *current assets* include its cash, as well as other items that will become cash generally within the next 12 months. These "soon-to-become-cash" items might include, in addition to the company's current cash position, its marketable securities, accounts receivable, and inventory. These are *assets,* things of value that a company owns or has owed to it. It owns its marketable securities and inventory, and is owed its accounts receivable. Most of these assets are quite liquid and may easily be converted to cash. The one current asset that isn't readily convertible into cash is its inventory. A company's *quick assets* include all of its current assets *except* inventory.

The company's *current liabilities* include those items that the company expects to pay out during generally the next 12 months. These would include, among other items, the company's accounts payable, salaries and wages, taxes and interest. Whereas current assets reflect where the cash is coming from, current liabilities show where the money is going. Here is only the "top" half of a balance sheet. It shows the company's current assets and current liabilities and, as shown, is far from being a complete balance sheet:

Cash	$1,100	Accounts payable	$700
Marketable securities	300	Salaries payable	400
Accounts receivable	800	Interest payable	25
Inventory	1,000	Accrued taxes	75
	$3,200		$1,200

It is obvious that a company should have more money coming in than it expects to pay out. Our "sample" company has $3,200 in current assets and $1,200 in current liabilities. It has $2,000 more than it needs to meet its current obligations ($3,200 − $1,200), and this amount, $2,000, is called the company's *working capital.* If we divide the current assets by the current liabilities ($3,200 ÷ $1,200), we get the company's *current ratio:* 2.7 to 1. This indicates that the company has $2.70 in current assets for every dollar of current liabilities; it has its short-term debts "covered" 2.7 times over. A very general rule of thumb is that a manufacturing company should have a current ratio of at least 2 to 1. So our illustrative company seems to be in good shape.

■ CAN THE CORPORATION PAY ITS WAY?

The most severe test of a company's ability to meet its short-term obligations is known as its *quick asset ratio,* also known as the *liquidity ratio.* This ratio measures the relationship between a company's *quick* assets and its current liabilities. We can easily calculate our company's quick assets by simply subtracting inventory (a nonliquidity asset) from total current assets and dividing by its current liabilities: ($3,200 − $1,000) ÷ $1,200 = 1.8 to 1. This is a respectable ratio, as 1 to 1 is the usual standard. At least for the near term, the company we have "analyzed" seems okay.

■ USING DEBT AND CAPITAL STRUCTURE OF A CORPORATION AS SOURCES OF LONG-TERM FUNDS

Corporations have found that issuance of debt and equity instruments to investors have proved a useful way of raising corporate funds. Often, long term debt, in the form of bonds and debentures, are issued. These represent long term liabilities or obligations of the corporation owed to investors, which often carry a related burden of paying interest expense.

Interest on the company's outstanding bonds *must* be paid; if not, the trustee for the bonds which every corporation must appoint to safeguard Bondholder interest, may force the company to liquidate. It is extremely important, therefore, that the company earn enough money to meet any interest and principal payments due on its bonds (its *debt service*). If the company is able to properly utilize its debt, by making more money on the borrowed funds than it is paying out to service the debt, things are fine. But when earnings are insufficient to pay debt service, it can be catastrophic. The "leveraged buyout" craze of the 1980s and early 1990s saw many companies fail because they were too heavily laden with debt. The "junk" bonds (unsecured high yield debt bonds) that were issued proved, in many cases, to be too great a debt burden. Companies that have a disproportionate amount of debt are considered speculative and should be avoided by the conservative investor.

Another way for corporations to raise funds is the issuance of stocks to shareholders. Capital accounts, often consisting of common and preferred stock authorized, issued, and/or outstanding, are found in the stockholder's equity section of the balance sheet. The stockholders' equity, or net worth, section of the balance sheet often displays the

- The par value of preferred stocks.
- The value of its common stock and the value that the company may have received through the sale of common stock (paid-in capital).
- Accumulated earnings (retained earnings) that the company has reinvested in additional assets rather than paying such earnings out to shareholders in the form of dividends.

The balance sheet shows what a company owns (its assets), what a company owes (its liabilities), and the difference between the two, its *net worth (for corportions, stockholders' equity)*. In theory, the sum of the balance sheet's last three items (the common stock account, paid-in-capital, retained earnings), show what total amount would be due the common stockholders if the company were to be liquidated. This liquidation value, per share of common stock, is known as *book value per share,* calculated again as assets, less liabilities, divided by shares outstanding. Investors should examine a corporate balance sheet to become familiar with these items, which are beyond the scope of this text.

■ THE INCOME STATEMENT

The financial statements of a corporation include its P&L (profit and loss), or income statement. The income statement shows how much the company took in (sales) and what it laid out in expenses. The famous *bottom line* is the company's *net income or net loss*. From the income statement we can derive, among other things, the company's profit margins, its cash flow, and its earnings per share.

The company's *net profit margin* is calculated as net income divided by net sales. *Net sales* are gross sales less both sales' discounts taken and sales' returns and allowances. Here in our example, as there are no sales' discounts nor returns and

Sales	$100,000,000
Less:	
Cost of goods sold	−55,000,000
Selling, general, and administrative expenses	−20,000,000
Depreciation expense	− 7,000,000
Operating income	18,000,000
Plus: Other income	+ 2,000,000
Total income	20,000,000
Less:	
Interest expense	− 1,000,000
Taxes	− 6,500,000
Net income	**$ 12,500,000**

FIGURE 13–1 INCOME STATEMENT (SIMPLIFIED VERSION)

allowances indicated, net sales are $100,000,000. Furthermore, as net income is $12,500,000, we can calculate the net profit margin as follows:

$$\text{Net Profit Margin} = \frac{\$12,000,000 \text{ net income}}{\$100,000,000 \text{ net sales}} = .125 = 12.5\%$$

Thus, with the net profit margin formula, it can be said that net income is 12.5 % of net sales.

The company's *gross profit margin* is calculated as gross profit divided by net sales. *Gross profit* is net sales less cost of sales. (Cost of sales is also known as cost of goods sold.) Here in our example, we just determined net sales to equal $100,000,000. As cost of goods sold equals $55,000,000, gross profit is calculated as $100,000,000 net sales less $55,000,000 cost of goods sold, or $45,000,000. Furthermore, gross profit margin is calculated as follows:

$$\text{Gross Profit Margin} = \frac{\$45,000,000 \text{ gross profit}}{\$100,000,000 \text{ net sales}} = .45 = 45\%$$

Thus, with the gross profit margin formula, it can be said that gross profit is 45% of net sales.

Cash flow is the sum of net income and depreciation: $12,500 + $7,000 = $19,500 cash flow.

Earnings per share (EPS), probably the most important measure of a company's success, is calculated as follows. Although there are variations of the earnings per share formula, financial papers, such as *The Wall Street Journal,* uses the formula that incorporates the concept of dilutive securities whereby net income less preferred dividends are divided by both common shares outstanding and dilutive securities. Dilutive securities are those securities that potentially can be converted into common shares as described in Chapter 12. Assuming for the corporate income statement presented in Figure 13-1 that there were $500,000 paid in preferred dividends, 6,000,000 common shares outstanding and no dilutive securities, its earnings would be $2.00 per share:

$$\text{EPS} = \frac{\$12{,}500{,}000 \text{ net income less } \$500{,}000 \text{ preferred dividends}}{6{,}000{,}000 \text{ common shares outstanding less } 0 \text{ dilutive securities}} = \$2.00 \text{ per share}$$

OR:

$$\text{EPS} = \frac{\$12{,}000{,}000}{6{,}000{,}000} = \$2.00 \text{ earnings per share}$$

Figure 13–2 shows the "Company Earnings" which is printed often in *The New York Times.* It shows how well, or how poorly, a company fared during the quarter (or year) covered. Note that the listing for Fox Entertainment Group Inc. shows net deficit earnings, or net *loss,* from the first quarter 2000 through and including September 30, 2000. Fox had a net profit of $0.06 per share in 1999, but experienced a decline in financial performance to a net loss per share of $0.63 at September 30, 2000. This figure shows the "bottom line" for the companies listed—which

COMPANY EARNINGS

For periods shown. In parenthesis, the first one to five letters before the comma are the company's stock ticker symbol. N after the comma indicates stock is listed on the New York Stock Exchange, A the American Stock Exchange, NNM Nasdaq National Market System, NSC Nasdaq Small Capitalization, and ECM Emerging Company Marketplace.

ArvinMeritor Inc. (ARM,N)

Qtr to Sept. 30	2000	1999
Sales	1,680,000,000	1,880,000,000
Net inc	29,000,000	b84,000,000
Share earns	.43	1.10
Shares outst	68,100,000	76,400,000

Year:

	2000	1999
Sales	7,722,000,000	7,491,000,000
Net inc	a287,000,000	c280,000,000
Share earns	4.02	3.67
Shares outst	71,400,000	76,300,000

a-Included income of $89 million related to sale of business and a loss of $30 million related to restructuring costs and other charges. Items totaled a gain of 46 cents a share.

b-Included a gain of 24 cents a share on the formation of a transmission and clutch joint venture with ZF Friedrichshafen AG.

c-Included income of $31 million related to sale of business and a loss of $35 million related to restructuring costs and other charges. Items totaled a loss of 1 cent a share.

AXA Financial Inc. (AXF,N)

3d qtr to Sept. 30	2000	1999
Revenue	1,742,900,000	1,483,700,000
Net loss	a106,400,000	b231,600,000
Share earns	(.26)	.51
Shares outst	441,400,000	441,900,000

a-Included gain of $107.5 million from investment banking and brokerage segment, and a loss of $407 million from a tax provision related to the planned disposal of the investment banking and brokerage segment.

b-Net income. Includes income of $84.9 million, or 18 cents a share, related to discontinued operations. Third quarter earnings exclude DLJ, which is now reported in net income as discontinued operations.

(Loss)

BP Amoco p.l.c. (BP,N)

3rd qtr to Sept 30	2000	1999
Net inc	a3,796,000,000	1,955,000,000
Share earns	1.01	.61
Shares outst	22,596,900,000	n/a

a-Included income of $289 million related to the integration of ARCO, Vastar, and Burmah Castrol and rationalization costs post the BP Amoco merger. Also included income of $449 million from adjustments related to the ARCO and Burmah Castrol acquisitions.

Share earnings figures reflect the price per American depository share, or ADS.

Cablevision Systems Corp. (CVC,N)

3d qtr to Sept. 30	2000	1999
Revenue	1,035,548,000	902,310,000
Net loss	a40,142,000	178,063,000
Share earns	(.23)	(1.17)
Shares outst	174,053,000	152,461,000

a-Included income of $130.8 million from the sale of cable assets.

b-Included a loss of $14 million, or 8 cents a share, related to discontinued operations.

c-Included a loss of $322 million, or $1.99 a share, related to discontinued operations

d-Included a loss of $22 million, or 14 cents a share, related to discontinued operations and a charge of $96 million, or 59 cents a share, on the divestiture of low-margin businesses and the realignment of service businesses.

(Loss)

Dell Computer Corp. (DELL,NNM)

3rd qtr to Oct. 27	2000	1999
Sales	8,260,000,000	6,780,000,000
Net inc	674,000,000	289,000,000
Share earns	.25	.11

Emerson Electric Co. (EMR,N)

Qtr to Sept. 30	2000	1999
Sales	4,065,000,000	3,620,100,000
Net inc	a371,000,000	c340,200,000
Share earns	.86	.78
Year sales	15,544,800,000	14,269,500,000
Net inc	b1,422,400,000	d1,313,600,000
Share earns	3.30	3.00

a-Included a loss of 9 cents a share related to goodwill amortization .

b-Included a loss of 33 cents a share related to goodwill amortization.

c-Included a loss of 7 cents a share related to goodwill amortization.

d-Included a loss of 27 cents a share related to goodwill amortization.

Encompass Services Corp. (ESR,N)

3d qtr to Sept. 30	2000	1999
Revenue	1,167,512,000	a969,741,000
Net inc	15,021,000	31,073,000
Share earns	.16	.38
Shares outst	64,946,000	82,321,000

a-Figures are pro forma to reflect the combined results of Encompass as if the merger of Building One and Group Maintenance America was completed January 1 Figures exclude all merger, integration and other related charges.

Federated Department Stores Inc. (FD,N)

3d qtr to Oct. 28	2000	1999
Sales	4,195,000,000	4,137,000,000
Net loss	a668,000,000	b123,000,000
Share earns	(3.32)	.56

a-Included Fingerhut asset impairment and restructuring charges of $795 million, or $3.58 a share.

b-Net income.

(Loss)

Fox Entertainment Group Inc. (FOX,N)

1st qtr to Sept. 30	2000	1999
Revenue	1,828,000,000	1,801,000,000
Net loss	a458,000,000	843,000,000
Share earns	(.63)	.06
Shares outst	724,000,000	714,000,000

a-Included a $494 million charge, or 58 cents a share, for an accounting change.

b-Net income.

(Loss)

a-Net income.

(Loss)

Loews Corp. (LTR,N)

3d qtr to Sept. 30	2000	1999
Revenue	5,776,400,000	5,513,800,000
Net inc	a679,600,000	b271,300,000
Share earns	a6.89	b2.52
Shares outst	98,600,000	107,600,000

a-Included income of $387.2 million, or $3.93 a share, related to investments gains.

b-Included income of $6.4 million, or 6 cents a share, related to investments gains.

Masco Corp. (MAS,N)

3d qtr to Sept. 30	2000	1999
Sales	1,893,000,000	1,704,000,000
Net inc	187,400,000	a64,900,000
Share earns	.41	.15
Shares outst	457,000,000	445,600,000

a-Included charges of $126 million related to pooling of interest mergers.

MetLife Inc. (MET,N)

3d qtr to Sept. 30	2000	1999
Revenue	8,017,000,000	6,219,000,000
Net inc	a241,000,000	b242,000,000
Share earns	.31	.31

a-Included net realized investment losses of $143 million.

b-Included demutualization expenses of $33 million and surplus taxes of $30 million.

News Corp. (NWS,N)

1st qtr to Sept. 30	2000	1999
Revenue	3,240,000,000	3,159,000,000
Net loss	a268,000,000	b165,000,000
Share earns	(.27)	.16

a-Included abnormal items which totaled a loss of $417 million, or 41 cents per American Depository Receipt.

b-Net income.

Share earnings figures reflect price per American depository share, or ADS.

(Loss)

OfficeMax Inc. (OMX,N)

3d qtr to Oct. 21	2000	1999
Sales	1,307,103,000	1,301,774,000
Net loss	a22,019,000	b37,440,000
Share earns	(.20)	(.33)
Shares outst	112,805,000	113,119,000

a-Included pretax charge of $19.5 million for a lawsuit settlement with Ryder Integrated Logistics Inc. Item totaled a loss of 10 cents a share.

b-Included a pretax charge of $83.3 million related to a supply-chain management initiative. Item totaled a loss of 47 cents a share.

(Loss)

UtiliCorp United Inc. (UCU,N)

3d qtr to Sept. 30	2000	1999
Sales	8,085,500,000	6,464,200,000
Net inc	a74,900,000	42,500,000
Share earns	.80	.46
Shares outst	93,900,000	92,500,000

a-Available to common shares.

Walt Disney Co. (DIS,N)

4th qtr to Sept. 30	2000	1999
Revenue	6,034,000,000	5,744,000,000
Net inc	240,000,000	b85,000,000
Share earns	.11	.04

FIGURE 13–2. COMPANY EARNINGS

companies *made* money (and how much) and which companies *lost* money (and how much).

Investors are understandably eager to purchase stocks that have ever-increasing earnings. They also look for "special situations" in which the company's earnings might be dramatically affected by a nonrecurring event such as a merger or a new discovery. Knowing how per-share earnings are derived, as well as how they are influenced by different circumstances, is part of being a well-informed investor in the stock market.

ONLINE TRADING IN THE STOCK MARKET
How Technology Has Changed the Financial Landscape

Trading in the stock market for the average individual investor has traditionally been conducted through personal contact directly with a broker, whether face to face or via the telephone. However, in the 1990s, with the growth of the modern version of the telegraph, that is, the Internet, plus the ready access it provides to a stream of communication and information, a revolutionary new technique was born that allowed direct market trading by individuals: online trading over the Internet.

Online trading became a household term in America during the mid-1990s. Online investing has paved the way for investors to easily access the market and has encouraged people from all walks of life to participate in the stock market. The popularity of investing in the stock market online is attributable to the fact that it offers direct trading benefits for a wide range of investors, from novices to the more sophisticated investors. With online trading, investors are provided with the opportunity to place an order to buy or sell stock, with lightening speed, at their convenience, whether at home, at work, or anywhere. A computer equipped with the proper software makes this possible, and the technology has even expanded to wireless handheld devices. The bottom line is that the market is always at an investor's fingertips no matter where he or she is.

Another feature of online investing is an investor's immediate access to his or her stock account information at any time—day or night, weekday or weekend—whether trading local or global, eliminating any mail time delay and the need to contact a live broker.

In this chapter, we'll focus on the benefits and drawbacks of online investing. In addition, we'll cover how the brokerage firms have adjusted the range of services to accommodate stock customers to this new wave of trading, and we'll discuss how an online trader can place trades and the safeguards that should be followed in doing so.

■ BROKERAGE FIRMS IN THE WORLD OF ONLINE TRADING

As online stock trading expands, many brokerage firms have felt the need to compete and implement individual online programs themselves. It is estimated that about 25% of all stock trades are executed online. This estimate is conservative as the number continues to grow every day. Forty percent of executions in the Nasdaq Stock Market and New York Stock Exchanges occur online. It is this growth that has prompted brokerage firms to initiate online trading services and make it available to the general public. Brokerage firms like TD Waterhouse, National Discount Brokers, E*Trade, DLJ Direct, Merrill Lynch, PaineWebber, Charles Schwab, and others currently offer online trading accounts. In fact, brokerage firms like these cumulatively handle about 15 million online accounts in the United States.

In their competition for market share, both discount and full service firms now offer online access to customers and compete heavily for customers. Commissions charged to customers by brokerage firms for executing an online trade will vary from approximately $10 to $30 per trade, depending on the balance maintained in the account.

Many brokerage firms offer many services to their online customers. Customer access to these services may be free or may be assessed a charge that varies in amount from one firm to another. These services include: (1) stock data research; (2)

optional help from a broker; (3) financial news reports, either general or customized; (4) record of current stock trading activity; (5) real-time stock quotes, whether for the general market or customized for selected stocks; (6) charts and analysis of trends; (7) current portfolio market valuation; (8) market averages and indexes; (9) availability of checking and credit card services; and (10) after-hours (extended hours) trading.

The types of services that brokerage firms offer may depend on whether the firm is discount or full service. In addition, the kind of services available may also depend on the size of the investor's initial investment, the current account balance, and the trading activity of the customer, especially in the case of day trading.

Day trading is the practice of initiating and liquidating a stock position in a brief time period, particularly within a single day. The aim of the day trader is to quickly capitalize on daily changes in a stock's market value. Brokerage services available to day traders because of their greater activity consist of more complex charting and, in some instances, access to a broader range of markets.

In addition, a day trader who wishes to receive stock data on his or her computer may subscribe to a company that is not a brokerage firm, but rather is merely a data service provider. Some examples of these data providers for day traders include eSignal and WindowOnWallStreet.com. These data services typically provide real time streaming quotes, advanced charting, research, and news services. In addition, they offer technical analysis services. Some also provide Internet links to online brokers through which day traders can have an account and place orders.

Day traders should consider using EDAT (Electronic Direct Access Trading). EDAT, which is provided by direct-access brokers, enables day traders to electronically initiate trades directly with ECNs, Nasdaq market makers, or exchange specialists of their preference, eliminating "middlemen." Buyers and sellers are then matched with one another within the selected market system.

EDAT is an advanced form of online trading. The advantage EDAT gives traders is the opportunity to immediately trade on newly released information—whether price movements are minimal or wide.

Brokerage firms provide a wide selection of the type of accounts through which investors can trade online. The kinds of accounts typically offered include joint or individual accounts, commercial accounts for businesses including partnerships and corporations, retirement accounts such as IRAs, and custodial accounts.

In addition, the online brokerage firms provide investors with personal security and protection for their financial investments. This includes:

(1) Brokerage membership with the insurance provided by the Securities Investor Protection Corporation (SIPC). SIPC insurance coverage against brokerage firm bankruptcy overall is $500,000 per customer, which includes $100,000 for cash within an investor's account.

(2) Secured computer software and encryption devices for the Internet. This allows for secured communications on the Internet in order to prevent unauthorized individuals and computer hackers from gaining access to investors' accounts and financial information over the Net.

(3) Password identification. Another means to maintain security and protection of the customers' investments is through secret identification passwords and codes to allow access to authorized individuals only.

Without a system of password codes, it would be possible for anyone to access a specific investor's online account and frivolously make stock trades adverse to the account owner's financial interests. The damage that an unauthorized individual could cause is unlimited, leaving the online account owner with a financial nightmare. The security measures taken by online brokerages give online investors a necessary degree of security.

■ HOW AN INVESTOR ESTABLISHES ONLINE TRADING

Once an investor decides which online brokerage service he or she desires to make stock trades through, the next step for the investor is to actually set up the online account. Before we discuss how an online account is established, let's briefly review the prerequisites that must be met in order for an investor to open an online account.

Obviously, the first prerequisite is to have a computer with Internet access through an online or internet service provider such as America Online (AOL), Compuserve, and Net Zero.

Once the investor is online, he or she can then visit the website of the brokerage firm and apply to open an account. An online account application form must be submitted to the brokerage firm selected, either electronically or by snail mail. Applications can be obtained by downloading them from the brokerage firm's Internet web site.

The applications to establish an online account for stock trades are commonly reviewed upon submission or within a short period of time thereafter. Once the brokerage firm is satisfied with the application information provided, including the credit history of the applicant, it will continue processing the application in order to set up the account.

To activate an approved online account, the investor must comply with the firm's initial funding and subsequent minimum balance requirements to trade online. These requirements vary greatly among brokerage firms.

Some firms will allow investors to begin immediately trading for a specified limited amount upon application approval before the investor initially funds the account. However, other firms will require initial funding first. The amount of funding and the minimum balance may range from a few thousand to several thousand dollars. In certain brokerage firms, these prerequisites along with the trading activity of an online investor, will affect the level of commissions charged and the range of services available.

After meeting the initial funding requirements, the investor can proceed to trade online by visiting the web site of the brokerage firm. The investor is able to browse the firm's web site before ordering the trade to access the services, that is, charting, financial and price information, and real time quotes.

Once the investor is ready to trade, her password and account identification must be entered online. The firm web site usually provides trading instructions and order entry instructions.

Once a stock trade has been ordered, it may be executed immediately, which is normally the case. In short, the procedure basically is point, click, and trade. However, it is possible that heavy trading volume or computer problems may delay execution. The web sites should provide an option to check the status of the order.

Some web sites will display a schedule of the status of all trades ordered. Information given includes the date the trade was ordered, the type of transaction, the quantity, trading symbol, the type of order, the execution price, and the trade status, that is, whether it has been executed, open or pending. Pending status means the order has been received but not yet accepted by the firm. Pending status changes to open status once the order has been sent by the firm to the exchange. Finally, it will be given an "executed" status once the trade has been completed.

An investor can cancel a trade that has not yet been executed. In addition, orders not yet executed may be modified. Once the trade is made, the investor's account is updated by the firm to reflect the transaction, and will be debited or credited accordingly.

■ WIRELESS AND TOUCH TONE TRADING

In addition, investors have other means to trade or check stock quotes once an online account is established. One way is through portable and handheld wireless devices. Such wireless devices include pagers, cell phones, and wireless PC organizers and allow market access anytime from anywhere. This will include obtaining Dow Jones Average and market index information and real-time quotes, and entering trade order information to buy and sell. However, certain features available through a PC or laptop, such as charting or trend analysis, are currently not available through wireless devices, but the technology is constantly evolving and these shortcomings may be eliminated in the not-too-distant future.

There are costs connected with using the wireless services, such as carrier airtime. There are also additional fees for extra features, such as news access.

In addition, some online brokerage firms also provide customers with touch tone trading. With the use of a touch tone telephone, an investor may obtain real-time stock price data and place orders for stock trades.

■ THE RISKS OF ONLINE TRADING

Online trading gives investors easy access to the financial markets, and while there are definite advantages to having instant access to stock markets around the globe, it also makes it easy to make impulsive investment decisions. Many online investors are lured by the prospect of instantaneous wealth with just a mere point and click of a computer mouse. This temptation to "gamble" in the stock market can be a real threat to the financial security of an overzealous investor. Many investors, often propelled by one successful trade, develop an overconfidence that leads them to make rash and unwise trades.

And as with any means of investment, a danger the online investor must be careful to avoid is a lack of diversification. Failure to have a diversified stock portfolio can wipe out an individual's entire investment if a stock's value experiences a serious downturn.

Another danger inherent with trading the market through online channels is the risk of overtrading. The ease and luxury of being able to order a trade at the touch of a button can tempt an investor to excessively trade, without a carefully considered strategy. Unnecessary or impulsive trading can result in increased losses. Further, an online trader may be unaware of margin calls on leveraged stocks. Many online investors have been dismayed to discover that the firm has sold their stock position for margin deficiency.

PLACING AN ORDER

As with traditional means of investing, cancellations cannot be made on executed orders. Thus it is important to be certain that the trade is a deliberate and desirable one before it is executed. Online investors are sometimes confused as to the status of trade execution once a buy or sell order has been placed. Some online investors may think a stock trade order is automatically executed upon receipt by the brokerage firm. Executions due to heavy market volatility may take some time to occur. Investors should verify the firm's particular policies involving the mechanics of trade execution and completion. They also should understand that a communication by the firm that an order has been received means only what it says, and does not verify the execution status.

Another common problem regarding order execution involves duplicate trades. Due to a system fault an online investor may mistakenly believe an execution did not occur after placing an order. The investor then initiates a duplicate trade online, causing a second transaction to occur. To avoid this problem, investors must clarify with their brokerage firm the proper procedures in order to avoid this problem and the havoc it can cause.

Conversely, every online investor must realize, especially when trading in fast moving, volatile markets, that although trading online is faster than the more traditional forms of stock trading, online brokerage firms cannot guarantee that trades will immediately be executed once a buy or sell order is placed.

Investors should review their agreements with their online brokerage firms to see what responsibility the firm has in situations when the execution is delayed by factors not at the control of the investor. That is, will the investor have to absorb losses incurred by the delays, or will the firm accept all, or part, of the responsibility?

ONLINE INVESTING AND SECURITIES FRAUD

Another major danger confronting online investors is securities fraud. Individuals looking to defraud investors may attempt to make contact via such communications methods as e-mail, chat rooms, bulletin boards, and online newsletters. They may present information appearing to be credible and try to lure investors into get-rich-quick schemes. Some well-known scams include pump and dump, fraudulent off-shore investment, no-risk fraud, pyramid schemes, and false online stock transactions. These frauds are dangers that anyone is susceptible to. However, because these frauds focus on financial risk takers, online investor should be extra wary as they may be particularly attractive targets for defrauders.

PUMP AND DUMP SCHEMES. In this type of securities fraud, information is sent online to investors by those claiming to have inside knowledge on a particular stock. Commonly, the stock is that of a small corporation whose stock price is easy to manipulate. These scammers create a lot of hype about that particular stock, thereby urging unsuspecting investors to buy into the company's stock. This pumps up the stock's value. The scammers then sell out of the investment and run off with their quick profits, leaving other investors to suffer when the stock price plummets. In short, it is the heavy selling off of stocks by the scammers that causes the stock price to fall to a point that victimizes investors, who are still holding onto their stock after the sell off.

OFFSHORE INVESTING SCAMS. In this type of investment scam, foreign predators try to entice investors (online or otherwise) to place their money in fraudulent schemes outside the U.S. Generally, if there is any kind of investment fraud being run by someone outside the jurisdiction of the United States, there is little recourse through the U.S. system for American victims of the scheme. It is very hard for American agencies to punish scammers who are located outside the United States but are able to reach victims in the United States via the Internet or through other means.

RISK-FREE INVESTMENT FRAUD. In this type of online investment scam, online scammers will guarantee a windfall to an investor who puts up money in order to fund an illusory scheme. For example, an investor may see an ad on the internet that says, "No Risk Money Making Opportunity! Sign up now and invest your money in a new company that will bring you guaranteed profits in one month." In this scenario, an investor may invest money in a company of questionable pedigree, or one that does not even exist. The investor may lose all of his or her money. Contrary to the claim in the ad, nothing is free of risk.

PYRAMID SCHEMES. Also known as Ponzi schemes, this type of investment fraud is based on luring investors with the promise of big profits proportionate to a ratio based on how many other investors they convince to sign on to the so-called investment program. "Investors" in this scheme usually lose the money they risked.

FALSE ONLINE STOCK TRANSACTIONS. In this scenario, investors are given the opportunity to invest in start-up companies. In some instances, those making the offer really are just individuals working out of their homes offering stock on a company that really does not even exist. Many times, these individuals have a past history of securities violations. Online investors who fall for these deals make payments for stock shares, only to discover that shortly after they've paid their money, the so-called company that sold them the stock becomes unreachable and that the product that was advertised does not exist.

This latter kind of Internet stock fraud has grown to be a major threat to online investors. In 1998 alone, the SEC filed almost 40 cases that alleged that hundreds of investors had been scammed out of millions of dollars. Deregulation of federal authority in favor of state responsibility for stock offerings has increased the possibility of this type of online investment scam.

■ PROTECTION FOR ONLINE INVESTORS

It is critical for online investors to be educated about the potential risks and dangers of online stock investing. Some steps that should be taken include:

1) Making certain that the computer system being used for online trading meets the necessary requirements for speed and Internet access.

2) Investors selecting an online brokerage firm should review popular, reputable financial publications and newspapers which often feature articles comparing the services and fees for competing online brokerage firms. Studying this information can go a long way to ensuring the best possible return on investment by reducing excessive or unnecessary fees.

3) Choosing an online brokerage should consider whether ECNs (electronic communications networks) are a means through which the brokerage carries out buy or sell orders. In an ECN, there is no dealer spread because sellers and buyers are automatically matched at one price. Accordingly, an ECN must have enough trading activity for the trade execution to occur.

4) Taking special care to protect their online passwords and codes.

5) Carefully reading all the terms of the agreement with the brokerage firm. It is important to know the rights of the investor and the brokerage firm, especially in the case of margin calls. An investor must understand what recourse he or she and the brokerage firm has in a margin call situation. Likewise, the investor must also understand what the responsibilities and liabilities are of all parties in such a scenario. These are especially important when computer tech-

nical problems interfere with the effectiveness of online stock trades.

6) Investors must take the time to learn the stock market procedures, terms, terminology, and the mechanics of placing orders, executions, and cancellations. They should understand the order entry procedures so as to avoid erroneously making double orders or attempting to cancel an order when it is too late.

7) When investing online, a limit order may be used to specify the particular price at which a stock order may be executed. However, although sometimes a useful tool, the limit order may prevent a stock execution if the market moves past the specified limit price too fast. Like any tool, it must be used with precision.

8) Online investors searching the Internet for financial data should take into consideration the source of the data. This is important to help determine the likelihood that the information is biased with the intention of selling a particular stock or product.

THE SEC AND ONLINE INVESTING

In addition to precautions online investors must follow to protect themselves, the Securities and Exchange Commission (SEC) is taking steps to create a safer environment for online investors. The SEC has watch groups that seek out perpetrators of Internet fraud. In addition to its own efforts, the SEC works in conjunction with other agencies, such as the FBI, to help eliminate investment fraud online.

Particularly important to online investors is the Office of Compliance and Inspections of the SEC. This division's main purpose is to conduct evaluations of brokerage firms who provide online investing in the market. Based on its inspections, the Office make recommendations to brokerage firms as to how they can improve with respect to their online investors.

The SEC, with its groups and committees, is studying ways it can improve its operations and the amount of resources available to give increased protection to investors with a strong focus on the impact of online trading and technology upon the market.

In addition, the SEC is striving to educate investors by making public on the Internet guidelines that online investors should consider before investing, as well as the dangers of Internet fraud.

■ CONCLUSION

The world of online trading offers many opportunities to investors. The speed and convenience with which one may make a connection to the financial markets virtually whenever one wishes are the underlying reasons for the success of online investing. The number of online market participants is continually growing and brokerage firms have adapted to this trend. However, there are also precautions that online investors must take to protect their investments. Individuals who are responsible and knowledgeable about the benefits and disadvantages of online trading can successfully use this technological advancement to increase their wealth.

GLOBALIZATION OF THE STOCK MARKET
Expanding Opportunities for Investors

As time goes on and technological advances are made, countries all around the world have become increasingly interconnected with one another. Computers, e-mail, and other media of mass communication have contributed to interdependence within the world. The Internet, specifically the World Wide Web, and the advantages it provides, demonstrates globalization at its best.

"Globalization" is a system that blends together the countries of the world, capitalistic markets, and technology. It is the interlinking of markets and technologies of multiple countries. It involves the increasing access and interdependence that countries and people within them have upon each other. Globalization is affecting the business world because investors, with increased communications and access to other countries and markets, have expanded opportunities to do business around the world. Globalization enables anyone to access information from anywhere in the world instantly. It is pervasive, particularly in the business world and the economy.

Around the globe, we are living more and more in an era of a worldwide market that is subject to both positive upswings and negative downturns with international financial crises. One recent example is the Asian financial crisis of the late 1990s. With a significant drop in the value of Asian stocks beginning with the Hong Kong stock market, the result was a ripple effect of stock selling that traveled from Asia, through Europe, and finally reaching North and South America. Major market averages and indexes of stock market activity around the world, including the Dow Jones, the DAX index of Germany, and Tokyo's Nikkei index fell as a result of the plummeting Asian markets. The event clearly illustrates the degree to which our economy has become global.

A major component of economic globalization is the globalization of the stock market. Global expansion of the stock market is the growing access that investors have to trade stocks of foreign and international companies in both foreign and domestic markets. With cross-border equity trading, geographic barriers are gradually fading away. Hundreds of major corporations are traded on several exchanges in various countries simultaneously.

A variety of factors has contributed to the globalization of the stock market. In this chapter, we will discuss the impact of after-hours or extended-hours trading upon globalization. We will learn how various exchanges are continually striving and competing to develop a global equity marketplace for investors, and we will discuss how access to worldwide stock markets has been made possible with online trading through the continuing growth of the Internet.

■ STOCK MARKETS AROUND THE WORLD

Before we discuss globalization of the investing world, it is important to touch upon the nature and developments concerning international stock markets.

A. EUROPE

The longstanding London Stock Exchange has undergone some major changes in the 1990s. Deregulation of markets and the emergence of organizations that offer self-regulation arose. Changes in the market technology used in the London Stock Exchange occurred, which is similar to the operations of Nasdaq, known as the Stock Exchange Automated Quotations system (SEAQ). This is screen based trading. In addition, the London

Stock Exchange in the mid-1990s created the AIM, that is, Alternative Investment Market. The AIM is akin to the OTC Bulletin Board in the United States concerning markets in smaller companies.

The 1990s saw the creation of exchanges in the former Soviet bloc, including Russia, and Eastern/Central Europe.

In Russia, with mass privatization of industries and rich natural resources, there is a developing market that may or may not be attractive to foreign investors. The market utilizes electronic technology similar to Nasdaq referred to as RTS, that is, the Russian Trading System.

In the Russian stock markets, there are currently problems with price valuation and financial reporting. However, these are typical problems with those of an emerging market. Despite this, the Russian markets still have potential for success.

In Eastern and Central Europe, new markets have opened. Emerging markets in this section of Europe include those in Poland, Slovakia, Hungary, and the Czech Republic. These markets have attracted investment on a global scale.

The Frankfurt Stock Exchange in Germany is a developed exchange, which has undergone some growth and changes since the reunification of East and West Germany with the tearing down of the Berlin Wall. Frankfurt is the home of German banking and the Deutsche Terminboerse, which is an electronic derivatives exchange. The Frankfurt Stock Exchange is currently electronically linked to other European national exchanges, trading stock simultaneously on more than one exchange. The exchange also participates in EURO.MN, an electronically linked network of small companies.

In France, the Paris Stock Exchange has implemented since 1989 an electronic trading system, replacing floor trading. France has also opened the Nouveau Marche, which is a market for smaller companies like London's AIM.

There are also other markets in Europe have also undergone various changes with respect to market operations and performance. Some are well-established exchanges while others are emerging. Countries include Italian, Nordic, Swiss, Beneleux, Nordic, and Iberian.

B. Asia/Pacific Exchanges

Like the other continents, Asia presents both emerging and well-established markets to investors.

In Japan, the Tokyo Stock Exchange is the leading developed market of Asia. The economic experience of this exchange has varied in the 1990s, with both bullish and bearish elements. For instance, on the upside, the Tokyo Stock Exchange had in the beginning of the 1990s exceeded the New York Stock Exchange in terms of market capitalization. However, by the middle of the decade, this had fallen to half of the market capitalization of the New York Stock Exchange. The negative downturn of the Japanese market was largely due in part to problems with an overvalued real estate market. In the later part of the decade, the bankruptcy of Japanese banks and some brokerage houses due to poor loans was another factor in the decline. In summary, there have been some upswings, but overall the 1990s has seen a decline in the market in Japan.

The markets in Korea and southeast Asia have grown strong over the last two decades. They have, however, experienced some economic problems in the later part of the 1990s. Some of these problems concerned issues with currencies and defaults on foreign debts. In the markets of Korea, Malaysia, India, Thailand, and Taiwan, the opportunity for investment by foreigners has been limited. Other countries, including Singapore, Philippines, and Indonesia, however, have offered greater access to their markets. Hong Kong, which is linked with China, has offered the most open Asian emerging market to Americans. Currently, the Chinese stock exchange is under development and has much potential as its businesses have Western ties.

C. Latin America

The markets of Latin America offer opportunities to investors for stock investment in both internationally established businesses as well as start ups and private companies. These markets, which include those in Argentina, Brazil, Chile, Colombia, Mexico, Peru, and Venezuela, are fast moving and volatile. Over the past decade, these markets have experienced quick and continuous growth, helped by the push for freedom in trading.

■ GLOBAL INVESTING

Individuals who wish to diversify their portfolios by investing in foreign markets have a variety of investments to choose from. One of the most popular ways of global investing is through mutual funds. Among the very broad variety of mutual funds are those that invest in foreign stocks. Some funds reflect a mix of foreign and domestic stocks. There are different funds with different combinations regarding foreign stock investing. A few examples of globally-oriented mutual funds include: Fidelity Advisor Overseas Fund, Putnam Global Equities and Growth Funds, Paine Webber Global Equities Fund, and Morgan Stanley Dean Witter Global Dividends Funds.

Although mutual funds are a very common means to invest in overseas markets, investors can also buy individual foreign stocks directly, subject, of course, to the laws of each country.

Another major form of investment in foreign global securities is available through American Depository Receipts (ADRs), which ease the difficulty of making foreign investments. Through an ADR, an investor can have an interest in share ownership of certain stocks of foreign companies. A U.S. bank holds the stocks. ADRs are commonly traded on American exchanges, and price variations are measured in U.S. dollars. The market value of an ADR is based upon trading in the U.S. stock market.

Global investing is also done through global equity indexes that are based on the economic performance of a select number of companies with global ties. More on the topic of global equity indexes will be discussed later in this chapter.

Regardless of the type of global investment made, an investor should consider which currency the stock is being invested in, that is, whether foreign or domestic. This is important because changes in the value of a particular currency affect the value of the investment. For instance, where the value of the stock itself remains stable but the value of the foreign currency in which it is invested declines, then as a result of the decline of the currency value, the overall investment declines despite the performance of the individual stock without respect to currency changes.

■ EFFECT OF EXTENDED/AFTER-HOURS TRADING ON GLOBALIZATION

In order to expand access of the stock markets to a broader range of people whose schedules often conflict with the market trading hours, many markets are providing for extended hours trading, also known as after-hours trading. In the past, after-hours trading was available only to institutional investors. However, it has become available to the general public. Regular market hours start at 9:30 A.M. and end at 4 P.M. (local time) on weekdays (except holidays). Thus, markets and exchanges located on the East Coast, for example, in New York, have normal market operations that currently run today from 9:30 A.M. to 4 P.M. in U.S. Eastern Standard Time. After-hours trading extends a few hours past the close of the regular trading session, depending on the particular market, and may even begin a few hours before the regular session in U.S.

After hours trading is made possible through electronic communication networks (ECNs). The ECNs are entirely computerized, enabling them to instantly match buy and sell orders for execution. ECNs dispense with the use of broker/dealers and market makers that receive orders from brokerage firms during the regular trading day. One of the major ECNs is Instinet, a leader in after-hours trading and one of the largest ECNs worldwide. Instinet is a globalized trading system that matches up orders of institutions without using the exchange. Many online brokerage firms offer extended hours trading to their clients through the use of ECNs, such as Instinet. In addition to ECNs, the stock exchanges, both electronic and floor-based, will or have already joined the wave of extended hours trading to better meet the needs of investors. For instance, the Nasdaq Stock Market offers select trading services after-hours from 4 P.M. to 6:30 P.M. SelectNet's after-hours sessions run from 4 P.M. to 5:15 P.M., Eastern Standard Time, and additional hours are currently planned.

There are advantages for extended hours trading. First, it makes available to a broader range of investors another opportunity to conveniently trade stock outside of normal trading hours. This may present opportunities for more favorable prices than if an investor had to wait for the next day.

After-hours trading does have some disadvantages. First, liquidity may be less than during the normal trading hours. Second, especially in a situation where important news is released after hours, there may be more rapid, volatile, dramatic price changes during this time period. Third, market fragmentation is another potential problem for extended hours traders. Market fragmentation refers to large price discrepancies in different markets. For example, a stock may be trading at a value of $15/share on one exchange while concurrently trading at $21/share on another market. To protect against unfavorable trade prices, investors engaging in after-hours trading should consider implementing limit orders. Many systems permit limit orders only during these hours.

■ GLOBALIZATION: THE STOCK EXCHANGES

The major stock exchanges have undergone efforts to contribute their share in expanding equity market access worldwide. They have engaged in competition among each other and in other instances have collaborated in joint projects. In addition, in order to make this possible, the various stock market exchanges continually update their systems and services to keep pace with technology.

Some of the efforts made by the exchanges in the push for market global expansion include opening new exchanges in other countries. For instance, as mentioned in Chapter 8, global-

LATE-TRADING SNAPSHOT 11/13/00

LATE-TRADING ACTIVITY (4 P.M.-6:35 P.M. Eastern Time)

	MONDAY	FRIDAY	THURSDAY	WEDNESDAY	TUESDAY
ISSUES TRADED	1,889	1,694	1,945	1,939	1,998
ADVANCES	515	571	493	770	520
DECLINES	565	476	584	525	794
UNCHANGED	809	647	868	644	684
ADVANCING VOLUME	16,297,700	28,499,100	8,704,800	18,697,900	22,957,060
DECLINING VOLUME	11,042,100	9,734,100	23,384,100	19,424,800	12,937,300
TOTAL VOLUME	41,409,300	48,518,600	51,144,400	47,666,000	45,704,560

LATE MOST ACTIVE ISSUES

ISSUE	EXCH	VOL(000)	LAST	NET CHG	% CHG	ISSUE	EXCH	VOL(000)	LAST	NET CHG	% CHG
Intel	(Nq)	1,823.0	38.19	....	....	VeritasSftwr	(Nq)	411.4	112.88	+ 0.13	+ 0.1
CiscoSys	(Nq)	1,227.1	50.50	+ 0.13	+ 0.2	PeregSys	(Nq)	401.6	19.38	+ 0.13	+ 0.6
Peoplesoft	(Nq)	1,107.6	39.88	+ 2.38	+ 6.3	Vivendi ADS	(N)	352.0	14.13	+ 0.06	+ 0.4
SmithfldFd	(N)	906.3	28.00	....	....	SunMicrsys	(Nq)	329.6	85.38	+ 0.06	+ 0.1
Microsoft	(Nq)	861.9	66.44	....	....	Compuware	(Nq)	324.0	8.75	....	....
OracleCp	(Nq)	779.9	24.81	+ 0.06	+ 0.3	TycoInt	(N)	314.1	49.63	– 3.31	– 6.3
UBS	(N)	776.5	136.43	....	....	EricsnTel	(Nq)	305.6	11.69	+ 0.19	+ 1.6
FlextronInt	(Nq)	658.2	28.75	– 0.06	– 0.2	Harmonic	(Nq)	289.6	10.94	– 3.31	– 23.2
WorldCom	(Nq)	625.7	16.44	+ 0.06	+ 0.4	Nextel	(Nq)	289.3	32.25	– 0.06	– 0.2
DellCptr	(Nq)	569.8	24.38	+ 0.25	+ 1.0	Novell	(Nq)	278.2	7.56	+ 0.03	+ 0.4
SnriseLvg	(Nq)	512.0	24.56	....	....	PacifiCare	(Nq)	269.3	12.77	+ 0.14	+ 1.1
Staples	(Nq)	495.3	11.25	– 0.13	– 1.1	VionPharm	(Nq)	255.0	9.94	– 0.19	– 1.9
PMC Sierra	(Nq)	456.7	115.38	+ 0.69	+ 0.6	AmFrtways	(Nq)	251.9	27.63	....	....
NASDAQ100	(A)	427.3	71.00	+ 0.94	+ 1.3	XO Comm A	(Nq)	247.7	21.06	....	....
WstrnMultiplx	(Nq)	415.0	9.00	....	....	Amgen	(Nq)	247.4	62.63	....	....

LATE PRICE PERCENTAGE GAINERS... AND LOSERS

ISSUE	EXCH	VOL(000)	LAST	NET CHG	% CHG	ISSUE	EXCH	VOL(000)	LAST	NET CHG	% CHG
Telescan	(Nq)	2.8	3.00	+ 1.06	+ 54.8	Harmonic	(Nq)	289.6	10.94	– 3.31	– 23.2
MP3.com	(Nq)	13.0	4.00	+ 0.63	+ 18.5	ClprTch	(Nq)	39.0	48.00	– 8.13	– 14.5
DirectFocus	(Nq)	12.2	49.25	+ 6.75	+ 15.9	Cognos	(Nq)	15.6	37.81	– 4.94	– 11.5
GadzooxNtwk	(Nq)	2.9	4.84	+ 0.41	+ 9.2	MobiusMgt	(Nq)	4.1	4.23	– 0.52	– 10.9
Affymtrix	(Nq)	54.1	75.13	+ 5.94	+ 8.6	Clarus	(Nq)	5.3	10.31	– 1.19	– 10.3
GalileoTch	(Nq)	3.1	25.75	+ 2.00	+ 8.4	Extensity	(Nq)	3.0	12.69	– 1.31	– 9.4
Amsurg A	(Nq)	2.2	15.75	+ 1.00	+ 6.8	Neurocrine	(Nq)	12.2	31.75	– 3.25	– 9.3
CatalSemi	(SC)	2.2	7.84	+ 0.47	+ 6.4	McLeodUSA A	(Nq)	188.3	14.50	– 1.44	– 9.0
Peoplesoft	(Nq)	1,107.6	39.88	+ 2.38	+ 6.3	Ligand B	(Nq)	25.0	12.25	– 1.19	– 8.6
GuilfrdPharm	(Nq)	3.5	23.75	+ 1.38	+ 6.1	AdvRdioTele	(Nq)	7.0	4.00	– 0.38	– 8.6
AcclrtdNtwk	(Nq)	5.1	12.38	+ 0.69	+ 5.9	XOMA	(Nq)	60.6	10.06	– 0.94	– 8.5
Net2000	(Nq)	50.0	4.88	+ 0.25	+ 5.4	SpectraLink	(Nq)	4.0	6.25	– 0.56	– 8.3
SeeBeyondTch	(Nq)	100.6	17.13	+ 0.88	+ 5.4	LatticeSemi	(Nq)	31.8	19.63	– 1.75	– 8.2
iBEAM	(Nq)	6.6	4.94	+ 0.25	+ 5.3	UnvlMfg	(SC)	4.0	5.00	– 0.38	– 7.0
PrimsKnldg	(Nq)	2.3	7.00	+ 0.34	+ 5.2	AlexionPharm	(Nq)	14.5	80.38	– 5.94	– 6.9

The Late-Trading Snapshot reflects trading activity after regular trading hours in NYSE and Amex issues reported by electronic trading services, securities dealers and regional exchanges between 4 p.m. and 6:35 p.m. Eastern time, and in Nasdaq NMS issues between 4 p.m. and 6:30 p.m., with a minimum price of $3 and volume of 2,000. The primary market is indicated for each issue. N-NYSE A-Amex Nq-Nasdaq SC-Nasdaq SmallCap

FIGURE 15–1. *WALL STREET JOURNAL,* TUESDAY, 11/14/00: AFTER HOURS ization of the Nasdaq, the pioneer of the electronic stock market, is occurring today.

Another example includes the consideration by seven stock exchanges around the world of a project to create a single world-wide global equity market. This market, if created, would continuously link the participating markets electronically. It would provide convenience to investors who would have access to the markets from a central web portal. Participation includes the New York Stock Exchange along with exchanges in Australia, Tokyo, Toronto, Mexico, and Brazil. In addition, also involved is the Euronext, which is comprised of the Amsterdam, Paris and Brussels exchanges.

The stock markets around the world have also contributed to globalization by listing stocks of foreign companies and domestic companies who conduct business in foreign countries or have other global ties. Many companies listed on the exchanges have undergone corporate structural changes on an international level, as evidenced by mergers and acquisitions between domestic and foreign companies. Some of the major corporations that have significant business ties to multiple countries have stock that is simultaneously listed on different exchanges worldwide.

One example of a security with multiple market listings is Daimler Chrysler, which is traded currently in 17 securities markets, including the New York Stock Exchange.

There are currently American securities being traded in the Stock Exchange of Hong Kong (SEHK) in a pilot program. The Nasdaq Stock Market is allowing seven stocks to be quoted and traded. These include Microsoft, Intel, Starbucks, and Dell. Because these stocks are not listed on the Hong Kong Stock Exchange but have received admission to the exchange to be traded only, their regulation remains the duty of Nasdaq.

In addition, the markets have contributed to globalization as they allow global indexes, such as the S & P Global 100 Index, to be listed on the exchange. Global indexes track the financial success of their members, and each can include up to several hundred international companies. Examples of indexes include the following: in London, the FTSE 100 Index; in Frankfurt, the Xetra DAX Index; in Tokyo, the Nikkei 225 Index, to name but a few.

A leading index that is truly global on an international scale is the Standard & Poors (S & P) Global 100 index. This consists of one hundred international companies, regardless of their geographical location. The stock value of these companies is often influenced by the global economy. This global index is being made possible through Standard & Poors, Deutsche Borse, the Tokyo Stock Exchange, and the New York Stock Exchange. Most importantly, the Global 100 portrays companies that conduct business all over the world and reflects their global trading opportunity. Today, the Global 100 members have a combined market capitalization of some $9.5 trillion dollars and seventy-one of the member companies trade on the New York Stock Exchange. In today's market, there is no question that national boundaries mean less to the equities market than in the past. Globalization is a market trend that is here and now, with many companies having a worldwide household-name presence.

Companies in the S & P Global 100 Index include America Online (United States), Barclays (Great Britain), Canon (Japan), Daimler Chrysler (Germany), Fiat (Italy), Royal Dutch (Netherlands), and Samsung Electronics (Korea), to name but a few.

Another good example of a global index is Merrill Lynch's Major 11 International Market Index Target-Term Securities(R), also known as MITTS(R). This is traded on the American Stock Exchange under the symbol EUM. This index is based on 11 foreign sub-indexes of various countries. These subindexes and their respective countries are as follows: the Amsterdam Exchanges Index of the Netherlands; the All Ordinaires Index of Australia; the Compagnie des Agents de Change 40 Index of France; the Deutscher Aktienindex of Germany; the Financial Times SE 100 Index of the United Kingdom; the Hong Kong 30 Index of Hong Kong; the IBEX 35 Index of Spain; the Milano Italia Borsa 30 Index of Italy; the Nikkei 225 Index of Japan; the Stockholm Options Market Index of Sweden; and the Swiss Market Index of Switzerland.

Other global indexes have been recently introduced by financial institutions and brokerage firms, include, Morgan Stanley Capital International, the London Stock Exchange, and Goldman, Sachs & Co, among others.

The globalization of the stock market is further accelerated by the web sites that many stock exchanges create and run. Investors from anywhere in the world can access a stock exchange's web site to obtain financial information. Since many such web sites contain links to other stock exchanges around the globe, it becomes easy for investors to find access to stock exchanges globally. Furthermore, some of the markets from around the world are working together to provide joint web sites with expanded financial information.

Finally, in an effort to promote global trading, some of the U.S. markets are changing their price quoting system from fractions to decimals. Price quotations in a majority of non-American stock markets is done in the decimal system, thus the change will help foreign investors to more readily comprehend market fluctuation in the price in American markets.

■ BROKERAGE FIRMS AND ONLINE ACCESS

Brokerage firms have taken advantage of the Internet in their efforts to expand worldwide. Online trading is another significant contributor to global expansion of the stock market. The Internet allows people from every part of the world to obtain immediate market information 24 hours a day. Brokerage firms allow investors to take advantage of such information by offering them the means to make investments and stock market trades based on this information. The number of investors worldwide is growing because of the benefits of the accessibility of investing online.

Through the Internet, a foreign investor, for example, can use a U.S. based online broker to trade shares of American companies. However, most U.S. brokerage firms are careful to avoid actively soliciting such customers so as not to attract the attention of foreign regulators. Some believe it is prudent to avoid the attention of such regulators as their restrictions may make it harder for the brokerage firms to conduct business in foreign countries. Furthermore, many foreign brokerage firms, which in some cases are actually banks that provide brokerage services in addition to banking, have begun to compete against their American counterparts. They, too, are offering online investing and financial services, such as real time quotes. These foreign financial institutions provide access for trading shares on the exchanges of their respective countries and as well as in the United States.

Besides the online brokerage services available to foreign investors through the Internet, many firms have opened offices and begun operations in major cities of foreign countries, such as Hong Kong, London, and Tokyo, and make themselves more accessible worldwide. These brokerage firms strive to be global financial services firms.

■ CONCLUSION

Globalization of the stock market is a continuing process, much of which has been made possible by ongoing technological advances. Globalization of this market is important to investors who want access to invest in foreign companies and markets. Likewise, it is important to companies who want to raise large amounts of capital by issuing stock to as wide of a range of investors as possible, both foreign and domestic. This world-wide expansion of the stock market is making it possible for all types of investors, regardless of size or wealth, to have greater choices and opportunities to invest. Globalization of the stock market is removing barriers that once existed for those looking to expand their investment choices into foreign lands and for those seeking foreigners to invest in their businesses.

TAXATION
How Dividends and Capital Gains Are Taxed

Investors are subject to taxation, both federal and state, on some or all of their income from existing securities. It is important to understand, at least in general, which of these distributions are taxable and by whom. Taxes can eat into an apparent "profit" and turn it into an "after-tax" loss. Tax loss carryforwards (described in this chapter) can ease the tax burden in years ahead. The broad rules relate to:

- The taxation of interest.
- The taxation of dividends.
- The taxation of capital gains.
- Tax loss carryforwards.
- Multiple positions.
- Stock gifts to minors.
- Stocks received as gifts or inheritances

This chapter will focus on relevant federal tax laws. It should be understood by the investor that state tax rules may vary from the federal rules. The state tax rules, although not discussed in depth for each of the fifty states in this chapter, must also be seriously considered by the investor for each of the issues discussed in terms of federal tax law.

■ THE TAXATION OF INTEREST

Most interest on municipal bonds (MUNIs) is federally tax-exempt, and generally is also free from state taxation, especially if investors own municipal securities issued in the state where they live. The interest earned on corporate bonds is subject to both federal and state tax. In addition, interest earned on United States government bonds generally is subject to federal tax but not state tax. The tax rates on these interest payments, if they are taxable, are about the same as the taxes levied on "regular" income such as your salary. The interest rate on tax-exempt municipal bonds is actually higher than it appears when you take the tax-free nature of the distributions into consideration.

■ THE TAXATION OF DIVIDENDS

Cash dividends are taxable, by both the federal government and state government, as received. Some dividends are optional, and the shareholder is given the choice as to whether to receive the dividend in cash or in additional shares. Even though the shareholder elects to receive shares instead of cash, the dividend *is* taxable! Optional dividends are taxable, whether cash or shares are received.

Non-optional stock dividends, where the shareowner receives additional shares, are not taxable at the time they are received.

Stock splits are also not taxable when received. The receipt of such additional shares changes the "tax cost" basis of your original holdings. The corporation distributing these stock dividends and splits will ordinarily explain their tax ramifications in a fair amount of detail.

Reinvested dividends, even though no cash is received, are still taxable. Most not-yet-retired investors in mutual funds elect to reinvest their dividend and capital gains distributions in additional fund shares, thus hoping to pyramid (compound) their overall profits. Although they do not receive any cash, these distributions are taxable at the time they are reinvested. All is not lost, however, since the "cost basis" of the shareowners' total fund holdings is increased, and the capital gain taxes payable when the shares are eventually sold and reduced proportionately.

■ THE TAXATION OF CAPITAL GAINS

When security positions are "closed out," a taxable event has taken place. A *close out* occurs when a long position is sold or a short position is covered. The difference between the purchase price and the sale price is the capital gain (or loss) on the transaction. Gains and losses can either be long-term or short-term, depending on the length of time elapsed between the date of purchase and the date of sale. The *trade dates* are used for both the buy and sell, not the settlement dates. When a stock has been held more than one year, the gain or loss is long-term. When a stock has been held for one year (exactly) or less, the gain or loss is short-term. A stock purchased on November 8, 1999 will result in a short-term situation if sold on or before November 8, 2000, and will be long-term if sold on or after November 9, 2000. This section of the tax law has been very flexible in the past, and the short-term/long-term period has varied from six to eighteen months. As of this writing it is one year.

Also very changeable is the tax treatment of capital gains. During most of the past 50 years, long-term capital gains have been afforded favorable tax treatment, currently at a federal tax rate of 20 percent. This is the government's way of encouraging investment in the U. S. corporate economy.

Investors who wish to trade securities, especially for the favorable capital gain/loss tax treatment advantages, should be aware that there are rules and restrictions concerning sales to related parties and wash sales which have tax consequences for him.

A. TAX LOSS CARRYFORWARDS

Investors should keep track of their capital gains and losses each year, and at year-end they will have either a *net* capital gain or loss. If they have a net capital gain, it is taxable. If they have a net capital loss, it is deductible for tax purposes, reducing the tax liability. There is a maximum limit to how much an investor can deduct for tax losses in a given year against ordinary income, and that limit is $3,000. (If a person, however, files his federal income tax return as married filing separately, then the maximum net capital loss that may be deducted against ordinary income is $1,500, not $3,000.) If the net capital losses exceed this $3,000 limit—assume a total of $5,000 net losses—then only the $3,000 is deducted in the current year, and the balance of the loss ($2,000) can be deducted in the subsequent tax year. The $2,000 "extra" loss becomes a *tax loss carryforward*.

■ MULTIPLE POSITIONS

If an investor owns several lots of stock, bought at different times and prices (multiple positions), and he or she elects to sell one of those lots, a question arises: Which of those lots is being sold as far as the taxing authorities are concerned? Unless the investor otherwise specifies, the oldest (first purchased) lot is considered to be the one sold. This is the *FIFO method*, first-in/first-out.

An investor, however, can choose to determine which long position is sold when multiple positions are held, such as specific identification of shares sold or even averaging.

ILLUSTRATION: FIFO

Here's an interesting example. Assume an investor has purchased two different 100-share lots of JKL: 100 shares at 92 8/16 in 1997 and 100 shares at 85 in 1998. It is now 2000 and JKL is trading at 89 12/16. If the investor instructs his or her broker to sell 100 shares, then (for tax purposes) he or she is considered to have sold the first lot he or she bought, the shares that cost 92 8/16. The investor will have a capital loss of $275 as a result of the sale (bought 100 shares for $9,250 and sold them for $8,975); he or she will be left with a remaining position of 100 shares at a cost of $8,500 (the shares he or she purchased in 1998).

But what if the investor would rather profit on the sale? If he or she does, he or she merely instructs the broker to sell 100 shares of JKL "versus purchase 1998." The tax authorities now consider the 1998 purchase to be the shares sold, and the investor will now show a capital gain of $475 (bought 100 shares for $8,500 and sold them for $8,975). He or she will be left with a remaining position of 100 shares at a cost of $9,250 (the shares purchased in 1997).

■ STOCK GIFTS TO MINORS

Stocks should not be registered directly in the name of a minor. They can be registered in a *custodian account*, however, for control purposes, but they must be re-registered in the child's name when he or she comes of age. In most cases this will be age 21. When someone wishes to give a gift of securities to a minor, a custodian account is usually set up. The new account form shows information about the custodian, with the single exception of the social security number used to identify the account. It's the *minor's* taxpayer number, not the custodian's number! This reflects the fact that the taxable consequences arising from the dividends, interest, and a capital gains generated by the account are the responsibility of the minor, not of the custodian. The securities actually belong to the minor. A gift of securities to a minor cannot be "recalled," because the gift is irrevocable. No margin transactions are permitted in a custodian account.

■ STOCKS RECEIVED AS GIFTS AND INHERITANCES: TAXABLE AMOUNTS AND BASIS

The receipt of securities as a gift or inheritance is not ordinarily a taxable event. Gift and estate taxes, if any, are the responsibility of the donor (for a gift) or of the estate of the deceased (for an inheritance).

Most estates and gifts made under a certain value are not subject to federal estate and gift taxes. (See Figure 16-1.) The federal non-taxable amount will increase until the year 2006, in which a maximum of $1,000,000 will be exempt. Generally, the specific valuation amounts that either an estate or gift must not exceed in order to be exempt from federal estate and gift taxation are as follows for decedents dying in or gifts made in 1999 onward:

In addition, a spouse can generally transfer property, regardless of value, to his or her spouse during life and/or after death *without* federal estate and gift consequences. This tax-free transfer to one's spouse is attributable to the *unlimited marital deduction*, which applies but for certain exceptions. Therefore, for instance, a surviving spouse generally can inherit any amount of securities or property from his or her deceased spouse without federal estate tax having to be paid on such transfer of property, even if the amount is in excess of the values set forth in Figure 16-1. However, when the surviving spouse eventually dies, his or her estate, which may include the property received from the predeceased spouse, may be subject to estate taxes.

With respect to the transfer of property of a decedent's estate, inherited stocks have a tax cost equal to their value at the time of the decedent's death, or six months later, whichever of those dates the estate's executor had chosen when the estate was settled. This is called a *stepped-up basis*. The holding period, for the inheritor, begins on the decedent's date of death.

Exempt Value of Gift or Estate	Year (s) in Which Specific Exempt Amount Applies
$650,000 or less	1999
$675,000 or less	2000, 2001
$700,000 or less	2002, 2003
$850,000 or less	2004
$950,000 or less	2005
$1,000,000 or less	2006 and thereafter

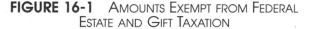

FIGURE 16-1 AMOUNTS EXEMPT FROM FEDERAL ESTATE AND GIFT TAXATION

With respect to the transfer of property in the form of a gift, a donee's tax cost basis for stock received as a gift depends on whether the donor had a "paper" loss or profit at the time he or she made the gift. The rules are as follows:

Rule # 1: Fair Market Value Of Gift (At Time Gift Is Made) Is Greater Than The Donor's Adjusted Tax Cost Basis

In this case, the donor's adjusted tax cost basis carries over to the donee. Thus, the donee determines gain or loss on sale of gifted property by using the following basis:

Donee's Adjusted Tax Cost Basis = Donor's Adjusted
Tax Cost Basis

Rule # 2: Fair Market Value Of Gift (at time gift is made) Is Lower Than The Donor's Adjusted Tax Cost Basis (OR Donor's Adjusted Tax Cost Basis Is Greater Than The Fair Market Value of Gift (at time gift is made)

Where this is the case, the donee's adjusted tax cost basis is also dependent upon the price at which he or she sells the gifted property at in the future. There are three sub-rules:

a) Donee's Selling Price Is Greater Than The Donor's Adjusted Tax Cost Basis Which Is Greater Than The Fair Market Value of Gift (At Gift Date)

In this case, where donee sells the gifted property for more than the donor's adjusted tax cost basis, and donor's basis is greater than fair market value of the gift at the time it is made, then the donee determines gain by using the following basis:

Donee's Adjusted Tax Cost Basis = Donor's Adjusted
Tax Cost Basis

b) Donor's Adjusted Tax Cost Basis Is Greater Than The Fair Market Value of Gift (At Gift Date) Which Is Greater Than The Donee's Selling Price

In this case, where donor's adjusted tax cost basis is greater than fair market value of gift at the time it is made, and donee sells the gifted property for less than this fair market value, then the donee determines loss using the following basis:

Donee's Adjusted Tax Cost Basis = Fair Market Value of Gift at Date Gift Is Made

c) Donor's Adjusted Tax Cost Basis Is Greater Than The Donee's Selling Price Which Is Greater Than The Fair Market Value of Gift (At Gift Date)

In this case, where donor's adjusted tax cost basis is greater than the price at which the donee sells the gifted property, and this selling price is greater than the fair market value of the gift at the time it was made, then the donee has no gain or loss on disposition (sale) of property.

Furthermore, the federal government allows those making gifts what is known as the annual exclusion. In short, under the annual exclusion, total gifts of an annual maximum $10,000 cash or fair market value of property to a donee are excluded from gift tax consequences. If total annual gifts made to a donee is worth more than $10,000, then the excess of cash or property over $10,000 may be subject to gift tax payable by the donor. In addition, there are rules applying to married couples which allow them to give up to a total $20,000 in tax-free gifts per donee per year.

Thus, a person can give away up to $10,000 in securities (for married couples, up to $20,000 in gifts) per individual each year to as many different individuals as he chooses *without incurring a federal gift tax!* These gifts to individuals are not deductible for the donor (as gifts to charitable institutions would be), but such gifts will lower the donor's taxable estate so that the ultimate tax bill (at the death of the donor) will be lower.

There are many other tax considerations having to do with securities transactions. Mutual funds, options, and futures all have their special tax rules. There are little-known practices that affect taxes, including short-against-the-box sales and wash sales, and special rules for short selling. Certain items on your "confirms" are considered part of your cost basis or proceeds of sale; some are not. It is prudent always to consult competent tax counsel. These few paragraphs have only scratched the surface of this very complex area.

IN THE TANK OR, EVEN WORSE, CRASH, BUT THEN A REVERSAL
How the Stock Market Works
Under Pressure

At about 7:00 A.M. on October 19, 1987, the usual Monday morning strategy conference at Merrill Lynch Pierce Fenner & Smith was attended by William A. Schreyer, the chairman, and Daniel P. Tully, the president. Their attendance was unusual, prompted by the pessimistic pall over the stock market in the past week or so. Robert J. Farrell, the chief stock market analyst at Merrill, warned that the market might be down by as much as 200 points, or about ten percent. Scenes like this one had been played out in most firms if not that same morning, then within the past week or so. Most analysts and traders knew that a "market correction" was due. The October 15th *Wall Street Journal*, in an article entitled "Stocks May Face More Than a Correction," stated: "Recent declines in stock prices, widely regarded as a mere correction in an underlying bull market, may not be reversed so readily."

For various reasons, everyone seemed to understand that the market had gone up for too long for a significant downturn not to happen. Many issues were overvalued in the headiness of the prolonged bull market. There was some gloom about inflation and interest rates. Investors were concerned about the U.S. trade deficit and the falling value of the dollar.

Takeovers did not have the appeal they did prior to the Tax Reform Act of 1986, which eliminated many of the tax benefits of borrowing to pay for takeovers. In fact, Carl C. Icahn, the renowned takeover speculator, said, "That was the match that ignited the dynamite." The market had to turn soon.

303

The morning trading session of October 19 seemed to prove all expectations correct. Even before the opening bell, sell orders flooded the order-handling system at the New York Stock Exchange. By 9:45 A.M., the Dow was down 13 points and continuing to slide. The supply side was dominating the market.

A little after 10:00 A.M., John J. Phelan, Jr., the then chairman of the NYSE, had spoken with David S. Ruder, SEC chairman, and held a meeting with representatives of leading brokerage firms. The decision was to keep the exchange open. A Reuters report on the decision had the opposite effect: traders assumed there was a possibility that the exchange would close. Rumors of a trading halt dashed cold water on the small rally that program trading *buy* orders had sparked. The market resumed its slide.

At about that time, the stocks of takeover target companies were dropping fast in value. Arbitrageurs, who seek to profit on price rises of such stocks, could not stay in the market. They bowed out of the trading. With them went over $10 billion in operating capital, at least some of which would have been put to use in buying stock.

By noon, the market had been down 200 points but had rallied over 70 points. The morning trading had been a roller coaster ride, all of it on heavy volume. Just about everyone in the market was shaken. One trader, whose firm normally handles 150,000 shares a day, had done a half-million shares by midday. "Everything is out of control," he commented, "clerks and teletypists will be here till 7 o'clock."

But the worst was yet to come. By 12:30 P.M., the Dow was down again by 165 points. From that point, it steadily lost 25 to 50 points every half-hour. The news at about 2:00 P.M. that corporations were buying back stock—with National Distillers being the first—had no visible effect on the slide. Volume tipped over 400 million shares just before the market went into an uncontrollable free-fall. By 3:00 P.M., the ticker was almost two hours late, and no one knew where the market was. By 3:30 P.M., the Dow was down another 104 points. By closing, one half-hour later, another 108 were lost.

As the peals of the closing bell died away, no one knew how bad things were. Traders stood quietly staring at others about them. A bear had rampaged through their market, which had become almost completely supply-driven. Only the specialists and market makers held the ground on the buy side—barely. During that unprecedented afternoon, nothing was normal. In the sales offices, phones were perpetually tied up, and clients could not get through on the phones to their AEs (account executives). Wire house order systems jammed, with unexecuted sell orders piling up. On the exchange floor, even the orders that made it to trading posts were executed only with difficulty. Floor traders peered helplessly at the electronic tickers and quotation screens. Specialist units were running out of money. In the OTC market, phones rang at trading desks without being answered. There were just too many orders to handle.

At the end of that fateful session, one floor trader remarked: "I thought there would be a correction in the market. But this is shocking. There's hysteria and fear. It's absolute fear."

Another said: "I've lost a sizable amount of money, and others have had losses that have left them speechless. This is the most staggering thing I've seen."

Others compared the afternoon's session to a free-fall drop in an elevator or to plummeting downhill in a car with no brakes.

At one trading desk, a magic-markered sign read, "To the lifeboats!"

By the end of trading, the Dow was off 508.32 points—22.6 percent of the whole market—on record volume of over 600 million shares. In one day, the stock market on the NYSE floor alone lost some $750 million. (It had lost $1 trillion in the month preceding October 19th.) Prices had retreated so far that Peter Eliades, a technical chartist of some 18 years, had to tape five pieces of graph paper top to bottom to follow the whole day. Ordinarily, he gets up to six months' worth of activity on one piece.

That evening, stockbrokers, traders, analysts, and many others went home not to sleep, but to wonder what Tuesday would bring. In the meantime, the lights were on in the back offices well into the night.

The next morning, the newspapers headlined one of the most newsworthy events of the century, each in its own way:

- "CRASH!" (*New York Post*)
- "PANIC!" (*New York Daily News*)
- "STOCKS PLUNGE 508.32 AMID PANICKY SELLING" (*Wall Street Journal*)

From that point forward, October 19, 1987 became Black Monday . . . Monster Monday . . . Meltdown Monday.

Perhaps the key question was highlighted in a subheadline in the *New York Times*: "Does 1987 Equal 1929?" The prevailing view, however, seems to be that, while the crash certainly dampened economic and securities activity, there are too many regulatory mechanisms in place for it to has caused the type of depression that we had in the 1930s. Black Monday, however, served at least several worthwhile purposes. For one thing, it was a crucible, in which the industry market structures and support systems were put to the test of fire. By and large, they passed the test. Second, the events of the day demonstrated the interdependence of stock markets, both nationally and globally. Third, it put the acid test to many of the assumptions on which program trading is based. Finally, it raised the significant question as to how much of an economic indicator the stock market is.

Let's look at these points one at a time.

■ THE FAIR AND ORDERLY MARKET

There's no doubt that the legal requirements put into place in the aftermath of the 1929 Crash prevented a national calamity in 1987.

For example, the Securities Exchange Act of 1933 and the Securities Exchange Act of 1934 have such rigid disclosure requirements that "bogus" corporations are few and far between. In the 1920s, a corporation could issue stock without disclosing anything about its financial status—whether it owned so much as a desk or had a dollar to its name. When the market plunged in 1929, these companies were blown away.

Worse, it became clear that they did not have the financial resources to get through times of adversity. Their collapse helped to escalate the panic and, later, personal bankruptcies of stockholders.

Such shams are almost impossible today. As a result, when prices took a nose dive, most issuers were able to ride out the storm. Some of the "big cap" companies even started creating additional treasury stock for themselves by buying. In one stroke, they retrieved their stock at bargain prices, acted as buyers in a supply-driven market, and cast a vote of confidence in the market and in their companies.

Because of regulatory requirements in a primary offering, the capital was there, backing the issues, to pull the market through. Investors were not left bankrupt because they had bought stock in "paper" corporations.

Brokerage firms are also required to keep certain levels of capital in reserve. Periodically, they must submit a report that reflects their net capital position. The report requires a firm to add up all the money that it has on loan to customers and all the money it has on hand in cash. The ratio of the loan amount divided by the cash amount represents how extended the firm is in terms of credit to its clients. Ratios of 2 to 1 or 3 to 1 are perfectly acceptable; 4 to 1 or more is questionable. Ratios approaching 10 to 1 often result in a firm being audited and even in its being forbidden to extend further credit until the ratio comes down.

Since brokerage firms, which generally own large inventories of securities, are "net holders" of stocks, they operate on billions of dollars of capital, but much of it is on loan from commercial banks. If the value of a firm's inventory is deflated across the board due to an overall market decline and it does not have money to operate, it has to sell some inventory to raise capital. The last thing the market needs in a panic is more selling by the brokerage firms themselves!

As a result, the net operating capital of a brokerage firm is monitored very closely. The underlying logic of the SEC's Rule 15c3-3, which is the rule that requires frequent reporting of a firm's net capital status, is that a broker/dealer should have enough cash on hand to wind down its operations, while protecting its customers, within a month. A firm must have enough capital, after making a series of deductions from its total capital, to compare well with safety margins established by the SEC. Although the purpose of this rule is to protect investors in the event of one firm's failure, its across-the-board effect is that all firms are obliged by law to have a minimum amount of operating capital in reserve. This capital (not generally available in 1929) no doubt moderated the effect of the 1987 crash.

Perhaps the most conspicuous safeguard against calamity in a down market is Regulation T. With this regulation, the Federal Reserve—the arbiter of credit in this country—requires that, to buy stock on margin, you have to deposit at least 50 percent of the market value of the stock with your broker. Exchange, NASD, and firm requirements are invariably higher. Margin and maintenance requirements strike a balance by preventing investors from becoming overextended. With this provision, some investors may not have been able to honor monster margin calls. But at least the margin departments were able to sell the margined securities, and minimize losses.

In this environment, investors who were hurt the worst violated prudent guidelines. For instance, the story goes around the street that an AE advised one or more clients to take out equity loans on their homes and use the money to buy stock on margin. That's not only illegal—for the stockbroker to suggest and for the clients to do—but it is also downright stupid. These clients, unable to meet the margin calls, saw their positions sold out and zero balances in their accounts. All they were left with were equity loans to pay off.

Although these cases were by far the exceptions in 1987, they were the norm in 1929. There was no Reg T, no margin regulation. You could buy stock with just a few dollars down. You didn't worry about making a margin call, because everyone knew that calls happen only in down markets. And the market in the late 1920s was going up, up, up. When the crash occurred, people were not only broke; they were in deep debt because the firms had loaned them most of the purchase price. There's no doubt that limiting the use of margin put a brake on the downhill careening of the market in 1987. The margin calls were big, and people lost money—especially those who used their buying power to increase their positions. But it could have been much, much worse.

It could have been worse still, many think, if commercial banks had been invested in the market, as they had been in the 1920s. Back then, banks were allowed to buy and sell stock with depositors' funds, as well as to underwrite primary offerings. As a result, much of the money that investors might have used to meet their margin calls or otherwise to deal with huge losses in the market was unavailable to them. The banks were losing the investors' deposited funds just as fast as investors were losing their investment funds. The Crash was draining both individuals and institutions dry of capital.

In 1933, the Glass-Steagall Act prohibited financial institutions from engaging in investment and commercial banking at the same time. That is, if a bank wanted to take deposits and make loans, it was legally a "commercial" bank. If it wanted to act as a corporate underwriter and carry an inventory of securities, it was an "investment" bank. By law, it could not be both. That is essentially the law today, but it is under siege and yielding rapidly.

Commercial banks for years had been lobbying for a repeal of the Act. Their primary argument is that the market would be *more* stable if investment banks were large, well-capitalized financial service firms.

At the same time, commercial banks have tested the law. In 1986, for example, a bank that was bailed out by the U.S. government in 1984, Continental Illinois Corporation, bought First Option of Chicago, a clearing service firm. Continental Illinois received government permission to become a "broker's broker," on the basis of the argument that First Option derived revenue not from trading profits, but rather from clearing fees. Hence its involvement in the securities industry was regarded as all but risk-free. On Black Monday, however, with capital running scarce, First Option customers found it harder and harder to meet their obligations. The charges for clearing, which, given the volumes involved, were going through the ceiling, were just going unpaid in many instances. Continental Illinois had to funnel some $90 million into First Option to keep it afloat. Without Continental's infusion, First Option might have gone out of business. Being owned by a bank did serve as a stabilizing factor, but where does the capital commitment end?

In another case, First Chicago Corporation (a bank) planned to by Wood Gundy, a major Canadian underwriting firm. The purchase would be legal because the Glass-Steagall restriction did not apply to foreign underwriters. Wood Gundy, however, was one of the underwriters in a huge stock issue being offered by British Petroleum, the government-owned oil company of Great Britain. The value of the stock, offered internationally, took a beating in late October. Wood Gundy lost $45 million on the offering. Although First Chicago walked away from the purchase, the question remains as to how much capital a bank can safely commit to underwriting and other securities-related transactions.

Another question is whether the business of commercial banking is compatible with that of investment banking. "Mega" banks, with enormous loans out to developing nations, make decisions and generally operate in a very different time frame from brokerage houses. A brokerage firm usually needs money in a matter of hours, sometimes minutes. Occasionally decisions involving large sums must be made instantaneously. It is questionable whether the two decision-making environments can mesh, so that the parent bank can act prudently, yet within the time constraints often imposed by the market.

Certainly, the legally mandated separation between commercial and investment banking undoubtedly helped to stabilize the runaway market in 1987. Yet these two examples illustrate the bear-traps in allowing commercial banks to participate in securities trading and underwriting. If any changes are to be made, they should be made carefully and wisely.

Of all the systems aimed at maintaining a fair and orderly market, however, the ones put to the severest tests were the exchange specialists and the OTC market makers. "The dealer (specialist and market maker) system," said an officer of a specialist unit, "was very close to the limits of what it could stand.

There's no question that by the 20th it had exhausted most of its resources."

The specialists, in their attempts to head off the worst market downturn in over half a century, suffered enormous financial losses. While their holdings normally totaled a maximum of $400 million, their accumulated holdings were between $11.5 and $2 billion by the end of trading on Meltdown Monday—almost all of it purchased in a sliding market. Indeed, a few specialists were put out of business, having had to sell their seats to meet their commitments. On October 22, to enable capital to move into the dealer system, the NYSE lifted its long-standing ban on the ownership of specialist units by brokerage houses. Merrill Lynch bought one right away.

So battered was the specialist and market maker system that the Fed had to assure commercial banks that there was enough "credit" in the system to go around. The banks needed the reassurance. They had many more times the amount of loans out to firms than they normally did, and many were ready to cut off short-term loans to brokers. Citicorp, for example, had some $1.4 billion on loan to brokerage houses, compared to its normal level of $200 million. Citicorp Chairman John S. Reed went along with the additional amounts only after a call from the New York Federal Reserve President, E. Gerald Corrigan.

The money was needed not only on the exchange floors but also in the OTC market. Most market makers were coping with volumes averaging more than 60 percent higher than usual. As usual, most of these orders had to be handled on the phone—and they were all sell, sell, sell. As dealers, they were obliged to make market by buying, but their capital was dwindling quickly. Many market makers stopped answering phones or giving quotes. Prices that others quoted were often way out of line with the market. "It's clear," said Edward J. Mathias, president of T. Rowe Price New Horizons Fund, "a number of market makers saw their capital impaired and ran for cover. I don't think anybody was willing to stand in front of a speeding train." The members of the dealer system held to their credit but just barely. Like a defensive line after a furious assault, there were the shell-shocked and the casualties among their numbers. On the night of October 19, the unanswered question was whether they could stand another assault. Yet, despite the losses and the thinly spread capital, the system withstood the pressure.

This was despite the possibility that not all specialist units acted forthrightly, in as much as price swings in a few stocks seemed unjustified. In January 1988, a specialist firm voluntarily withdrew as specialists for J. P. Morgan & Company because of such an allegation.

Other questions persisted. Clearly, should another crash occur at any time in the future, the dealers needed an emergency reservoir of capital. David S. Ruder, SEC chairman of only a few months, applauded the firms that came to the aid of specialists but called for a formal system to assure the presence of such capital in the future.

In the OTC sector of the stock market, the concern of officials was equally high. On the evening of October 22, a NASD official called a meeting of the managers of the top firms' OTC trading desks at Harry's Bar at Hanover Square. The purpose of the meeting was to come up with proposals on improving access to, and liquidity in, the over-the-counter market. The memo that emerged from that meeting, called "Where Were You When I Needed You?", addressed the criticism that phones were unanswered. Numerous improvements were implemented. One thing is certain. The general lack of capital in the dealer system was compounded in the OTC market by its lack of automated order handling. If the specialists could console themselves with anything, it was the fact that their order-handling systems held up under the deluge. The NYSE's order-relay computers are so redundant with backup systems, and their fault tolerance so high, that the enormous volumes of orders were getting through to the floor.

The only breakdowns that did occur were in the Intermarket Trading System, a computerized network that links regional exchanges and the NYSE. This system did slow down to the point that specialists on the regional floors could not get orders executed on the New York Stock Exchange.

Over-the-counter order handling was a different story. Not only were some dealers unable to get orders executed, but also many orders (most of them phoned in by clients) were not getting to the trading desks because the phones were jammed. Those market makers that were still accepting orders and doing their best to execute them could only take so many calls. After that, the phones went unanswered. Before long, the overwhelming supply pressure and lack of market-maker response created huge "unnatural" spreads. Despite the cracks in the wall that the exchange and OTC dealers quickly erected between a tidal wave of sell orders and total panic, the wall held, but it was close. Perhaps there should be an emergency capital pool for dealers to draw on. Perhaps greater automation is necessary. Perhaps some broke ranks and ran before the wave. The fact remains that, without the dealer system, the capital markets and the economy as a whole would have been in a very different state after October 19.

■ PROGRAM TRADING MYTHS

Computerized programs are used basically for three investment goals. When employed to hedge large stock positions, this type of trading is called "portfolio insurance". When aimed at conducting arbitrages (that is, taking profits on market price differences), program trading is referred to as "stock index arbitrage." Finally, there is "speculative" program trading. (None of these should be confused with "package traders," which are largely institutional accounts buying quantities of stock on a daily, weekly, or monthly basis, as they receive infusions of capital.)

Computerized trading systems originated in the early 1980s, when personal computers and their related miniaturized circuitry made possible the nearly immediate use of trading information. Clearly, this technology has made the market more efficient; that is, current trading includes, more than ever, the very latest information. Such systems also promised to enable hedgers, arbitrageurs, and speculators alike to act instantaneously on the most up-to-date of information. That was the theory. The actuality was very different.

■ THE GLOBAL CRASH

Given the high-tech linkages of markets all around the world, it is not surprising that the U.S. market was not alone when it crashed. In fact, the momentous event that fills our perspective from horizon to horizon is only one aspect of a global phenomenon.

For the week preceding October 19, every major stock market in the world was feeling the weight of the decline in American stock prices, as well as its own. Many exchanges resisted the tug to decline, but on that next Monday, they caved in. During the week of October 12, the Nikkei index on the Tokyo exchange plunged 12 percent. In London, the Financial Times-Stock Exchange index dropped 20.36 percent. West German shares were down 11.19 percent, the Swiss 16.56 percent, and so on. Again, technology turned from benefactor to demon. Under normal conditions, global networks enable traders to execute huge transactions by pressing several buttons at a terminal and watching the computer's screen flicker with the execution. Some $750 billion worth of stocks are traded this way, internationally, 24 hours a day, every year. That's the potential upside of global trading. The demon emerges during down markets. At such times, a bear market can be handed around the world, from exchange to exchange, without intermission. A bad trading session at any one major center affects them all. This synchrony is what happened in early October, and what continues to happen, as long as the markets are so closely linked. In the words of Carl F. Adams, managing director of Carl Marks & Company, "It (the worldwide bear market) certainly shows you the downside of globalization of markets."

The bleak Monday in October spotlighted one or two basic flaws in the program trading approach. Traditionally, computerized portfolios were supposed to be almost "self-adjusting," that is, buy or sell orders would be activated automatically as the market dictated. All the planning and thinking was supposed to have been done long before the orders were put into position. The assumption was that no thinking had to be done if the market moved; the orders would simply be activated like mousetraps. But let's see what actually happened.

Portfolio "insurance" is not really insurance. It is a form of money management that makes use of stock index futures to protect the value of a portfolio. In theory, when the market value of the stock declines, managers offset most of the losses through short sales in the futures contract obligation. In practice, not all the losses are offset because stock index futures prices are expected to track actual stock prices closely but not exactly.

On October 19, several assumptions were proven wrong. For one thing, futures and stock prices were soon widely out of synchronization, and no one knew for sure exactly where stock prices were going. Most portfolio managers who were lulled into believing that the computers would do the right thing could not absorb, analyze, and act fast enough on this unexpected set of circumstances. Many, of course, did start selling futures contracts.

When they did, two things happened. First, with so many managers and other investors creating supply by selling, futures prices started to drop dramatically. Then the second thing started to happen. The abrupt decline in futures prices scared stockowners into selling, which added fuel to the selling flames in both the futures and the stock markets.

The basic error on the part of money managers was that they relied on the performance of the program, not on their assessment of the fundamentals. They got away from making up their own minds, depending instead on "the computer" to adjust to market conditions.

Arbitrageurs base their trading techniques on the same basic assumption: That the difference in prices between futures and stocks will be small and fleeting. Using sophisticated programs, arbitrageurs look for discrepancies between futures and stock prices. When they find such gaps, they simultaneously sell the higher-priced instruments and buy the lower-priced one. They thereby lock in guaranteed profits in what is known as "riskless arbitrage." Under normal circumstances, arbitrageurs, which account for about 20 percent of stock market trades, tend to close such gaps very quickly.

As the market plunged, however, these gaps widened and should have become an arbitrageur's dream-come-true. But both markets were losing value too fast, orders were too difficult to get executed at all, much less simultaneously, and the conditions were changing far too quickly for most traders to react quickly enough. Consequently, arbitrage trading on October 19 is estimated to be only 9 percent, most of it probably in the morning, before the "arbs" bowed out and in many cases were blown out of the market. When they ceased trading, they further deflated the buy side of the market.

Like arbs, speculators represent buying pressure in a bear market because they often trade against the direction of the market. Yet speculators also rely on the same assumptions: close tracking of futures and stock prices, prompt order execution, a reasonably adequate demand side, and enough time to react to the market. When all of these requirements went out the window, speculators had to stand back, thus denying the market even more would-be buyers.

The raging bear market was frustrating program traders of all kinds. Yet the widespread fear was that these participants would enter the market as a group and create a highly volatile witching hour that would knock the market on its ear. For a couple of months after the Crash, it was believed that program traders were in too great a disarray for any such thing to happen. Witching hours could occur only in relatively orderly markets, when all the day-to-day conventions hold. Under extreme conditions, they seemed to have no more or less effect than any other supply factors.

Yet, critics of program trading persist by saying that the percentage of trades is not as influential as their timing. Certainly the speed of events not only on October 19, but normally in today's stock market, is a factor: "We are learning," said Robert A. Brusca, chief economist at Nikko Securities, "that when we compress the time in which things happen, they happen differently." So it was conceivable that a limited amount of concerted trading at a critical point might have a different effect than it would under normal circumstances.

In addition, computer technology, while making the market more efficient, also makes it all but impossible for traders to react to all the available information. "Overnight," said Allen Sinai, chief economist of Shearson Lehman Hutton, as the firm was then known, "the reaction time to market-influencing events dropped from months or days to minutes and seconds. Unless you could evaluate all this data instantly, you were out of business."

For a while after October 19, no one knew for sure what role program trading really played. The circumstances were just too chaotic for anyone to know. SEC Chairman Ruder stated that index futures trading "occurred in significant amounts" and even that various forms of index futures trading played an important role in the collapse on October 19 and 20. He went on to question whether there is enough capital behind index futures trading, for which you need to put up only 5 percent of the value of the contract. (Compare this with the Reg T 50 percent requirement on a stock purchase.) When calls go out to index futures traders for more money in a declining market, there is less of a guarantee that the obligation will be honored. Whatever its real effect, program trading was banned from the NYSE on October 20. Only on November 9 was it allowed to resume, with money-market watchers holding their breath. The effect of its return was barely noticeable.

In January of 1988, the task force appointed by President Reagan issued a report that placed the blame squarely on program trading. The report went on to make a number of suggested changes, including limits on stock price swings, trading halts, and giving the Federal Reserve Board overseer duties for both the stock and the futures markets (now regulated separately). There was little doubt that program trading would undergo regulatory changes.

■ THE STOCK MARKET AND THE ECONOMY

Many people equate the well being of the stock market with that of the economy. Others regard the market as at least an all-important economic indicator. The underlying, almost instinctive, assumption is that the fate of one is inextricably linked with that of the other. This perception is prevalent enough that on

Meltdown Monday, President Reagan felt compelled to state publicly that, while the stock market might be undergoing a correction, the economy was sound.

Given this linkage, fears of recession, inflation, unemployment, and worse were understandably heightened after the Crash. Suddenly the budget and trade deficits, the value of the dollar, and other economic factors were hyped in the news.

There is some basis for this view. The stock market has acted as an indicator nine times since World War II. In each instance, it has presaged recession by a sustained decline, with lead times of about nine months. What is a "sustained decline?" A month or even two of retreating prices is not necessarily significant—three, four, or more months are. But we hadn't had a crash since 1945, when these records were started, and so the cause-effect relationship between a stock market crash and a recession remains to be seen.

Suffice it to say that the Commerce Department uses an index of several economic indicators, of which the stock market is only one. For some reason, however, we do not become as excited over a decline in the gross national product as we do a sudden drop in the stock market. Such is the visibility of the stock market that we regard it as a far more telling indicator than perhaps it really is. Yet, its significance, yesterday, today, and tomorrow will always be with us.

Since Meltdown Monday of October 1987, there have been several highly volatile down days and periods in which the market declined drastically and tanked. The universal cause: fear and anxiety ridden reaction to news. The result: heavy selling.

A quick summary to date of some newsworthy events that fueled the fire of market volatility:

- the Desert Shield build up;
- the Asian crisis;
- the tech and dot.com decline (some say disaster); and
- currently, as of this writing, the 2000 U.S. presidential election fiasco, which has the United States, the global world, and Wall Street so unsettled that the market is skidding into the tank.

The above events are but a few disaster stories among several; however, in each case, there was no bubble that burst as in October 1929's market crash that caused and preceded the Great Depression of the 1930s.

It is natural that people will herd and panic together, and selling will always cause more selling. We are all human. Each and every one of us will attempt to save our wallets and abandon ship immediately. However, on a positive note, short selling, call writing, and put buying enable us to profit or to, at least, hedge our losses in a down market. Remember, all market decisions are immediate and most importantly, technical analysis teaches us to predict the reversal. The key to profiting in the market is timing, enabling us to call every shot right. Higher market highs always generate from lower lows. Each of us loves to buy at discount, a statement that almost describes a human being, in all our wonder. This is why every market professional, analyst, investor, trader, or student should know both the fundamental and technical approaches to the market by studying the force: the force of supply, the force of demand.

■ CONCLUSION

I hope that you enjoyed reading the book, but more importantly, that you learned the essentials of the stock market process. And to each of you, as you go on with your investment career, may the force be with you.

GLOSSARY

ACCOUNT EXECUTIVE (AE). A brokerage firm employee who advises clients and handles orders for them. The AE must be registered with the National Association of Securities Dealers (NASD) known as Series Seven before taking orders from clients. Also known as registered representative (RR), Financial Advisor or stockbroker.

ACCOUNT STATEMENT. A statement sent periodically (at least quarterly) to clients, showing the status of their accounts with a broker/dealer.

ADJUSTED DEBIT BALANCE. The net money borrowed by a brokerage customer in a margin account as a result of both settled and unsettled transactions. It includes Special Miscellaneous Account (SMA).

ADVANCE-DECLINE THEORY. A market theory that uses the relative number of advances versus declines in relation to total issues traded to make buying and/or selling decisions. Formula = A - D/V.

AE. *See* Account Executive.

AFFILIATED PERSON. Anyone in a position to influence decisions made in a corporation, including officers, directors, principal stockholders, and members of their immediate families. Their shares are often referred to as "control stock."

AFTERMARKET. A market for a security either over the counter or on an exchange after an initial public offering has been made. *See* Free-Riding; Hot Issue; Stabilization; Withholding.

ALL-OR-NONE (AON) OFFERING. A "best-efforts" offering of newly issued securities in which the corporation instructs the investment banker to cancel the entire offering (sold and unsold) if all of it cannot be distributed.

ALL-OR-NONE (AON) ORDER. An order to buy or sell more than one round lot of stock usually in block size of 10,000 shares or more at one time and at a designated price or better. It must not be executed until both conditions can be satisfied simultaneously.

ALTERNATIVE (EITHER/OR) ORDER. An order to do either of two alternatives such as either buy at a limit or buy stop for the same security. Execution of one part of the order automatically cancels the other. *See* One-Cancels-the-Other Order.

AMERICAN STOCK EXCHANGE PRICE CHANGE INDEX. An "unweighted" market index for all common stocks listed on the ASE, prepared hourly.

AMERICAN STOCK MARKET VALUE INDEX. A market index for all common stocks listed on the ASE, prepared daily and grouped by geographic locale and industrial category.

AMEX. An acronym for American Stock Exchange, Inc.

AMEX RULE 411. The American Stock Exchange's version of the "know your customer" rule of the NYSE. *See* Rule 405.

AON OFFERING. *See* All-or-None (AON) Offering.

AON ORDER. *See* All-or-None (AON) Order.

ARBITRAGE. The simultaneous purchase and sale of the same or equal securities in such a way as to take advantage of price differences prevailing in separate markets, that is, buying the security in one market and selling it at a higher price in the other, or buying a convertible security such as a convertible bond or Preferred Stock which is exchangeable into common stock and selling the receivable common stock at a profit. *See* Risk Arbitrage.

ARBITRAGEUR. One who engages in arbitrage.

AS AGENT. The role of a broker/dealer firm when it acts as an intermediary, or broker, between its customer and another customer, a market maker, or a contrabroker. For this service the firm receives a stated commission or fee. This is an "agency transaction." *See* As Principal.

AS PRINCIPAL. The role of a broker/dealer firm when it buys and sells for its own firm proprietary account. In a typical transaction, it buys from a market maker or contrabroker and sells to a customer at a fair and reasonable markup; if it buys from a customer and sells to the market maker at a higher price, the trade is called a markdown. *See* As Agent.

ASK-BID SYSTEM. A system used to place a market order. A market order is one the investor wants executed immediately at the best prevailing price. The market order to buy requires a purchase at the lowest offering (asked) price, and a market order to sell requires a sale at the highest (bid) price. The bid price is what the dealer is willing to pay for the stock, while the ask price is the price at which the dealer will sell to individual investors. The difference between the bid and ask prices is the spread. *See* Bid-and-Asked Quotation (or Quote).

AT-THE-CLOSE ORDER. An order to be executed, at the market, at the close, or as near as practicable to the close of trading for the day.

AT-THE-MARKET. (1) A price representing what a buyer would pay and what a seller would take in an arm's-length transaction at the current market or quote assuming normal competitive forces; (2) An order to buy or sell immediately at the currently available price. *See* Market Order, Quote.

"AT THE MONEY." A put or call option with no intrinsic value; the exercise price and current market value of the underlying stock are equal to each other.

AT-THE-OPENING (OPENING ONLY) ORDER. An order to buy or sell at a limited price on the initial transaction of the day for a given security; if unsuccessful, it is automatically canceled.

AUCTION MARKETPLACE. A term used to describe an organized exchange where transactions are held in the open and any exchange member present may join in.

AUTHORIZED STOCK. The maximum number of shares that the corporation is permitted to issue.

AVERAGE. A stock market indicator based on the sum of market values for a selected sample of stocks, divided either by the number of issues or by a divisor that allows for shares outstanding (sold) or other changes in capitalization. The most widely used average is the Dow Jones Industrial Average.

AWAY FROM ME. When a market maker does not initiate a quotation, transaction, or market in an issue, he says it is "away from me."

AWAY FROM THE MARKET. An order where the limit bid is below (or the limit offer is above) the current quote for the security. For example, if a quote for a security is 20 Bid, 20 1/4 offered, a limit order to buy at 19 is "away from the market."

BACK OFFICE. An industry expression used to describe non-sales departments of a brokerage concern, particularly a firm's P&S cashier departments and margin departments involved in post trade processing, delivery, settlement, and payment.

BACK UP. A reverse in a stock market trend.

BACKING AWAY. The practice of an OTC market maker who refuses to honor his or her quoted bid-and-asked prices for at least 100 shares, or 10 bonds, as the case may be. This action is outlawed under the NASD Rules of Fair Practice.

BALANCE ORDERS. The pairing off of each issue traded in the course of a day by the same member to arrive at a net balance of securities to receive or deliver. The net difference between buyers and sellers on the opening of the market allows the specialist to open the market appropriately.

BAR CHART. In technical analysis, a chart used to plot stock movements with darkened vertical bars indicating all prices. Most charts are issued daily, weekly, or monthly.

BARRON'S CONFIDENCE INDEX. A market index that measures investors' willingness to take risks according to yields on rated bonds.

BASE MARKET VALUE. In the construction of a market index, the average value of securities traded at a certain time. All movement is usually reported in terms of a dollar or percentage change from an original value, or "base."

BASKET SESSION. Also known as Crossing Session II of the NYSE, this trading session starts at 4 PM and ends at 5:15 PM, Eastern Standard Time, and is open to every NYSE member. This session allows "baskets" of multiple securities to be traded. To be eligible for crossing during this session, each basket must have at least $1 million in cumulative market value and possess at least 15 different stocks that are listed on the NYSE. Prices are established in aggregate combined totals. At the end of the session, information concerning every basket order that was executed, specifically, the totals of dollar value and quantity of shares executed is made available.

BEAR MARKET. A securities market characterized by declining prices. *See* Bull Market.

BEAR RAIDERS. Groups of speculators who pool capital and sell short to drive prices down and who then buy to cover their short positions—thereby pocketing large profits. This practice was outlawed by the Securities Exchange Act of 1934. *See* Raiders.

BEARISH. An adjective used to describe an opinion or outlook where one anticipates decline in price of the general market, of an underlying stock, or of both. *See* Bullish.

BENEFICIAL OWNER. The owner of securities who receives all the benefits, even though they are registered in the "street name" of a brokerage firm or nominee name of a bank handling his or her account.

BEST-EFFORTS OFFERING. An offering of newly issued securities in which the investment banker acts merely as an agent of the corporation, promising only his "best efforts" in making the issue a success but not guaranteeing the corporation its money for any unsold portion. *See* All-or-None (AON) Offering.

BEST EXECUTION RULE. This is a SEC (Securities and Exchange Commission) rule that mandates that reasonable diligence to get the best price possible is to be used by brokers/dealers when executing a trade for customers. If the stock is an over the counter market stock, the broker/dealer must get quotes from at least three dealers. If there are less than three dealers available, then quotes must be obtained from all dealers.

BETA. A measure of risk by calculating the percentile change in a stock's price compared to the percentage change of a market index, usually the S & P 500 Index. A stock with a beta of 1.5 should refer to the stock's expected ability to change 50%, up or down, compared to the movement of the Index. Due to volatility, the beta of a stock will always change.

BID-AND-ASKED QUOTATION (OR QUOTE). The bid is the highest price anyone has declared that he or she wants to pay for a security at a given time; the asked is the lowest price anyone will accept at the same time and is also called the offer. *See* Offer.

BIG BOARD. A popular slang term for the New York Stock Exchange.

BLOCK. A large amount of securities, generally a minimum 10,000 shares of stock.

BLOCK POSITIONER. A broker/dealer who takes positions for his or her own account and risk in order to facilitate a large purchase or sale of securities by customers that would otherwise be disruptive to the market. A block positioner may be given relief under Regulation T to assist the financing of such positions.

BLOWOUT. A securities offering that sells out almost immediately.

BLUE-CHIP STOCKS. Common stocks of well-known companies with histories of profit growth and dividend payment, as well as quality management, products, and services. Blue-chip stocks are usually high-priced and low-yielding. The term "blue chip" comes from the game of poker in which the blue chip holds the highest value.

BLUE ROOM.   One of the small trading areas just off the main trading floor of the New York Stock Exchange.

BLUE-SKY LAWS.   State securities laws pertaining to registration requirements and procedures for issuers, broker/dealers, their employees, and other associated persons of those entities.

BLUE-SKYING THE ISSUE.   The efforts of the underwriters' lawyers to analyze and investigate state laws regulating the distribution of securities and to qualify particular issues under these laws.

BOARD BROKER.   A member of an options exchange appointed by that exchange to handle public limit orders left in his or her care by floor brokers. In performing this function, he or she is said to be running the "public book." These brokers' prime responsibility is to ensure that a fair, orderly, and competitive market exists in the classes of options to which they are assigned. *See* Market Maker; Specialist.

BOARD OF ARBITRATION.   (1) A three-to-five-member NASD board, appointed ad hoc by the Board of Governors, to arbitrate disputes involving transactions among members, nonmembers, and customers. *See* Code of Arbitration. (2) A board appointed by the chairman of the NYSE Board of Directors, comprised of members and allied members who serve in various ways and numbers to settle disputes arising among members or between members, allied members, and nonmembers.

BOARD OF GOVERNORS.   The governing body of the NASD, most of whom are elected by the general membership; the remainder are elected by the board itself.

BOILER ROOM SALES.   The use of high-pressure sales tactics to promote purchases and sales of securities.

BOOK VALUE.   The accounting value of a common stock's tangible worth, calculated as assets less liability divided by shares outstanding. Book value = $A-L$. Sometimes called Net Asset Value.

BORROWING POWER OF SECURITIES.   (1) The money invested in securities on margin, shown in the customer's monthly statement. The margin limit is usually 50 percent of their stock values, 30 percent of their bond values, and full value of their cash equivalent assets. (2) The securities pledged to a lender as collateral for a loan.

BOT. (1) Industry abbreviation for "bought." (2) Abbreviation for balance of trade. (3) Abbreviation for board of trustees (mutual savings bank industry).

BOUGHT DEAL. A commitment by a group of underwriters to guarantee performance by buying the securities from the issuer themselves, usually entailing some financial risk for the underwriters (or syndicate).

BOX. A section of a cashier department where securities are stored temporarily. The department's responsibilities are sometimes subdivided to monitor both an active box and a free box for securities held by the firm.

BREADTH INDEX. The net securities advanced or declined for a given day's trading dividend by the total issues traded. For example:

Advances	500
Declines	600
Unchanged	200
	1,300

$$\frac{600 - 500}{1,300} = 7.69\%$$

BREAKOUT. In technical analysis, the rise through a resistance level or the decline through a support level by the market price of a security.

BROKER. An agent, often a member of a stock exchange firm or the head of a member firm, who handles the public's orders to buy and sell securities and commodities, for which service a commission is charged. The definition does not include a bank. *See* As Agent; As Principal.

BROKER BOOTH SUPPORT SYSTEM. Also known as the BBSS, this a system used by the NYSE used for the delivery of orders of member firms to the exchange.

BROKER'S BROKER. A person who is a Stock Exchange Member and who deals only with other securities brokers and dealers, and not directly with the general public. Also referred to as *A Two Dollar Broker*.

BUCKET SHOP. An organization that accepts customer orders but does not immediately execute them. It waits until, and if, the market acts contrary to the customer's expectations, then executes the order but confirms it to the customer at the price prevailing originally. This practice is outlawed by the National Association of Securities Dealers.

BULK IDENTIFICATION/SEGREGATION. A system for segregating customer securities in accordance with SEC Rule 15c3-3 in which all certificates and/or depository positions of an issue are identified as belonging to all customers. For example, a broker has ten customers each owning 100 shares, and the broker segregates one certificate for 1,000 shares.

BULL MARKET. A securities market characterized by rising prices. *See* Bear Market.

BULLISH. Describing an opinion or outlook that a rise in price is expected either in the general market or in an individual security. *See* Bearish.

BUNCHING ODD-LOT ORDERS. The combination of several odd-lot orders into round lots so they can be handled by a commission house broker, specialist, or two-dollar broker, thereby eliminating the odd-lot differential.

BUY-IN. On any day on or after a prescribed settlement date, the purchasing firm that has failed to receive the certificates can give written notice to the selling firm that the contract is in default, and (1) after giving notice, purchase the security in the marketplace, and (2) hold the seller responsible for any money loss that may be incurred. *See* Sell-Out.

BUY MINUS. This term refers to a price lower than the last sale, known as a minus tick or at a price equal to the last sale but lower than the last different priced sale on a zero minus tick.

BUY STOP ORDER. The instructions with a buy order for a broker or specialist on the exchange floor to execute the order at the best available price when the market price touches the customer's price or when a transaction takes place above the price. Upon execution, the transaction activates (elects or triggers) the order, making it a market order to buy.

BUY THE BOOK. An instruction to buy, at the current offer price, all available shares from the specialist in a security and/or from other broker/dealers. This instruction usually comes from traders or institutions.

BUYING POWER. The dollar amount of equity securities a customer could purchase without additional funds and continue to meet the initial margin requirements of Regulation T of the Federal Reserve. Computed as Reg T excess divided by Reg T initial margin requirements. For example: $10,000 divided by 50% = $20,000.

CAGE (THE). A slang expression used to describe a location where a brokerage firm's cashier department responsibilities are satisfied.

CALAMITY CALL. *See* Catastrophe (Calamity) Call.

CALL MONEY RATE. The percentage of interest a broker/dealer pays on a broker's collateral loan.

CALL OPTION. This is an option contract in which the holder has the right to buy the underlying stock upon exercise.

CANCELLATION. Revocation of a buy or sell order, an action that is permissible at any time prior to execution. After execution, it is allowed only with the consent of the other party to the trade and with the approval of an NYSE floor official.

CAPITAL STOCK. A corporation's total equity capital. This is a synonym for the more popular term, "common stock."

CAPITALIZATION. *See* Total Capitalization.

CARRYING COST. Expense of the interest paid on a debit balance when a position is established.

CASH ACCOUNT. An account in a brokerage firm in which all transactions are settled in full on a cash basis and only lone stock, i.e., stock owned, may be sold; short selling is not permitted by a cash account owner.

CASH CONTRACT. A securities contract by which delivery of the certificates is due at the purchaser's office the same day as the date of the trade. *See* Regular-Way Contract: When Issued/When Distributed Contract.

CASH COW. A colloquial term for any business that generates an ongoing cash flow. These businesses have well-known products and pay dividends reliably.

CASH DIVIDEND. Any payment made to a corporation's shareholders in cash from current earnings or accumulated profits. Cash dividends are taxable as income.

CASH ON DELIVERY (COD). *See* Delivery Versus Payment.

CASH TRADE. A transaction involving specific securities, in which the settlement date is the same as the trade date.

CATASTROPHE (CALAMITY) CALL. An issuer's call for redemption of a bond issue when certain events occur, such as an accident at a construction site that severely affects the completion of the project.

CCS. *See* Central Certificate Service.

CENTRAL BANK. (1) A Federal Reserve Bank situated in one of twelve banking districts in the United States. (2) The Federal Reserve System.

CENTRAL CERTIFICATE SERVICE (CCS). Former name of the Depository Trust Company.

CERTIFICATE. The actual piece of paper that is title evidence of ownership or creditorship in a corporation. Watermarked certificates are finely engraved with delicate etchings to discourage forgery.

CERTIFICATED SECURITY. A security whose ownership may be represented by a physical document. Also known as being available in "definitive form."

CHARTER. A document written by the incorporators of a corporation and filed with a state. The state approves the articles and then issues a certificate of incorporation as the license that gives the corporation its existence. Together, the two documents become the charter and the corporation is recognized as a legal entity. The charter includes such information as the corporation's name, purpose, and the amount of shares authorized for sale. Internal management rules are written by the founders in the *bylaws*.

CHECK KITING. The illegal practice of drawing a check upon a demand deposit account that contains no money or has insufficient funds. It is so called even if the person deposits someone else's check into his account prior to clearance of the check previously drawn and presented as payment for an obligation.

CHURNING. A registered representative's improper handling of a customer's account: He or she buys and sells securities for a customer while intent only on the amount of commissions generated, ignoring the customer's interests and objectives.

CIRCUIT BREAKERS. These refer to NYSE Rule 80B, in which trading halts are implemented based upon drastic declines in the DJIA (Dow Jones Industrial Average).

CLEAN. When block positioners can match customers' buy-and-sell orders for a security, they don't have to take the security into inventory. This kind of trade is said to be "clean." If the transaction appears on the exchange tape, the term "clean on the tape" is often used. Also sometimes referred to as "natural."

CLEARANCE. (1) The delivery of securities and monies in completion of a trade. (2) The comparison and/or netting of trades prior to settlement.

CLIMAX (BUYING/SELLING). A large increase or decrease in the price of a security accompanied by large volume. The price change should gap, indicating a completion of a price increase or decrease cycle. *See* Gap.

CLOSE. The final transaction price for an issue on the stock exchange at the end of a trading day.

CLOSED-END FUND. This is a kind of management investment company consisting of a portfolio and which does not issue shares to new investors. In addition, they do not redeem shares from sellers. They are bought and sold in the open-market on stock exercises and through Nasdaq.

CLOSE-OUT PROCEDURE. The procedure taken by either party to a transaction when the contrabroker defaults; the disappointed purchaser may "buy in," and the rejected seller may "sell out" or liquidate. *See* Reclamation; Rejection.

CLOSING TRANSACTION. Any trade that reduces an investor's current position.(1) Purchase: The purchase of a listed option so as to close or eliminate an existing short/written position.(2) Sale: The sale of a listed option so as to close or eliminate an existing long position. *See* Opening Transaction.

CNS. *See* Continuous Net Settlement.

COD TRADE. Cash on delivery. A general term to describe a transaction in which a seller is obliged to deliver securities to the purchaser or the purchaser's agent to collect payment.

COD TRANSACTION. A purchase of securities in behalf of a customer promising full payment immediately upon delivery of the certificates to an agent bank or broker/dealer.

CODE OF ARBITRATION. Rules established and maintained by the NASD Board of Governors to regulate arbitration of intramember and customer/member disputes involving securities transactions. *See* Board of Arbitration.

COLLARS. These refer to NYSE Rule 80A, in which index arbitrage orders are market either "buy minus" or "sell plus" depending on the amount of advances or declines in the Dow Jones Industrial Average during a trading session.

COLLATERAL. Securities and other property pledged by a borrower to secure repayment of a loan.

COMMINGLING. The act of using various customer securities in the same loan arrangement with the firm's securities. This practice is prohibited.

COMMISSION. A broker's fee for handling transactions for a client in an agency capacity.

COMMISSION HOUSE BROKER. A member of the NYSE executing orders in behalf of his or her own organization and its customers.

COMMITTEE ON UNIFORM SECURITY IDENTIFICATION PROCEDURES (CUSIP). An agency of the NASD responsible for issuing identification numbers for virtually all publicly owned stock and bond certificates.

COMMON STOCK. A unit of equity ownership in a corporation. Owners of this kind of stock exercise control over corporate affairs and enjoy any capital appreciation. They are paid dividends only after preferred stock. Their interest in the assets, in the event of liquidation, is junior to all others.

COMMON STOCK EQUIVALENTS. (1) Debt and/or equity securities capable of subscription, exchange, or conversion into common stock of the company. (2) Convertible bonds and convertible preferred stock may be so classified at the time of issuance, based on many factors.

COMMON STOCK RATIO. The relationship of common stock outstanding to the total capitalization of a corporation.

COMPETITIVE BIDDING. A sealed envelope bidding process employed by various underwriter groups interested in handling the distribution of a securities issue. The contract is awarded to one group by the issuer on the basis of the highest price paid, interest rate expense, and tax considerations.

COMPETITIVE TRADER. A member of an organized exchange who may, subject to certain rules and restrictions, trade for his or her own account and risk while on the trading floor.

CONGESTION AREA. In technical analysis, a period of trading during which the market reacts in alternating directions with great frequency. This area is characterized by small peaks and dips without any clear trend in either direction.

CONSOLIDATED TAPE. A system of reporting all trades in New York Stock Exchange-listed securities on one ticker tape.

CONTINGENT ORDER. One order given to the trading desk of a brokerage firm to buy stock and then sell a covered call option. Also called a "net order" and a "not held" order. *See* Market Not Held Order; Switch (Contingent or Swap) Order.

CONTINUING COMMISSIONS. The practice of paying commissions to registered representatives after they have left the employment of the broker/dealer or to their heirs after a registered representative has died.

CONTINUOUS NET SETTLEMENT (CNS). A procedure used by all clearing corporations to simplify processing daily transactions and correspondingly to reduce the number of certificate deliveries required. The clearing corporation interposes itself on each transaction, crediting or debiting each member's total holdings in each issue. The net balance is carried forward from day to day.

CONTRABROKER.   A term used to describe the broker with whom a trade was made.

CONTRACT SHEET.   A complete list of each member's daily transactions arranged by issue and prepared by the clearing house for members to check for accuracy of detail and approval of settlement terms.

COOLING-OFF PERIOD.   *See* Twenty-Day (Cooling-Off) Period.

CORNERING THE MARKET.   A situation in which a party or group has acquired a substantial quantity of the available shares and, as a result, exerts considerable influence on the shares' market price.

CORPORATION.   A business organization chartered by a state secretary as a recognized legal institution of and by itself and operated by an association of individuals, with the purpose of ensuring perpetuity and limited financial liability. *See* Certificate of Incorporation; Charter.

CREDIT BALANCE.   (1) In a customer's account of a broker/dealer, the credit balance indicates that the broker/dealer owes money to the customer either conditionally or unconditionally. (2) The opposite of debit balance.

CROSS (CROSSING STOCK).   A broker/dealer's pairing off of a purchase order with a sell order in the same security at the same time and price for different customers.

CROSSING SESSIONS.   There are two crossing sessions offered by the NYSE, known as the "Fixed Price Session" (Crossing Session I) and "Basket Session" (Crossing Session II).

CROWD.   *See* Trading Crowd.

CUM DIVIDEND.   A term applied to stock at a time when the purchaser will be entitled to a forthcoming dividend.

CUM RIGHTS. A term applied to a stock trading in the marketplace "with subscription rights attached," which are reflected in the price of that security.

CUMULATIVE PREFERRED STOCK. A preferred stock that accrues any omitted dividends as a claim against the company. This claim must be paid in full before any dividends may be paid on the company's common stock.

CUMULATIVE VOTING. A voting privilege that allows a stockholder to multiply the shares he or she owns by the number of vacancies to be filled on the board (or proposals to be resolved). The stockholder can then apportion his or her total votes accordingly in the manner he or she prefers. This procedure is particularly advantageous for minority stockholders.

CURBSTONE BROKER. An historic reference for a member of the American Stock Exchange.

CURRENT YIELD. This is a formula that is expressed as a percentage of the price of the stock by dividing the dollar and cents dividend per common share by the current market value of the stock.

CUSHION THEORY OF INVESTMENT. A theory of investment that views the short seller as a stabilizing influence on either a bull or bear market.

CUSIP. *See* Committee on Uniform Security Identification Procedures.

CYCLICAL STOCK. Any stock, such as housing industry-related stock, that tends to rise in price quickly when the economy turns up and fall quickly when the economy turns down.

DAISY CHAIN. A series of purchases and sales of the same issue at successively higher (or lower) prices, by the same group of people. Its purpose is to manipulate prices and draw unsuspecting investors into the market, leaving them defrauded of their money or securities.

DATE OF RECORD. The date set by the corporate board of directors for the transfer agent to close the agency's books to further changes in registration of stock and to identify the recipients of a forthcoming distribution. Also known as record date. *See* Ex-Dividend (Without Dividend) Date.

DAY ORDER. A transaction order that remains valid only for the remainder of the trading day on which it is entered.

DAY TRADING. The act of buying and selling a position during the same day.

DEALER. An individual or firm in the securities business acting as a principal rather than as an agent. *See* As Agent; As Principal.

DEBIT. Money paid out of an account. In a debit transaction, the net cost is greater than the net sale proceeds.

DEBIT BALANCE. The balance owed by a customer in his or her account as reflected on the brokerage firm's ledger statement of settled transactions.

DELAYED OPENING. The delay of the opening of trading in a security when buy and sell orders are grossly out of balance with each other.

DELIVERY DATE. The day delivery of securities is made, which may be on or subsequent to settlement date.

DELIVERY VERSUS PAYMENT. The purchase of securities in a cash account with instructions that payment will be made immediately upon the delivery of the securities, sometimes to the contrabroker but usually to an agent bank. *See* COD Trade.

DEPOSITORY TRUST COMPANY (DTC). An independent corporation owned by broker/dealers and banks responsible for: (1) holding deposit securities owned by broker/dealers and banking institutions; (2) arranging the receipt and delivery of securities between users by means of debiting and crediting their respective accounts; (3) arranging for payment of monies between users in the settlement of transactions. The DTC is generally used by option writers because it guarantees delivery of underlying securities if assignment is made against securities held in DTC.

DEPTH. (1) The amount of general investor interest in the market, comparing the number of issues traded with the number of issues listed:

the more that are traded, the greater the "depth" of the market. (2) The "depth" of a security depends on how large a buy or sell order it can absorb without its price changing greatly.

DESCENDING TOPS. In technical analysis, a chart pattern element in which each new high price for a security is lower than the preceding high—indicating a bearish trend.

DESCENDING TRIANGLE. A major chart pattern in technical analysis indicating consecutive highs until a leveling-off point is reached.

DESIGNATED ORDER TURNAROUND (DOT). A computerized order routing system used by the New York Stock Exchange to match and automatically execute small market orders that is located at the trading post location for the particular stock in the presence of the specialist.

DIFFERENTIAL (DIFFERENTIAL RETURN). The dealer's compensation for handling an odd-lot transaction. The dealer adds the differential to the price of the first possible round-lot sale and fills a customer's buy order at that somewhat higher price (or at a somewhat lower price for sell order). The differential is generally one-eighth of a point and is not itemized separately on the trade confirmation.

DILUTIVE SECURITIES. Those securities that have the potential to become common shares, that is, those securities, such as convertibles or warrants that potentially can be converted into common stock.

DIP. Any slight drop in security prices during an ongoing upward trend. It is advisable to buy on dips when the price is temporarily low.

DIRECT PLACEMENT. Any direct sale of securities to one or more investors, typically life insurance companies.

DISCOUNT BROKER. A broker/dealer whose commission rates for buying and selling securities are markedly lower than those of a full-service broker. These brokers usually provide execution-only services.

DISCRETION. *See* Limit Order; Market Not Held Order.

DISCRETIONARY ACCOUNT. A customer's account in which an employee of a member firm has authority to act arbitrarily. This term does not authorize the use of judgment as to time or price of execution for an order prompted by a customer.

DISCRETIONARY ORDER. An order that empowers a registered representative or other brokerage firm employee to use his or her own judgment on the customer's behalf with respect to choice of security, quantity of security, and whether any such transaction should be a purchase or sale. *See* Discretionary Account.

DISTRIBUTION. The sale of a large block of stock, through either an underwriting or an exchange distribution.

DISTRIBUTION AREA. In technical analysis, a relatively narrow price range for a security for a long period, typically a month or more.

DISTRIBUTION STOCK. Publicly sold stock offered by persons affiliated with the issuer pursuant to an effective shelf registration.

DISTRIBUTOR. *See* Underwriter.

DIVERSIFICATION. (1) Spreading investments and contingent risks among different companies in different fields of endeavor. (2) Investing in the securities of one company that owns or has holdings in other companies. (3) Investing in a fund with a portfolio containing many securities.

DIVIDEND PAYOUT. The percentage of dividends distributed in terms of what is available out of current net income.

DIVIDENDS. Distributions to stockholders declared by the corporate board of directors.

DK. A slang expression for "Don't Know," as applied to a securities transaction on which transactional data are missing when the brokers exchange comparison sheets. Also called a "QT" for a "questioned trade."

DNR. *See* Do Not Reduce (DNR) Order.

DO NOT REDUCE (DNR) ORDER. A limit order to buy, a stop order to sell, or a stop-limit order to sell that is not to be reduced by the amount of a cash dividend on the ex-dividend date because the customer specifically requested that it be entered that way.

DON'T FIGHT THE TAPE. Colloquial expression meaning "don't trade against the market trend."

DON'T KNOW. *See* DK.

DOT. *See* Designated Order Turnaround.

DOUBLE BOTTOM. In technical analysis, a chart pattern showing that the price of a security has twice declined to its support level and risen again. It indicates that there is a demand for securities at that level and that the security shouldn't drop any farther.

DOUBLE TOP. In technical analysis, a chart pattern showing that the price of a security has twice risen to its resistance level and fallen back. It indicates that there is a supply of securities at that level and that the security, in trying to move higher, is running into resistance at that price.

DOW JONES AVERAGE. A market average indicator consisting individually of (1) 30 industrial, (2) 20 transportation, and (3) 15 public utility common stocks; the composite average includes these 65 stocks collectively.

DOW THEORY. A theory predicated on the belief that the rise or fall of stock prices is both a mirror and a forecaster of business activities.

DOWNGRADE. Lowering a bond rating by a rating service, such as Moody's or Standard & Poor's.

DOWNLOADING. Is the process through which retrieval of a computer file is accomplished so that it becomes accessible to the individual user.

DOWNTICK. The sale of a listed security at a lower price than that of the last regular-way transaction. For example, if a stock last sold at 27, the next regular-way transaction at 26 7/8 is said to be a downtick.

DOWNTREND. A type of trend in a pattern in which each price peak is lower than the previous peak. Earnings Per Share (EPS). Corporate net earnings, less any preferred dividends, divided by outstanding common stocks and those unissued common shares that would be outstanding upon conversion to common stock from a convertible security or warrant.

DTC. *See* Depository Trust Company.

DUE BILL. A document evidencing the fact that one party owes another a dividend or other distribution along with the Delivery of Stock.

DUMPING. (1) In the securities market, the offering of large amounts of stock without regard for the effects on prices or the market. (2) In international finance, the selling of goods overseas below cost to get rid of a surplus or to gain a competitive edge on foreign firms.

DVP. *See* Delivery Versus Payment.

E&OE. Errors and omissions excepted. This legend often appears on a customer's statement. It is intended to absolve the firm of liability if it makes a mistake in preparing that statement.

EARLY WARNING SYSTEM. A system of financial reports made by broker/dealers under various exchange and SEC rules designed to provide information on the broker/dealer's financial condition.

EFFECTIVE DATE. The date on which a security can be offered publicly if no deficiency letter is submitted to the issuer by the SEC. It is generally no earlier than the twentieth calendar day after filing the registration statement. The first date that a new securities offering may be sold.

EFFICIENT MARKET HYPOTHESIS. A theory stating that market prices reflect the knowledge and expectations of all investors. Seeking undervalue stocks or forecasting any kind of market movement is futile because new developments are already reflected in the corporation's stock price, making it impossible to beat the market. Making the right investment is based purely on chance.

EFFICIENT PORTFOLIO. A portfolio, arrived at mathematically, with a maximum expected return for any level of risk or a minimum level of risk for any expected return.

EITHER/OR ORDER. *See* Alternative (Either/Or) Order.

ELECTING SALE. The round-lot transaction that activates (triggers) a stop order.

ELECTRONIC COMMUNICATIONS NETWORKS (ECNS). Are a means through which the brokerage can execute an order to buy or sell stock. In an ECN, there is no dealer spread because sellers and buyers are automatically matched at one price. Accordingly, an ECN must have enough trading activity for the trade execution to occur.

ELECTRONIC DIRECT ACCESS TRADING (EDAT). Enables day traders to directly initiate trades electronically with ECNs, Nasdaq market makers, or exchange specialists of their preference. Buyers and sellers are then matched with one another within the selected market system. EDAT is basically an advanced form of on-line trading. With EDAT, eliminated are the "middlemen" who interact between the time an order is placed until execution.

EXCHANGE DISTRIBUTION. The marketing of a large block of stock by one or two member organizations under special terms and conditions. Buy orders are solicited informally and then crossed with the large block of stock at the current market price on the floor of the exchange.

EX-CLEARING HOUSE. A term used to describe a transaction that is to be settled (i.e., paid for and delivered) without benefit of clearing corporation facilities.

EX-DISTRIBUTION. The security is trading so that the buyer will not be entitled to a distribution that is to be made to holders.

EX-DIVIDEND (WITHOUT DIVIDEND) DATE. A date set by the Uniform Practice Committee or by the appropriate stock exchange, upon which a given stock will begin trading in the marketplace without the value of a pending dividend including the contract price. It is closely related to and dependent on the date of record. It is often represented as "X" in the stock listing tables in the newspapers.

EXECUTION. Synonym for a transaction or trade between a buyer and seller.

EXERCISE DATE. The date when the sale or purchase of an option takes place according to the contract.

EXERCISE PRICE. This is the price at which the option buyer and seller will exchange the underlying stock of the option contract if the buyer exercises his rights under the contract on or before the expiration date.

EXPIRATION DATE. The date an option contract becomes void. The expiration date for listed stock options is the Saturday after the third Friday of the expiration month. All holders of options who wish to exercise must indicate their desire to do so by this date.

EX-RIGHTS. A term applied to stocks trading in the marketplace for which the value of the subscription privilege has already been deducted and which therefore no longer bears such a right; it is literally trading "rights off."

EX-WARRANTS. The security is trading so that the buyer will not be entitled to warrants that are to be distributed to holders.

FACE AMOUNT CERTIFICATES. These certificates are contracts in which investors make one or more periodic payments, the total of which are less than the face amount the investor receives on maturity.

FACE VALUE. The redemption value of a bond appearing on the face of the certificate. Also sometimes referred to as par value, or the principal value.

FAIL CONTRACT. A transaction between brokerage concerns that is not completed by delivery and payment on a settlement date.

FAIR AND REASONABLE. *See* Five Percent Guideline.

FAIR MARKET VALUE. The price, based on the current market value determined by supply and demand, for which a buyer and seller are willing to make a transaction.

FILL-OR-KILL (FOK) ORDER. An order that requires the immediate purchase or sale of a specified amount of stock, though not necessarily at one price. If the entire order cannot be filled immediately, it is automatically canceled (killed).

FINANCIAL AND OPERATIONAL COMBINED UNIFORM SINGLE (FOCUS) REPORT. A report required periodically of brokers by various regulatory authorities that gives vital statistics regarding the firm's capabilities to handle its business.

FIRM MARKET (PRICE, QUOTE). In the OTC market, a quotation on a given security rendered by a market maker at which he or she stands ready and able to trade immediately.

FIRM QUOTE RULE. This is a rule of the SEC (Securities and Exchange Commission) that mandates that brokers/dealers generally cannot offer to sell or purchase at a stated price. However, a broker/dealer can make this offer only if he is prepared to trade at the stated price under the terms and conditions stated when the offer is made. Furthermore, under the firm quote rule, a broker/dealer must correctly set forth and specify the details, i.e., nature, concerning quotes that others may obtain. Broker/dealers must also prepare to handle questions during the business day.

FIVE PERCENT GUIDELINE. A general guideline established by the NASD Board of Governors to define "fair" in a random trading transaction; it is not a rule or regulation and is used only as an approximate criterion for markups, markdowns, and commissions.

FIXED PRICE SESSION. Also known as Crossing Session I of the NYSE, this is a trading session that occurs from 4:15 to 5 PM Eastern Standard Time. It is accessible to member broker-dealers of the NYSE who are SUPERDOT subscribers who enter orders into the SUPERDOT system for execution of specific stock securities at 5 o'clock P.M. New York time. Matching and execution of these orders occurs at the closing price of the regular session of that day for that specific stock.

FLASH PRICES. When reporting falls six or more minutes behind activity on the stock exchange floor, transactions in 30 representative issues are periodically culled from their proper sequence and immediately published on the ticker tape.

FLOAT. The number of shares issued and outstanding that is sold by the Corporation held by the investing public and not by management.

FLOOR. The securities trading area of an exchange. *See* Trading Post.

FLOOR BROKER. A person who is a member of the exchange and works on the exchange floor executing the orders of public customers or other investors who do not have physical access to the area.

FLOOR BROKERAGE. A fee paid to a specialist or to a two-dollar broker on the floor for executing a trade as agent.

FLOOR DEPARTMENT. The department of the NYSE responsible for the administration and supervision of trading rules and regulations on the floor of the exchange.

FLOOR ORDER TICKETS. Abbreviated forms of order tickets, used on the floor of the exchange for recording executions.

FLOOR TRADER. *See* Registered (Floor) Trader.

FOCUS. *See* Financial and Operational Combined Uniform Single (FOCUS) Report.

FOK ORDER. *See* Fill-or-Kill (FOK) Order.

FOURTH MARKET. A term referring to the trading of securities between institutional investors without the use of broker/dealers.

FREE BOX. A bank vault or other secure location used to store fully paid customer securities. The depositories of the NCC and DTC serve as free boxes for many member firm customers.

FREE-RIDING. As used in credit activities within the securities industry, the illegal practice of purchasing and selling an issue without showing ability and intent to pay for the transaction. The penalty for this practice is to freeze the account for 90 days.

FREE-RIDING AND WITHHOLDING. As defined by the NASD in distributions of hot issues, the failure of a member to make a bona fide offering of a security that the member is distributing as an underwriter or selling group member.

FREE SECURITIES. A term used to describe securities unencumbered by a lien.

FROZEN ACCOUNT.   A special cash account in which a customer sells a security he or she had purchased but not paid for, and then either (1) fails to pay by the seventh business day after the transaction, or (2) withdraws any portion of the proceeds before payment for the purchase. Full payment is required before any further purchase executions for 90 days.

FULL DISCLOSURE ACT.   The Securities Act of 1933.

FUNDAMENTAL ANALYSIS.   A method for analyzing the prospects of a security through the observation of accepted accounting economic measures such as earnings, sales, assets, and so on. *See* Technical Analysis.

FUTURES.   Short for "futures contract," which is an agreement to make or take delivery of a commodity at a specified future time and price. The contract is transferable and can therefore be traded like a security.

GAP.   In technical analysis, a "break" between the trading ranges of a stock's price for two successive days. That is, the two ranges do not overlap. A gap usually signals a reversal because the market is overbought or oversold.

GARAGE.   One of the small trading areas just off the main trading floor of the New York Stock Exchange.

GATHER IN THE STOPS.   A tactic in stock trading in which enough stock is sold to drive its price down to a point where stop orders are known to exist. The stop orders become market orders, in turn creating movement and setting off more stop orders. This process is called *snowballing.*

GENERAL ACCOUNT.   *See* Margin (General) Account.

GIVE UP.   The practice by the payer of a commission or fee directing the recipient to "give up" part of the fee to another broker. In some situations the practice may be illegal.

GLOBALIZATION.   Refers to the interconnection and interdependence among countries throughout the world. It is the expansion of that which is local to the international level.

GOING AWAY. A term applied to the purchase of one or more serial maturities of an issue either by an institution or by a dealer.

GOING PRIVATE. Moving a company's shares from public to private ownership, either through an outside private investor or by the repurchase of shares. A company usually decides to go private when its shares are selling way below book value.

GOING PUBLIC. A private company is "going public" when it first offers its shares to the investing public.

GOLDEN HANDCUFFS. A contract between a broker and a brokerage house, offering lucrative commissions, bonuses, and other benefits, as long as the broker stays with the firm. Upon leaving, the broker must return much of the compensation.

GOOD DELIVERY. Proper delivery by a selling firm to the purchaser's office of certificates that are negotiable without additional documentation and that are in units acceptable under the Uniform Practice Code.

GOOD NAME. A slang expression used to denote the registration of securities so as to permit good delivery.

GOOD-TILL-CANCELED (GTC OR OPEN) ORDER. An order to buy or sell that remains valid until executed or canceled by the customer. *See* Limit Order; Stop Limit Order.

GRAVEYARD MARKET. A bear market in which selling investors are faced with large losses, while prospective investors keep their money in cash until the market gets better.

GREENMAIL. In response to a corporate takeover attempt, the "target" corporation buys back its shares from the potential acquirer at a premium. The would-be acquirer then abandons the takeover bid.

GREEN SHOE. In an underwriting agreement, a clause that allows the syndicate to purchase additional shares at the same price as the original offering, normally conditioned on the syndicate member first selling its allotted shares.

GROUP SALES. Sales of securities by a syndicate manager to institutional purchasers from "the pot."

GROWTH COMPANY (STOCK). A company (or its stock) that has made fast gains in earnings over the preceding few years and that is likely to keep on showing such signs of growth.

GTC. *See* Good-till-Canceled (GTC or Open) Order.

GUARANTEED STOCK. Preferred stock whose dividend is guaranteed by someone other than the issuer.

GUN JUMPING. (1) Illegally soliciting orders before an SEC registration is effective. (2) Buying a security based on information that is not yet public (that is, "inside information").

HAIRCUT. The amount taken off the value of securities for the purpose of computing a broker/dealer's net capital. The range of percentages taken off—the "haircuts"—ranges from 0 percent for U.S. government obligations to 100 percent for fail contracts.

HAMMERING THE MARKET. The intensive sale of stocks to drive prices down.

HARD DOLLARS. The dollars that a brokerage firm pays for analysis, research, or other client-related services.

HEAD AND SHOULDERS. In technical analysis, a bar chart pattern of a stock's price movement marked by a shoulder line, a neck line, and a head line resembling a person's upper torso. As the price moves toward the shoulder line, the analyst considers the trend bearish. This is known as a *head and shoulders top*. The reverse pattern, with the head at the bottom, is called a *head and shoulders bottom*. This pattern is considered bullish.

HEAD AND SHOULDERS TOP PATTERN. This is a trading pattern that signals a reversal, that is, an upward to downward trend, or vice versa, in the market. This pattern is so named because of the shape of a head and shoulders outlined on the chart.

HEAVY MARKET.   A market for a stock that contains many more sellers than buyers. This market is characterized by falling prices.

HEDGE.   Any combination of a long and/or short positions taken in securities, options, or commodities in which one position tends to reduce the risk of the other.

HEMLINE THEORY.   Theory stating that the trend in stock prices goes hand-in-hand with the trend in the hemlines of women's dresses: If hemlines drop, so do stock prices.

HIGHBALLING.   The illegal act of swapping securities with a customer at price levels above that prevailing for those same issues under competitive conditions.

HIT THE BID.   Term applied to the situation in which a seller accepts the buyer's highest bid. For example, if the ask price is 34 1/4 and the bid 34, the seller "hits the bid" by accepting 34.

HOLDER OF RECORD.   The party whose name appears on a company's stockholder register at the close of business on the record date. That party will receive a dividend or other distribution from the company in the near future.

HOLDING THE MARKET.   Going into the market with enough buy orders to generate price support for a security. The purpose is to offset a downward trend. Viewed by the SEC as a form of illegal manipulation (except in the case of a new issue cleared by the SEC).

HOME PAGE.   The initial web page which appears when a web site is accessed over the Internet.

HORIZONTAL MARKET.   Also known as a sideways market, this is a market without uptrends and downtrends. Rather, in this market, prices fall within a trading range, in which prices are relatively constant and hard to predict in which direction they are going, sometimes referred to as a dead cat bounce.

HOME RUN.   Any large gain by an investor in a short period, commonly the result of takeover bids.

HORIZONTAL PRICE MOVEMENT. In technical analysis, a string of transactions in which the prices change little. This pattern, if sustained, indicates no trend.

HOT ISSUE. A security that is expected to trade in the aftermarket at a premium over the public offering price. *See* Withholding.

HOT STOCK. (1) A security whose price rises quickly on the first day of sale. (2) Stolen stock.

HOUSE ACCOUNT. An account managed by a firm's executive and/or handled at the firm's main office. No salesperson receives a commission on transactions in a house account.

HOUSE CALL. Notification of the customer by the brokerage house that the equity in a margin account is below the maintenance level.

HYPOTHECATION. The act of borrowing money to finance purchasing or carrying securities while using those securities as collateral for the loan.

IMMEDIATE OR CANCEL (IOC) ORDER. An order that requires immediate execution at a specified price of all or part of a specified amount of stock: the unexecuted portion has to be canceled by the broker.

"IN THE MONEY." *See* Intrinsic Value.

IN THE TANK. Colloquial expression for a security or group of securities that is quickly losing value.

INACTIVE MARKET. See Narrow Market.

INDEX. A stock market indicator, derived in the same way as an average, but from a broader base of securities.

INDEX OPTIONS. Options on stock indexes.

INDICATION. On the ticker tape, an approximation of the current quotes.

INDICATOR. A unit of measurement used by the securities market analyst to help forecast market direction, volume of trading, direction of interest rates, or buying and selling by corporations.

INDIVIDUAL PROPRIETORSHIP. *See* Proprietorship (Individual).

INITIAL MARGIN REQUIREMENT. The minimum equity requirement (in 1993, $2,000) a customer must furnish his brokerage firm, as established by New York Stock Exchange Rules, at the time a margin account is opened.

INSIDE MARKET. The favorable, wholesale market price for a security available only to a market maker and other members of the NASD.

INSIDER. An officer, director, or principal stockholder of a publicly owned corporation and members of their immediate families. This category may also include people who obtain nonpublic information about a company and use it for personal gain.

INSTINET. Is a privately operated, computerized system that is a leader in after hours trading and is the one of the largest ECNs worldwide. It is a globalized trading system which matches up orders of institutions without using the exchange.

INSTITUTION. A large organization engaged in investing in securities, such as a bank, insurance company, mutual fund, or pension fund.

INSTITUTIONAL DELIVERY. *See* National Institutional Delivery System.

INTERNET. Also known as the Net; is a system of interconnected networks and computers which enable users to access information and communicate with other Internet users throughout the world.

INTERNET WEB PAGE. A page on the Internet which provides information and may connect the user to other pages through available links.

INTERMARKET TRADING SYSTEM. Also known as the ITS and the National Market, this is an order routing and tape reporting system available to traders. It connects various exchanges for trade data dissemination to all market participants. It links stock exchanges, such as New York, American, Chicago, Cincinatti, Boston, Philadelphia, and

Pacific, in addition to the Chicago Board of Options and the NASD Third Market.

INTRADAY. Meaning "within the day," this term is most often used to describe daily high and low prices of a security or commodity.

INTRINSIC VALUE. This is the actual value of the option at exercise. It is also how much the option contract is "in the money." For a put option contract, it is the excess of exercise price over the current market value of the underlying stock. For a call option contract, it is the exercise price over the current market value of the underlying stock.

INVESTMENT ADVISOR. A person, company, or institution registered with the SEC under the Investment Advisors Act of 1940 to manage the investments of third parties.

INVESTMENT ADVISORS ACT OF 1940. A federal law requiring those who charge a fee for investment advice to register with the SEC. Exceptions include banks, some brokers, and newspapers with broad-based readership.

INVESTMENT BANKER. A broker/dealer organization that provides a service to industry through counsel, market making, and underwriting of securities.

INVESTMENT COMPANY ACT OF 1940. Federal statutory law concerning rules and requirements applicable to investment companies and funds.

INVESTMENT HISTORY. Under NASD interpretation with regard to a hot issue, certain customers must have made at least 10 purchases over a three-year period with an average dollar value equal to that of the hot issue allocated.

IOC ORDER. *See* Immediate or Cancel (IOC) Order.

ISSUE (ISSUANCE). (1) Any of a company's class of securities. (2) The act of distributing securities.

ISSUED-AND-OUTSTANDING STOCKS. That portion of authorized stock distributed among investors by a corporation.

ISSUER. A corporation, trust, or governmental agency engaged in the distribution of its securities.

JOINT ACCOUNT. An account including jointly two or more people.

LAST TRADING DAY. Options cease trading at 3:00 P.M. Eastern Standard Time on the third Friday of the expiration month.

LATE TAPE. The exchange tape when it is late in reporting completed transactions. When the tape falls behind, the first digit of transactions is deleted. For example, 47 1/2 becomes 7 1/2.

LEGAL DELIVERY. A delivery of securities that is not a good delivery because of the way in which registration of the certificates was carried out.

LEVERAGE. Using less money as in options, or borrowed money as in margin to obtain a greater percentage of profit.

LEVERAGE STOCK. Any stock bought with credit, such as in a margin account.

LEVERAGED BUYOUT. Taking over a controlling interest in a company using borrowed money.

LIMIT ORDER. An order in which a customer sets a maximum price he or she is willing to pay as a buyer and a minimum price he or she is willing to accept as a seller. *See* Market Order; Stop Order.

LIMIT ORDER DISPLAY RULE. This is a rule applicable to the Nasdaq Stock Market that concerns situations where a Nasdaq investor has placed a limit order. If the price of the limit order is either the same or better than the market maker's current quotation and there is not immediate execution of the order, the maker is required to display the limit order to the entire market on the trading screen. The maker could instead, for display, send this order to an ECN or a different market maker.

LIMIT ORDER PROTECTION RULE. *See* Manning Rule.

LIMIT PRICE. A modification of an order to buy or sell. With a *sell* limit order, the customer is instructing the broker to make the sale at or

above the limit price. With a *buy* limit order, the customer is instructing the broker to make the purchase at or below the limit price.

LINE CHARTS. These are charts that are utilized to show the pattern or trend of one statistic, such as price.

LINKS. Through which multiple pages on the Internet may be connected with one another.

LIQUIDATION. The voluntary or involuntary closing out of security positions.

LIQUIDITY. (1) The ability of the market in a particular security to absorb a reasonable amount of trading at reasonable price changes. Liquidity is one of the most important characteristics of a good market. (2) The relative ease with which investors can convert their securities into cash.

LISTED STOCK. The stock of a company traded on a securities exchange and for which a listing application and registration statement have been filed with the SEC and the exchange itself.

LOAN VALUE. The maximum permissible credit extended on securities in a margin account, presently 50 percent of the current market value of eligible stock in the account.

LOCKED MARKET. A highly competitive market in which the bids and prices are temporarily the same—that is, they are "locked."

LONG MARKET VALUE. The market value of securities owned by a customer (long in his or her account).

LONG POSITION. The ownership of securities.

MAINTENANCE CALL. A broker/dealer's notice to a customer to deposit additional equity in his or her account to meet either New York Stock Exchange or the broker/dealer's own minimum maintenance requirements.

MAJOR MARKET INDEX. An index prepared by the American Stock Exchange and upon which futures contracts are traded.

MANAGEMENT COMPANIES. These are investment companies that are comprised of open-end and closed-end funds with diversified, managed portfolios that can vary day to day. The funds also may reinvest distributions and dividends.

MANIPULATION. Making securities prices rise or fall artificially, through aggressive buying or selling by one investor or in connection with others. This is a severe violation of federal securities laws.

MANNING RULES. Also known as limit order protection rules, these are rules applicable to the Nasdaq Stock Market that are designed to give security to Nasdaq investors by mandating that NASD member firms cannot trade ahead of them.

MARGIN. The amount of money or securities that an investor must deposit with a broker to secure a loan from the broker. Brokers may lend money to investors for use in trading securities. To procure such a loan, an investor must deposit cash with the broker.

MARGIN (GENERAL) ACCOUNT. An account in which a customer uses credit from a broker/dealer to take security positions. *See* Margin.

MARGIN CALL. A demand on the customer to deposit money or securities with the broker when a purchase is made or when the customer's equity in a margin account declines below a minimum standard set by an exchange or the firm.

MARK TO THE MARKET. As the market value of a borrowed security fluctuates, the lender may demand more in cash collateral for a rise in value, or the borrower may demand a partial refund of collateral for a decline. The written notice for either demand is a "mark" to the market.

MARKDOWN. The fee charged by a broker/dealer acting as a dealer when he or she buys a security directly from a customer for themselves. *See* As Principal; Five Percent Guideline.

MARKET FRAGMENTATION. This term refers to large price discrepancies existing for the same stock in different markets. For instance, a stock may be trading at a value of $15/share on one exchange while concurrently trading at $21/share on another market.

MARKET-IF-TOUCHED ORDER. An order allowable only on the Commodity Futures Exchange and also the CBOE. Such a buy order is activated when a series declines to a predetermined price or below. Such a sell order is activated when a series rises to a predetermined price or higher.

MARKET INDEX. A general measurement of market movement, that, unlike an average, includes weighting of prices in terms of outstanding shares.

MARKET MAKER. (1) An options exchange member who trades for his or her own account and risk. This member is charged with the responsibility of trading so as to maintain a fair, orderly, and competitive market. He or she may not act as an agent. (2) A firm actively making bids and offers in the OTC market.

MARKET NOT HELD ORDER. An order to buy or sell securities at the current market with the investor leaving the exact timing of its execution and the price up to the floor broker. If the floor broker is holding a "market not held" buy order and the price could decline, he or she may wait to buy when a better price becomes available. There is no guarantee for the investor that a "market not held" order will be filled.

MARKET ORDER. An order to be executed immediately at the best available price, that is at the current quote by buying at the offer or selling long to the bid.

MARKET PRICE. (1) The last reported sale price for an exchange-traded security. (2) For over-the-counter securities, a consensus among market makers.

MARKET VALUE. The price that would be paid for a security or other asset.

MARKETABILITY. How easily a security can be bought and sold. *See* Liquidity.

MARKING. Manipulative action at the close by a trader during the execution of an option contract or by creating a fictitious trade. The purpose of this action is to improve the equity position in the client's account, even if the transactions do not represent the fair value of the contract.

MARKUP.   The fee charged by a broker/dealer acting as a dealer when he or she buys a security from a market maker and sells it to a customer at a higher price. *See* As Principal; Five Percent Guideline.

MATCHED ORDERS.   Sales and purchases by the same beneficial owner of the same security at the same time and price, giving the impression of extensive trading in that security. This is a violation of the Securities Exchange Act of 1934.

MEMBER.   A term used to describe a member of the New York Stock Exchange or other organized exchange or clearing corporation.

MEMBER FIRM.   A term used to describe a company that has as an officer or partner a member of the New York Stock Exchange, another organized exchange, or clearing corporation.

MEMBER TAKEDOWN.   A situation in which a syndicate member buys bonds at the takedown (or member's discount) and then sells them to a customer at the public offering price.

MERGER.   The nonhostile and voluntary union of two corporations. *See* Takeover.

MINIMUM MAINTENANCE MARGIN.   The minimum equity customers must have in their accounts as defined by NASD or Stock Exchange Rules, currently 25 per cent minimum.

MINIMUM TRADING VARIATION.   The minimum amount of variation allowable in the trading values in an exchange, usually one-sixteenth of a point (described as a "teeny"). *See* Point.

MINUS TICK.   A transaction on an exchange at a price below the previous transaction in a given security.

MISSING THE MARKET.   The failure by a member of the exchange to execute an order due to his or her negligence. The member is obliged to reimburse the customer promptly for any losses due to the mistake.

MIXED ACCOUNT. A margin account continuing both long and short positions in securities.

MOODY'S INVESTORS SERVICE. One of the best-known bond rating agencies, owned by Dun & Bradstreet.

MUTILATION. A term used to describe the physical condition of a certificate, note, bond, or coupon when the instrument is no longer considered negotiable.

MUTUAL FUND. Also known as an open-end fund, this is a type of investment management company comprised of a portfolio of diversified securities that are managed professionally. Its ability to raise capital is "open-ended," as it has the ability to issue shares to new investors, and redeem shares from sellers.

N. (1) "Newly listed" when used in lowercase with a stock transaction report in the newspaper. (2) "New York Stock Exchange" when used as a capital next to a stock transaction report.

NARROW MARKET. Light trading and great price fluctuations with regard to the volume on a securities or commodities market. Also known as an "inactive market."

NASD. *See* National Association of Securities Dealers.

NASDAQ. *See* National Association of Securities Dealers Automated Quotations.

NASDAQ-100 INDEX. Since 1985, this index represents the 100 of the biggest Nasdaq, non-financial companies with the greatest growth throughout major industry sectors. All the companies upon which this index is based are listed on the Nasdaq National Market. Securities participation in this index requires that the company has a minimum market capitalization of $500 million. In addition, the average trading volume of the companies is a minimum 100,000 shares.

NASDAQ COMPOSITE INDEX. A very popular, major market index introduced in 1971 that is based on the financial success and market valuation of all common stocks, both foreign and domestic, which are listed on the Nasdaq Stock Market. Approximately 5,000 different companies of various industries, especially technology, have stock comprising this index, often used as a reference for the "new economy."

NASDAQ NATIONAL MARKET INDEX. This index is similar to the Nasdaq Composite Index. It is comprised of all Nasdaq National Market listed companies that are part of the Nasdaq Composite Index.

NASDAQ OTC PRICE INDEX. *See* National Association of Securities Dealers Automated Quotations Over-the-Counter Price Index.

NATIONAL ASSOCIATION OF SECURITIES DEALERS (NASD). An association of broker/dealers in the over the counter securities organized on a nonprofit, non-stock-issuing basis. Its general aim is to protect investors in the OTC market by adopting Rules of Fair Practice and Compliance Standards.

NATIONAL ASSOCIATION OF SECURITIES DEALERS AUTOMATED QUOTATIONS (NASDAQ). A computerized quotations network by which NASD members can communicate bids and offers and execute orders directly and immediately online within the automated system.

NATIONAL ASSOCIATION OF SECURITIES DEALERS AUTOMATED QUOTATIONS OVER-THE-COUNTER PRICE INDEX. A computer-oriented, broad-based indicator of activity in the unlisted securities market, updated every five minutes.

NATIONAL CLEARING CORPORATION (NCC). The organization responsible for arranging a daily clearance of transactions for members by means of a continuous net settlement process.

NEGOTIABILITY. In reference to securities, the ability to easily transfer title upon delivery.

NEGOTIATED MARKETPLACE. The over-the-counter market, in which transactions are negotiated between two parties. The opposite of auction marketplace.

NEGOTIATED UNDERWRITING. The underwriting of new securities issues in which the spread purchase price and the public offering price are determined through negotiation rather than through bidding.

NET CHANGE. The last column in a listed stock or bond table showing the difference between the closing prices of that day and the previous day of the security traded, adjusted for dividends and other distributions.

NET PRICE. The proceeds of a sale or the gross payment on a purchase after deducting or adding, respectively, all expenses.

NET PROCEEDS. The contract price less all expenses incurred on a sale execution. *See* Net Price.

NEW ACCOUNT REPORT. A mandatory document for broker/dealers who conduct a customer business, this is a record of inquiry probing into the essential facts relative to the background, financial circumstances, and investment objectives of each customer.

NEW ISSUE. (1) Any authorized but previously unissued security offered for sale by an issuer. (2) The resale of Treasury shares.

NEW YORK STOCK EXCHANGE INDEX. A "weighted" market index consisting of all common stocks listed on the Big Board, reporting price movements in dollars and cents.

NEXT-DAY CONTRACT. A security transaction calling for settlement the day after trade date.

NH. *See* Not Held (NH) Order.

NO-ACTION LETTER. In response to a query as to whether an activity is in violation of securities regulations, the SEC may issue a letter stating that it will take no action, criminal or civil, if the activity is not in violation.

NOMINAL QUOTATION. A quotation that is an approximation of the price that could be expected on a purchase or sale, and that is not to be considered firm in the event that a purchase or sale is consummated. *See* Numbers Only.

NONCUMULATIVE PREFERRED STOCK. Preferred stock on which omitted dividends do not accrue and the shareholders have no claim to them in the future.

NONPURPOSE LOAN. A loan involving securities as collateral that is arranged for any purpose other than to purchase, carry, or trade margin securities. *See* Purpose Loan.

NORMAL MARKET. In futures trading, a market with adequate supply. In this type of market, the price of a commodity for future delivery should be equal to the present cash price plus the amount of carrying charges needed to carry the commodity to the delivery date.

NORMAL TRADING UNIT. The accepted unit of trading in a given marketplace: On the NYSE it is 100 shares (round lot) for stocks and $1,000 par value for bonds. In some relatively inactive stocks, the unit is 10 shares. For NASDAQ traded securities it is 100 shares for stocks and $10,000 par value for bonds. *See* Odd Lot; Round Lot.

NOT HELD (NH) ORDER. An order that does not hold the executing member financially responsible for using his or her personal judgment in the execution price or time of a transaction. *See* Market Not Held Order.

NUMBERS ONLY. A dealer's response to a request for a quote with just numbers; the dealer is not obligated to make a transaction. *See* Nominal Quotation.

ODD LOT. An amount of stock less than the normal trading unit, normally a trade of one to ninety-nine shares. *See* Round Lot.

ODD-LOT DIFFERENTIAL. Generally, the dealer who facilitates an odd-lot transaction will buy the securities 1/16, 1/8 or 1/4 point below the next round-lot trade, or *sell* the securities 1/16, 1/8 or 1/4 above the next round-lot trade.

ODD-LOT THEORY. A theory of market activity stating that small (odd-lot) investors frequently become heavy buyers as the market peaks and that they sell heavily in a declining market, just prior to a rally.

OFF-BOARD. An expression that may refer to transactions over the counter in unlisted securities or to transactions involving listed shares that were not executed on a national securities exchange.

OFFER. The price at which a person is ready to sell. *See* Bid-and-Asked Quotation (or Quote).

OFFERING (ASKED) PRICE. The lowest price available for a round lot.

OFFERING CIRCULAR. (1) A publication that is prepared by the underwriters and that discloses basic information about an issue of securities to be offered in the primary market. (2) Sometimes used to describe a document used by dealers when selling large blocks of stock in the secondary market.

OFFERING DATE. When a security is first offered for public sale.

OFFER WANTED (OW). Notation made, usually in the pink or yellow sheets, by a broker/dealer who wants another dealer to make an offer for a security.

OFF-FLOOR ORDER. An order that originates and is executed off the floor of the NYSE.

OFFICE ORDER TICKETS. Transaction order forms filled out in great detail at each sales office of member firms. *See* Floor Order Tickets.

ON-FLOOR ORDER. An order originating and executed on the floor of the exchange.

ON-THE-QUOTATION ODD-LOT ORDER. An odd-lot order that must be executed immediately; the price is therefore based on the existing round-lot quotation on the floor of the New York Stock Exchange or on some other exchange.

ON THE TAPE. A trade reported on one of several ticker tapes.

ONE-CANCELS-THE-OTHER ORDER. Two or more orders to be treated as a unit. If one order is executed, the other is canceled.

ONLINE. The stage during which a user has accessed and is connected to the Internet.

ONLINE COMPARISON SYSTEM. Also known as OCS, this is a system utilized by the NYSE which gives its clearing members an opportunity to compare real time trades. It is useful to help solve problems that occur after trade execution.

ONLINE INVESTING. Also known as online trading, is the way through which investors can place orders and have brokerage firms execute such through using the Internet online.

OPD. Appearing next to a ticker symbol, these letters indicate an issue's initial transaction during a trading session, or the ticker price of the transaction did not get published shortly after execution. The symbol is used to report the correct opening price.

OPEN BOX. *See* Active Box.

OPEN-END FUND. *See* Mutual Fund.

OPEN ON THE PRINT. Term used when a block positioner takes the contra side of the trade from an institution. The transaction is printed on the tape, but buyers and sellers are still needed to offset the risk.

OPEN ORDER. *See* Good-till-Canceled (GTC or Open) Order.

OPENING. (1) The price at which a security or commodity starts trading. (2) A short period during which interest rates drop and corporations can issue bonds at reduced prices.

OPENING AUTOMATED REPORT SERVICE. Also known as OARS, this is utilized by the NYSE to take pre-market opening orders that are no greater than 30,000 shares in size, and match buy and sell orders together.

OPENING ONLY ORDER. *See* At-the-Opening (Opening Only) Order.

OPENING TRANSACTION. Any trade that increases an investor's position. (1) *Purchase:* An opening purchase transaction, so as to establish a new long position, adds long securities to the account. (2) *Sale:* The writing or selling of a listed option, so as to establish a new short position, adds short securities to the investor's net position. *See* Closing Transaction.

OPTION. A contract wherein one party (the option writer) grants another party (buyer) the right to demand that the writer perform a certain act.

OPTION PREMIUM. This is the price of the option contract. It is also the sum of intrinsic value and time value of the option.

OPTIONS CLEARING CORPORATION. Also known as the OCC, it secures issues and guarantees every option contract traded on the exchanges, especially with respect to issuance and pricing of options contracts. Members of the OCC include the American, Pacific, and Philadelphia Stock Exchanges, in addition to the Chicago Board of Options (CBOE).

OTC MARGIN STOCK. A stock traded over the counter whose issuer meets certain criteria that qualify the stock for margined purchases or short sales, as governed by Regulation T.

"OUT OF THE MONEY." This is a put or call with no intrinsic value. In the case of a put option, the exercise price is less than the current market value of the underlying stock of the contract. In the case of a call option, the current market value is less than the exercise price of the underlying stock of the contract.

OVERNIGHT POSITION. The inventory in a security at the end of a trading day.

OVERSOLD. In technical analysis, a security that is expected to go down in price or that went down too fast. This situation usually manifests itself as a "gap" or a "selling climax," where the closing price is much below the previous day's close.

OVER THE COUNTER BULLETIN BOARD. Also known as the OTC Bulletin Board or OTCBB, this is a service which, since its introduction by the NASD in 1990, provides investors with data concerning non-listed Nasdaq market securities. Generally, OTCBB listed stocks are over the counter equities of companies not large enough to meet the listing and trading requirements of the Nasdaq Stock Market. In addition, they include stocks not traded nor listed on national securities exchanges. Presently, there are over 6,500 OTCBB stocks. The stocks include Direct

Participation Programs (DPPs), American Depository Receipts (ADRs), foreign equity issues, units, and warrants.

OVER-THE-COUNTER (OTC) OPTION. (1) A market, conducted mainly over the telephone, for securities made up of dealers who may or may not be members of a securities exchange. Thousands of companies have insufficient shares outstanding, stockholders, or earnings to warrant listing on a national exchange. Securities of these companies are therefore traded in the over-the-counter market between dealers who act either as agents for their customers or as principals. The over-the-counter market is the principal market for U.S. government and municipal bonds and for stocks of banks and insurance companies. (2) A market for options traded directly between buyer and seller, unlike a listed stock option. These options have no secondary market and no standardization of striking prices and expiration dates. *See* Secondary Market.

OVERTRADING. A practice in violation of NASD principles. A broker/dealer overpays a customer for a security to enable the customer to subscribe to another security offered by that broker/dealer at a higher markup than the loss to be sustained when the firm sells the customer's first security at prevailing market prices.

OVERVALUED. (1) In securities trading, a security whose market price is higher than it should be in the opinion of fundamental analysts. (2) In options trading, a security trading at a higher price than that indicated by the mathematical models. *See* Fair Market Value; Undervalued.

OW. *See* Offer Wanted.

P/E RATIO. *See* Price/Earnings (P/E) Ratio.

PAINTING THE TAPE. An individual or group making numerous transactions without any real change in ownership. The purpose is to dupe investors into thinking the security is being actively traded and joining in that activity.

PAIRED SHARES. When the common stock of two companies that are run by the same management is sold as one unit, it is said to be "paired," "stapled," or "Siamese."

PAPER LOSS/PROFIT. An unrealized loss or profit on a security still held. Paper losses and profits become actual when a security position is closed out by a purchase or sale.

PAR (VALUE). The face nominal value of a security.(1) A dollar amount assigned to a share of common stock by the corporation's charter. At one time, it reflected the value of the original investment behind each share, but today it has little significance except for bookkeeping purposes. Many corporations do not assign a par value to new issues. For preferred shares or bonds, par value has importance insofar as it signifies the dollar value on which the dividend/interest is figured, the original issuance price of the security and for bonds the amount to be repaid upon redemption. (2) Preferred dividends are usually expressed as a percentage of the stock's par value.

PARKING. The practice by a dealer of selling a security to another dealer to reduce the seller's net capital. The securities are sold back to the first dealer when a buyer is found, and the second dealer recoups any carrying charges.

PARTIAL DELIVERY. A delivery of fewer securities than the amount contracted for in the sales transaction.

PARTICIPATE BUT DO NOT INITIATE (PNI) ORDER. On large orders to buy or sell, an instruction given to a broker from institutional buyers or sellers not to initiate a new price, but either to let the market create a new price or obtain a favorable price through gradual and intermittent transactions.

PARTICIPATING PREFERRED STOCK. A preferred stock that is entitled not only to its stated dividend, but also to additional dividends on a specified basis if dividends are declared after payment of dividends on common stock. The extra dividends are shared equally by common and participating preferred stockholders.

PARTNERSHIP. A type of business organization typified by two or more proprietors.

PEGGING. Also known as stabilization. Keeping a security's offer price at a certain level by means of a bid at or slightly below the price. Pegging is legal only in underwriting.

PENNANT. In technical analysis, a roughly triangular chart pattern whose apex points to the right. Pennants do not indicate any clear trends because the stock may rise or fall near the apex.

PENNY STOCKS. Colloquial term for—but not limited to—low-priced, high-risk stocks that usually sell for less than $1 per share. These shares usually require a special margin maintenance requirement, and purchases are often limited to unsolicited orders.

PENNY STOCK RULES. These are rules applicable to the OTCBB market that are designed to provide protection to investors. Under the rules, broker/dealers must do two things before executing an investor's penny stock order: (1) approve the account of the investor for penny stock, and (2) give the investors important information, including market information.

PERPETUAL WARRANT. A warrant with no expiration date.

PICTURE. The prices at which a broker/dealer or specialist is ready to trade. For example, "The picture on XYZ is 18 1/2 to 18 5.4, 1,000 either way."

PINK SHEETS. A list of securities being traded by over-the-counter market makers, published every business day by the National Quotation Bureau. Equity securities are published separately on long pink sheets. Debt securities are published separately on long yellow sheets.

PLACE. A securities distribution to a buyer, either publicly or privately.

PLUS TICK. A transaction on a stock exchange at a price higher than the price of the last transaction. Also known as an uptick.

PLUS-TICK RULE. An SEC rule stating that a short sale of a round lot has to be made at a price that was an advance over the last different regular-way sale of that security. For example, if the last transaction was at 40, the next short sale must be at 40 1/16 or higher. If the last sale was itself an advance, then a sale at the same price is a zero plus tick and legitimate for a short sale. For example, if the last two transactions were at 40 and 40 1/8, then the next sale could be at 40 1/8—a zero plus tick.

PNI ORDER. *See* Participate but Do Not Initiate (PNI) Order.

POINT. (1) In stocks, $1. (2) In market averages, it means simply a point—a unit of measure.

POINT AND FIGURE (P&F) CHART. In technical analysis, a chart of price changes in a security. Upward price changes are plotted as "X's," and downward prices are plotted as "O's." Time is *not* reflected on this type of chart.

POISON PILL. Any kind of action taken by a takeover target company to make its stock less palatable to an acquirer. Tactics include issuing new preferred stocks that give shareholders the right to redeem at premium price if a takeover does occur. This makes acquisition much more expensive for the would-be acquirer.

PORTFOLIO. Holdings of securities by an individual or institution. A portfolio may include preferred and common stocks, as well as bonds, of various enterprises.

PORTFOLIO THEORY. A theory based on an investment approach that permits investors to classify, estimate, and control the kind and amounts of return and risk in their own portfolios.

POS. *See* Preliminary Official Statement.

POSITION. (1) The status of securities in an account—long or short. (2) To buy or sell a block of securities so that a position is established. *See* Facilitation.

POT, THE. A pool of securities, aside from those distributed amount individual syndicate members, that is allocated by the manager for group or institutional sales. When "the pot is clean," the portion of the issue reserved for institutional (group) sales has been completely sold.

POT IS CLEAN. *See* Pot, The.

PREEMPTIVE RIGHT. *See* Subscription Privilege (Preemptive Right).

PREFERENCE STOCK. *See* Prior Preferred (Preference) Stock.

PREFERRED STOCK. Owners of this kind of stock are entitled to a fixed dividend to be paid regularly before dividends can be paid on common stock. They also exercise claims to assets, in the event of liquidation, senior to holders of common stock but junior to bondholders. Holders of preferred stock normally do not have a voice in management.

PRELIMINARY AGREEMENT. An agreement between an issuing corporation and an underwriter drawn up prior to the effective date and pending a decision by the underwriter on the success potential of the new securities.

PRELIMINARY OFFICIAL STATEMENT (POS). Also known as the preliminary prospectus, the preliminary version or draft of an official statement, as issued by the underwriters or issuers and subject to change prior to the confirmation of offering prices or interest rates.

PRELIMINARY PROSPECTUS. *See* Preliminary Official Statement (POS).

PRESOLD ISSUE. A completely sold-out issue of municipal or government securities prior to the announcement of its price or coupon rate. This practice is illegal with regard to registered corporate offerings, but it is not illegal in the primary distribution of municipals or Treasuries.

PRICE/EARNINGS (P/E) RATIO. A ratio used to gauge the relative value of a security in light of its current market price. The P/E ratio or multiple refers to the relationship of the current market value of a stock divided by the corporations earnings per share; for example, if a stock is trading at 24, and the annual earnings per share is $2, the P/E ratio is $12 ($24 divided by $2). A high P/E Ratio usually implies more of a risk. Ratio = Market price divided by earnings per share.

PRICE RANGE. The range defined by the high and low prices of a security over a given period.

PRIMARY DISTRIBUTION (OFFERING). The original sale of a company's securities. The sale of authorized but unissued shares of stock is a primary sale, while the resale of Treasury shares is a secondary sale.

PRIMARY MARKET. The new issue market as opposed to the secondary market.

PRIMARY MOVEMENT. A long-term (one- to five-year) movement or direction in the market.

PRINCIPAL, AS. *See* As Principal.

PRINCIPAL TRADE. Any transaction in which the dealer or dealer bank effecting the trade takes over ownership of the securities.

PRINCIPAL TRANSACTION. *See* As Principal.

PRINCIPALS (STOCKHOLDERS). The investors in a corporation with an equity interest, entitled to voting privileges, dividends, access to books and records, ready transferability· of stock, proportionate shares of assets in liquidation, and subscription privileges.

PRINCIPAL VALUE. The face value of an obligation that must be repaid at maturity and that is separate from interest. Often called simply "principal."

PRIOR PREFERRED STOCK. Preferred stock whose claim on corporate assets takes precedence over other issues of preferred stock should the issuer be dissolved. It also has priority on its claim on earnings when dividends are declared.

PRIOR PREFERRED (PREFERENCE) STOCK. A kind of preferred stock entitling the owner to prior claim to forthcoming dividends or claim to assets in liquidation proceedings.

PRIVATE PLACEMENT. The distribution of unregistered securities to a limited number of purchasers without the filing of a statement with the SEC. Such offerings generally require submission of an investment letter to the seller by all purchasers.

PROCEEDS SALE. A secondary market sale whose proceeds are used for another purchase. The two transactions are considered as one transaction, and the total sales charges must be less than 5 percent. *See* Five Percent Guideline; Switch (Contingent or Swap) Order.

PROFIT TAKING. A drop off in general market prices after a sharp increase, in the absence of any adverse socioeconomic influence. Traders are assumed to be taking short-term profits.

PROPRIETARY.   A term applied to the assets of a brokerage firm and those of its principals that have been specifically pledged as their capital contribution to the organization.

PROPRIETARY ACCOUNT.   An account used by broker/dealers for trading securities, options, or commodities for their own account and risk, as opposed to trading for their customers.

PROPRIETORSHIP (INDIVIDUAL).   A type of business structure consisting of one owner, who is personally responsible for all debt liabilities but who also can manage the business as he or she sees fit.

PROSPECTUS.   A document that contains material information for an impending offer of securities (containing most of the information included in the registration statement) and that is used for solicitation purposes by the issuer and underwriters.

PROXY.   (1) A formal authorization (power of attorney) from a stockholder that empowers someone to vote in his or her behalf. (2) The person who is so authorized to vote on behalf of a stockholder.

PROXY CONTEST.   The situation in which a person or group of people, other than a company's management, attempts to solicit shareholders' proxies, usually to change the management of the company.

PROXY STATEMENT.   Material information required by the SEC to be given to a corporation's stockholders as a prerequisite to solicitation of votes. It is required for any issuer subject to the provisions of the Securities Exchange Act of 1934.

PRUDENT MAN INVESTING.   Investing in a fashion that is exemplified by the conduct of a conservative person managing his or her own assets. In certain cases this type of investing is limited to the "legal list." Some states use the "prudent man" rule as a legal guideline for investing others' money.

PUBLIC BOOK (OF ORDERS).   A book that contains the buy or sell orders entered by the public away from the current market and that is kept by the board broker or a specialist. Only the specialist knows at what price and in what quantity the nearest public orders are. *See* Board Broker; Market Maker; Specialist.

PUBLIC OFFERING (DISTRIBUTION).   The offering of securities for sale by an issuer.

PUBLICLY HELD.   Term applied to a corporation whose shares are traded according to either SEC rules or New York Stock Exchange rules.

PURCHASING (BUYING) POWER.   The amount of security value available in a margin account solely from the use of existing equity in excess of current federal requirements.

PURE HEDGE.   A buying hedge used to lock in an interest rate and thereby protect against a decline in interest rates.

PURPOSE LOAN.   A loan, using corporate securities as collateral, that is used to purchase, trade, or carry margin securities. *See* Nonpurpose Loan.

PUT OPTION.   This is an option contract in which the purchaser obtains the right to sell, at the strike price, the underlying stock of the option.

PYRAMIDING.   Using profit generated by a position to add to that position.

QUESTIONED TRADE.   *See* DK.

QUOTATION OR QUOTE.   *See* Bid-and-Asked Quotation (or Quote).

RAIDERS.   Persons or groups of persons who attempt to buy a controlling share in a company's stock for the purpose of voting in new management, not for investment purposes. *See* Bear Raiders.

RALLY.   A brisk rise following a decline in the general price level of the market or in the price of an individual stock.

RANDOM WALK THEORY.   A hypothesis stating that historical prices, because they react to random influences on the market, are of no use in forecasting price movements. Espoused in 1900 by the French mathematician, Louis Bachelier, and revived in the 1960s, this theory contradicts the principals used in technical analysis. *See* Technical Analysis.

RANGE.   A set of prices consisting of the opening sale, high sale, low sale, and latest sale of the day for a given security.

RATING AGENCIES. Organizations that publicly rate the credit quality of securities issuers, the most often cited being Moody's Investors Service, Inc. and Standard & Poor's Corporation.

READING THE TAPE. Appraising a security's performance by monitoring the price changes on the ticker.

RECLAMATION. The privilege of a seller in a transaction to recover his or her certificates and return the control money, or of a buyer to recover his or her contract money and return the certificates, should any irregularity be discovered upon delivery and settlement of the contract. *See* Rejection.

RECORD DATE. *See* Date of Record.

RECTANGULAR BASE PATTERN. In technical analysis, this is a pattern or model that illustrates the principle of support and resistance. In such a pattern, in a tight trading range, there are alternating peaks and bottoms over several months. There is much volume until prices begin to go up and down. This is followed by a combination of falling prices and high volume with a possible heavy volume in price advances. This combination of activity signals a sell off in stocks. Rising prices are then accompanied by heavier trading volume which eventually go in sync with a movement in prices; this demonstrates resistance.

REG T CALL. A notice to a customer of a broker/dealer that additional equity is needed in his or her account to meet the minimum standards set by Regulation T of the Federal Reserve.

REG T EXCESS. The amount of equity in a customer's account above the minimum requirements of Regulation T of the Federal Reserve.

REGISTERED FORM. A term applied to securities that are issued in a form allowing the owner's name to be imprinted on the certificate and that allow the issuer to maintain records as to the identity of the owners. Opposite of bearer form.

REGISTERED REPRESENTATIVE. *See* Account Executive.

REGISTERED SECONDARY DISTRIBUTION. An offering of securities by affiliated persons that requires an effective registration statement to be on file with the SEC before distribution may be attempted.

REGISTERED SECURITY. (1) A certificate (stock or bond) clearly inscribed with the owner's name. (2) A stock or bond that is registered with the SEC at the time of its sale. If such an initial registration does not take place, then the term also includes any security sold publicly and in accordance with the SEC's rules.

REGISTERED (FLOOR) TRADER. A member of the NYSE who buys and sells stocks for his or her own account and risk on the floor of the exchange.

REGISTRATION STATEMENT. A document required to be filed with the SEC by the issuer of securities before a public offering may be attempted. The Securities Act of 1933 mandates that it contain all material and accurate facts. Such a statement is required also when affiliated persons intend to offer sizable amounts of securities. The SEC examines the statement for a 20-day period, seeking obvious omissions or misrepresentations of fact.

REGULAR SPECIALIST. A member of the NYSE who continually solicits and executes orders in listed stocks assigned to him or her. The specialist also maintains an orderly market and provides price continuity and liquidity by means of transactions for his or her own account and risk on those stocks assigned to them by the exchange.

REGULAR-WAY CONTRACT. The most frequently used delivery contract. For stocks and corporate and municipal bonds, this type of contract calls for delivery on the third business day after the trade, soon to be on the first business day after the trade. For U.S. government bonds and options, delivery must be made on the first business day after the trade.

REGULATION T. A Federal Reserve Board regulation that explains the conduct and operation of general and special accounts within the offices of a broker/dealer firm, prescribing a code of conduct for the effective use and supervision of credit.

REJECTION. The privilege of the purchaser in a transaction to refuse a delivery lacking in negotiability or presented in the wrong denominations, without prejudice to his or her rights in the transaction. *See* Reclamation.

RELATIVE STRENGTH. This is a measure of the performance and activity of a particular stock or category of stocks as compared or related to the performance and activity of the entire market. The purpose of relative strength is to make a determination as to whether the movement of a stock(s) is (are) consistent with the rest of the market, and to what degree of upward or downward variance there exists.

REPEAT PRICES OMITTED.   A ticker tape announcement to signify that the tape has fallen three minutes behind transactions on the trading floor. Sequential transactions at the same price are then purposely eliminated from the tape; only the first trade prices in a string of transactions appear.

RESISTANCE.   This is a chart price line or level above the current market price where selling pressure has historically overcome buying pressure and price advances have been turned back.

RESISTANCE LEVEL.   *See* Resistance.

RESTRICTED ACCOUNT.   (1) A margin account in which the equity is less than the current federal requirement. (2) The cash account of a customer who has failed to pay for a purchase under Regulation T and must have cash in the account for a period of 90 days prior to executing a buy.

REVERSAL.   In technical analysis, a substantial, and/or long-term, countermovement of a trend.

REVERSAL ARBITRAGE.   A riskless arbitrage involving the sale of the stock short, the writing of a put, and the purchase of a call with the options all having the same terms.

RIGGED MARKET.   The manipulation of a security price in an attempt to attract buyers and sellers. *See* Manipulation.

RIGHT.   *See* Subscription Right.

RIGHTS OFFERING.   A right that is granted by a corporation and that enables shareholders to purchase a number of shares of a new issue of common stock, usually at a lower price than the market price of the existing shares. The offer is made to the shareholders before the issue is offered to the public.

RISING BOTTOM. In technical analysis, a chart pattern, usually on a daily chart, indicating a rising trend in a security's price.

RISK ARBITRAGE. A purchase and short sale of potentially equal securities at prices that may realize a profit.

ROUND LOT. A unit of trading or a multiple thereof. On the NYSE, stocks are traded in round lots of 100 shares for active stocks and 10 shares for inactive ones. Bonds are traded in units of $1,000. *See* Normal Trading Unit; Odd Lot.

ROUNDING BOTTOM. In technical analysis, a chart pattern suggesting the shape of a saucer. Also called a saucer. The trend is considered upward.

ROUNDING TOP. In technical analysis, a chart pattern suggesting the shape of an inverted saucer. A rounding top indicates a downward trend.

RR. *See* Account Executive.

RUN. (1) A market maker's list of offerings, including bid-offer prices (and, for bonds, par values, and prices). (2) In technical analysis, a quick movement of prices, usually in reference to an uptrend.

RUNNING AHEAD. An AE's entering a personal buy/sell order before entering a customer's order. This activity is not ethical.

RUNNING THROUGH THE POT. In a distribution, the syndicate manager can take securities back from the group members and put them into "the pot" for institutional sales. Usually this is done if institutional sales are doing better than retail sales. *See* Pot, The.

S. A symbol on the ticker tape meaning the actual quantity if preceded by more than one digit. For example: T2s50 1/2 means 200 shares of AT&T at 50 1/2

S: S A symbol on the ticker tape meaning actual quantity in a security that trades in round lots of 10 shares.

S: T A symbol on the ticker tape meaning "stopped."

SAFEKEEPING.   A protected condition maintained as a service by a brokerage firm for its customers' fully paid securities registered in the customers' own names. The practice entails use of vault space to store those certificates until they are withdrawn or sold.

SAME DAY SUBSTITUTION.   A provision of Regulation T of the Federal Reserve that allows a customer to sell securities and buy securities of a lesser or equal amount without having to deposit separate initial margin requirements on the purchase.

SAUCER.   *See* Rounding Bottom.

SCALE ORDERS.   Multiple limit orders entered by investors at various prices but at the same time. The purpose is to obtain an overall, or average, favorable purchase or sale price. Multiples of round lots may be either *bought* at prices scaled down from a given value or *sold* at prices scaled down from a given value or *sold* at prices scaled up from a given value.

SCALPER.   A market maker who puts heavy markups or markdowns on transactions. *See* Five Percent.

SCREEN (STOCKS).   To look for stocks that meet certain predetermined investment and financial requirements.

SCRIP.   Document evidencing the fractional share of a stock distributed by a company because of an exchange of stock, split, or spin-off. The owner can then buy the remaining fraction to make a full share.

SEASONED ISSUE.   An issue, once distributed, that trades actively and that has great liquidity.

SEC.   *See* Securities and Exchange Commission.

SEC RISK DISCLOSURE RULES. These are rules applicable to the OTCBB market designed to give investors protection. These set forth requirements that the broker/dealers obtain from investing customers a writing, which must acknowledge that the investors have a Risk Disclosure Document. This document states the meaning of "penny stock." It also sets forth some of the risks of penny stock investing.

SECONDARY DISTRIBUTION (OFFERING). A public offering of stock by selling it to stockholders.

SECONDARY MARKET. (1) A term referring to the trading of securities not listed on an organized exchange. (2) A term used to describe the trading of securities other than a new issue.

SECONDARY MOVEMENT. A short-term movement in the market in the opposite direction from the primary movement.

SECURITIES ACT OF 1933. Federal legislation designed to protect the public in the initial issuance and distribution of securities by providing to prospective purchasers full and accurate information about an issue. The law that governs the primary market.

SECURITIES ANALYSIS. The historical study of stock movements and trends by means of charting. Most brokerage firms now employ an analyst to aid them in predicting the financial condition of a company or group of companies.

SECURITIES AND EXCHANGE COMMISSION (SEC). A government agency responsible for the supervision and regulation of the securities industry.

SECURITIES EXCHANGE ACT OF 1934. Federal legislation designed to protect the public against unfair and inequitable practices on stock exchanges and in over-the-counter markets throughout the United States. The law that governs the secondary market.

SECURITIES INVESTOR PROTECTION CORPORATION (SIPC). Formed by the Securities Investors Protection Act of 1970, a government-sponsored, private, nonprofit corporation that guarantees repayment of money and securities to customers in amounts up to $100,000 cash equity and $500,000 overall per customer in the event of a broker/dealer bankruptcy.

SECURITY. A transferable instrument such as a common stock evidencing ownership, or in the case of a note, bond, evidence of debt. The term is broad and also includes interest or participation in a profit-sharing agreement, investment contract, voting trust certificate, fractional undivided interest in oil, gas, or other mineral rights, or any warrant to subscribe to, or purchase, any of the foregoing or other similar instruments.

SEEK A MARKET. Look to make a buy or sale.

SEGREGATE. To keep customer securities physically separate from those owned by the broker/dealers.

SEGREGATED SECURITIES. Customer-owned securities fully paid for or representing excess collateral in a margin account that are locked away and cannot be used in the conduct of the firm's business.

SEGREGATION. A protected condition maintained by a brokerage firm for its customers' fully paid securities and those representing excess collateral in margin accounts.

SELL THE BOOK. An instruction to the broker/dealer to sell as many shares as possible at the best available bid.

SELL-OUT. Upon failure of the purchasing firm to accept delivery of the security and lacking the proper rejection form, the seller can without notice dispose of that security in the marketplace at the best available price and hold the buyer responsible for any financial loss resulting from the default. *See* Buy-In.

SELL PLUS. This term refers to a price higher than the last sale on a plus tick or at a price higher than the last different sale on a zero plus tick.

SELL STOP ORDER. A memorandum that becomes a market order to sell if and when someone trades a round lot at or below the memorandum price.

SELLING CONCESSION. A fraction of an underwriter's spread granted to a selling group member by agreement. It is payment for services as a sales agent for the underwriters.

SELLING DIVIDENDS. The unfair and unethical practice of soliciting purchase orders for mutual fund shares solely on the basis of an impending distribution by that fund.

SELLING GROUP. Selected broker/dealers who contract to act as selling agents for underwriters and who are compensated by a portion of the sales charge (selling concession) on newly issued stocks. They assume no financial liability for the unsold balance, nor do they share in profit from syndicate residuals.

SELLING OFF (SELL-OFF). Selling commodities or securities to avoid losses from continued drops in price.

SELLING ON THE GOOD NEWS. Practice of selling a stock right after good news has pushed the stock price very high. The investor thinks that the stock has reached its top price.

SEPARATE ACCOUNT. A specialized legal entity created by an insurance company to incorporate contracts offered by the company under a variable annuity plan.

SEPARATE CUSTOMER. As defined by SIPC, the accounts of a given customer at a single brokerage firm. Different types of accounts held by the same person do not constitute "separate customers."

SETTLEMENT (DELIVERY) DATE. The day on which certificates involved in a transaction are to be delivered to purchaser.

SHADOW CALENDAR. Forthcoming issues that are registered with the SEC but that are not offered yet, usually because of a backlog at the SEC.

SHARE. A stock certificate—a unit of measurement of the equity ownership of a corporation.

SHARE BROKER. A discount broker who charges a commission that decreases as the number of shares traded increases.

SHAREHOLDER. *See* Principals (Stockholders); Stockholder (Shareholder).

SHARK REPELLANT. Any step taken by a "target" corporation to discourage a takeover. Also called a porcupine provision. *See* Poison Pill.

SHARK WATCHER. A company whose business is to detect takeover attempts by watching trading patterns in a client's stock.

SHELF DISTRIBUTION. A privilege written in a registration statement enabling an affiliated person to dispose of sizable amounts of securities from his or her portfolio (shelf) over a nine-month period following the effective date. For OTC transactions, order tickets must be marked "distribution stock"; for exchange sales, "Dist."

SHOP/SHOPPING THE STREET. (1) "Shop" is slang for the broker/dealer's office. (2) "Shop" or "shopping the street" means a broker/dealer's gathering quotations from OTC market makers to form a basis for negotiating a transaction. *See* Firm Market (Price, Quote); Subject Market (Price, Quote); Workout Market.

SHORT-AGAINST-THE-BOX. A situation in which a person is both long and short in the same security at the same time in his/her account, a practice usually employed to defer tax liability on capital gains. Although the customer sells the stock short, he/she actually owns the security, which is held in the broker's "box." The aim is to protect a capital gain in owned shares, while deferring the taxes due if the shares were actually sold and the capital gain reported. This way, the investor can wait until he or she is in a more favorable tax situation to sell the securities.

SHORT INTEREST THEORY. Short interest positions are reported each month as of the fifteenth. The theory postulates that an increase in the short interest is bullish since those customers who are short must buy back that position, causing a demand for securities. A decline in short interest would be bearish.

SHORT MARKET VALUE. The market value of security positions that a customer owes to a broker/dealer (short in the account).

SHORT POSITION. (1) The number of shares in a given security sold short and not covered as of a particular date. (2) The total amount of stock sold short by all investors and not covered as of a particular date. (3) A term used to denote the writer of an option.

SHORT SALE. The sale of a security that is not owned at the time of the trade, necessitating its purchase some time in the future to "cover" the sale. A short sale is made with the expectation that the stock value will decline, so that the sale will be eventually covered (i.e., repurchased) at a price lower than the original sale, thus realizing a profit. Before the sale is covered, the broker/dealer borrows stock (for which collateral is put up) to deliver on the settlement date.

SHORT SELLING POWER.   The dollar amount of equity securities a customer may sell short without additional funds and continue to meet the initial margin requirements of Regulation T of the Federal Reserve. Short selling power is equal to the Reg T excess divided by the Reg T initial margin requirements. For example, $10,000/50% = $20,000.

SHORT-STOP (LIMIT) ORDER.   A memorandum that becomes a limit order to sell short when someone creates a round-lot transaction at or below the memorandum price (electing sale). The short sale may or may not be executed since the rules then require that it be sold at least one-eighth above the electing sale as well as high enough in value to satisfy the limit price.

SHORT-TERM CAPITAL TRANSACTION.   The sale of securities held for six months or less, or a short sale and a purchase to cover at a profit within any time period.

SIAMESE STOCK.   *See* Paired Shares.

SIDEWAYS MARKET.   *See* Horizontal Market.

SILENT PARTNER.   A member of a partnership represented only by capital and not entitled to a voice in management, a limited partner.

SIMULTANEOUS (RISKLESS) TRANSACTION.   A transaction in which the broker/dealer takes a position in a security only after receipt of an order from a customer, and only for the purpose of acting as principal so as to disguise his or her remuneration from the transaction.

SINKER.   Slang for a bond with a sinking fund. *See* Sinking Fund.

SINKING FUND.   (1) An annual reserve of capital required to be set aside out of a current earnings to provide monies for retirement of an outstanding bond issue and, sometimes, preferred stock. Such a feature has a favorable effect on the market value of that issue. (2) A separate account in the overall sinking fund for monies used to redeem securities by open-market purchase, by request for tenders or call, or in accordance with the redemption schedule in the bond contract.

SL.   Stockbroker shorthand for "sold."

SNOWBALLING. *See* Gather in the Stops.

SOFT MARKET. The market for securities with low demand.

SOFT SPOT. Term used to describe the weakness in a select stock or group of stocks during a generally strong and advancing market.

SOLD SALE (SLD). A transaction appearing on the ticker tape out of its proper sequence.

SOLD TO YOU. Term used by over-the-counter traders to confirm the acceptance of their offer.

SPECIAL BID. A New York Stock Exchange procedure for facilitating bids for a large block of stock. Regulations are similar to those regarding a special offer.

SPECIAL CASH ACCOUNT. An account in which the customer is required to make full payment on the fifth business day after the trade date, and in no case later than the seventh calendar day, or arrange for COD payment on the fifth business day. The account is defined in Regulation T. *See* Frozen Account.

SPECIAL OFFERING. The disposal of a large block of stock in accordance with certain terms and conditions, by inviting members of the exchange to place buy orders on the floor to be executed by crossing in the normal procedure. The seller pays a special commission.

SPECIALIST. A member of the NYSE with two essential functions: First, to maintain an orderly market, insofar as reasonably practicable, in the stocks in which he or she is registered as a specialist. To do this, the specialist must buy and sell for his or her own account and risk, to a reasonable degree, where there is a temporary disparity between supply and demand. To equalize trends, the specialist must buy or sell counter to the direction of the market. Second, the specialist acts as a broker's broker, executing orders when another broker cannot afford the time. At all times the specialist must put the customer's interest before his own. All specialists are registered with the NYSE as regular, substitute, associate, or temporary.

SPECIALIST BOOK. The chronological Orderbook of Exchange specialists used to keep a record of the buy and sell orders they received for execution at specified prices. It also includes their own inventory of securities.

SPECTAIL. A combination of "speculator" and "retail." A broker/dealer who does more speculative trading for his or her account than handling of client orders.

SPECULATION. The employment of funds in high-risk transactions for relatively large and immediate gains in which the safety of principal or current income is of secondary importance.

SPIN OFF. A distribution of stock in a company that is owned by another corporation and that is being allocated to the holders of the latter institution.

SPLIT. A division of the outstanding shares of a corporation into a larger number of shares, by which each outstanding share entitles its owner to a fixed number of new shares. Individual shareholders' overall equity remains the same, but they own more stock, since the total value of the shares remains the same. For example, in a two-for-one split, the owner of 100 shares, each worth $100, would be given 200 shares, each worth $50.

SPLIT COMMISSION. When one AE executes a transaction that was brought in by another AE, they split the commission between them.

SPLIT DOWN. A corporate reorganization whereby the holder of a security must return the certificate to the issuer and receive proportionately fewer shares in the exchange.

SPLIT OFFERING. An offering combining both a primary and secondary distribution.

SPLIT ORDER. The periodic purchase or sale of small parts of a large block of securities to avoid market upset and price fluctuations.

SPLIT RATING. A term used to describe the situation in which a corporation has been given different credit ratings by different services.

SPLIT UP. A corporate recapitalization in which the holder of a security receives proportionately more shares from the issuer in relation to his or her current ownership in the company.

SPONSOR. *See* Underwriter.

SPOT SECONDARY DISTRIBUTION. A secondary distribution that does not require an SEC registration statement and may be attempted on the spot, without delay.

SPREAD. (1) The difference in value between the bid and offering prices. (2) Underwriting compensation.

STABILIZATION. The syndicate manager is empowered by the members of his group to maintain a bid in the aftermarket at or slightly below the public offering price, thus "stabilizing" the market and giving the syndicate and selling group members a reasonable chance of successfully disposing of their allocations. This practice is a legal exception to the manipulation practices outlawed by the Securities and Exchange Act of 1934.

STAG. A speculator who buys and sells stocks rapidly for fast profits.

STAGFLATION. The combination of sluggish economic growth, high unemployment, and high inflation.

STAGNATION. (1) A period of low volume and inactive trading on a securities market. (2) The economic doldrums resulting from retarded economic growth.

STANDARD & POOR'S (S&P) CORPORATION. A source of investment services, most famous for its *Standard & Poor's Rating* of bonds and its composite index of 425 industrial, 20 transportation, and 55 public utility common stocks, called *Standard & Poor's Index*.

STANDBY COMMITMENT. *See* Standby Underwriting Agreement.

STANDBY UNDERWRITING AGREEMENT. An agreement between an investment banker and a corporation whereby the banker agrees for a negotiated fee to purchase any or all shares offered as a subscription privilege (rights offering) that are not bought by the rights holders by the time the offer expires.

STAPLED STOCK. *See* Paired Shares.

STATUTORY VOTING. A means by which a stockholder is given the right to cast one vote for each share owned in favor of or against each of a number of proposals or director/nominees at a formal meeting convened by the corporation.

STICKERING. Changing the official statement of a new issue by printing the altered information on adhesive-backed paper and "stickering" onto the statement.

STICKY DEAL. An underwriting that, for one reason or another, will be hard to market.

STOCK AHEAD. An expression used on the floor of the New York Stock Exchange to signify that one or more brokers had made a prior bid (or offer) at the same price as an order you had entered. Sometimes a customer's order remains unexecuted for this reason. In other words, there is "stock ahead" of the order.

STOCK DIVIDEND DISTRIBUTION. A distribution to shareholders made upon declaration by a corporation's board of directors. This distribution differs from the usual disbursement in that it is given in the form of additional shares of stock instead of money.

STOCKHOLDER (SHAREHOLDER). The owner of common or preferred stock.

STOCKHOLDER OF RECORD. Person named on the issuer's stock books as the owner.

STOCKS. Certificates representing ownership in a corporation and a claim on the firm's earnings and assets; they may yield dividends and can appreciate or decline in value. *See* Authorized Stock; Common Stock; Issued-and-Outstanding Stocks; Preferred Stock; Unissued Stock.

STOCK WATCHER. A computerized service in the stock watch department of the NYSE that keeps track of the trading activity and movements of listed stocks.

STOP LIMIT ORDER. A memorandum that becomes a limit (as opposed to a market) order immediately after a transaction takes place at or through the indicated (memorandum) price.

STOP LOSS ORDER. A customer's order to set the sell price of a stock below the market price, thus locking in profits or preventing further losses.

STOP ORDER. A memorandum that becomes a market order only if a transaction takes place at or through the price stated in the memorandum. Buy stop orders are placed above the market, and sell stop orders are placed below it. The sale that activates the memorandum is called the electing (activating or triggering) sale. *See* Buy Stop Order; Market Order; Sell Stop Order.

STOP-OUT PRICE. The lower dollar price at auction for which Treasury bills are sold.

STOPPED OUT. An expression reflecting a broker's unsuccessful attempt to improve upon the price of a transaction after having been guaranteed an execution price by the specialist.

STOPPING STOCK. A specialist's guarantee of price to a broker, thus enabling the broker to try to improve upon that price without fear of missing the market.

STREET. "Wall Street"—that is, the New York financial community, as well as the exchanges throughout the country.

STREET NAME. When securities have been bought on margin or when the customer wishes the security to be held by the broker/dealer, the securities are registered and held in the broker/dealer's own firm (or "street") name.

STRIKE PRICE. *See* Exercise Price.

SUBJECT MARKET (PRICE, QUOTE). In the OTC market, a range of buying or selling prices quoted by market makers at which they are unable to trade immediately. Such prices are subject to verification by the parties whose market they represent.

SUBSCRIPTION. An agreement to buy a new issue of securities. The agreement specifies the *subscription price* (the price for shareholders before the securities are offered to the public). This right is called the *subscription privilege or subscription right*.

SUBSCRIPTION PRIVILEGE (PREEMPTIVE RIGHT).   A shareholder's right to purchase newly issued shares or bonds (before the public offering). It must be exercised within a fixed period, usually 30 to 60 days, before the privilege expires and becomes worthless.

SUBSCRIPTION RATIO.   The ratio of old stock to new stock offered as a subscription privilege.

SUBSCRIPTION RIGHT.   A privilege granted to owners of certain stocks to purchase newly issued securities in proportion to their holdings, usually at values below the current market price. Rights have a market value of their own and are actively traded. They differ from warrants in that they must be exercised within a relatively short period of time.

SUBSIDIARY.   A company whose voting shares are owned by another company.

SUBSTANTIAL NET CAPITAL.   Each member of the New York Stock Exchange is required to maintain "substantial net capital."

SUBSTITUTION (SWAP).   The sale of one security in an account to use the proceeds to pay for the purchase of another security on the same trade date. *See* Switch (Contingent or Swap) Order.

SUITABILITY.   The appropriateness of a strategy or transaction, in light of an investor's financial means and investment objectives.

SUNSHINE LAW.   Law giving the public access to the meetings and records of government agencies (such as the SEC and the Commodities Futures Trading Commission).

SUPER-RESTRICTED ACCOUNT.   An old term no longer in use. A margin account in which the equity is less than 30 percent of the market value of the adjusted debit balance in the account.

SUPERDOT. This is an electronic system utilized by the NYSE to manage orders on the exchange. It is used to transmit and deliver orders from NYSE member firms to specialists on the exchange.

SUPPORT. This is a chart price line or level below the current market price where buying interests have historically turned back and reversed selling pressure.

SUPPORT LEVEL. *See* Support.

SUSPENDED TRADING. The temporary ceasing of trading of an issue.

SUSPENSE ACCOUNT. A record maintained by a broker/dealer to reflect unreconciled money and securities differences in its business activities.

SWAP ORDER/TRANSACTIONS. *See* Switch (Contingent or Swap) Order.

SWEETENER. A special feature in a securities offering, such as convertibility, that encourages the purchase of the security.

SWITCH (CONTINGENT OR SWAP) ORDER. An order to buy one security and then sell another at a limit, or to sell one security and then to buy another at a limit. The transaction may also be called a proceeds sale, if as is usually the case the proceeds of the sell order are applied against the expenses of the buy order.

SYNDICATE. A group of investment bankers who purchase securities from the issuer and then reoffer them to the public at a fixed price. The syndicate is usually organized with one or more members acting as *syndicate manager*, to ensure the successful offering of a corporation's securities.

TAILGATING. An account executive's purchase of a security for his/her own account right on the heels of a purchase of the same security for a customer.

TAKE A BATH. Slang meaning to incur a large loss.

TAKE A FLIER. Slang meaning to enter into a highly speculative investment.

TAKE A POSITION. (1) To hold stocks or bonds, in either a long or short position. (2) To purchase securities as a long-term investment.

TAKE DELIVERY. In securities, accepting a receipt of stock or bond certificates after they have been purchased or transferred between accounts.

TAKEDOWN. In an underwriting, the number of securities that a syndicate member is supposed to sell.

TAKE OFF. The summary of daily changes in a security that is posted to the stock record.

TAKE OUT. The money that an investor "takes out" from an account when there is a net credit balance.

TAKEOVER. The assumption of control over a corporation by another corporation, through acquisition or merger. *See* Poison Pill; Shark Watcher; Tender Offer.

TANK. A downward move in the market.

TAPE. A financial news service that reports the prices and sizes of transactions. Although this information was once reported on a paper tape from a "ticker tape" machine, it is now displayed on electronic screens. The name "tape," however, persists.

TAPE RACING. An account executive's executing personal orders before executing a sizable customer order, to take advantage of the large order's effect on prices.

TECHNICAL ANALYSIS. An approach to market theory stating that previous price movements, properly interpreted, can indicate future price patterns.

TECHNICAL SIGN. A movement in a security's price that, under certain circumstances, indicates a short-term trend.

TELEPHONE BOOTHS. Booths or cubicles ringing the stock exchange trading rooms that are used by member organizations to (1) receive orders from their offices, (2) distribute orders to brokers for execution, and (3) transmit details of the executed orders back to their offices.

TEMPORARY SPECIALIST. An experienced member of the exchange appointed by a floor official to act as a specialist only in an emergency situation. His or her responsibilities are the same as those of a regular specialist.

TENANTS BY ENTIRETY. A form of ownership by which assets legally transfer to the surviving spouse upon the death of either party in a marriage. If a securities account were so owned jointly by husband and wife, it would transfer to the surviving spouse upon the death of either tenant.

TENDER OFFER. A formal proposition to stockholders to sell their shares in response to a large purchase bid. The buyer customarily agrees to assume all costs and reserves the right to accept all, none, or a specific number of the shares presented for acceptance.

THIRD MARKET. Transactions in exchange-listed stocks by broker/dealers directly beween themselves, off the floor of a stock exchange.

THIRD-PARTY ACCOUNT. A brokerage account carried in the name of a person other than a customer. The practice is prohibited by NYSE regulation.

THIRD-PARTY CHECK. A check drawn to the order of one person who endorses it to another person, who subsequently presents it to someone else in satisfaction of an obligation.

THROWAWAY OFFER. A nominal (approximate) bid or offer that should not be considered final.

TICK. A transaction on the stock exchange. *See* Minus Tick; Plus Tick; Zero Minus Tick; Zero Plus Tick.

TICKER TAPE. A trade-by-trade report in chronological order of trades executed, giving prices and volumes. Separate tapes exist for various markets. The mechanism used to be mechanical, but it is now some sort of electronic display.

TIGHT MARKET. An active, vigorous market with narrow bid-offer spreads.

TIGHT MONEY. An economic condition characterized by scarce credit, generally the result of a money supply restricted by the Federal Reserve.

TIME VALUE. This is the excess of option premium over intrinsic value of an option.

TIP.   A suggestion as to what to buy or sell.

TOMBSTONE.   The type of newspaper advertisement used for public offering. The ad simply and drably lists all the facts about the issue. Also called the offering circular.

TOTAL CAPITALIZATION.   The aggregate value of a corporation's long-term debt, preferred, and common stock accounts—or, put, another way, funded debt plus shareholders' equity.

TOTAL COST.   The contract price plus all expenses incurred on the purchase execution.

TOTAL VOLUME.   A column in the listed stock tables showing total shares of stocks traded (omitting the last two zeros).

TRADE DATE.   The date a trade was entered into, as opposed to settlement date.

TRADER.   A person or firm engaged in the business of buying and selling securities, options, or commodities for a profit.

TRADING AUTHORIZATION.   The legal right conferred by a person or institution upon another to effect the purchase and/or sale of securities in the former's account.

TRADING CROWD.   Members of an exchange involved in the purchase and sale of a particular issue. They gather the specialist's position. Each specialist is responsible for monitoring its own crowd.

TRADING FLOOR.   The location at any organized exchange where buyers and sellers meet to transact business.

TRADING POST.   The physical place on the exchange floor where a stock is located.

TRANSFER AND SHIP.   Customer instructions to have securities transferred into his or her name and sent to his or her address.

TREND.   Movement, up or down, in a security's market price, or in the market itself.

TRENDLINE. The line superimposed by technical analysts on price plot-tings to indicate a price trend. Drawn beneath the prices, the line reflects an upward trend; above the prices, it means the trend is down-ward.

TRIANGLE. In technical analysis, a chart pattern of stock price move-ments with the base at the left and the apex at the right. Also called a flag, coil, wedge, or pennant, depending on the price movements.

TRIGGERING SALE. *See* Electing Sale.

TURKEY. A security that is not doing an investor any good.

TWENTY-DAY (COOLING-OFF) PERIOD. A period of 20 calendar days following the filing of a registration statement with the SEC, during which (1) the SEC examines the statement for deficiencies; and (2) the syndicate prepares for the successful distribution of the impending issue. The final day of the period is normally considered the effective date.

TWO-DOLLAR BROKERS. Members of the New York Stock Exchange who execute orders in any security for any organization, in return for which they receive a brokerage fee, which is negotiable, but previously was $2 each 100 share per trade. They are also known as independent brokers or agents.

UNDERLYING SECURITY. The security that an investor has the right to buy or sell according to the terms of a listed option contract.

UNDERVALUED. A term used to describe a security that is trading at a lower price than it should. *See* Overvalued; Fair Market Value.

UNDERWRITER. Also known as an "investment banker" or Syndicate Member acting as a " middleman" between an issuing corporation and the public. The managing underwriter usually forms an underwriting group, called a syndicate, to limit risk and commitment of capital. In the distribution of mutual funds, the underwriter may also be known as a "sponsor," "distributor," or even "wholesaler." Investment bankers also offer other services, such as advice and counsel on the raising and investment of capital.

UNDERWRITER'S RETENTION. The percentage of a total issue to which each member of an underwriter's group is entitled and which it distributes to customers. The retained amount is usually equal to about 75 percent of the member's total financial commitment. The syndicate manager decides, on behalf of the other members, how to distribute the rest of the issue (or "the pot") and how it is to be sold to institutional investors (group sales) or reserved for handling by selling groups.

UNDERWRITING COMPENSATION (SPREAD). The gross profit realized by an underwriter equal to the difference between the price he paid to the issuing corporation and the price of the public offering.

UNDIVIDED ACCOUNT. In an underwriting agreement, an arrangement for the sharing of liability in which each member of the syndicate is liable for any unsold portion of an issue. The degree of liability is based on each member's percentage of participation. *See* Syndicate.

UNISSUED STOCK. That portion of authorized stock not distributed among investors.

UNLISTED SECURITY. A security that is not traded on an exchange. Usually called an over-the-counter security.

UNWIND A TRADE. (1) To undo a transaction, such as "unwinding" a short sale with a purchase. (2) To correct an erroneous transaction.

UPGRADE. Raising a security's rating by improving the credit quality of the issue or issuer.

UPTICK. *See* Plus Tick.

UPTREND. Any generally upward movement in a security's price. A type of trend that occurs in a pattern in which each trough/peak is higher than the previous one.

UNIT INVESTMENT TRUST. Also known as a unit trust or UIT, this is an investment company in which securities are structured by a management firm and consisting of a fixed set of investments with a fixed expiration date. It is managed by a trustee, such as a bank, which also secures the securities within the trust.

VAULT CASH.   All the cash in a bank's vault.

VENTURE CAPITAL COMPANY.   An investment company whose objective is to invest in new or underdeveloped companies.

VOLATILE.   Price movement in a stock, or the market, that is excessive.

VOLATILITY.   This is an erratic and very often a wild market with wide price swings and price variations; the opposite of liquidity.

VOLUME.   Number of bonds or shares traded during specific periods, such as daily, weekly, or monthly.

VOLUME DELETED.   A ticker tape announcement to signify that quantities of less than 5,000 shares per transaction will not appear until the ticker tape can stay abreast of trading activity on the stock exchange floor. It appears when the tape falls two minutes behind.

VOLUME RESUMED.   The volume-deleted condition is no longer in effect.

VOLUNTARY UNDERWRITER.   An individual or corporation that purchases a security from an issuer or affiliated person and offers it for public sale under an effective registration statement.

WALLFLOWER.   A stock that investors are, by and large, just not attracted to.

WAR BABIES.   Securities of corporations engaged in defense contracts. Also known as war brides.

WAREHOUSING.   The illegal sale of a corporate security with a provision for its repurchase by the seller at some future date and at a prearranged price.

WARRANT.   A security issued by the corporation that allows the owner to purchase a fixed number of common stock, usually one warrant for one share, at a fixed price within a set period of time.

WASH SALE.   (1) For regulatory purposes, the purchase and sale of the same security at the same time and price without any real change of ownership. This practice is outlawed under the Securities Exchange Act of 1934. (2) For tax purposes, a sale at a loss and repurchase of the same or a similar issue, within 30 days before or after the first transaction, while intending to use that loss to offset capital gains or taxable income in that year. The loss is generally not allowed as a tax deduction. *See* Manipulation.

WATCH LIST.   A list of securities, established by a broker/dealer or an exchange, that is under scrutiny for evidence of illegal or unethical practices.

WATERED STOCK.   A corporation's issuance of additional shares without increasing its capital. Also called "diluting the shares."

WD.   *See* When Issued/When Distributed Contract.

WEAK MARKET.   A market characterized by a greater number of sellers than buyers, which creates a general downtrend in prices.

WEDGE.   *See* Triangle.

W FORMATION.   *See* Double Bottom.

WHEN ISSUED/WHEN DISTRIBUTED CONTRACT.   A delivery contract involving securities (stocks or bonds) that have been proposed for distribution but not yet issued. The date of delivery is set for some time in the future by the NASD Uniform Practice Committee or the appropriate stock exchange, as the case may be.

WHITE KNIGHT.   Colloquial expression for a person or firm who blocks a hostile takeover attempt by taking over the target company itself.

WHOLESALER.   *See* Underwriter.

WI.   *See* When Issued/When Distributed Contract.

WINDOW SETTLEMENT.   Transactions that are not cleared through the SCC or NCC and that are completed in the office of the purchasing firm by means of certificate delivery versus immediate payment.

WIRE HOUSE.   Any large exchange member firm.

WIRE ROOM. An area in each branch office and in the home office where messages may be received and sent using machinery that creates a printed copy of the messages. Message traffic normally consists of order data, reports of order executions, trade settlement information, and other sales data.

WITH OR WITHOUT A SALE ORDER (WOW). An odd-lot limit order to buy or sell either at a price derived from an effective round-lot quotation (with a sale) or at the existing round-lot quotation plus differential (without a sale), whichever occurs first in accordance with the customer's limit.

WITHHOLDING. A failure by a broker/dealer to make a bona fide distribution of a hot issue, thus encouraging demand at a premium price. This practice is a violation of the NASD Rules of Fair Practice. *See* Free-Riding.

WITHOUT DIVIDEND. *See* Ex-Dividend (Without Dividend) Date.

WOODEN TICKET. Confirming execution of a customer's order without actually executing it.

WORKOUT MARKET. In the OTC market, a range of prices quoted by a market maker who is not certain that a market is available, but who feels he or she can "work one out" within a reasonable period of time.

WOW ORDER. *See* With or Without a Sale Order.

WRINKLE. Colloquial term for a feature in a security that could benefit the holder.

WRITE. The process of selling an option. The writer is the investor who sells the option.

WRITE-OUT. An exchange floor procedure by which specialists are allowed to buy stock for themselves from a customer's offering in their books, or sell from their accounts to a customer's bid. They must, however, allow the broker who entered the order to execute and "write out" the confirmation of the transaction and earn the contingent brokerage fee.

X. *See* Ex-Dividend (Without Dividend) Date.

XCH. *See* Ex-Clearing House.

XD. Shorthand notation meaning "ex-dividend." *See* Ex-Dividend (Without Dividend) Date.

X DIS. *See* Ex-Distribution.

XRT. *See* Ex-Rights.

XW. *See* Ex-Warrants.

YO-YO STOCK. A stock whose price rises and drops often and quickly.

ZERO MINUS TICK. A transaction on the exchange at a price equal to that of the preceding transaction but lower than the last different price.

ZERO PLUS TICK. A transaction on the exchange at a price equal to that of the preceding transaction but higher than the last different price.

INDEX

A

Account executive (AE), 55–56
  sales orientation of, 56
  selecting, 62–66
Accounting department, operations
    of, 212–214 (*see also* Back
    offices)
Activating sale, 84
ACTS, 152–153
Actual market, 129
ADRs, 286
Advanced Computerized
    Execution System
    (ACES), 152
After-hours trading, 89–91 (*see
    also* Secondary market)
  effect of, 272–288, 289 (*see also*
    Globalization)
Agents, 76
AIM, 284
All or none (AON) order, 86
Allocation Committee of NYSE,
    120–121
Alternative Investment Market
    (AIM), 284
Alternative order, 88
Alternative Trading Systems
    (ATS), 155–157

American Depository Receipts
    (ADRs), 286
American Stock Exchange (Amex),
    33–34, 96, 101–104, 171
    (*see also* Secondary
    market)
  Market Value Index, 227
  merger of with NASD, 146–147
  Post Execution Reporting (PER),
    110
Analysts, 231–241 (*see also* Stock
    market theories)
Analyzing stock, 260–268
  balance sheet, 260
  book value per share, 264
  cash flow, 266
  current assets/liabilities,
    261–262
  current ratio, 262
  debt and capital structure, using,
    263–264
  debt service, 263
  dilutive securities, 266
  earnings per share (EPS), 266
  income statement, 264–268
    gross profit margin, 265–266
    net income/loss, 264
  liquidity ratio, 262–263
  net worth, 264

Analyzing stock (*continued*)
profit and loss (P&L) statement, 260
quick asset ratio, 262–263
quick assets, 261
stockholders' equity, 264
working capital, 262
AON, 86
Arbitrageurs, 315–316
Archipelago, 155–156
Arithmetic scale for charting, 249
Asia/Pacific Exchanges, 285
Tokyo Stock Exchange, 285
Assets, 261–262
Assigning securities to specialist, 120–121
At-the-close order, 87–88
in odd-lot trading, 119–120
"At-the-money," 182, 183–185
Auction system of NYSE, 80–83
Automated Confirmation
Transaction Service (ACTS), 152–153
Automation, specialist and, 110–112
(*see also* Specialist)
Authorized stock, 37

B

Back offices, 194–219
accounting department, 212–214
"E&OE" legend, 214
15c3–3 report, 212–213
Financial and Operational Combined Uniform Single (FOCUS) report, 212
statements of account, 213
clearing house, 196–198
dividend department, 214–218
declaration date, 215

due bills, 217–218
ex-distribution date, 216–217
ex-dividend date, 215–216
payment date, 215
record date, 215
margin department, 206–210
cash account, 207
equity, 207–208
excess equity, 207–210
maintenance requirement, 208–209
margin account, 207–210
Regulation T, 207
order department, 198–199
discretionary account agreement, 198
margin account agreement, 198
new account agreement, 198
P&S (Purchase and Sales) department, 199–206
bank loan section, 202
"cage," 201–202
conversions, 204–205
disposition of clients' rights, 205–206
exchanges, 205
figuration, 200
involuntary exchange, 205
merger, 205
preemptive rights offering, 205
recording trade, 200
redemption call, 204
registrar, 201
reorganization department, 204–206
"in seg," 202
short cover, 204
short sale, handling, 202–204
stock power, 201

subscription privilege
offering, 205
tender offer, 206
ticket charges, 200
transfer agent, 201–202
voluntary exchange request,
205
warrants, 206
process prior to 1960s, 194–195
proxy department, 218–219
stockholder solicitation, 219
reorganization, 205
securities depository, 196–198
setup, typical, 195
SIAC (Securities Industry
Automation
Corporation), 196–197
stock record department, 210–212
break, 211
daily stock record, 211–212
position lists, 211
weekly stock record, 212
wire room, 199
Balance sheet, 260
Banks, inability of to make new
business loans, 39–40
Bar charts, 233, 246
Basis price order in odd-lot
trading, 120
Basket Session, 90
BBSS, 78, 79–80
Beneficial owner, 22
Best-efforts offering, 40–41, 46
Best execution rule, 132
Bid, 81
"Bid cap" companies, 237
"Bid wanted" (BW), 129
"Big Board," 69
"Black Monday," 240, 303–319
Black-Scholes Option Pricing
formula, 185

Block sales, specialist and, 112, 115
Blue room of NYSE, 73
Blue-skying, 46
Board brokers of CBOE, 121
Bond mutual funds, 168–169
Bonds, 3, 16, 238–239, 263
The "Book," 102
Book value (BV), 12, 238
per share, 264
Boutique forms, 60
Breakpoints, 167
Broker Booth Support Systems
(BBSS), 78, 79–80
Brokerage accounts, insurance of,
8
Brokerage firm, inside, 55–67
account executive (AE),
55–56
sales orientation of, 56
selecting, 62–66
boutique firms, 60
carriage trade house, 59
commission rates, negotiability
of, 57
discount houses, 57, 60
full service versus discount,
57–61
advantages/disadvantages
of each, 61
clearing, 58
management accounts,
57–58
what full service provides,
57–58
institutional investors, 56
interdepartmental relationships,
59
"May Day," 57
money, earning, 55–57
in online trading, 270–272,
292–293

Brokerage firm, inside (*continued*)
  registered representative, 55 (*see*
     also ...account executive)
  research department, role of, 57
  sales assistant, 66–67
  selecting, 62–66
  Series 7, 55
  specialized firms, 59
  stockbroker, 55
  wire houses, 58
Budget deficits, effect of, 239–240
Bull spreads, 193
Buy-low, sell-high principle, 6
Buy minus order, 88, 97
Buy stop sale, 84

C

"Cage," 201–202
Calendar spreads, 193
Callable preferred stock, 14–15
Calls, 172, 179–182
  "at the money, " 184–185
  covered/uncovered call
    writing, 180
  "in the money," 184–185, 189
  negatives about, 181–182
  "out of the money," 184–185
Cancellation, 88
Capital gains, 5–6
  taxation of, 296–297
    close out, 296
    tax loss carryforwards, 296–297
Capital statement in corporate
    charter, 36–38
Capital structure, using as source
    of corporate long-term
    funds, 263–264
Carriage trade house, 59
Cash accounts, 20–21 (*see also*
    Financial press)

regular way settlement, 20
settlement date, 20
street name stock, 21
Cash cows, 6
Cash flow, 266
CBOE, 96, 121, 171 (*see also*
    Chicago Board)
Certificate of incorporation,
    36–38 (*see also* Initial
    public offering)
  capital statement, 36–38
  general purpose clauses, 36
  purpose statement, 36
Charter, 36–38 (*see also* Initial
    public offering)
Charting, 232–234, 245–249
  arithmetic scale, 249
  bar charts, 233, 246
  line charts, 246, 247–248
  point and figure charts, 246,
    247
  semilog scale, 249
Chartists, 242–259 (*see also* Stock
    market theories *and*
    Charting)
"Cheap" stock, 238
Chicago Board of Options
    Exchange (CBOE), 96,
    121, 171
  market-maker system, 121
"Chinese Wall," 221
Circling the stock, 44–45
"Circuit breaker" restrictions in
    NYSE rules, 98–99
Clearance date, 20
Clearing, 58
Clearing house, 196–198
Close out, 296
Closed-end fund, pricing, 163
"Collar" restrictions in NYSE
    rules, 97–98

Commercial bank as source of
    expansion funds, 35
  vs. investment bank, 310
  problems with, 39–40
Commission house brokers, 76
Commission rates, negotiability
    of, 57
Common stocks, 10–12
  corporations, requirement of, 10
  as equity security, 10, 18
  new companies, issued by, 37
  outstanding shares, 10
  par value of, 12
  preemptive rights feature, 17–18
  rights of common stockholder,
    10–12 (*see also* Rights of
    common stockholder)
  subscription price, 17
Competitive market makers, 76,
    77
Competitive traders, 76–77
Composite Index of NYSE, 96–97
Computer Assisted Execution
    System (CAES), 157
Continental Illinois Corp., 309–310
Contingent order, 88
Contrarian opinion theory, 245
Conversion arbitrage, 17
Conversions, 204–205
Conversion ratio, 16
Convertible preferred stock, 15–17
Cooling-off period for IPO, 44–46
Covered call writing, 180
The Crash of 1987, 303–319
Crossing Session, 79, 89–91 (*see
    also* Secondary market)
Crossing stock, 88–89
Crowd, 89
Cumulative preferred stock, 14
Cumulative voting, 11
The Curb, 33, 101

Curbstone brokers, 33, 101
Current assets/liabilities, 261–262
Current ratio, 262
Current yield, 237
  calculating, 27–28
Cushion theory, 113–114
Custodian account for stock gifts
    to minors, 298

D

Daily stock record, 211–212
Data service provider, 271
Day order, 85
Day trading, 5, 271
Debt, using as source of corporate
    long-term funds, 263–264
Debt service, 263
Decimalization, 95, 157–158, 292
Declaration date, 215
Depository, securities, 196–198
Deutsche Borse, 291
Deutsche Terminboerse
Differential, 116–117
Dilutive securities, 235–236, 266
Disclosure statement, 41–43
Discount brokerage houses, 38–40,
    57, 60 (*see also* Brokerage
    firm)
  advantages/disadvantages, 61
Discretionary account agreement,
    198
Display Books, 79, 80
Diversifiable risk, 229
Diversification:
  lack of as risk in online trading,
    275
  principle of, 160
Dividend department, operations
    of, 214–218 (*see also* Back
    offices)

Dividends, 4–5
  receipt of by common
    stockholders, 11
  reinvesting, 160
  taxation of, 295–296
DJIA, 97, 257
Dow, Charles, 222
Dow Jones Company, 222
Dow Jones Industrial Average
  (DJIA), 97, 257
Dow Jones-Irwin, 222
Dow theory, 222–223
Downtrends, 249–251
Due bills, 217–218
Due date, 20
Due diligence meeting, 46–47

E

"E&OE" legend, 214
Earnings, analysis of, 235
Earnings per share (EPS), 235, 266
  dilutive securities, 235–236
ECNs, 99, 279
EDAT (Electronic Direct Access
  Trading), 271–272
EDGAR, 130
Effective sale, 116
Efficient market theory,
  220–221
Either/or order, 88
Electing sale, 84, 119
Electronic communication
  networks (ECNs), 99,
  155–157, 287–288
  advantages, 156
  qualified, 156
  "top of book," 156
Electronic Direct Access Trading
  (EDAT), 271–272
Equity, 207–208

Equity instruments, using as
  source of corporate long-
  term funds, 263–264
Estate taxes, 298–302 (*see also*
  Taxation)
EURO.MN, 284
Euronext, 290
Europe, stock markets in, 283–284
  Deutsche Terminboerse, 284
  EURO.MN, 284
  Frankfurt Stock Exchange, 284
  London Stock Exchange, 283–284
    Alternative Investment
    Market (AIM), 284
    Stock Exchange Automated
    Quotation (SEAQ)
    system, 283–284
  Paris Stock Exchange, 284
    Nouveau Marche, 284
  Russian Trading System (RTS),
    284
Ex-distribution date, 216–217
Ex-dividend date, 215–216
Excess equity, 207–210
Exchange acquisition/
  distribution, 93
Exchanges, 205
Execution of orders in online
  trading, 276–277
Exercise price, 172–174, 177
Extended (after-hours) trading,
  effect of, 287–288 (*see
  also* After hours)

F

Face amount certificate companies,
  160, 161
False online stock transactions,
  278–279
15c3-3, 212–213, 307–308

Fill or kill (FOK) instruction, 86
Financial and Operational
 Combined Uniform
 Single (FOCUS) report,
 212
Financial press, reading, 20–31
 cash accounts, 20–21
 regular way settlement, 20
 settlement date, 20
 street name stock, 21, 22
 figuration of current yield, 27–28
 investor's return, 27
 margin accounts, 21–23
 beneficial owner, 21
 dangers in, 22
 debit balance, 22
 leverage, 22
 maintenance call, 22
 owner of record, 22
 newspaper listings, 28–31
 pricing stocks, 25–27
 point, 26
 round/odd lots, 26–27
 security positions, 23–25
 flat, 23–24
 long, 23
 receives, 24
 short, 24–25
Firm quote rule, 132
Flat, 23–24, 25
Float, 226
Floor brokerage, 76, 84, 106–107
FOCUS report, 212
FOK instruction, 86
Foreign companies, NYSE criteria
 for, 70–71
Fourth-market transactions on
 OTC market, 135
Frankfurt Stock Exchange, 284
FTSE 100 Index, 290
Full disclosure statement, 41–43

Full service brokerage firms, 57–61
 (see also Brokerage firm)
Fundamental analysis, 232
Fundamentalists, 231–241 (see also
 Stock market theories)
Futures contracts on index, 227–231

G

Garage of NYSE, 73
General purpose clauses in
 corporate charters, 36
Gifts, taxation of stocks received
 as, 298
Glass-Steagall Act, 38–40,
 309–310
Global crash of 1987, 314–317
Global equity indexes, 286
Globalization of stock market,
 282–293
 after-hours (extended) trading,
 287–288, 289
 advantages/disadvantages,
 288
 electronic communications
 networks (ECNs),
 287–288
 Instinet, 287
 market fragmentation, 288
 Asian financial crisis of 1990s,
 ripple effect of, 282–283
 brokerage firms and online
 access, 292–293
 conclusion, 293
 definition, 282
 investing, 286–287
 American Depository
 Receipts (ADRs), 286
 currency, importance of,
 286–287
 global equity indexes, 286

Globalization of stock market, (*continued*)
    mutual funds, 281
  stock exchanges, 288–292
    decimalization, 292
    Euronext, 290
    Hong Kong Stock Exchange (SEHK), 290
    Merrill Lynch's Major 11 International Market Index Target- Term Securities(R) [MITTS(R)], 291
    S&P Global 100 Index, 290–291
    web sites, 292
  stock markets around world, 283–286 (*see also* under particular heading)
    Asia/Pacific Exchanges, 285
    Europe, 283–284
    Latin America, 285–286
Glossary, 320–397
Good-till-cancelled (GTC) order, 85–86
Green shoe privilege, 50
Gross profit margin, 265–266
Growth stocks, 5, 235
GTC order, 85–86

H

Hand signals, trading by, 33
"Head and shoulders top" pattern, 253–255, 257, 258
Hedging tool, options as, 190–192
Hong Kong Stock Exchange (SEHK), 290
Horizontal spreads, 193
Hot issues, 48–50
  green shoe privilege, 50
How the Bond Market Works, 3
How the Options Markets Work, 193

I

Immediate or cancel (IOC), 87
"In the money," 182–185, 187, 189
Income statement, 264–268 (*see also* Analyzing stock)
Income stocks, 4–5
Incorporating business, process of, 35–40 (*see also* Initial public offering)
Independent brokers, 76
Indexes, 225–231 (*see also* Stock market theories)
Indicators, sentiment and technical, 243–244
Inefficiencies in market, 221
Inheritance, taxation of stocks received as, 298–302
Initial public offering (IPO), 32–54
  after completion of offer, 54
  "broken syndicate," meaning of, 54
  history, 32–34
    American Stock Exchange (AMEX), 33–34
    The Curb, 33
    Curbstone brokers, 33
    hand signals, trading by, 33
    over-the-counter market, 32, 34
  incorporating business, 35–40
    authorized stock, 37
    banks, inability of to make loans, 39–40
    capital statement, 36–38
    certificate of incorporation (charter), 36–38
    discount brokerage, 38–40
    general purpose clauses, 36
    Glass-Steagall Act, 38–40
    issued and outstanding stock, 37

purpose statement, 36
initial public offering (IPO),
    40–54
    allocating issue by lead
        manager, 46–47
    "best-efforts" basis, 40–41, 46
    "blue-skying," 46
    "circling the stock," 44–45
    cooling-off period, 44–46
    date, effective, 47–50
    due diligence meeting, 46–47
    finalizing agreements, 44
    full disclosure statement,
        41–43
    green shoe privilege, 50
    hot issues, 48–50
    lead manager in syndicate, 45
    offering circular, 53
    penny stocks, 53
    "pot," 46–47
    price, setting, 47
    prospectus, 44, 48, 49, 50
    purchase agreement, 44
    "red herring," 43–44
    registration process, 41–44
        (see also Registration
        process)
    Securities and Exchange
        Commission, 41
    selling group, 45
    stabilizing the market, 48
    syndicate, forming, 45–46
    tombstone, 50–54
    underwriter, 45
    underwriting agreement,
        44
    underwriting securities,
        40–41
primary market, 34–35
    expansion funds, three
        sources of, 35
"Inside market," 126

Instinet, 155–156, 287
Institutional investors, 56
Institutional sales, 93–95 (see also
        Secondary market)
Institutional Xpress, 100–101
Interest, taxation of, 295
Interest rates, effect of on stock,
        239
Intermarket Trading System (ITS),
        95–96, 111, 157, 312
    problems with, 111–112
Internet, 269–281, 282–293 (see
        also Online trading and
        Globalization)
Investment banker as source of
        expansion funds, 35,
        39–40
    commercial banks, inability of,
        39–40
Investment Company Act of
        1940, 159
Investment vs. commercial banks,
        310
Investment companies,
        159–169
    conclusion, 169
    face amount certificate
        companies, 160, 161
    investment portfolio, forming,
        159–160
        diversification, principle of,
        160
    management companies,
        160–169 (see also
        Management companies)
    mutual funds, 159
    types, three, 160–162
    Unit Investment Trust (UITs),
        160, 161
Investment return, determining,
        20–31 (see also Financial
        press)

Investments, advantages of
  stocks as, 3–4
 as investment medium
  outpacing inflation, 8
Involuntary exchange, 205
IOC, 87
"Irrational exuberance," 237
Issued and outstanding stock, 37
Issuing stock as sole right of
  corporate entity, 34

J

Jones, Edward, 222
"Junk" bonds, 159, 263

L

Latin America, stock markets in,
  285–286
Lead manager in building
  syndicate, 45
Letter of intent, 167
Leverage, 22, 170
Liabilities, 261–262
Limit order, 83–84, 280
 in odd-lot trading, 118
 in OTC market, 133–135
Limit order to buy in odd-lot
  trading, 118
Limit order display rule, 131
Limit order to sell long in odd-
  lot trading, 118
 to sell short in odd-lot trading,
  118–119
Line charts, 246, 247–248
Liquid, definition, 2
Liquidity ratio, 262–263
London Stock Exchange, 283–284,
  291 (see also Europe)
Long, 23, 25
Long-term profits, 5

M

Maintenance call, 22
Maintenance requirement, 208–209
Maloney Act, 135
Management accounts, 57–58
Management companies, 160–169
 breakpoints, 167
 closed-end fund, pricing, 163
 letter of intent, 167
 liquidating value, 163
 mutual funds, 163–168
 net asset value per share, 163
 open-end fund, 163–168
 premium/discount prices, 163
 self-directed annuities, 167
 withdrawal plans, 167
Margin accounts, 21–23, 92
 agreement, 198
 beneficial owner, 22
 dangers in, 22
 debit balance, 22
 leverage, 22
 limitations on, 308–309
 maintenance call, 22
 owner of record, 22
Margin department, operations
  of, 206–210(see also Back
  offices)
Marital deduction, unlimited, 299
Market continuity, 102, 106
Market fragmentation, 288
Market-maker system of CBOE,
  121
Market makers, OTC firms as,
  123, 126
Market order, 83
 in OTC market, 133–135
Market risk, 229
MarkeTrac of NYSE, 100
Markups/markdowns, 123–124
"Meltdown Monday," 303–319

Merger, 205
Merrill Lynch Major 11
    International Market
    Index Target-Term
    Securities (R),
    [MITTS(R)], 291
Minors, taxation of stock gifts to,
    298
Minus tick, 109
"Missing the market," 83
Money market, 3
Moving average, 250–251
Multiple positions, taxation of,
    297–298
Municipal bonds (MUNIs), 295
Mutual funds, 159, 163–168
foreign stocks in, 286
Myths, program trading, 313

N

NASD, 55, 65, 128 (*see also*
    National Association of
    Securities Dealers)
Nasdaq, 2, 71, 126–128, 140–158 (*see
    also* Over-the-counter)
  conclusion, 158
  globalization, 149
  growth, 151
  indexes, major, 147–149
    Nasdaq Composite, 147, 148,
      227
    Nasdaq Financial-100 Index,
      147
    Nasdaq National Market
      Composite Index, 147,
      148
    Nasdaq-100 Index, 147,
      148–149
  monitoring markets, 150–151
    Nasdaq MarketWatch
      Department, 150

      StockWatch, 150
      TradeWatch, 150
  Nasdaq Canada, 149
  Nasdaq International, Ltd., 149
  Nasdaq Japan, 149
  Nasdaq-100 Index Tracking
    Stock, 147, 149
  Nasdaq-100 Trust ownership,
    147
  QQQ, 147, 149
  requirements for listing,
    142–146
    Nasdaq National Market,
      142, 143–145
    Nasdaq SmallCap Market,
      142, 145–146
  Stock Market and OTCBB,
    difference between,
    131–133 (*see also* Over-
    the-counter)
  structure of NASD and
    subsidiaries, 140–142
  technological developments,
    151–158
    Advanced Computerized
      Execution System
      (ACES), 152
    after-hours trading services,
      158
    alternative trading systems
      (ATS), 155–157
    Automated Confirmation
      Transaction Service
      (ACTS), 152–153
    Computer Assisted
      Execution System
      (CAES), 157
    electronic communications
      networks (ECNs),
      155–157
    Intermarket Trading System
      (ITS), 157

Nasdaq (*continued*)
   Nasdaq Intermarket, 157
   Nasdaq Workstation, 152
   Nasdaq Workstation II, 153,
      154
   RADAR, 153
   Reuters Instinet, 155
   SEC rules, new, 154–155
   SelectNet, 153, 157, 158
   Small Order Execution
      System (SOES), 152, 153
   trading in 1/16ths and
      decimals, 157–158
National Association of Securities
      Dealers (NASD), 55, 65,
      128
   and American Stock Exchange,
      merger with, 146–147
   banks not eligible, 136
   Board of Governors, 142
   exclusions, 136
   globalization, 149
   as independent membership
      association, 135
   Maloney Act, 135
   Market Regulation, 150–151
      RADAR (Research and Data
         Analysis Repository),
         151
      SWAT (StockWatch
         Automated Tracking
         System), 151
   membership, 136
   NASD Regulation, Inc, 142
   objectives, 136
   as regulatory agency of OTC
      trading, 124
   compliance regulations,
      135–136
   Rules of Fair Practice, 137–139
      "reasonable diligence," 137

      suitability rule, 139
   self-regulator, largest in US
      securities industry, 142
   structure, 140–142
   subsidiaries, 142
NASD Regulation, Inc., 142
National Association of
      Securities Dealers
      Automated Quotations
      (NASDAQ) service,
      126–128 (*see also*
      NASDAQ)
National Market System:
   NYSE and, 95–96
   stocks, 127–128
National Quotation Bureau,
      129–130
Net income/loss, 264
Net worth, 264
New account agreement, 198
New York Stock Exchange (NYSE),
      2, 55, 68–101, 291
   Allocation Committee, 120–121
   auction system, 80–83
      bid, 81
      offer, 81
      "price for size," 82
      quote, 81
      "size at price," 82
      spread, 81
   "Big Board, " 69
   biggest and oldest exchange,
      68–69
   "Circuit Breaker" rule (80B),
      98–99
   "Collar" rule (80A), 97–98
      buy minus, 97
      sell plus, 98
   Composite Index, 96–97, 227
   delisting from, 71–72
   delivery of orders, 78–80

Broker Booth Support Systems
(BBSS), 78, 79–80
Crossing Session, 79
Display Book, 79, 80
Opening Automated Report
Service (OARS), 79
SUPERDOT system, 78–79
through high tech
communication devices,
80
floor, 72–78
blue room, 73
garage, 73
membership, 73–78 (see
also....membership)
players, 73–78
round lots, 73
trading posts, 73
history, 32–33
and Intermarket Trading
System (ITS), 95–96
listing requirements and
criteria, 69–71
distribution standards,
minimum, 70
for foreign companies, 70–71
quantitative criteria,
minimum, 69
maintenance listing
requirements, 71–72
membership, 73–78
agents, 76
commission house brokers,
76
competitive market makers,
76, 77
competitive traders, 76–77
floor brokerage, 76
floor brokers, 76
independent brokers, 76
schematic, 74–75

specialists, 76, 77–78, 81
two-dollar brokers, 76
Network NYSE, 99–101
anonymity, 100
and electronic
communication
networks (ECNs), 99
Institutional Xpress, 100–101
NYSE Direct +, 99–100
NYSE e-broker, 101
NYSE MarkeTrac, 100
Online Comparison System
(OCS), 80
options, 171
and OTC market, difference
between, 126
rules, 97–99
80A ("Collar"), 97–98
80B ("Circuit Breaker"), 98–99
New York Times, 51, 266–267
Network NYSE, 99–101 (see also
NYSE)
Newspaper listings, 28–31
NexTrade, 155
Nikkei 225 Index, 290, 291
"No-load"mutual funds, 164
bond mutual funds, 168–169
Nonconvertible preferred stocks,
16
Non-diversifiable risk, 229
Non-systematic risk, 229
Not held (NH), 86
Nouveau Marche, 284
*The NYIF Vest-Pocket Guide to Stock
Brokerage Math*, 261

O

OARS, 79, 113
OCS, 80
Odd-lot theory, 245

Odd-lot trading, 116–120
  charges to customer, two, 116
  differential, 116–117
  effective sale, 116
  specialist, role of, 116
  types, 117–120
    at-the-close order, 119–120
    basis price order, 120
    electing sale, 119
    limit orders, 118
    limit order to buy, 118
    limit order to sell long, 118
    limit order to sell short,
      118–119
    on-the-quotation order, 119
    short seller, 118
    stop order, 119
    stop limit order, 119
Odd lots, 26–27
  definition, 116
  specialist and, 116–120 (*see also*
    Odd-lot trading)
Off-hours trading, 89–91 (*see also*
    Secondary market)
Offer, 81
Offering circular, 53
"Offering wanted" (OW), 129
Offerings of stock market, 1–19
  bonds, 3
  brokerage accounts, insurance
    of, 8
  capital gains, 5–6
    Day Trading, 5
  common stocks, 10–12 (*see also*
    Common stocks)
  dividends, 4–5
    stock dividends, 4
  growth stocks, 5
  income stocks, 5
  for individuals and institutions,
    3–4

  as investments, 3–4
    outpacing inflation, 8
  listed securities, 2
  long-term profits, 5
  money market, 3
  New York Stock Exchange, 2
  over-the-counter market, 2
  patience, role of, 8
  preemptive rights feature of
    common stocks, 17–18
  preferred stocks, 12–17 (*see also*
    Preferred stocks)
  primary markets, 1, 2
  publicly held stocks, 2
  risks/rewards of investing, 8–9
  secondary, 1
  short sale, 5–7
  short-term profits, 5
  size of market, 2
  stock dividends, 4
  stock rights, 17–18, 19
  stock warrants, 18, 19
  why stocks are offered, 1–2
  subscription price, 17
  volatility, 9
  warrants, 18, 19
  yield, 4–5
Offshore investing scams,
    277–278
On-the-quotation order, odd-lot
    trading and, 119
Online brokerage services,
    292–293
Online Comparison System
    (OCS), 80
Online trading, 269–281
  accounts, types of, 272
  benefits, 269–270
  brokerage firms and, 270–272
  day trading, 271
  conclusion, 281

data service provider, 271
EDAT (Electronic Direct Access
    Trading), 271–272
and global expansion of stock
    market, 292
pending status, 274
prerequisites for, 273
process to establish, 273–274
protection, 279–281
risks, 275–279
    diversification, lack of, 275
    in execution of order,
        276–277
    false transactions, 278–279
    fraud, 277–279
    offshore investing scams,
        277–278
    overconfidence, 275
    overtrading, 275–276
    Ponzi schemes, 278
    pump and dump schemes,
        277
    pyramid schemes, 278
    risk-free investment fraud,
        278
SEC, role of, 280–281
    Office of Compliance and
        Inspections, 280
SIPC(Securities Investor
    Protection Corp.), 272
wireless and touch tone
    trading, 274–275
Open order, 85–86
Opening Automated Report
    Service (OARS), 79, 113
Opening of market, specialist
    and, 112–113
Operations, 194–219 (*see also*
    Back offices)
Options, 170–193 (*see also* Stock
    options)

Options Clearing Corp. (OCC), 171
    (*see also* Stock options)
Order department, operations of,
    198–199 (*see also* Back
    offices)
Orders, executing, 83–88 (*see also*
    Secondary market)
"Out of the money," 182,
    183–185, 186
Outstanding shares, 10
Over-the-counter market, 2
    history, 32, 34
Over-the-counter trading, 122–139
    actual market, 129
    "bid wanted" (BW), 129
    broker/dealers, 123
    Bulletin Board (OTCBB), 130–133
        best execution rule, 132
        EDGAR, 130
        firm quote rule, 132
        halts, activation of, 133
        not an issuer service, 130
        limit order display rule, 131
        manning/limit order
            protection rule, 131
        and Nasdaq Stock Market,
            differences between,
            131–133
        penny stock rules, 131– 132
        SEC filings, 132–133
        SEC risk disclosure rules,
            131–132
    compliance regulations of
        NASD, 135–136 (*see also*
        National Association)
    Rules of Fair Practice, 137–139
    and exchange market, difference
        between, 126
    firm bids/offers, 128
    fourth-market transaction, 135
    how it works, 122–123

Over-the-counter trading (*continued*)
"inside market," 126
limit orders, 133–135
market-makers, 123, 126
market orders, 133–135
markup/markdown, 123–124, 126
NASD, compliance regulations of, 135–136 (*see also* National Association)
Rules of Fair Practice, 137–139
NASDAQ (National Association of Securities Dealers Automated Quotations) System, 126–128
levels, three, 127
National Market System stocks, 127–128
Small Order Execution System (SOES), 127
success of, 128
National Quotation Bureau, 129, 130
as negotiated market, 126
"offering wanted" (OW), 129
order being executed, process for, 126–129
pink sheets, 122, 130
"reasonable diligence, " obligation for, 137
regulatory agency (NASD), 124
5% guideline, 124–125
riskless transaction, 124
shopping the street, 128
street name, 137–138
subject quotes, 129
supply and demand rule predominant, 139
third-market transactions, 135
types of orders, 133–135
workout quote, 129

Overconfidence as risk in online trading, 275
Overtrading, risk of in online trading, 275–276
Owner of record, 22
Ownership, common stocks and, 10

P

P&S (Purchase and Sales) department, operations of, 199–206 (*see also* Back offices)
Pacific Stock Exchange, 171
Package traders, 313
Par value of common stock, 12
of preferred stock, 13
Paris Stock Exchange, 284
Nouveau Marche, 284
Participate but not initiate (PNI) instruction, 86
Password codes, 272, 279
Patience, role of, 8
Payment date, 215
Peak, 253
Penny stocks, 53
rules in OTCBB market, 131–132
Philadelphia Stock Exchange, 171
Pink sheets, 122, 130
Players at NYSE, 73–78 (*see also* New York Stock Exchange)
Plus tick, 109
Point, 26
Point and figure charts, 246, 247
Ponzi schemes, 278
Portfolio insurance, 313, 315
Post Execution Reporting (PER) system of American Stock Exchange, 110

"Pot," 46–47
Preemptive rights feature of
        common stocks, 17–18
Preemptive rights offering, 205
Preferred stocks, 12–17
    Conversion Arbitrage, 17
    conversion ratio, 16
    corporations, not requirement
        for, 12
    as equity security, 18
    names of issues, 12–14
    par values, 13
    senior aspects of, 14
    types, 14–17
        callable preferred, 14–15
        convertible preferred, 15–17
        cumulative preferred, 14
        nonconvertible preferred, 16
        straight preferreds, 16
Premium, 172, 177–178, 182–190
        (*see also* Stock options)
Prestige as reason for tombstone,
        51–52
Price for IPO, setting, 47
"Price for size," 82
Price-earnings ratio (P/E), 235–237
Pricing stocks, 25–27
    point, 26
    round/odd lots, 26–27
Primary market, 1, 2, 34–35
Proceeds sale, 88
Profit and loss (P&L) statement,
        260
Profit potential of stock,
        unlimited, 8
Program trading myths, 313
Prospectus, 44, 48, 49, 50
Proxy department, operations of,
        218–219 (*see also* Back
        offices)
Publicly held stocks, 2

Publicly traded fund, pricing,
        163
Pump and dump fraud schemes,
        277
Purpose statement of corporate
        charter, 36
Puts, 172, 176–179
    "at the money," 183–184
    "in the money," 183–184, 187
    "out of the money," 183–184
Pyramid schemes, 278

Q

QQQ, 147
Quick assets, 261
    ratio, 262–263
Quote, 81

R

RADAR (Research and Data
        Analysis Repository),
        151, 153
Random walk theory, 220–221
Reaction high (peak), / low
        (trough), 253
Receives, 24
Record date, 215
"Red herring," 43–44
Redemption call, 204
Registered representative, 55–56
Registrar, 201
Registration process for IPO, 41–44
Regular way settlement, 20
Regulation T of Federal Reserve
        Board, 207, 308
Relative strength of market, 257
Reorganization, 205
Reorganization department (reorg),
        operations of, 205–206

Research and Data Analysis
Repository (RADAR),
151, 153
Residual rights of common
stockholder, 11–12
Reuters Instinet, 155–156, 287
Rights of common stockholder,
10–12
dividends, receipt of, 11
liquidity, 19
residual rights, 11–12
voting, 10–11
Risk-free investment fraud, 278
Riskless arbitrage, 315
Riskless transaction, 124
Risks/rewards of investing, 8–9
Round lots, 26–27, 73, 116
Rules of Fair Practice of NASD,
137–139
Russian Trading System (RTS),
284
Russell 2000 Index, 227

S

S&P 500 Common Stock Index, 227
Sales assistant, 66–67
Scale order, 87
Seats on exchange, 73–78 (see also
New York Stock
Exchange)
SEC, role of in online investing,
280–281
Office of Compliance and
Inspection, 280
SEC risk disclosure rules in
OTCBB market, 131–132
SEC Rule 15c3–3, 212–213,
307–308
Secondary distribution, 93–95 (see
also Secondary market)
Secondary market, 1, 68–104

after (off) hours trading
(a/k/a crossing
sessions), 89–91
basket session, 90
fixed price session, 90
purpose, 89–90
SUPERDOT system
restriction to, 90
American Stock Exchange
(Amex), 101–104
"the Book," 102
"The Curb," 101
floor layout, 103
liquidity, 102
market continuity, 102
specialist system, 102
crossing stock, 88–89
"crowd, " 89
decimalization, 95
institutional sales, 93–95
exchange acquisition, 93
exchange distribution, 93
secondary distribution, 93–95
how orders are executed in
crowd, 83–88
activating sale, 84
all or none (AON), 86
alternative, 88
at the close, 87–88
buy minus, 88
buy stop order, 84
cancellation, 88
contingent, 88
day order, 85
either/or, 88
electing sale, 84
fill or kill (FOK), 86
GTC (good-till-cancelled)
order, 85–86
immediate or cancel (IOC),
87
limit order, 83–84

market order, 83
"missing the market," 83
not held (NH), 86
open order, 85–86
participate but not initiate
    (PNI), 86
proceeds sale, 88
scale order, 87
sell plus, 88
sell stop order, 85
stop order, 84–85
swap, 88
switch, 88
New York Stock Exchange,
    68–101 (see also New
    York Stock Exchange)
over-the-counter trading,
    122–139 (see also Over-
    the-counter)
short sale, 91–92
    dividends in, 92
    margin account, 92
    upticks, 92
    "zero plus tick," 92
Securities, assigning to specialist,
    120–121
Securities Act of 1933, 41, 306
Securities Exchange Act of 1934,
    135, 219, 306
Securities and Exchange
    Commission (SEC), 41,
    65
Securities Industry Automation
    Corp. (SIAC), 196–197
Securities Investor Protection
    Corp. (SIPC), 272
Security positions, 23–25
"In seg," 202
SelectNet, 153
Self-directed annuities, 167
Sell plus order, 88, 98
Sell stop order, 85

Selling group, 45
Semilog scale for charting, 249
Sentiment indicators, 243–244
Series 7, 55
Settlement date, 20
Share value, determining, 20–31
    (see also Financial press)
Shopping the street, 128
Short cover, 204
Short interest theory, 113–114
Short sales, 5–7, 9, 24–25, 84,
    91–92, 112, 113–114
    "cushion" or "short interest"
    theory, 113–114
    danger in, 9
    handling of by cashier
    department, 202–204
    and investing, difference
    between, 7
    specialist and, 112, 113–114
Short-term profits/trading, 5
SIAC, 196–197
SIPC, 272
"Size at price," 82
Small Order Execution System
    (SOES), 127, 152–153
Specialists, 76, 77–78, 81, 94–95,
    105–121
    at Amex, 102
    assigning securities to,
        120–121
        Allocation Committee of
        NYSE, 120–121
        market-maker system of
        CBOE, 121
    automation and
        telecommunication, role
        of, 110–112
    Intermarket Trading System
        (ITS), 111
    pre-opening notification,
        problem of, 111–112

Specialists (*continued*)
  Super Designated Order
      Turnaround
      (SUPERDOT), 110–111
  third market, 111
  conclusion, 121
  definition, 106
  duties, other, 112–120
    block sales, 112, 115
    odd-lot trading, 112, 116–120
      (*see also* Odd-lot trading)
    Opening Automated Report
      Service (OARS), 113
    opening of market, 112, 113
    short sales, 112, 113–114
    stopping stock, 112, 114–115
  and market continuity, 106
  role of, 106–110
    "book," 107
    floor brokerage, 106–107
    functions, two, 106–107
    minus tick, 109
    order "on the book," 107
    plus tick, 109
    stabilizing market, 109, 110,
      114
    zero minus tick, 109
    zero plus tick, 109
  telecommunication, role of,
      110–112 (*see also*
      automation)
  volume, 105–106
Specialized firms, 59
Specific risk, 229
Speculative program trading, 313
Spreads, 81, 192–193
  bull, 193
  horizontal (calendar), 193
Stabilizing the market, 48
Standard & Poor's Global 100
    Index, 290–291

Statutory voting rights, 10–11
Stepped-up basis, 299
Stock dividends, 4
Stock Exchange Automated
    Quotation (SEAQ)
    system, 283–284
Stock index arbitrage, 313
Stock issuance as sole right of
    corporate entity, 34
Stock market:
  advantages of stock as
      investment, 3–4
  brokerage accounts, insurance
      of, 8
  capital gains, 5–6
  common stocks, 10–12 (*see also*
      Common stocks)
  Crash of 1987, 303–319
  Day Trading, 5
  dividends, 4–5
  and economy, 317–319
  income stocks, 5
  as investment medium
      outpacing inflation, 8
  listed securities, 2
  long-term profits, 5
  New York Stock Exchange, 2
  over-the-counter market, 2
  preferred stocks, 12–17 (*see also*
      Preferred stocks)
  under pressure, 303–319
  primary market, 1
  profit potential, unlimited, 8
  regulations about, 306–313
    Regulation T, 308
    reserve capital, 307
  risks/rewards of investing, 8–9
  secondary market, 1
  Securities Act of 1933, 306
  Securities Exchange Act of
      1934, 306

short sale, 5–7, 9
  danger in, 9
  and investing, difference
    between, 7
short-term profits, 5
short-term trading, 5
size, 2
stock dividends, 4
stock rights, 17–18
stock warrants, 18
subscription price, 17
volatility, 9
warrants, 18
why stocks are offered, 1–2
working under pressure, 303–319
around world, 283–286 (*see also*
    Globalization)
yield, 4–5
Stock market theories, 220–259
  American analyst, first, 222
  analysts, 231–241
    bonds, 238–239
    book value (BV), 238
    budget deficits, 239–240
    charting, 232–234
    "cheap" stock, 238
    deficits, 239–240
    dilutive securities, 235–236
    earnings, 235
    earnings per share (EPS), 235
    fundamental and technical
      analysis, need for both,
      257–259
    fundamentalists, 231–241
    growth stock, 235
    interest rates, 239
    "irrational exuberance, " 237
    price-earnings (P/E) ratio,
      235–237
    technical, 232 (*see also* technical
      approach)

trade deficits, 240
  yield, 237–238
"bid cap" companies, 237
"Black Monday," 240
"Chinese Wall," 221
Dow theory, 222–223
Dow Jones averages, 224–225
efficient market theory,
    220–221
indexes, 225–231
  American Stock Exchange
    Market Value Index, 227
  float, 226
  Nasdaq Composite index,
    227
  New York Stock Exchange
    Composite Index, 227
  options, 230–231
  Russell 2000, 227
  Standard & Poor's 500
    Common Stock Index,
    227
  as underlying instruments
    for futures, 227
  weighted, 225–226
  Wilshire 5,000 Equity index,
    227
inefficiencies in market, 221
random walk theory, 220–221
relative strength, 257
technical approach, 241–259
  "breadth" of market, 243
  chartists, 242–249 (*see also*
    Charting)
  contrarian opinion theory,
    245
  definition, 242
  and fundamental approach,
    need for both, 257–259
  indicators, sentiment,
    243–244

Stock market theories (*continued*)
   indicators, technical, 243
   new highs/lows, as
      indicator, 243
   odd-lot theory, 245
   present price movements/
      future levels, 243
   resistance level, 244–245,
      253, 254– 256
   support level, 244–245, 253,
      254– 256
   trends, 249–257
      "head and shoulders top"
         pattern, 253–255, 257, 258
      moving average, 250–251
      reaction high (peak), 253
      reaction low (trough), 253
   triple witching hours, 231
   witching hour, 231
Stock options, 170–193
   advantages, 171
   American Stock Exchange, 171
   Black-Scholes Option Pricing
      formula, 185
   calls, 172, 179–182
      "at the money," 184–185
      covered/uncovered call
         writing, 180
      "in the money," 184–185, 189
      negatives about, 181–182
      "out of the money," 184–185
   Chicago Board of Options
      Exchange (CBOE), 171
   conclusion, 193
   covered call writing, 180
   definitions, 172
   duration of contract, 175–176
   exercise price, 172–174
   exercising, 174–175
   expiration date of contract,
      175–176

   as hedging tool, 190–192
   intrinsic value and time value,
      recap, 186–190
   leverage, 170
   liquidating options positions,
      175
   Option Clearing Corporation
      (OCC), 171
   Pacific Stock Exchange, 171
   Philadelphia Stock Exchange,
      171
   positions, 192
      combination, 192
      straddle, 192
   premium, 172, 177–178,
      182–190
      Black-Scholes Option Pricing
         formula, 185
      definition, 182
      formula, 182
      "in the money," 182–185
      intrinsic value of option
         contract, 182–185,
         186–190
      time value, 185–190
   purposes, 170
   puts, 172, 176–179
      "at the money," 183–184
      "in the money," 183–184, 187
      "out of the money," 183–184
   rights and obligations under
      option contract, 174
   spreads, 192–193
      bull, 193
      horizontal (calendar), 193
   strike price, 172–174
   time value of option contract,
      185–190
      and intrinsic value, recap,
         186–190
   types of contracts, 176–182

calls, 179–182
puts, 176–179
uncovered call writing, 180
wasting assets, 190
Stock power, 201
Stock record department,
operations of, 210–212
(*see also* Back offices)
Stock rights, 17–18
Stock splits, taxation of, 295
Stock warrants, 18
Stockbroker, 55 (*see also*
Brokerage firm)
Stockholder solicitation, 219
Stockholders' equity, 264
StockWatch, 150
SWAT (StockWatch Automated
Tracking System), 151
Stop limit order in odd-lot trading,
119
Stop order, 84–85
in odd-lot trading, 119
Stopping stock, 114–115
Straddle position of option, 192
Straight preferred stocks, 16
Street name stock, 21, 22, 137–138,
214
STRIDES, 148–149
Strike price, 172–174, 177
Subject quotes, 129
Subscription price, 17
Subscription privilege offering, 205
SUPERDOT (Super Designated
Order Turnaround)
system, 78–79, 110–111
Display Books, 79, 80
Support and resistance principle,
244, 253, 254–256
Sustained decline, 318
Swap/ switch order, 88
Syndicate for IPO, forming, 45–46

Systematic risk, 229

T

Taxation, 294–302
of capital gains, 296–297 (*see
also* Capital gains)
of dividends, 295–296
gifts and inheritance, stocks as,
298–302
of interest, 295
minors, stock gifts to, 298
custodian account, 298
multiple positions, 297–298
municipal bonds (MUNIs), 295
rules, 294
state rules, 294
stepped-up basis, 299
of stock splits, 295
tax loss carryforwards, 296–297
unlimited marital deduction,
299
Tax loss carryforwards, 296–297
Tax Reform Act of 1986, 303
Technical analysts, 232, 241–259
(*see also* Stock market
theories)
Technical indicators, 243
Technology, effect of on trading,
269–281 (*see also* Online
trading)
Telecommunications, specialist
and, 110–112 (*see also*
Specialist)
Tender offer, 206
Theories about stock market,
220–259 (*see also* Stock
market theories)
Third market, 111
Third-market transactions on
OTC market, 135

Ticket charges, 200
Time value of option contract, 185–190
Tokyo Stock Exchange, 285, 291
Tombstone, 50–54
"Top of book," 156
Touch-tone trading, 274–275
Trade deficits, effect of, 240
TradeWatch, 150
Trading posts, 73
Transfer agent, 201–202
Trends, 249–257 (*see also* Stock market theories)
Triple witching hours, 231
Trough, 253
Two-dollar brokers, 76

U

Uncovered call writing, 180
Underwriter, 45
Underwriting agreement, 44
Underwriting securities in IPO, 40–41
Unit Investment Trust, 160, 161
Upticks, 92
Uptrends, 249–250

V

Value line, 14
Venture capital firm as source of expansion funds, 35
Volatility, 9
Voluntary exchange request, 205

Voting rights of common stockholder, 10–11

W

Wall Street Journal, 28–31, 51, 222, 266, 289, 303
Warrants, 18, 206
Wasting assets, options as, 190
Weekly stock record, 212
Wilshire 5,000 Equity Index, 227
Wire houses, 58–59
Wire room, 199
Wireless trading, 274–275
Witching hour, 231, 316
Withdrawal plans, 167
Wood Gundy, 310
Working capital, 262
Workout quote, 129
World Wide Web, 282 (*see also* Globalization)

X

Xetra DAX Index, 290

Y

Yield, 4–5, 237–238
current, calculating, 27–28

Z

Zero minus tick, 109
Zero plus tick, 92, 109

AUTHOR BIOGRAPHY

John M. Dalton is a practicing attorney with offices in Staten Island, New York, and an instructor at the New York Institute of Finance. Formerly with the American Stock Exchange, Inc., he was the Assistant Director of the Floor Rules Department, Director of the Trading Analysis Department, and a Senior Compliance Attorney. A well-known lecturer, Mr. Dalton has often been called upon to appear at trials and arbitration hearings to explain Wall Street practices and procedures.

7/22